GOD SO LOVED THE WORLD

Robert J. Spitzer, S.J., Ph.D.

GOD SO LOVED
THE WORLD

Clues to Our Transcendent Destiny
from the Revelation of Jesus

Volume Three of the Quartet:
Happiness, Suffering, and Transcendence

IGNATIUS PRESS   SAN FRANCISCO

Nihil Obstat: Hugh Barbour, O. Praem.
　　　　　　　Censor Librorum
Imprimatur: + The Most Reverend Kevin J. Vann, J.C.D., O.D.
　　　　　　　Bishop, Diocese Orange

Cover design by John Herreid

© 2016 by Ignatius Press, San Francisco
All rights reserved
ISBN 978-1-62164-036-3 (PB)
ISBN 978-1-68149-701-3 (eBook)
Library of Congress Control Number 2015939073
Printed in the United States of America ∞

*In loving memory of my mother, who introduced me to
the Person and love of Jesus Christ, and my father,
who showed me how to express my faith in action.*

*And to my wonderful nieces and nephews—
Kristin, Nicholas, Meghan, Alex, Michelle, Kellie, and Andrew—
who show me the face of Christ in their love.*

*For God so loved the world that he gave his only-begotten Son,
that whoever believes in him should not perish but have eternal life.
For God sent the Son into the world, not to condemn the world,
but that the world might be saved through him.*

—John 3:16–17

CONTENTS

Appendix Two: Making Sense of the Trinity and Incarnation

ACKNOWLEDGMENTS

I am most grateful to Joan Jacoby—whose invaluable work transformed my thoughts once again into a full manuscript—for typing multiple copies of each chapter, making helpful editing suggestions, and helping with research. I am particularly grateful for her appreciation of the subject, and her undying patience.

I am also grateful to Joe Miller and Karlo Broussard for their important input and assistance on the manuscript, and Juliana Gerace for her help in preparing it.

I would also like to express my appreciation to the board and friends of the Magis Institute who gave me the time and resources to complete this Quartet.

INTRODUCTION

In the previous volume we examined the evidence for a supreme transcendent deity and our transcendent nature. We first explored the evidence of interior experience—the numinous experience, the religious intuition of the sacred, the authority behind conscience, and the myth of a cosmic struggle between good and evil. We then set out Lonergan's proof of a unique, unconditioned, unrestricted act of thinking that is the Creator of everything else in reality ("God") and then showed that this God was the source of our horizon of complete and unrestricted intelligibility, giving rise to our unrestricted desire to know. We then showed that the unique unrestricted act of thinking must also be perfect love, perfect justice or goodness, and perfect beauty, and that it must therefore be the source of our desire for them. Next we examined the latest medical evidence for survival of bodily death from near-death experiences, revealing a transphysical ground of self-consciousness ("soul"), and then gave an explanation for how a transphysical soul could interact with the physical brain. This then showed the inadequacy of physicalist and protomentalist explanations for heuristic notions, the horizon of unrestricted intelligibility, Gödel's proof, near-death experiences, and the hard problem of consciousness. We concluded by giving a summary of evidence for an intelligent Creator from contemporary physics as well as an exposition of Dawkins' "complexity error" through a metaphysical proof of God. Thus, our investigation led us to four kinds of interior evidence, two logical-metaphysical proofs of God, three indications of transcendental awareness and desire, verified accounts of near-death experiences, and scientific evidence for intelligent creation. This encompassed eleven sources of evidence coming from five methodologies.

This remarkable confluence of sources and methods forms a strong probative case for the existence of an ultimate transcendent Being as well as our transcendental and transphysical nature. At this juncture experience and reason (natural explanation) can go no further. Yet, questions about our transcendent *destiny* still abound. Does God grant eternal life? If so, what is that life like? Does God redeem suffering? If so, how? Does God answer prayers? Does He heal us interiorly? Is He unconditionally good and loving? Does He inspire and guide us? Can we be eternally separated from God? What is our path to salvation? Since these questions are beyond reason, we must look to the only other available source of answers—God Himself. We must seek the possibility and reality of God's *self*-revelation.

I. Would God Reveal Himself to Us *Personally* and *Ultimately*?

In the conclusion to Volume II, we reasoned that a *good and loving* God would not leave us in a state of radical incompleteness, without the self-revelation we need to answer the above questions, and so we concluded that He *would* want to reveal Himself to us in a special way. Such special revelations would have to be subject to particular times and places, which means that God would have to reveal Himself through many different religions and many different times, places, and cultures. After noting Heiler's seven similarities among world religions (and the major differences in interpreting these seven similarities), we asked whether God would pick a *particular* time, place, culture, and religion to make a *personal and ultimate* revelation of Himself—not to undermine other religions, but to bring them to their fulfillment.

We suggested that Christianity would be a major candidate for this personal and ultimate revelation because of its radical claim that God is unconditional love, and that He sent His only Son into the world to reveal the fullness of that love both in word and action. This Son carefully defines love in parables and Beatitudes; gives that love freely to sinners, the needy, friends, and enemies; and finally gives Himself to the whole of humanity for all time in an unconditional act of self-sacrifice, which He calls the greatest love (Jn 15:13).

Some readers may feel uneasy about considering the question of an *ultimate* revelation because it seems to suggest that one religion is better than another—or at least has access to a revelation that the others do not. Isn't this inconsistent with an unconditionally loving God who would not show favoritism in the manifestation of His love? Clearly an unconditionally loving God does not show favoritism; He does not love one culture or religion more than another.

However, the question about the particularity of a personal and ultimate revelation is not about favoritism. It is about the *necessary* conditions for the Divine to become *personally incarnate* ("embodied" and subject to space-time particularity). If God wants to be incarnately present in the human condition, He will have to enter into a *particular* place and time, because humanity is conditioned by space and time. Furthermore, He would have to enter into a culture that would undoubtedly have a religion, because we live in *particular* cultures with *particular* religious traditions.

Why would God want to do this? Why would He want to be *personally incarnately* present, which would force Him to choose a particular place, time, culture, and religion? Jesus answers this question on behalf of Himself and His Divine Father by revealing that they are *unconditional* love. He, as Divine Son, wants to be with us *as we are*, because this will enable us to apprehend directly (in both mind and heart) His empathy, compassion, affection, forgiveness, patience, support, and willingness to give Himself totally to us. His intention goes beyond the needs of our hearts' appropriation of His personal love; He *wants* to give Himself *unconditionally* to us—in the restrictions of our space and time, our embodiment, cultural limitations, suffering, debilitation, and death. He wants this because He views self-sacrifice as gift of self and views unconditional gift of self as unconditional love. He wants to love us concretely and completely, not just to *show* us His love, but to *infuse* that love into us—as a light that will overcome darkness, a fullness that will overcome emptiness, a companionship that will overcome alienation and loneliness, and an unconditional goodness that will break the spell of evil, which will open the path to eternal unconditional love with Him. If the unconditionally loving God really wants to do all this, He will have to become incarnate, and if He becomes incarnate, then He will have to choose a particular place, time, culture, and religious tradition.

This leaves God with only two choices: He can incarnate Himself at *one* particular place, time, culture, and religious tradition for the redemption of *all* times, places, cultures, and religious traditions, *or*

He can incarnate Himself over and over again for every time, place, culture, and religion, not only in the world, but in the universe. If we suppose that one complete self-sacrifice is enough—not only for the world but for the universe—then the unconditionally loving God will have to pick a particular place and time to incarnate Himself, and in so doing, overcome any possible thought of favoritism or preference.

How might He make this selection amid so many good and beautiful cultures, religions, times, and places? One can only speculate about this, but it seems that He might pick a religion in which a sense of His love and care has been increasingly revealed (such as one revealed by the patriarchs and prophets of Judaism). He would also pick a culture and time that would have access to logic, philosophy, and systematic methodology that would optimize the use of reason (such as the Hellenistic culture). At the same time He would pick a place and time that had connections to the rest of the world and could provide the infrastructure to spread the good news far and wide (such as the Roman Empire).

Similarly, the unconditionally loving God would want to pick a cultural setting that was humble (and even humbled), not powerful, glorious, arrogant, and proud. He would also want to choose a place within that culture that was equally humble—a small town with religious significance, but not the central point of a religion. He would also want to choose a place in that town that was humble, like a stable or cave, to make His appearance, and choose a humble mother and father, and be surrounded by humble people like shepherds. It seems to me that if an unconditionally loving God were to become incarnate, and to give Himself completely to humanity, in one particular place, time, and culture, He would do it in the most humble and unobtrusive way possible—in a stable in the town of Bethlehem in Israel.

If the unconditionally loving God picked Israel—with its prophetic preparation as well as its Hellenistic influences amid Roman roads and infrastructure—He could work through their religious and philosophical apparatus to articulate and spread the good news about His unconditional love and to help us follow the path of that unconditional love in humility, gentleness, compassion, forgiveness, and reconciliation.

We can be sure that if an unconditionally loving God did this, He would not have done so because He loved one group more than another. Rather, He would have done it to meet the *necessary* condition for His Incarnation—a *particular* place, time, culture, and religious tradition—so that He could reveal Himself personally and ultimately, and more importantly, *give* Himself completely to His beloveds throughout the world for *all time*.

II. An Overview of This Book

As noted above, this volume is concerned with whether the intelligent Creator (God)—manifest in logical proofs, scientific evidence, and near-death experiences, and who is the source of the numinous experience, our desire for the sacred, and the four transcendental desires for truth, love, goodness, and beauty—would *want* to reveal Himself to us *personally and ultimately*. In Chapters 1 and 2, we show that this is reasonable not only in light of our interior experience of a transcendent reality, but also the likelihood that a completely intelligent reality is completely positive, implying its possession of a completely positive virtue—namely, "love" (defined as *agapē*).

This leads us to ask whether God might be *unconditionally* loving, and if He is, whether He would want to make a personal appearance to us in a perfect act of empathy—peer-to-peer and face-to-face. In Chapter 2, we examine the rational evidence for this and then begin our search of world religions to see if there is one that reveals such a God, an unconditionally loving God who would want to be with us in perfect empathy and love (gift of self). This leads us to the extraordinary claim of Jesus Christ, who taught that God is "Abba" (the unconditionally loving, affectionate, gentle, trustworthy Father), who can be compared to the father in the Parable of the Prodigal Son.

Jesus' claims go further. He says that *He* is also unconditional love, and that His mission is to give us that love through an act of complete self-sacrifice. He does this through a Eucharistic banquet with His disciples, after which He allows Himself to be captured by adversaries and persecuted. He also claims that He is the exclusive Son of the Father, the eschatological Son of Man sent by God to judge the world, and the one who possesses divine power and authority in

Himself. If Jesus' claims are true, then He truly is the "unconditionally loving God with us". Is there some way of probing the veracity of Jesus' claims?

Recent New Testament historical research has uncovered considerable evidence for these claims. In Chapter 3, we examine the evidence for Jesus' unconditional love of sinners, the poor, and His disciples, as well as the meaning and significance of His Eucharistic banquet and self-sacrificial gift (from Joachim Jeremias, Raymond Brown, John P. Meier, and N. T. Wright). In Chapter 4, we investigate the apostolic Church's claim that Jesus was risen in glory, focusing on Gary Habermas' survey of exegetical opinion and N. T. Wright's comprehensive study of the uniqueness of the prolific Christian messianic movement and his study of the Christian mutations of Second Temple Judaism's view of the Resurrection. In Chapter 5, we examine the historical evidence for Jesus' miracles, focusing on Raymond Brown's analysis of the uniqueness of those miracles and John P. Meier's thorough examination of the historicity of Jesus' exorcisms, healings, and raising the dead. We then consider the significance of and evidence for Jesus' gift of the Holy Spirit that enabled His disciples to perform miracles in His name, and conclude with the evidence for the presence of the Holy Spirit today. In chapter 5, when we consider the likelihood of each of these remarkable incidents (in light of the above historical evidence), the legitimacy of Jesus' claim to be the exclusive Son of the Father, and the "unconditionally loving God with us", becomes increasingly apparent.

All the evidence in the world will not suffice to lead anyone to *faith* in "Jesus Christ as Lord and Son of God", because such faith requires a movement of the heart—that is, an affinity for Jesus' teaching on love and a desire to be healed and saved by Him. Without this affinity and desire, we would have no intrinsic motivation to examine the evidence, let alone assent to it. However, if we do believe that Jesus' view of love is our ultimate meaning and destiny, and as a result desire His saving presence in our lives, the evidence will be more than sufficient to galvanize the Holy Spirit within us to show that Jesus is "the way, and the truth, and the life" (Jn 14:6).

This faith in Jesus as Lord and Savior enables us to answer the many questions going beyond the domain of reason and experience. In Chapter 7, we look at the revelation of Jesus concerning

God's *universal* offer of salvation, the nature of eternal life with God ("Heaven"), the reason why God would allow Hell, and the path to salvation. If we believe that Jesus is Lord and Savior, it will transform and enhance everything we think about our nature, dignity, and destiny, as well as how we live, endure suffering, contend with evil, and enter into community and society; it will affect the ideals, values, and virtues we embrace, the friendships and relationships we pursue, and the legacy we will ultimately leave. It will be the most important decision of our lives.

If you, the reader, sense an affinity for Jesus' teaching on love (see Chapter 1), and desire to move toward eternal and unconditional love through His grace, healing, and redemption, you will want to consider carefully the evidence presented in this volume to solidify your belief and clarify the path toward salvation. If you are confirmed in your belief and trust in Jesus, then profess that faith within a Christian community, share it with others, pursue Jesus' path to salvation, and enter into the hope and destiny prepared for you from the beginning of time.

Chapter One

The Supremacy of Love

Introduction

It may seem more than a bit ironic that we entitle this chapter "The Supremacy of Love" because "supremacy" implies power and hierarchy, while "love"—at least in its best sense—implies gentleness and humility. Yet, the combination of these concepts is not "illogical", according to the logic of love, which is not so much concerned with analytical consistency as with actualizing what is ultimately positive, ultimately healing, ultimately fulfilling, ultimately transformative, and therefore ultimately victorious. Though the greatest rational philosophers, such as Socrates, Plato, and Aristotle, recognized love to be an essential part of one's happiness and fulfillment, they did not recognize the breadth and depth of love as humble and gentle compassion and forgiveness, in the way that Jesus defined it, and so they did not recognize that this compassionate love was our highest happiness and fulfillment. Since they only had experiential and rational access to God, they did not recognize that God *is* unconditionally *humble*, *gentle*, and *compassionate* love, and that such a God would want to bring us to our ultimate happiness and fulfillment with Him—to a place where we cannot bring ourselves. They had reached the limits of reason, and now the world awaited the coming of someone who could define love as humble and gentle and who would know about the unconditionally loving God.

There was a man who came three hundred years after Socrates, Plato, and Aristotle who claimed to be more than a man; indeed, He claimed to be the exclusive Son of His Divine Father and claimed to bring the definitive revelation about love and God, which He delivered in both word and action. Is Jesus *really* the ultimate revelation of God, the exclusive Son of God, the "unconditionally loving God personally and ultimately present to us"? The answer to this question lies in a historical examination of His words and actions, but before we can begin we must probe deeply into the meaning of love and the remarkable impact that Jesus had on its definition and actualization throughout the centuries.

In the previous consideration of God through experience and natural reason (Volume II) we discovered hints about the importance of love in the numinous experience, conscience, and particularly in our desire for perfect and unconditional love, which shows that love is linked to our happiness. But these hints do not add up to the affirmation of love as the *central* meaning and purpose of life. If we are to decide that love is the central meaning of life, we will have to consider it in the light of other candidates for life's central meaning and fulfillment.

How can we go about making such a decision about ultimate meaning in favor of love or something else such as success, reputation, security, material comfort, athletic prowess, beauty, or some combination of them? We must first and foremost define what we mean by "love", for without such a definition, we would not know what we are choosing (or rejecting). We will have to make sure that our definition is comprehensive enough, that it touches not only the *intellectual* domain, but also the emotional, intuitive, interpersonal, and transcendent domains. Once we have formulated a comprehensive definition, we will make distinctions within it so that we can classify the different kinds of love. This will enable us to make well-informed decisions about the highest principle, meaning, and fulfillment of our lives.

I. General Characteristics and Definition of Love

If we are to follow the classical model of the definition of love, we will want to begin with characteristics of love on which many thinkers (e.g., philosophers, theologians, psychologists, and literary masters) would agree. I will begin with three very well-known lists of the characteristics of love coming from the Christian tradition, because they permit at least partial agreement among many members of other religions as well as philosophers, psychologists, and literary masters:

1. The characteristics of love in Saint Paul's First Letter to the Corinthians (Chapter 13)
2. Jesus' definition of love—the Beatitudes (Mt 5:3–11)
3. The definition of love implicit in the Prayer of Saint Francis

Saint Paul lists both interior attitudes and behaviors that come from Jesus' teaching, the Beatitudes emphasize interior attitudes central to the heart of love, and the Prayer of Saint Francis focuses on the healing and restorative power of love. After examining these characteristics, we will be able to form a general definition of love acceptable to a large segment of the Christian and non-Christian population.

Let us begin with Saint Paul's definition of love in 1 Corinthians 13:4–8:

> Love is patient, love is kind. It does not envy, it does not boast, it is not proud. It does not dishonor others, it is not self-seeking, it is not easily angered, it keeps no record of wrongs. Love does not delight in evil but rejoices with the truth. It always protects, always trusts, always hopes, always perseveres. Love never fails. (My translation.)

In this list, Saint Paul has captured much of Jesus' teaching on love, trying to interpret it for both a Jewish and Gentile audience. Though Paul mentions positive interior dispositions (e.g., patience, kindness, protection, perseverance, and trust), he also lists attitudes and behaviors that should be avoided (e.g., envy, pride, boasting, anger, self-seeking, carrying grudges, and dishonoring others). This stands in contrast to six of the eight Beatitudes that are focused solely on positive interior dispositions. Each of these Beatitudes was explained in detail in Volume I, Chapter 9, Section II.A. The following gives a brief summary of that interpretation:

- poor in spirit (humble-heartedness)
- meek (gentle-heartedness)
- hunger for righteousness (readiness for salvation of self and others)
- mercy
- forgiveness of others and compassion toward the needy and marginalized

- purity of heart (authenticity and truth to self)
- peacemaking (reconciliation)

The prayer attributed to Saint Francis[1] focuses on the healing power and ministry of the loving person, and combines the interior dispositions and behaviors mentioned in 1 Corinthians 13 and the Beatitudes:

> Lord, make me an instrument of Your peace;
> Where there is hatred, let me sow love;
> Where there is injury, pardon;
> Where there is discord, harmony;
> Where there is error, truth;
> Where there is doubt, faith;
> Where there is despair, hope;
> Where there is darkness, light;
> And where there is sadness, joy.
> O Divine Master, Grant that I may not so much seek
> To be consoled as to console;
> To be understood as to understand;
> To be loved as to love.
> For it is in giving that we receive;
> It is in pardoning that we are pardoned;
> And it is in dying that we are born to eternal life.

As we reflect on these lists, we can see three dimensions of love:

1. Attitudes that will free us from self-centeredness, pride, and antipathy (humble-heartedness, hungering for righteousness, purity of heart, and avoiding envy, anger, boasting, and pride)
2. Attitudes that recognize the intrinsic dignity and goodness of others (gentle-heartedness, forgiveness, and patience, as well as not dishonoring others, not being easily angered, and not holding grudges)

---

[1] Though this prayer captures much of the teaching of Jesus and Saint Francis and is attributed to the latter, it was probably composed by a French priest, Fr. Esther Bouquerel, in 1912.

3. Attitudes and actions of compassion and service (kindness, peacemaking, and bringing care, light, hope, joy, peace, harmony, truth, and faith)

The following diagram shows the dynamic relationship among these three dimensions of love.

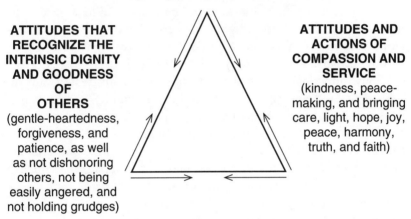

ATTITUDES THAT WILL FREE US FROM SELF-CENTEREDNESS, PRIDE, AND ANTIPATHY
(humble-heartedness, hungering for righteousness, purity of heart, and avoiding envy, anger, boasting, and pride)

ATTITUDES THAT RECOGNIZE THE INTRINSIC DIGNITY AND GOODNESS OF OTHERS
(gentle-heartedness, forgiveness, and patience, as well as not dishonoring others, not being easily angered, and not holding grudges)

ATTITUDES AND ACTIONS OF COMPASSION AND SERVICE
(kindness, peace-making, and bringing care, light, hope, joy, peace, harmony, truth, and faith)

As the diagram indicates, each of these dimensions of love is interrelated. Thus being freed from self-centeredness, pride, and antipathy will help us to recognize the goodness and dignity of others—and vice versa. Freedom from self-centeredness, pride, and antipathy will also help us to be compassionate and bring compassion to others—and vice versa. We can also see that recognizing the goodness and dignity of others will help us to be compassionate to them—and vice versa. So where should we begin the process of deepening our interior disposition so that we will be free to be caring and compassionate? Where can we find the interior power to *want* to do these things, let alone actually do them? We have two basic options: we can empower love from within *ourselves* (through a stoic act of will) or we can focus on the unique goodness and lovability of *others*.

The stoic approach to virtue (through an act of will) is not the approach of Jesus, Saint Paul, and Saint Francis. As we watch Jesus in many New Testament passages, we can see how He opens Himself to the goodness and dignity of others, especially sinners and the poor and the sick. He is not concerned with their outward appearance, but rather with their goodness, dignity, and transcendent mystery, which makes them uniquely lovable. This vision of the unique lovability of the other fuels His empathy, care, compassion, and desire to help them.

Jesus teaches us His way to love in the Parable of the Good Samaritan. The Samaritan's openness to the goodness and lovability of the man who had been beaten by the robbers—beyond all *appearances*—empowers his compassion. The Samaritan saw right through the bloody, half-dead figure lying on the side of the road—to a good and precious individual who had been unjustifiably mistreated, not just robbed of his belongings but of his intrinsic dignity and humanity. This vision moves the Samaritan to compassion, moving him to care about and even care for this stranger (who was an enemy of the Samaritan people). The vision of the stranger's intrinsic goodness and dignity moves the Samaritan to sadness and compassion, which in turn moves him to care about and for his "Jewish neighbor".

Notice that a stoic act of will proceeds in the opposite fashion. Seeing little (or no) goodness, dignity, transcendent mystery, or lovability in the other, the stoic must depend on *himself* to summon an act of will sufficient to love the unlovable, to help the wretched, and to tolerate the undignified. As he helps a poor person, he is drawn into the logic of the famous Roman Stoic philosopher Seneca:

> Consider, further, that the wise man uses foresight, and keeps in readiness a plan of action; ... he, consequently, will not suffer pity, because there cannot be pity without mental suffering.... He will bring relief to another's tears, but will not add his own; to the shipwrecked man he will give a hand, to the exile shelter, to the needy alms; ... he will do these things with unruffled mind, and a countenance under control. The wise man, therefore, will not pity, but will succor.... Pity is akin to wretchedness; for it is partly composed of it and partly derived

from it.... Pity is a weakness of the mind that is over-much perturbed by suffering, and if anyone requires it from a wise man, that is very much like requiring him to wail and moan at the funerals of strangers.[2]

Seneca views a compassionate heart as something weak, preferring to help the other out of a sense of duty and strength. Jesus teaches the opposite—that compassion for the unfortunate is the power that leads not only to bringing corporal assistance, but also to the restoration of the other's dignity and spirit. Seneca's mode of helping is focused primarily on the *self* (and attitudes to preserve strength within the self). Though he advocates giving assistance such as alms and hospitality, he treats the other with almost callous indifference—despising, instead of sympathizing with, the other's pain. Jesus holds that respect for the *other's* goodness and transcendent mystery will naturally lead to *sympathy* for the other's pain, and this in turn will lead to both corporal assistance and restoration of the other's dignity and lovability.

For Jesus, the beginning of love is the vision of the Good Samaritan that recognizes the goodness, lovability, and transcendent mystery of the other within his miserable outward appearance (Lk 10:25–37). If we can see the "good news" in the other, it will not only help us to be compassionate, but also to be free from self-centeredness, pride, and antipathy. Can we use a stoic approach to get to this kind of freedom? Can we will ourselves out of self-centeredness, pride, and antipathy? This project seems to be inherently contradictory—willing my*self* out of *self*-centeredness and pride. The minute we use the power of *self* to overcome the self, we ironically build up the self. The more we try to will ourselves to diminish ourselves, the more we increase ourselves, and so it seems that we need *another* person to free us from ourselves, our self-centeredness, and our pride.

Let's review where we have come. There are three interrelated dimensions of love, but it seems that one of them—"the recognition of the unique goodness and dignity of the other"—is the key to the other two; the impetus for love must come from the beloved. If we can see the unique goodness and lovability of the other, an act

---

[2] Lucius Seneca, *De Clementia*, in *World Essays*, trans. John W. Basore, vol. 1, The Loeb Classical Library (London: W. Heinemann, 1928), 2.6–7.

of empathy occurs, which breaks down the barrier between us and the other, allowing us to care about and for the other; this, in turn, enables us to see the other, no longer as "other", but as "beloved". When this unity occurs, we can become not only a source of corporal help to the other, but a source of genuine love, which can restore lost dignity and lovability, and through this, bring joy, hope, consolation, and peace.

Moreover, it turns out that virtue is its own reward, for the more we see the belovedness of the other, and the more we desire to help the other, the more we can become free from self-centeredness, pride, and antipathy. We no longer have to use the power of the self to overcome the self; we can use our vision and love of others to loosen the grip of self-centeredness, for we do not want our pride or antipathy to harm the one that we love.

The more deeply we see the goodness of the other, the more we are naturally inclined to empathize and care for them, and the more we care for them, the more we will not want to hurt or harm them. We will know the damage that our self-centeredness, pride, and antipathy can do, and we will be naturally inclined to move away from these things—attractive as they sometimes can be—for the *sake of the other*.

Though the unique goodness and lovability of the other is a strong motivator for freeing ourselves from self-centeredness, pride, and antipathy, all of us need additional assistance—namely, the grace of God. As with loving our neighbor, loving God proceeds naturally from recognizing the unconditional goodness and lovability of God and His unconditional empathy and care for us. The more deeply we recognize this—through Scripture, worship, prayer, inspiration, and God's providential guidance in our lives—the more we respond with gratitude and love. This is explained in detail in Volume I, Chapters 7–9.[3]

The more deeply we love the unconditionally loving God, the more we want to be in perfect relationship with Him, and the more

---

[3] Chapter 7 (Volume I) addresses contemplative prayer, particularly Ignatian contemplation on Scripture that emphasizes entering into biblical scenes in which Jesus manifests His love. Chapter 8 (Volume I) concerns following the Holy Spirit and discernment of spirits, particularly in times of suffering, and Chapter 9 (Volume I) discusses the Prayer of Gratitude (within the Examen Prayer) that allows us to appreciate our lives more deeply and God's action in it. All of these prayers help us to recognize and appreciate God's loving action in our lives.

we want others to be in this perfect relationship as well. Love has a remarkable way of moving beyond itself, because it seeks not only the good of one person, but of every person. The more we give ourselves over to the dynamic of love, the more it universalizes us. Of course we do not do this in a perfectly equal way; we commit ourselves to family and friends more than to strangers (because we do not have an infinite amount of time and psychic energy). However, the universalizing quality of love does help us to see the unique goodness and lovability in everyone, whether they be attractive, useful, esteemed, or wise (Aristotle's criteria for friendship), or not.

The love of God can also assist us with inspiration, spiritual strength, and providential guidance, which help to sustain and deepen our love for both friends and strangers. Once again we are getting ahead of ourselves, for if we are to affirm these truths about the power of God's love, we will have to make a *choice* about love and God, which may very well bring us face-to-face with the Person and revelation of Jesus Christ. Before we can move to these two fundamental choices, we will first want to complete our definition of love (in this section), make some distinctions within our general definition (Section II), address the power of love (Section III), and examine the potential of unconditional love as life's central meaning (Section IV).

Let us now return to our general definition of love. We saw that love involves three interrelated dynamics. It begins with opening ourselves to the unique goodness, dignity, lovability, and transcendent mystery of others (even strangers), which has a way of first capturing our attention. As we open ourselves more deeply to the goodness and mystery of others, we begin to empathize with them, which has the curious effect of mitigating what we formerly termed "the bad news" in them (what is irritating, insensitive, unkind, weak, and unintelligent).[4] As empathy grows, we begin first to care *about* them, but if we continue to open ourselves to them, their goodness and mystery seems to radiate from their eyes (the windows to their souls) and from the quality of their voices. This eventually results in care *for* others. They begin to have an emotional impact

---

[4] See Volume I, Chapter 4, Section III, which develops the distinction between looking for the good news versus the bad news in the other, showing the immense power of initial intentionality.

on us. As this occurs, we genuinely wish them well and feel discord (even a kind of sickness) about their suffering. At this point, we are gripped by compassion, the compassion of the Good Samaritan,[5] and are willing to make *sacrifices* for the good of the other, even a total stranger.

The reader may now be thinking, "Do everyday people use the word 'love' in this way? Is this general definition of love applicable to every kind of love?" The brief answer is that the above definition describes the *ideal* of love—that is, the end or goal (*telos*) toward which love strives, what Aristotle would call "what it was meant to be". We use the term "love" in many ways, and in most of these ways, it strives for its ideal—as "gift of self"—finding its perfection in the compassion capable of complete self-sacrifice. We may now proceed to a discussion of four distinct kinds of love, noting how each relates to the ideal specified above. As we shall see, the fourth kind of love, *agapē*, best reflects this ideal.

II. Four Kinds of Love

In his well-known work *The Four Loves*,[6] C. S. Lewis describes the four classical terms used for love: *storgē*, *philia*, *eros*, and *agapē*, noting that the first three kinds of love are widely present in classical Greek works of literature and philosophy, though *agapē* is not. This is the reason why the early Christian Church used it to refer to Jesus' unique and original meaning for "love"[7] (which is reflected in the above general definition and in Jesus' Parable of the Good Samaritan). I will briefly examine each kind of love and then concentrate on

[5]The Greek word used by Luke to translate Jesus' Aramaic is *esplagchnisthē*. The root *splagchnon* has the general meaning of "the bowels, which were thought to be the seat of the deeper affections, and could refer to pity or sympathy—inward affection, tender mercy". See James Strong, *New Strong's Exhaustive Concordance* (New York: Thomas Nelson), no. 4697. An online concordance is available at http://lexiconcordance.com/greek/4145.html. It signifies being deeply moved by the suffering of another. See also Jesus' reaction to the widow of Nain who has lost her only son (Lk 7:11–17).

[6]C. S. Lewis, *The Four Loves* (New York: Harcourt, 1960).

[7]For the unique and original meaning of love in Christianity, see John L. McKenzie, *Dictionary of the Bible* (New York: Macmillan, 1965), p. 521.

agapē (the uniquely Christian love), showing how it can bring *philia* and *eros* to their ideal expressions.[8]

Storgē (Affection)

Storgē (affection) is a spontaneous emotional response to someone or something we find to be outwardly lovable, delightful, or cute. Children immediately elicit affection (when they are in a good mood). The smile of a cherished friend, or even a pet, can elicit this spontaneous *emotional* response. This feeling can be quite fleeting or, in the case of parents, enduring. It lacks depth, does not necessarily result in action or commitment, and may not elicit the same response from others. It is dependent upon mood and a perception of the likeability and delightfulness of another. As will be seen, *agapē* is quite different from affection. Though affection may accompany *agapē*, *agapē* can occur without it.

Philia (Friendship)

Philia (friendship) expects mutuality or reciprocity, and when it occurs it is open to various degrees of commitment and depth. So, for example, if we deepen our commitment to a friend (perhaps through a pledge of time, shared concern, physical energy, psychic energy,

[8] Plato's classical work on love is the *Symposium*, but large sections of the *Phaedrus* and the *Timaeus* are also dedicated to this theme. See *The Collected Dialogues of Plato*, ed. Edith Hamilton and Huntington Cairns (Princeton, N.J.: Princeton University Press, 1961). Jesus' emphasis on love (*agapē*) is everywhere reflected in Christian Scripture and can be considered a central theme of virtually every book in the New Testament. Christian philosophers and theologians have also made this theme central to their writings, and it occupies a central place not only in spiritual works, but also in systematic and moral works. Later writers combined philosophical and theological material with insights from psychology and anthropology. In addition to C.S. Lewis' *The Four Loves*, there are two truly outstanding volumes on the nature of *agapē*: Martin D'Arcy, *The Mind and Heart of Love: Lion and Unicorn; A Study in Eros and Agape* (New York: Meridian Books, 1956), and Josef Pieper, *About Love*, trans. Richard Winston and Clara Winston (Chicago: Franciscan Herald Press, 1974). Other excellent works on *agapē* are Léon Joseph Cardinal Suenens, *Love and Control* (Westminster, Md.: Newman, 1962); Ignace Lepp, *The Psychology of Loving* (New York: Mentor-Omega Books, 1963); and Robert Johann, S.J., *The Meaning of Love* (Glen Rock, N.J.: Paulist Press, 1966).

or even our future), it acts as an invitation to our friend to make a commitment on a similar level back to us. If reciprocal commitment occurs, the friendship grows in depth. This depth reaches its natural limit only when both parties have committed themselves totally to each other. However, depth of friendship can increase only as much as each party is willing to reciprocate.

A certain state of being occurs conjointly with increased depth of friendship. There is a sense of caring and being cared for, a sense of being completed by the other and completing the other, a sense of being at home through the other and the other being at home through us, and a sense of intimate connection, which carries with it a sense of stability and well-being. A heightened degree of reciprocity and commitment requires considerable sensitivity and work, and so it should not be surprising to find occasional lapses in friendship manifested by frustration, impatience, anger, and dashed expectations.

Notice that *philia* has an inbuilt reward in its reciprocity—we not only care for another; they care for us. Similarly, we not only provide a home for the other; the other provides a home for us. We not only provide security, loyalty, and joy to others; they provide these things to us. Though our participation in friendship requires effort and discipline, it also provides us with reciprocal rewards. As will be seen, *agapē* is different from friendship in this respect because *agapē* neither anticipates nor seeks a reward.

Most of the time, we do not pursue friendships merely for the reward, but the reward is nonetheless anticipated and given. Though some friendships are pursued out of need, most of them originate from discovering something good, likeable, or lovable in another person, which elicits a desire for greater contact and collaboration.

Eros (Romantic/Sexual Love)

Eros is concerned with romance and romantic feelings. Romance is a complex phenomenon much broader than sexual feelings and satisfaction. It involves many dimensions of the psyche, including intimacy, generativity, the reception of generativity, anticipation of deep friendship and commitment, the perception of beauty, complementarity of function, anticipation of family, and a sense of adventure.

Hence, *eros* has a very wide range of feelings and psychological engagement coming from both personal maturity and decisions about life's meaning.

Recall from the discussion of happiness (Volume I, Chapter 4, Section I) that a Level One or Level Two view of happiness or purpose tends to emphasize *personal* gratification and satisfaction of *self*, while Levels Three and Four tend to emphasize empathy, contribution, and transcendental purpose. Thus, a person who has a Level One or Level Two meaning in life (who is likely to be less personally mature) will have a very different (more superficial) view of *eros* than a person in Levels Three and Four (who is more mature and is open to an intimate, generative, and committed relationship).

Recall also the discussion of "freedom from" and "freedom for" (Volume I, Chapter 4, Section V), in which it was shown that individuals on Levels One and Two are likely to have a view of "freedom from", which focuses on immediately attaining strong urges and desires, escaping constraint and commitment, "keeping their options open", and resenting unreciprocated sacrifices. Conversely, individuals on Levels Three and Four are likely to view freedom as "freedom for", which focuses on the most pervasive, enduring, and deep purpose in life, one that goes *beyond* self and makes a genuine contribution to family, friends, community, organizations, church, the Kingdom of God, and even the culture. In this view, constraint and commitment for the sake of achieving life's higher purpose is seen as worthwhile. Likewise, foreclosing options to pursue some truly good directions is deemed essential, and unreciprocated sacrifices are accepted and expected. Once again, these different views of freedom radically affect individuals' views of a romantic relationship, as well as their feelings and expectations from it.

We may now give a general profile of the focus and expectations for a romantic relationship in the perspectives of Level One-Two and Level Three-Four. As might be expected, the Level One-Two perspective of *eros* emphasizes what is more apparent, immediately gratifying, intense, and ego-fulfilling. Hence, its focus is predominantly on the sexuality, beauty, and gender complementarity, as well as being focused on romantic excitement and adventure. Furthermore its expectations are fairly short-term and focused on immediate gratification, keeping options open, increased levels of romantic excitement, and avoiding commitments and unreciprocated sacrifices. As a consequence, it resists movement to Level Three-Four, and the intimacy and generativity intrinsic to them (discussed below in this section).

In contrast to this, a Level Three-Four perspective of *eros* focuses on making a difference beyond the self, and in mature individuals on making the most pervasive, enduring, and deep contribution possible. It is also open to empathy and care for others (in its quest to make an optimal positive contribution to the world). Though it does not abandon the dimensions of *eros* emphasized in Levels One and Two (sexuality, beauty, gender complementarity, and romantic excitement), it contextualizes these desires within concomitant desires for intimacy, generativity, complementarity, collaboration, common cause, deep friendship, loyalty, commitment, and family. As noted above, a Level Three-Four perspective is not enough to bring about these desires; there must also be psychological stability and personal development and maturation. When these factors are co-present, the expectations of romantic relationships broaden and deepen. As a consequence there is a willingness to foreclose options, and to invest more fully in the romantic relationship (and ultimately to make this relationship exclusive). There is willingness to make the other a "first priority" in the expenditure of physical and emotional resources, which anticipates a lifelong commitment as well as unreciprocated sacrifices. The chart on page 37 summarizes the outlooks of both perspectives.

When romantic relationships occur in Level Three-Four individuals who are stable and mature, the intimate friendship becomes deeper and deeper. Recall that when *philia* is reciprocated, it tends to deepen and become more committed. When we commit more of our time, future, and physical and psychic energy to a friend, and that friend reciprocates with a deeper commitment to us, the friendship becomes closer, more supportive, more fulfilling, and more emotionally satisfying. When it is appropriate, this deep friendship can incite intimacy, generativity, and romantic feelings, which in turn can deepen the friendship even more—but now it is not just a deep friendship; it is an *intimate, romantic,* deep friendship. This distinctive kind of friendship can continue to deepen until both parties are not only ready for but desirous of making the other their *no. 1* priority. From a logical point of view there can only be one no. 1 priority; everything else is

LEVEL	FOCUS	EXPECTATIONS
Eros *(Romantic Love)* **3 and 4**	Openness to the importance and inclusion of intimacy, generativity, complementarity, collaboration, common cause, deep mutual friendship, long-term commitment, and family (note: sexuality, beauty, and romantic excitement are still important, but contextualized by the above).	Pervasive, enduring, and deep meaning, foreclosing of options to secure "best option", mutually supportive communion, constraints for the sake of intimacy, depth, and commitment, unreciprocated sacrifice
Eros *(Romantic Love)* **1 and 2**	Emphasis on sexual feelings and gratification, beauty of the other, romantic adventure, excitement of the relationship, and control within the relationship	Immediate and heightened gratification, fulfillment of the desire to be admired and loved, keeping options open, greater levels of excitement, and no unreciprocated sacrifices

a contradiction. Hence the desire to make a deep intimate friend a no. 1 priority is tantamount to wanting an *exclusive* commitment, which cannot be given to anyone else.

Furthermore, this deep friendship anticipates a *lifelong* commitment in which the couple enters into common cause—that is, to do some good through their mutual efforts for the world *beyond* themselves. The most significant dimension of common cause for a couple who are intimately related (anticipating sexuality) is the creation of a *family*. Recall from above that love moves *beyond* itself; we seek to do the good for *the other*, the community, the world, and the Kingdom of God. Just as loving individuals move beyond themselves, so also loving couples move beyond themselves. Though it is very important that the couple have their "alone time" to develop their closeness, affection, generativity, and mutual support, it is likewise important that they do not *stay* within the relationship *alone*. A couple staring into each other's eyes can be as mutually self-obsessive as Narcissus looking at his image in the pool; they can simply fade away doing nothing else. This illustrates the need for intimate friendships to move from "*within* the relationship" to "*beyond* the relationship". The deeply committed romantic relationship cultivates a complementary and collaborative strength, a synergy to move beyond itself to make a positive difference through common cause. Family is the most fundamental aim of such a relationship. But there can be many other objectives as well—for community, church, culture, Kingdom of God, and so forth. Though the most fundamental objective (family) must come first, it too must move beyond itself, to make a positive difference in ways that will not undermine its depth and cohesiveness.

In sum, the ideal of a Level Three-Four romantic relationship is to bring intimate friendship to its highest level—to make the intimate friend a no. 1 priority through an exclusive and lifelong commitment to enter into mutually supportive and collaborative common cause toward family and other positive objectives that will serve not only friends, but community, culture, church, and the Kingdom of God.

We can now see an inherent conflict between Level One-Two *eros* and Level Three-Four *eros*. The emphasis on beauty, adventure, and sexual feelings in Level One-Two *eros*, without the dimensions of generativity, friendship, and commitment, can incite individuals to be both sexually permissive and promiscuous. Sexual stimulation (from sexual activity to pornography) is frequently addictive.[9] Sexuality can become an end in itself, and when it does, romantic desires can only be accentuated by more sexual activity, more partners, or more excitement (amplified by aggressiveness, risk, and alcohol or drugs, etc.).[10] These activities can enhance sexual

---

[9] Activation of the reward pathways (dopamine system) in the lower brain by sexual activity, pornography, aggression, and drugs all form memories and habits of pleasure that can become gradually addictive. See Donald L. Hilton Jr., "Pornography Addiction—A Supranormal Stimulus Considered in the Context of Neuroplasticity", *Socioaffective Neuroscience and Psychology* 3 (July 19, 2013), http://www.socioaffectiveneuroscipsychol.net/index.php/snp/article/view/20767/29179. See also Frances Prayer, "What Drives a Sex Addict? Is Sex Addiction about Love or an Insatiable Craving?" *Psychology Today*, October 7, 2009, http://www.psychologytoday.com/blog/love-doc/200910/what-drives-sex-addict.

[10] Both sexual activity and aggression activate reward pathways in the hypothalamus. There is also evidence of an interrelationship between sexual desires and aggression (even violence) through the hypothalamus. See Dayu Lin et al., "Functional Identification of an Aggression Locus in the Mouse Hypothalamus", *Nature* 470 (February 10, 2011): 221–26, and Ewen

addiction[11] and desensitize the individual to higher dimensions of relationship and psychic satisfaction (e.g., intimacy, generativity, collaboration, common cause, friendship, commitment, exclusivity, and family). As a result, the long-term practice of Level One-Two *eros* can become addictive, callous, and aggressive,[12] leading to objectification ("thingification") of the other, "using" the other as an object of gratification, and dominating the other for ego satisfaction. This can lead to a state of mind in which intimacy, generativity, and mature friendships are hard to recapture. The addictive quality of lower-brain activities can make it difficult to move from Level One-Two to Level Three-Four happiness and meaning. The longer individuals reinforce Level One-Two *eros*, the more difficult it will be for them to grow in levels of maturity and development, and to seek genuinely intimate, generative, and exclusive romantic relationships. It is difficult to maintain and deepen marital and family relationships with a narrow Level One-Two perspective and focus.

Agapē (Compassionate Love)

The central meaning of *agapē* is captured by our general definition of love: looking for the unique goodness and lovability and transcendent mystery of the other that incites empathy for the other, whereby doing the good for the other is just as easy if not easier than doing the good for oneself. This empathy with the other can lead to caring about the other and caring for the other to the point of self-sacrifice (even complete self-sacrifice). The attitude of the Good Samaritan shows all of these qualities.

Agapē has four distinctive qualities:

1. *Agapē* is its own reward; it does not have a secondary reward, as do the other three kinds of love.

Callaway, "Sex and Violence Linked in the Brain", *Nature News*, February 9, 2011. If sexuality is connected to generative (higher cerebral) functions, it will likely mitigate the aggressive components originating in the hypothalamus.

[11] See Hilton, "Pornography Addiction", and Prayer, "What Drives a Sex Addict?"

[12] See ibid.

2. *Agapē* can be as powerfully manifest with strangers as with friends, spouses, and children.
3. *Agapē* is not concerned with the appearance of the other.
4. *Agapē* can be directed toward negative individuals in negative situations.

Each of these points deserves attention.

With respect to the first distinctive quality, *agapē* expects no secondary reward beyond protecting, maintaining, and fostering the good of the *other*. There is no need to obtain a good for the self at the same time. Thus, *agapē* does not need the affectionate feelings of *storgē*, or the mutuality, support, and feelings of friendship, or the romantic feelings and commitments of *eros* (which are reflected back to the loving person from the beloved). *Agapē*'s fulfillment terminates in the good of the other, which is its own reward.

With respect to the second distinctive quality, *agapē* requires no familiarity with the beloved. It is directed toward anyone in need. Recall that *agapē* seeks not just to alleviate a person's need or pain, but to do this in a way that treats the other with respect and communicates that he is intrinsically good and lovable (deserving of the good received). Once again we see that the focus of *agapē* is the *other*, specifically his *intrinsic* goodness, lovability, and transcendent mystery. As we saw, the Parable of the Good Samaritan reveals this quality.

With respect to the third distinctive quality, *agapē* is unconcerned with appearances, which is frequently not the case for the other three kinds of love—*storgē* (affection) seeks the appearance of adorableness or delightfulness, *philia* (friendship) frequently seeks companions who are pleasant in appearance and behavior, and *eros* (romance) is inevitably connected with beauty (even if it is in the eyes of the beholder). Since *agapē* focuses on the good of the other alone, it begins with looking for the unique dignity, lovability, and transcendent mystery of the other—*beyond* all appearances. Thus, when people are moved by *agapē*, they can see beyond repudiation, sickness, poverty, destitution, and any other form of *apparent* indignity. The perspective of *agapē* invests dignity in the goodness, lovability, and transcendent mystery of the other in himself, which is always present, irrespective of *every apparent* indignity. The Good Samaritan's compassion is incited by the worthiness, lovability, and mystery of the other, even though he is beaten, robbed, and half-dead. Blessed Teresa of Calcutta (Mother Teresa) saw the presence of Christ and transcendent beauty in every physically damaged person she served. Saint Francis of Assisi, who began his life in a wealthy family, gave away that wealth to work for the poor and sick. He originally had an aversion to leprosy and other ghastly wounds, but his strong sense of the intrinsic dignity of the sick (and Jesus' presence in them) turned that aversion into complete dedication. In a famous transitional incident, he kissed the face of a leper who was asking for alms, and this led to a breakthrough to "the *agapē* of Jesus".

With respect to the fourth distinctive quality, *agapē* does not lose its power in a *negative* environment, but rather gains it. *Storgē* feels no affection or delight for an enemy or someone offensive. *Philia* can expect no mutuality or reciprocity from an offender or enemy, and of course, no one (except perhaps a masochist) seeks romance with someone offensive, harmful, or destructive. However, *agapē* is not daunted by the negating, offensive, or even evil qualities of others, because it is seeking the unique goodness and transcendent mystery of the other alone, and so it attempts to break through even the most dark qualities in order to allow a person's intrinsic light to be rekindled.

Since *agapē* seeks the good of the *other* alone, it is the only kind of love that can be the source of forgiveness, toleration of insult and injury, and love of enemies. Without a doubt, these three dimensions of *agapē* are the most difficult among Jesus' teachings, because they require going beyond another virtue: *justice*, which is acknowledged to be primary by many philosophers and non-Christian religions. *Agapē requires* justice, for it is impossible to seek the good of the other while being unjust to him (taking away what belongs to him or is due to him). However, *agapē* goes beyond justice by asking its adherents to give up their rights to retribution for injustice.

Since justice concerns equity, it must always have two sides: giving others their due, and expecting our due from others. If others do not respect what belongs and is owed to us, justice grants us a right of retribution or retaliation. The principal case of this is the ancient edict "an eye for an eye, and a tooth for a tooth" (the *Lex Talionis*). In religious circles, the principle of retributive justice (a punishment corresponding to the kind and degree of a harm or injustice) may be seen not only in the ancient Mesopotamian Code of Hammurabi, but also in the Old Testament (Lev 24:19–21; Ex 21:22–25; Deut 19:16–21). Later rabbis humanized it so that it did not exact a harm for a harm, but rather gives compensation of some equivalent value for a harm.

Philosophers beginning with Socrates, Plato, and Aristotle articulated the two sides of justice as the proper distribution of goods (the positive side) and the proper distribution of punishments (the negative side). Plato advocated retributive justice, both for the common good (see *Republic*) and for the individual offender (see *Gorgias*). Aristotle also believed that retributive justice is necessary for the common good (see *Nichomachean Ethics*, Book V).

However, *agapē*, according to Jesus, naturally transcends the negative side of justice. Though *agapē* entails the positive side of justice (the proper distribution of goods), it does not seek punishment as a necessity or an intrinsic good for either individuals or society. It seeks to replace retribution with mercy and forgiveness, though it allows for protection of individuals and society by incarceration or other nonretributive means. This dimension of *agapē* goes beyond natural philosophy, for one must see beyond the negative deeds and qualities of the individual to the intrinsic goodness and transcendent mystery of the individual himself.

III. The Power of *Agapē*

For Jesus, forgiveness and the remission of retaliation or punishment have a remarkably positive and healing power. This power comes from the goodness of love itself and from the Spirit of God working through this goodness. It has the power to heal individuals, communities, culture, and society. Though the power of forgiveness and remission of punishment may seem to be counterintuitive, history is replete with examples of its immense good. The contrast between the Versailles Treaty and the Marshall Plan testifies to this. The Versailles Treaty punished the German people severely for their aggression in the First World War. As a result, the German economy collapsed, opening the way for Hitler and the Nazi party to assume power. In contrast to this, the Marshall Plan forgave the immense debt of

Germany for the Second World War and offered economic assistance to rebuild its economy. This resulted in a long-standing military ally that has become the cornerstone of the European economy.

The leadership of South Africa (most notably Nelson Mandela and Desmond Tutu) also showed remarkable forgiveness and compassion after the dissembling of apartheid when the African National Congress came into power after the free multiracial elections in 1994. The "winners" could have exacted a terrible vengeance on the perpetrators of apartheid, but they chose not to do so. Instead they instituted an almost ritualistic path to forgiveness and reconciliation, which not only averted violence and atrocities, but led to partnerships with white farmers and businessmen, thereby preserving the economy and assuring a peaceful transition to black leadership in every area of government, education, and commerce. When this approach is compared to the violence and forcible redistribution of land by despots throughout the world, the results speak for themselves. Love is more powerful than retribution, terror, and death.

The power of *agapē* is manifest not only in history's social dynamics, but also in individual lives. There are literally hundreds of cases of people like Viktor Frankl and Louis Zamperini who have been tortured severely or callously mistreated for years, and who have recovered from their experiences and transformed their lives into a positive cultural force through the power of forgiveness (*agapē*). Viktor Frankl was a Jewish Austrian psychiatrist who was interred in several Nazi concentration camps (along with his wife and parents), during the Second World War. He was sent to Auschwitz and ultimately to Kaufering (Dachau), where he was compelled to be a slave laborer under the harshest conditions. During that time he had an epiphany while on a veritable slave march back to the concentration camp. Visualizing his wife, he thought:

I heard her answering me, saw her smile, her frank and encouraging look. Real or not, her look was then more luminous than the sun which was beginning to rise.

A thought transfixed me: for the first time in my life I saw the truth as it is set into song by so many poets, proclaimed as the final wisdom by so many thinkers. The truth—that love is the ultimate and the highest goal to which Man can aspire. Then I grasped the meaning of the greatest secret that human poetry and human thought and belief have to impart: *The salvation of Man is through love and in love.*[13]

This insight led Frankl to crystalize his thoughts about the meaning of suffering, and the necessity to give positive meaning to life through even the most dreadful experiences. It became the foundation for his school of existential psychotherapy called "logotherapy" (recognized as the "Third Viennese School of Psychotherapy"). For Frankl, the power of love and positive meaning enabled him to transform suffering into a life of service for the world, bringing him closer to God (whom he considered to be a Supermeaning associated with a Superbeing who is the epitome of our interior longing). Frankl went on to publish thirty-nine books, many of which were translated into forty languages.

A less heralded figure, Louis Zamperini had a similar experience as a prisoner of war. He was an Olympic athlete in the 1936 Olympics in Germany who held collegiate records in long-distance running. He was captured by the Japanese in World War II and was sent to the Ōfuna Camp, a prisoner-of-war camp where he was badly beaten and tortured for over two years—particularly by ruthless guard Watanabe. When he was released and returned to the United States, he suffered from posttraumatic stress disorder and tried to sedate himself with alcohol and extreme living. He was consumed by hatred for his oppressors and overwhelmed by his memories of the camp. By happenstance (Providence?) he came upon a Billy Graham revival and decided to become a Christian. Through his faith and the power of prayer and forgiveness, he decided to let go of his hatred and sought out the guard who had inflicted the greatest cruelties and degradation upon him. He wrote a letter to Watanabe telling him that he forgave him, but Watanabe died before it reached him. He then proceeded to turn his life into a ministry to help those like himself to move from darkness to light through forgiveness. He gave countless speeches around the world and built a summer camp to help young people learn early the power of forgiveness, resilience, and faith.[14]

---

[13] Viktor Frankl, *Man's Search for Meaning: An Introduction to Logotherapy* (New York: Beacon Press, 1992), p. 48.

[14] His life is beautifully chronicled by Laura Hillenbrand in the best-selling biography *Unbroken: A World War II Story of Survival, Resilience and Redemption* (New York: Random House, 2010).

The power of *agapē* is also enshrined in one of Victor Hugo's classic works, *Les Misérables*, in which Jean Valjean is thrown into prison for many years for trying to steal bread for his starving sister. After being released from prison, he can find no means of employment, or even a place to stay because of his past incarceration. The bishop of Digne (Myriel) allows Valjean to stay at his home, for which Valjean "repays" him by stealing his silver. He is caught almost immediately and tells the police that he was given the silver by Bishop Myriel. The police bring him to Myriel, who supports Valjean's lie and then gives him two additional candlesticks, as if to say that he had forgotten to take them. He later asks Valjean to use the money from the candlesticks to do some good. This initiates twenty years of generosity and self-sacrifice, which is frequently met by greed and hatred.

Valjean starts a factory and becomes mayor of the town in which his factory was built. He begins to do good works with his wealth, and one day his generosity leads to trouble. He rescues a man caught under a cart, which arouses the suspicions of a police official, Javert, who pursues him throughout his life. Valjean helps a former factory worker by rescuing her daughter (Cosette) from greedy innkeepers (the Thénardiers) who have made her an indentured servant. In the complex tapestry that follows, he becomes a man of compassion, helping people at great risk to himself. In addition to rescuing Cosette, he rescues her prospective husband, Marius, from the barricades. Then in his most remarkable act of compassion and forgiveness, he rescues his adversary Javert from being executed by members of the rebellion. He then turns himself in to Javert and asks for some time to say good-bye to Cosette and Marius. While doing this, Javert experiences the power of Valjean's compassion and falls victim to an existential dilemma between his duty to strict justice and the law versus the compassion shown him by Valjean. He cannot bring himself to betray Valjean's compassion or to fail in his duty to the law, and so he throws himself into the Seine River, allowing Valjean to go free. Conversely, Valjean dies a contented man, keeping his promise to Bishop Myriel and to Cosette's mother, after giving Marius and Cosette his wealth.

Hugo does not believe that compassion will put an *end* to darkness, evil, greed, and social injustice. Indeed, these negative forces within the human condition follow Valjean wherever he goes. Yet, he responds to these acts of injustice with even greater compassion and forgiveness. So what is Hugo's point? Compassion may not eliminate evil and injustice, but it will slow them down—sometimes curbing their momentum, sometimes winning converts (such as Valjean and Javert), and often creating its own momentum of goodness that can last for generations.

For Hugo, compassion (*agapē*) can only work its wonders through a willing heart—at minimum, a partially willing heart—but it is rendered powerless in an unwilling heart. Hugo illustrates this "unwilling heart" in the Thénardiers (the greedy innkeepers), who seem to reappear in Valjean's life over and over again, not only unmoved by his compassion, but all the more anxious to exploit what they consider to be his weakness. In the end Valjean gives them enough money to go to America, where they can reach their heart's "highest" aspiration: to become slave traders. This tragic irony of the "success" of the evil heart should not be interpreted as a true success for Hugo, for even though they have deluded themselves into thinking they have success, the whole of their lives is one gigantic dark negation, a lie that expresses the full meaning of Socrates' philosophy: "The unexamined life is not worth living."

As can be seen from the above examples—from history (the Marshall Plan and the South African response to apartheid), the biographies of Victor Frankl and Louis Zamperini, and literature (e.g., Hugo's *Les Misérables*)—*agapē* holds out a tremendous power to curb the momentum of evil, overcome the momentum of injustice, and restore dignity to the oppressed and tortured. But this power is not limited to these social, societal, and cultural domains. It is equally effective in our families,[15] and our organizations and communities, in which acts of forgiveness and gratuitous kindness can overcome a history of neglect and abuse.[16]

The negative effects of "unforgiveness" are even more obvious; history is replete with examples of how vengeance begets vengeance,

[15] Virtually every Christian denomination offers several books on the importance and power of forgiveness and *agapē*. Catholics may want to consult R. Scott Hurd, *Forgiveness: A Catholic Approach* (Los Angeles: Pauline Books, 2011).

[16] See the many examples in Shan Ray Ferch, *Forgiveness and Power in the Age of Atrocity: Servant Leadership as a Way of Life* (Lanham, Md.: Lexington Books, 2011). See also Robert Greenleaf, Larry C. Spears, and Stephen R. Covey, *Servant Leadership: A Journey into the Nature of Legitimate Power and Greatness* (Mahwah, N.J.: Paulist Press, 2002).

and violence begets violence. In every culture in every age there are literally dozens of examples of feuds that have become warring factions, and warring factions that have incited civil and global wars. Injustice not only produces a desire for retribution, but also the potential to escalate through the forces of "anti-forgiveness"—pride, anger, contempt, and brooding. When these escalating effects occur, there are only three possible outcomes: mutual destruction, exhaustion (from overfighting), or forgiveness. If we make recourse to forgiveness, it will no doubt take an act of humility and we will probably have to pay a price—we will have to give up the prized possession of "as much retribution as we deserve". Yet, if we embrace this cost of forgiveness, we find that the price is much, much smaller than the alternative of violence begetting violence. Moreover, the good momentum it produces within individuals, families, organizations, communities, and societies can endure for many generations. Humility and relinquishing the right to punish are a small price to pay for the blessings of forgiveness, but this can only be recognized by someone who is open to the positive power of *agapē*.

IV. Unconditional Love as the Central Meaning of Life

Before considering the question of unconditional love as the central meaning of life, we will want to return for a moment to the four kinds of love discussed above (Section II), for we have left an important question unanswered—namely, how the four kinds of love are interrelated. Recall that *storgē* (affection) is only a spontaneous *feeling*; it is not an action, a state of being, or the internal dynamic of a relationship. Though feelings are important, they do not express the full reality and power of love. The other three kinds of love often include feelings of affection, but feelings need not always be present for these other loves to be real, powerful, and dynamic.

As noted above, *philia* can evolve into *eros* when romantic-sexual feelings are present and there is a mutual desire to make each party a no. 1 priority, anticipating an exclusive, lifelong commitment. However, most of the time, friendships do not move to this stage of *eros*, because friendships can produce mutual benefits and common cause without a single romantic feeling. Furthermore, if friends do feel romantic feelings, but do not have an interest in moving their friendship to an exclusive lifelong commitment, they will be better served—in both the present and the future—by refraining from expressing them sexually. As noted above (Section II), sexual expression without the concomitant intimacy, generativity, complementarity, deep friendship, and common cause evoked by the anticipation of exclusive lifelong commitment can make sexuality an end in itself, which not only implies using another (and being used by another), but also can block the mature development of intimacy, generativity, complementarity, and common cause. Furthermore, repeated sexual expressions—unconnected to deep friendship and commitment—can become aggressive, in order to enhance the excitement of the sexual act, which has become an end in itself.[17] It is best to let *philia* be *philia*, and to let *eros*, which is directed to exclusivity, be *eros*.

Additionally, *philia* can involve *agapē*. Most of us, looking back upon our long-term friendships, will recognize times when we had to be forgiving, and our friends had to forgive us; when we had to make sacrifices far beyond the reciprocity intrinsic to the friendship; or when we remained loyal to friends who changed for the worse— even "beyond recognition". It was not *philia* that provided the dynamic to remain connected with and do good for the other, but *agapē*, the love that is concerned exclusively with the other, which allows us to accept a cost to ourselves. Thus, we can say that friendships can be brought to their highest self-sacrificial level by *agapē*, but *agapē* does not need the reciprocity or feelings of friendship.

Eros can involve *agapē* in the same ways as *philia*, more frequently and more intensely. Every exclusive lifelong commitment will require moments of genuine forgiveness—giving undeserved compassion and self-sacrifice to another throughout a multitude of negative moods, through "tough times", and through changes of personalities and family dynamics. Much of the time, the romantic-sexual feelings of *eros* will not be able to carry a couple through these inevitable challenges. Without the power of *agapē* it will be difficult to break through the negative momentum and achieve a positive result from experiences of deprivation, suffering, and degradation. If we affirm the positivity

---

[17]See Hilton, "Pornography Addiction"; Prayer, "What Drives a Sex Addict?"; Lin et al., "Aggression Locus in Mouse Hypothalamus"; and Callaway, "Sex and Violence Linked in Brain". See also the explanation of *philia* and *eros* in Section II above.

of *agapē*, and we anticipate its necessity in friendships and in marriage, it can be transformative by bringing light out of darkness, goodness out of evil, and even generative love out of resentment, hatred, and contempt. For this reason, romantic relationships fortified by *agapē* (with a realistic sense of the challenges that life can bring) are likely to succeed in fostering intimacy, generativity, deep friendship, common cause, and good families.

In conclusion, *agapē* may be viewed as the purest form of love because it is concerned with the good of the other alone (without expectation of reciprocity, repayment, or reward) and because its power is derived from the unique goodness, lovability, and transcendent mystery of the other. This is what gives it its capacity to be compassionate without regard to the appearance of the other, to sacrifice for a stranger, and to forgive the most undeserved degradation and cruelty. This pure quality of *agapē* enables it to rescue friendships and marriages, to heal organizations and communities, and to allow cultures and countries to recover from unspeakable cruelties (without repeating the cycle of violence begetting violence). Accordingly, *agapē* can bring *philia*, *eros*, justice, and peace to fruition, and if we let it, bring them to their ideal: "what they were meant to be".

So, is love the central meaning of life? Are *agapē*, *philia*, and *eros* (as defined above) capable of bringing us personally to our fulfillment ("what we meant to be")? Is love capable of bringing community and culture to its fulfillment? Is it capable of bringing all individual aspirations, including the other transcendentals (perfect truth, perfect justice, and perfect beauty), to its fulfillment? Is it capable of producing perfect happiness in all four levels (as described in Volume I)? Is it the central meaning of life?

We cannot give a complete answer to this question by merely affirming or assenting to the strong evidence for the positivity of love in every dimension of life and culture; we will also have to make it part of our lives, not only in thought, but also in action. This reveals three layers of assent in answering the question of whether love is the central meaning of life:

1. An *intellectual affirmation* that love is our most positive power, which is the only one capable of bringing us to happiness and fulfillment on all four levels

2. A *decision* to make this threefold love (*philia-eros-agapē*) the main purpose and goal of one's life
3. The *choice* to actualize this goal every day and in every relevant decision

Do we have to assent to the centrality of love on all three levels in order to approach our original question about Jesus as God's ultimate self-revelation? I do not think so, because in my life, I had not attained the second and third levels of assent when I decided that Jesus truly was (and is) God's ultimate self-revelation. In retrospect I do not believe I could have come to those levels without the revelation of Jesus, the guidance of the Church, and the grace of God. I don't just *believe* this; I *know* it.

No doubt many people have attained the second and third levels of "assent to love" without faith in Jesus, but I am not one of them. As noted in Volume I, I did not make a natural transition from the second level of happiness to the third, but instead moved from the second level to the fourth level (the transcendent level), and then back to the third level. In many respects, I followed the examples of Saint Paul and Saint Augustine, who sought first the ultimate, perfect, and eternal in life's meaning and destiny—only to discover in an *intellectual affirmation* that love is integral to that meaning and destiny.

As I contemplated the transcendental desires of truth, love, justice, and beauty in college, I could sense the positive power of love. I recognized it not only in good friendships, but also in my anticipation of marriage and family (which was based on the experience of my own great family). Yet, I knew that there was more to love than *philia* and *eros*, for I had experienced forgiveness as well as undeserved compassion, loyalty, and self-sacrifice—not only from my friends and family, but from God, whom I sensed was not indifferent to me, but who cared for me. This awareness of God's love came from my Catholic faith, both in its ordinariness and also in special times of prayer (on one particular Christmas Eve, a particular Good Friday liturgy, and a particular moment of insight at school—see Volume I).

This experience of transcendent love made my first level of assent to love more lucid and certain. It added a dimension of ultimate significance and eternity to my experience of family and friends—an experience that revealed undeserved kindness, forgiveness, and love's potential for positivity, happiness, and fulfillment. This brought me to perhaps the most important realization of my life. I saw an intrinsic connection between the fulfillment of my nature and destiny in *this world* and the fulfillment of my *eternal* and *transcendental* nature and destiny through the love of Jesus Christ.

Later in college, I had a strong conviction about God's existence through physics and logic, a strong sense of God's inner presence and my transcendental nature that could only be satisfied by perfect truth, love, goodness, and beauty and a concomitant conviction that love held the key to my happiness, purpose, and destiny. I also had a sense of love that went beyond *philia* and *eros*—an incipient sense of the power of *agapē*. When I listened to the New Testament passages read during Mass, I became aware of two interrelated dimensions of happiness—that the highest level of love is *agapē*, and that God is unconditional love.

I subsequently learned that these two teachings were unique and original to Jesus, but I did not need to know this in order for those New Testament readings to bind together my conviction about love and eternal life. It occurred to me that Jesus held the key to *ultimate love*, which I believed to be the only one true fulfillment of my nature and destiny. At that point I needed only one assurance—that God was unconditional *agapē* and that He was calling me to be with Him in this love (as well as everyone else who was open to it).

I was truly fortunate to have all the pieces of the puzzle of ultimate happiness, purpose, fulfillment, and destiny come together catalytically and synthetically, truly fortunate to have discovered the power of love, recognized my transcendental nature, and to have heard the teaching of Jesus; but I wondered, what if I had only known the first two pieces of the puzzle and had not been fortunate enough to hear those New Testament passages? Would I still have been able to find my way to Jesus' revelation about *agapē* and the unconditional love of God? Though Jesus was central to *my* recognition of these truths, I saw a way in which others might be able to come to them by experience and reason—and in so doing, discover Jesus and even enter into a relationship with Him.

There is something built into our experience of love and our transcendental nature that points us to their fulfillment. If we probe them deeply, they tell us what they "need" to be ultimately fulfilled—namely, perfect love (particularly, perfect *agapē*) and the unconditionally loving God.

These two truths of experience and reason (the importance of love and our transcendental nature) seek their ultimate meaning and fulfillment in Jesus' revelation of *agapē* and the unconditional love of God. This will be the topic of the next chapter.

Chapter Two

The Unconditional Love of God

Introduction

We concluded the last chapter by saying that two of the highest truths in experience and reason are

1. love is integral to happiness, purpose, fulfillment, and destiny, and
2. we have a transcendental nature—revealed not only in our interior awareness of the transcendent, but also in our transcendental desire for perfect truth, love, justice, and beauty.

We also saw that these two truths seek the two central revelations of Jesus as their ultimate fulfillment—namely,

1. *agapē* as the purest form of love, and
2. God is *unconditional* love (*agapē*).

These two central revelations are unique and original in the teaching of Jesus. When these two revealed truths complement the two high truths of natural reason, they manifest the fulfillment of human nature, happiness, purpose, and destiny (as indicated in the diagram on page 54).

At the end of the last chapter, I posed the question of whether someone could discover that Jesus is the ultimate revelation of God by recognizing what the two major truths of experience and reason were seeking as their fulfillment: *agapē* and the unconditionally loving God. The following reflection (Section I) will show that it is possible. I have used this reflection many times to help students recognize that Jesus holds the key to their highest yearnings, fulfillment, and destiny.

Human nature
as transcendent
(desire for perfect
truth, love, justice,
and beauty)

God (the Father)
is unconditional love
(the Father of the
Prodigal Son)

NATURAL TRUTHS OF EXPERIENCE AND REASON

God, Jesus, and *agapè* are
ultimate fulfillment of happiness,
purpose, and destiny

REVEALED TRUTHS OF JESUS

Love as integral to
happiness, purpose,
destiny

Purest form of
love is *agapē*
(the Good Samaritan)

I. From Natural Reason to God's
Ultimate Self-Revelation

If we grant that God exists, that we have a transcendent nature, and that love is integral to our nature, happiness, purpose, and fulfillment, might we expect that God is unconditionally loving, and that He would want to be perfectly present to us, to bring us to our fulfillment? I think we can discover the answer to this from a logical assessment of evidence within ourselves. If we believe that love is the central meaning and fulfillment of our lives, it will lead us right into the reality and presence of the unconditionally loving God—to Jesus Emmanuel ("the unconditionally loving God with us").

A. Six Steps from the Creator to Jesus

When I was teaching at Georgetown University, I was privileged to direct a physics and philosophy student on an Ignatian retreat. He was exceptionally bright and good-willed and had the capacity to express what was on his mind in a very straightforward way. At the beginning of our first conference he said, "Could I ask you something very elementary which has been bothering me for several years? I don't have any real difficulty believing in God, because I think the evidence of physics points to the finitude of past time, implying a beginning and a creation.[1] My real problem is Jesus—I don't get it. If I believe in God, why do I need anything more, like Jesus? Can't we just stick with a 'Creator outside of space-time asymmetry'?"

I thought about it for a couple of minutes and said to him, "Jesus is about the *unconditional love* of God. He is about God's desire to be with us in a perfect act of empathy, about God wanting to save us unconditionally and to bring us to His own life of unconditional love. A Creator alone, indeed, even a Creator with infinite power, could be tantamount to Aristotle's God. Once He has fulfilled His

---

[1] See Robert J. Spitzer, *New Proofs for the Existence of God: Contributions of Contemporary Physics and Philosophy* (Grand Rapids, Mich.: William B. Eerdmans, 2010), Chapters 1–3, and also Robert J. Spitzer, *Indications of Creation in Contemporary Big Bang Cosmology*, vol. 10 of *Philosophy in Science* (Tucson: Pachart, 2003). See also Volume II, Appendix I, which summarizes the evidence for an intelligent Creator from physics.

purpose of ultimate, efficient, and final causation, He is detached from the affairs of rather base and boring human beings. The God of Jesus Christ is about the desire to be intimately involved in the affairs of human beings made in His image and destined for His eternity—and that makes all the difference."

He said in reply, "This all seems a bit too good to be true. I would like the Creator to be the God of Jesus Christ, but do you have any evidence that this is not just wishful thinking—evidence showing that this is really the way God is? Is there any reason why we would think that God is loving instead of indifferent?" I responded by noting that it would be better for *him* to answer six questions rather than have *me* give an extended discourse, because the six questions could reveal not only what was in his mind, but more importantly, what was in his heart—what he thought about love, life's purpose, others, and his highest imaginable state of existence. If he answered these six questions (from his heart) in a manner commensurate with "the logic of love", then the unconditional love and divinity of Jesus (Jesus being Emmanuel, "God with us") would become evident.

Question no. 1: What is the most positive and creative power or capacity within you? At first glance, one might want to respond that this power is intellect, creativity, wisdom, or artistic or literary genius, but further reflection shows that the capacity to apprehend truth or knowledge, or to create beauty, *in and of itself*, is not necessarily positive. Knowledge and beauty can be misused, and therefore be negative, destructive, manipulative, inauthentic, and thus undermine both the individual and the common good. There is but one personal power that contains its own end of "positivity", one power that is directed toward the positive by its very nature, and therefore one power that directs intellect and artistic creativity to their proper, positive end. As may by now be evident, that power is love (*agapē*, as defined in Chapter 1). Love's capacity for empathy, its ability to enter into a unity with others leading to a natural "giving of self", forms the fabric of the common good and the community, and so it seeks as its end the good of both individuals and the community.

Recall that *agapē* seeks the good of the *other* and derives its power from looking for the intrinsic goodness, lovability, and transcendent mystery of the other. For this reason, it needs no rewards like the mutuality of friendship or the romantic dimensions of *eros*. The good of the other *is* its own reward. Thus it is not deterred by the appearance of the other, whether the other is a stranger, or even whether the other has been offensive or harmful. This enables *agapē* to be the dynamic of forgiveness, compassion, and self-sacrifice—for anyone and everyone.

Agapē by its very nature unifies, seeks the positive, orders things to their proper end, finds a harmony amid diversity, and gives of itself in order to initiate and actualize this unifying purpose. This implies that love (*agapē*) is naturally oriented toward perfect positivity and perfect fulfillment.

Furthermore, love (*agapē*) would seem to be the one *virtue* that can be an end in itself. Other virtues do not *necessarily* result in positivity or culminate in a good for others. So, for example, courage left to itself might be mere bravado or might lead to the persecution of the weak. Self-discipline, left to itself, might lead to a disdain for the weak or a sense of self-sufficiency, which is antithetical to empathy. Even humility can be overbearing and disdainful if it is not done out of love. Even though these virtues are necessary means for the actualization of love (i.e., authentic love cannot exist without courage, self-discipline, and humility), they cannot be ends in themselves, for they can be the instruments of "unlove" when they are not guided by the intrinsic goodness of love. Love seems to be the only virtue that can be an end in itself and therefore can stand by itself.

Now, if *you*, the reader, affirm the existence of this power within yourself and further affirm that it is the guiding light of both intellect and creativity—that its successful operation is the only way in which all your other powers can be guided to a positive end, that it is therefore the only way of guaranteeing positivity for both yourself and others, and that it therefore holds out the promise of authentic fulfillment, purpose in life, and happiness—then you will have acknowledged *love* to be the highest of all powers and the central meaning of life. You will then want to proceed to the next question.

Question no. 2: If love is the one power that seeks the positive in itself, and we are made to find our purpose in life through love, could God (the unique unrestricted act of thinking that creates everything else), who created us with this loving nature, be devoid of love? If the Creator were devoid of love, why would that Creator create individuals not only with the capacity for love, but to be fulfilled only when they are loving? If the Creator is devoid of love, why make love the fulfillment of all individual powers and desires, and therefore of human nature? If the Creator is not loving, then the creation of "beings meant for love" seems absurd. However, if the Creator *is* love, then creating a loving creature (i.e., sharing His loving nature) would seem to be both intrinsically and extrinsically consistent with what (or perhaps better, "who") He is. Could the Creator be any less loving than the "loving nature" He has created? Furthermore, if the Creator is perfectly intelligent—a unique unrestricted act of thinking[2]—wouldn't that perfection extend to the highest perfection (love)?

If you, the reader, can reasonably affirm the love of the Creator from the above, then proceed to the third question.

Question no. 3: Is your desire to love and to be loved merely conditional or unconditional? Recall from Volume I, Chapter 4, Section I that we not only have the power to love (i.e., the power to be naturally connected to another person in profound empathy, care, self-gift, concern, and acceptance); we have a "sense" of what this profound interpersonal connection would be like if it were perfect. This sense of perfect love has the positive effect of inciting us to pursue ever more perfect forms of love. However, it has the drawback of inciting us to *expect* ever more perfect love from others. This generally leads to frustrated expectations of others and consequently to a decline of relationships that can never grow fast enough to match this expectation of perfect and unconditional love.

The evidence for our awareness of and desire for perfect love can be seen in our capacity to recognize *every* imperfection of love in others and in ourselves.[3] How could we have this seemingly unlimited capacity to recognize imperfection in love without having some sense of what perfect love would be like? Without at least a tacit awareness of perfect love, we would be quite content with any manifestation of affection that just happens to come along.

---

[2] See Lonergan's proof of God in Chapter 3 of Volume II of the Quartet.

[3] See the detailed exposition of this point in Chapter 4 of Volume II of the Quartet.

Do you, the reader, have a capacity to recognize imperfection of love in others and yourself? Do you do this seemingly without limit? If so, could you do this without some sense of what perfect love would be like? And if you have this awareness of and desire for perfect love, would you be content with anything less? Do you want to continue the pursuit of love until you have arrived at what you truly desire? If so, then you will have also affirmed within yourself the intrinsic desire for unconditional love, which leads to the next question.

Question no. 4: If our desire for love can only be ultimately satisfied by unconditional love, then could the Creator of this desire be anything less than unconditional love? A simple response to this question might run as follows: if we assume that the Creator does not intend to frustrate our desire for unconditional love, it would seem that His creation of the desire would imply an intention to fulfill it, which would, in turn, imply the very presence of this quality within Him. This would mean that the Creator of the desire for unconditional love is Himself unconditional love.

The converse is a contradiction. Why would God create us with a desire for unconditional love, only to allow it to go unfulfilled in everyone? Such a God would be a trickster and abjectly cruel, which contradicts the love of the Creator affirmed above in question no. 2. The argument may be summed up as follows: if God is really the Creator of our desire for unconditional love, and He does not intend to frustrate it in us, then He intends to fulfill it; and if He intends to fulfill it, He must have the capacity to do so, which means that He must be unconditionally loving. So did God really create our desire for unconditional love?

Recall from above that we have the capacity to recognize every imperfection of love in others and ourselves, revealing at least a tacit *awareness* of perfect love, which brings these imperfections to light. This tacit awareness of unconditional love seems to be beyond any specifically known or concretely experienced love, because every manifestation of love we encounter is *imperfect*. How can we have an awareness of unconditional love that we have not experienced? How can we even extrapolate to it if we do not know what we are looking for? So it seems that there must be some source of our awareness of unconditional love that is capable of unconditional love.

Is God the source of our tacit awareness of unconditional love? Recall from Lonergan's proof of God (Volume II, Chapter 3, Sections III and IV) that there must be a *unique*, unrestricted act of thinking to create everything else. Recall also from our investigation of the transcendentals (Volume II, Chapter 4, Section I.B) that perfect thinking must be a perfect unity and so also must be perfect love. Yet, as we saw, there can only be *one* perfect unity, and so, perfect thinking and perfect love must be the *same* reality (otherwise, there would be *two* perfect unities). If this reasoning is correct, then God must be the *one and only* perfectly loving reality, and therefore must be the *one and only* source of our tacit awareness of perfect and unconditional love.[4]

If you are in agreement with "God being unconditional love", then you will want to proceed to the next question.

Question no. 5: If the Creator is unconditional love, would He want to be with us and enter into a personal empathetic relationship with us face-to-face? Would He be Emmanuel ("God with us")? If one did not attribute unconditional love to God, then the idea of God wanting to be with us would seem implausible. If God were not loving, He would not bother to relate to creatures, let alone actually be among them and enter into an empathetic relationship with them. However, in the logic of love, or rather, in the logic of unconditional love, all this changes.

If we attribute the various parts of the definition of *agapē* (given in the previous chapter) to an unconditionally loving Creator, we might obtain the following result: God would be focused on what is uniquely good, lovable, and mysterious in each one of us, and in seeing this perfectly would enter into a perfect empathetic relationship with us, whereby doing the good for us would be just as easy if not easier than doing the good for Himself. Thus God would empathize with and do the good for us unconditionally, without expecting the "reward" of the other three kinds of love. He would

---

[4]Karl Rahner expresses this explicitly in his *Foundations of Christian Faith* (New York: Crossroad, 1982), pp. 123–24 (see the quotations in Volume II, Chapter 4, Section IV.B). See also Bernard Lonergan, *Method in Theology* (New York: Herder and Herder, 1972), p. 111; Josef Pieper, *About Love*, trans. Richard Winston and Clara Winston (Chicago: Franciscan Herald Press, 1974); and John Powell, *Unconditional Love* (New York: Argus, 1978).

love us unconditionally even if we did not love Him—even if we resented and rejected Him. He would love us unconditionally even if we had sinned terribly, so terribly that we had no hope of being excused, but only forgiven. His unconditional love would seek as deep a relationship with us as *we*, in our freedom, would allow. He would not only want to be with us in deepest intimacy; He would even sacrifice Himself for us—sacrifice Himself *unconditionally* for us even if we did not deserve it, *particularly* if we did not deserve it. If God were unconditional love, and the purest form of love is *agapē*, then God's love would naturally extend itself to us in an unmitigated act of compassion and affection, irrespective of our transgressions. If we open ourselves and respond to His love, He will deepen it until He brings us into the fullness of relationship with Him, which is perfect joy. If God truly is unconditional *agapē*, then it would be perfectly consistent with His nature (and heart) to want to be perfectly present to us, as Emmanuel.[5]

If God is truly unconditional love (*agapē*), then He is also unconditional empathy; and if He is unconditional empathy, He would want to enter into a perfectly empathetic relationship with us, "face-to-face" and "peer-to-peer", where the Lover and beloved would have an equal access to the uniquely good and lovable personhood and mystery of the other through empathy. A truly unconditionally loving Being would want to give *complete* empathetic access to His heart and interior life in a way that was proportionate to the receiving apparatus of the weaker (creaturely) party. Thus it seems that an unconditionally loving Creator would want to be Emmanuel in order to give us complete empathetic access to that unconditional love through voice, face, touch, action, concrete relationship, and in every other way that love, care, affection, home, and felt response can be concretely manifest and appropriated by us. If God really is unconditional love, and *agapē* is the perfection of love, then we might expect that this God would want to be perfectly present to us as Emmanuel. If this resonates with the reader's thoughts and feelings, you will want to proceed to the next question.

---

[5] Even though an unconditionally loving God would never stop loving us, He would give us the freedom to reject His love, because He would not want to force it upon us. Therefore, He would have to make some accommodation for those who wanted to live without Him and without love—even eternally. See Chapter 7, Section III of this volume.

Question no. 6: Inasmuch as the unconditionally loving God would want to be perfectly present to us, is Jesus the One? To answer this question, we will want to examine three dimensions of His teaching and life:

1. Jesus' proclamation of the unconditional love of God (Section III below)
2. Jesus' life of unconditional love (Chapter 3)
3. Jesus' manifestation of divine authority and power, in His Resurrection, gifts of the Spirit, and miracles (Chapters 4–5)

In other words, the rest of this book will be devoted to answering the following question: Is Jesus Emmanuel?

As we reflect on these three dimensions of Jesus' revelation in both our minds and hearts, it will impart a gradual freedom to believe. Instead of thinking, "God with us is too good to be true", we begin to think that an unconditionally loving God would *really* want to be with us, and if He were to come, that Jesus would be His perfect presence to us.

Since this is a truth of the heart, we will have to enter with our hearts into the mystery of Jesus' teaching and life of love. As we do so, we are likely to feel a deeper affinity for Him and recognize His love for us personally. This will galvanize the truth about *agapē*, Jesus' identity, and the Father's love within our hearts.

B. Can We Know the Unconditional Love of God by Reason Alone?

The reader may be thinking, "If we can show by reason alone that God is unconditional love, and that an unconditionally loving God would want to be with us in a perfectly empathetic relationship (as in the above reasoning process), why do we need a special self-revelation of God such as Jesus?" Though the above reasoning process has considerable probative force, it is dependent on two propositions that did not manifest themselves in history prior to the time of Jesus:

1. Love is the highest, purely positive, central meaning of life.
2. The purest, most excellent expression of love is what the Christians call "*agapē*" (see Chapter 1, Sections II and III).

Surprising as it may seem, great philosophers such as Socrates and Plato, and the world's great religions and sages, simply did not see these truths prior to the preaching and life of Jesus. After Jesus reveals them (see below in this chapter and Chapter 3), the philosophical world catches the implication—namely, the conclusion we just drew above (that God is unconditionally loving).

Notice that the two truths revealed by Jesus do not come from what Blaise Pascal called "the *mind's* reasons" (empirical and a priori evidence assembled through logic, mathematics, and scientific method), but rather through the *heart's* reasons (our intuitions and feelings of love, goodness, beauty, the numinous, and the sacred) as well as our *choice* to make love the first priority. Think about it: Could you have affirmed the answer to question no. 1 (above), concerned with love as the highest and most central meaning of life, without the involvement of your heart and your will? If you had not grasped with your intuition, feelings, and will how supremely positive and elevating love is, would you have ever considered it or chosen it to be the most central meaning of life? For myself, I do not think it would have been possible.

The same question might be asked with respect to knowing that the purest form of love is *agapē*. Would you have really known this without intuiting and feeling its importance and goodness in your *heart*? Would you have really chosen this very challenging form of love that includes forgiveness of enemies and compassion for a stranger if you did not have some inner sense of its excellence (an inner sense that did not come from rationality alone)? Again speaking for myself, I don't think I could have discovered this by my reason alone. I needed a movement of the heart.

Now here is the rub. If I could not have discovered these two remarkable truths of the heart by my experience and natural reason alone, how would I have ever come to be aware of them sufficiently to make my heart (intuition, feelings, and will) soar? How could I have known it sufficiently to be drawn to it and fed and transformed by it? After years of reflection, I can only answer, "Without the *revelation* of Jesus, I would have been as unaware of these two truths as the entire philosophical and religious world prior to the time of Jesus. I would have aspired to the justice of Socrates and Plato and to the truth of Aristotle, but I would have been completely in the dark about love and its primacy in life's meaning."

The curious conclusion I have arrived at is this: once Jesus revealed the centrality of love and its perfection in *agapē*, it became intuitively obvious, obvious to the heart's reasons that love *is* the central meaning of life, that the logic of love is not only true, but *the* truth, and that each person's unique goodness, lovability, and transcendent mystery (that animates forgiveness, compassion, and self-sacrifice) is the ground of that truth.

I have asked myself many times, "How could the whole of history have missed this truth prior to the time of Jesus?" I keep coming back to the words of Pascal: "The heart has its reasons that the mind (reason) does not know." I then add my personal conclusion that Jesus is the *first* light and inspiration of the heart's greatest reason, that love's perfection is *agapē*, and that this is not only the central meaning of life, but hope for the world and the destiny of everyone who chooses to accept it. Jesus not only provided the initial inspiration and light of our hearts; He continues to inspire and liberate them generation after generation.

Could we have reasoned to an unconditionally loving God (with the above reasoning process) *without* Jesus? Speaking personally, I do not think so because I do not think I could have gotten beyond question no. 1 without Jesus. I wouldn't have found my heart, recognized the goodness and beauty of its fulfillment in *agapē*, and as a consequence, chosen love as the central meaning of life. I would have been satisfied with truth and justice as the meaning of life and been oblivious to the ultimate meaning and power of love.

Once Jesus reveals the centrality of love and its purest form (*agapē*), we can answer question no. 1; and when we do this, we can then answer questions 2–5 from *experience* and *natural reason*. Though reason can carry us from love as our central meaning in life, to the existence of an unconditionally loving God, it cannot reveal or prove that love *is* our central meaning in life. Without Jesus to reveal this, and our hearts to affirm it, we remain in the state of the world prior to the time of Jesus. However, Jesus' revelation of the centrality of love enables our hearts to liberate reason so that it can move from the centrality of love to the unconditionally loving God who would want to be with us in perfect empathy. Revelation and the heart liberate reason so that reason can find its ultimate fulfillment.

II. A Brief Introduction to the Historical Jesus

Before examining Jesus' revelation of the unconditional love of God, it may prove helpful to consider three points about the historical Jesus:

1. The evidence for Jesus outside Christian Scripture
2. The apostolic proclamation (*kerygma*)
3. A brief portrait of Jesus according to the third historical quest

Volumes have been written on each of these three topics, but our purpose is simply to introduce them so that readers can have a basic background of the historical evidence for Jesus.

A. Evidence of Jesus outside of Christian Scripture

There are three major extratestamental sources of the historical Jesus:

1. The Roman historian Cornelius Tacitus
2. The Jewish historian Flavius Josephus
3. The Babylonian Talmud

Cornelius Tacitus

The Roman historian Cornelius Tacitus makes explicit reference to the Crucifixion of Jesus in the *Annals*, when speaking about Nero's blaming the Christians for the burning of Rome:

> Consequently, to get rid of the report, Nero fastened the guilt and inflicted the most exquisite tortures on a class hated for their abominations, called Christians by the populace. Christus, from whom the name had its origin, suffered the extreme penalty [crucifixion] during the reign of Tiberius at the hands of one of our procurators, Pontius Pilatus, and a most mischievous superstition, thus checked for the

moment, again broke out not only in Judaea, the first source of the evil, but even in Rome, where all things hideous and shameful from every part of the world find their center and become popular.[6]

There has been considerable discussion about the authenticity of this passage, but the majority of mainstream scholars concur with Kirby that

> the most persuasive case is made by those who maintain that Tacitus made use of a first century Roman document concerning the nature and status of the Christian religion. As to the reliability of that source, following normal historical practice, it is prudently assumed to be accurate until demonstrated otherwise. The reference from Tacitus constitutes *prima facie* evidence for the historicity of Jesus.[7]

Flavius Josephus

Flavius Josephus (a Jewish historian writing a history of the Jewish people for a Roman audience in approximately A.D. 93) provides the most impressive and detailed evidence for the historical Jesus outside Christian Scripture. Many historians and exegetes have written extensively on Josephus' testimony about Jesus because there were obvious Christian edits and interpolations of this text. Luke Timothy Johnson,[8] Raymond Brown,[9] and John P. Meier[10] have a very balanced (and somewhat minimalistic) approach to the critical passage. All three scholars believe that the beginning part of the passage from Josephus' *Antiquities* has not been significantly changed or edited, though later parts clearly were. The passage (sometimes called the

---

[6] Cornelius Tacitus, *Annals*, in *Complete Works of Tacitus*, ed. Alfred John Church and William Jackson Brodribb (New York: Random House, 1942), Book 15, Chapter 44, Perseus Digital Library, http://www.perseus.tufts.edu/hopper/text?doc=Perseus%3Atext%3A1999 .02.0078%3Abook%3D15%3Achapter%3D44.

[7] Peter Kirby, "Cornelius Tacitus", *Early Christian Writings*, accessed October 16, 2015, http://www.earlychristianwritings.com/tacitus.html.

[8] See Luke Timothy Johnson, *The Gospel according to Luke*, Sacra Pagina Series, ed. Daniel J. Harrington, vol. 3 (Collegeville, Minn.: Liturgical Press, 1991), pp. 113–14.

[9] See Raymond Brown, *An Introduction to New Testament Christology* (New York: Paulist Press, 1994), pp. 373–76.

[10] See John P. Meier, *A Marginal Jew: Rethinking the Historical Jesus*, vol. 2, *Mentor, Message, and Miracles* (New York: Doubleday, 1994), pp. 592–93.

Testimonium Flavianum) appears directly below. The italicized portions represent those which many scholars believe are part of the original text of Josephus. The unitalicized parts are either probably or definitely Christian additions or interpolations.

> *Now there was about this time Jesus, a wise man,* if it be lawful to call him a man; *for he was a doer of wonderful works, a teacher of such men as receive the truth with pleasure. He drew over to him both many of the Jews and many of the Gentiles.* He was [the] Christ. *And when Pilate, at the suggestion of the principal men amongst us, had condemned him to the cross,* those that loved him at the first did not forsake him; for he appeared to them alive again the third day; as the divine prophets had foretold these and ten thousand other wonderful things concerning him. *And the tribe of Christians, so named from him, are not extinct at this day.*[11]

Johnson provides a mainstream-minimalistic view of the matter:

> Stripped of its obvious Christian accretions, the passage tells us a number of important things about Jesus, from the perspective of a 1st-century Jewish historian.... Jesus was both a teacher and a wonder-worker, that he got into trouble with some of the leaders of the Jews, that he was executed under the prefect Pontius Pilate, and that his followers continued to exist at the time of Josephus' writing.[12]

"Wonder-worker" in the above passage refers to Jesus' miracles, and it is one of the most explicit references to miracle working in Josephus' works. Meier explains it as follows:

> Thus, Jesus of Nazareth stands out as a relative exception in *The Antiquities* [*of Josephus*] in that he is a named figure in 1st-century Jewish Palestine to whom Josephus is willing to attribute a number of miraculous deeds (*Ant.* 18.3.3 Sec. 63: *paradoxōn ergōn poiētēs*). That Josephus did not transform 1st-century religious figures into miracles-workers in an irresponsible fashion is shown not only by his presentation of the "sign prophets" but also by the intriguing contrast between Jesus and the Baptist in Book 18 of *The Antiquities*. The Baptist receives the longer and more laudatory notice (18.5.2 Sec.16–19), but without

---

[11] Flavius Josephus, *Jewish Antiquities*, ed. and trans. Louis H. Feldman, Loeb Classical Library (Cambridge, Mass.: Harvard University Press, 1965), 18.3.3.

[12] Johnson, *Gospel according to Luke*, pp. 113–14.

benefit of miracles, while Jesus is presented as both miracle-worker and teacher. The distinction implied in Josephus is mirrored perfectly in the Four Gospels.[13]

Babylonian Talmud

The Babylonian Talmud refers to Jesus in several references that can be dated between A.D. 70 and A.D. 200. It uses the terms "Yeshu", "Yeshu ha-Notrzri", "ben Satda", and "ben Pandera" to refer to Jesus. In view of the fact that the passages indicate rabbinical hostility toward Jesus and cast His Crucifixion in a negative light, they may be considered to be free of later interpolation. One of the passages states that Jesus was accused of "witchcraft", indicating that Jesus was known to have some kind of extraordinary and otherworldly power.[14]

In sum, Tacitus speaks to the historicity of Jesus' trial and Crucifixion, naming both Pontius Pilate as procurator and Tiberius as Caesar. Josephus also speaks to Jesus' Crucifixion and Pontius Pilate, adding Jesus' miracle working, "wisdom" (authority), and teaching. The Babylonian Talmud affirms Jesus' Crucifixion and miracle working.

B. The Apostolic Proclamation (Kerygma)

The *kerygmas* represent the earliest extant proclamations of the primitive Church (late A.D. 30s and 40s).[15] They are brief texts that resemble very simple creedal statements and are to be found mostly in the Pauline letters and the Acts of the Apostles (particularly in the speeches of Peter and Paul). These texts predate the Pauline letters and the Acts of the Apostles, in which they are contained. They are identifiable through form-critical methods, which were elucidated by C. H. Dodd and his predecessors.[16]

---

[13] Meier, *Marginal Jew*, pp. 592–93.

[14] See Babylonian Talmud, Tractate "Sanhedrin", 43a.

[15] C. H. Dodd, *The Apostolic Preaching and Its Developments* (New York: Harper and Brothers, 1962), p. 16.

[16] Four of the key elements here are (1) its formulaic character; (2) in the Acts of the Apostles, the occurrence of doublets in a style diverging from Luke's; (3) the absence of any theological interpretation from a later era of the Church; and (4) a Semitic and Aramaic background (identified originally by Charles Cutler Torrey in *The Composition and Date of Acts* [Cambridge: Harvard University Press, 1916]). For a fuller explanation, see Dodd, *Apostolic Preaching*, pp. 19–22.

There are nine major *kerygma* statements: Acts 2:14–39; Acts 3:13–26; Acts 4:10–12; Acts 5:30–32; Acts 10:36–43; Acts 13:17–41; 1 Thessalonians 1:10; 1 Corinthians 15:1–7; and Romans 8:34.

When we combine the content of these *kerygmas*, we find eight major repeated themes:

1. Jesus was a descendent of David.
2. Jesus was predicted by the prophets.
3. Jesus worked miracles.
4. Jesus was crucified and buried for our sins (in all major *kerygmas*).
5. Jesus rose in glory (in all major *kerygmas*).
6. Jesus gave His disciples the Holy Spirit.
7. Jesus is now exalted in God.
8. Jesus is, therefore, Messiah and Lord.

There is considerable historical evidence to substantiate four of these apostolic themes:

1. *Jesus worked miracles*—extratestamental sources (see II.A above), the Jewish polemic to explain Jesus' miracles ("It is by Beelzebul ..."), and historical verification by Raymond Brown and John P. Meier (see Chapter 5)
2. *Jesus was crucified and buried*—extratestamental sources (see above, II.A), archaeological evidence, historical verification by Brown and N.T. Wright (see Chapter 3)
3. *Jesus rose in glory*—Wright's assessment of messianic movements, Saint Paul's witness dilemma, and Wright's analysis of Second Temple Judaism (see Chapter 4)
4. *Jesus gave the Holy Spirit*—Dunn's analysis of miracles in the early Church and contemporary evidence of the power of the Spirit (see Chapter 5)

When this evidence is combined, it reveals why the early Church believed that Jesus is the exclusive Son of the Father (the Son of God), and why it was willing to make so many sacrifices to proclaim Him not merely risen from the dead, but the Lord (*ho Kurios*, the Greek Septuagint translation of the divine name "Yahweh").

The attribution of divinity to Jesus cost the apostolic Church dearly, because it ran contrary to the strict monotheism of Second

Temple Judaism and was viewed as blasphemous and repugnant to most Jewish audiences. This eventually led to Jewish Christians being banned from the synagogue (which they did not want), a loss of social and financial status, and even persecution and death.[17]

At the very least, the proclamation of Jesus' divinity was apologetically unappealing. Both Jewish and Gentile audiences would have been repulsed by the divinization of a crucified man, tried as a criminal. Why would the apostolic Church have selected a doctrine that was viewed so unfavorably by the very audience that it wanted to attract?

As Joachim Jeremias remarks, this was wholly unnecessary, for the apostolic Church did not have to proclaim or even imply that Jesus was divine (or raised in glory) in order to bestow great favor upon Him within the culture of the day. It could have proclaimed Him to be a "martyr prophet",[18] which would have allowed converts to worship at His tomb and to pray through His intercession. This more modest claim would have made Him acceptable to Jewish audiences, who could then have ranked Him high among the "holy ones".

Why then did the leaders of the apostolic Church go so unapologetically and dangerously far to proclaim that "Jesus is Lord" (Rom 10:9; see Rom 14:9; Phil 2:11)? Why did they suffer social and financial loss, religious alienation, and even persecution and death, when it all could have been avoided by simply giving up the implication of His divinity? The most likely answer is that they believed Him to be *truly* divine.

So why did the apostolic Church believe Him to be divine and even to share a unity with the Father throughout all eternity? How could they be so sure of this radical proclamation that had so many negative consequences, when they could have taken the "easier road" in proclaiming Him to be a martyr prophet? Was it simply because

---

[17] For a general context in which these events occurred, see James D. G. Dunn, *The Partings of Ways between Christianity and Judaism and Their Significance for the Character of Christianity* (London: SCM, 1991); Martin Hengel, *Acts and the History of Earliest Christianity*, trans. John Bowden (Philadelphia: Fortress Press, 1980); and N. T. Wright, *Jesus and the Victory of God*, vol. 2 (Minneapolis: Fortress Press, 1996).

[18] Joachim Jeremias, *Heiligengräber in Jesu Umwelt (Mt. 23, 29; Lk. 11, 47): eine Untersuchung zur Volksreligion der Zeit Jesu* (Göttingen: Vandenhoeck and Ruprecht, 1958), and Hans Küng, *On Being a Christian*, trans. Edward Quinn (Glascow: Fount Paperbacks, 1978), p. 371.

of Jesus' claim to be the exclusive Son of the Father or something more? When we read the nine major *kerygmas*, we see the "something more": His glorious Resurrection, the gift of the Holy Spirit (the power of God), His miracles (by *His* own power and authority), and the love He shares with the Father for all eternity.

These experiences showed the apostolic Church that Jesus shared in God's power, authority, and love, making it the *truth* that could not be compromised, a truth worth sacrificing everything for—financially, socially, and religiously, even to the point of death.

C. A Brief Portrait of Jesus according to Mainstream Historical Scholarship

Allowing temporarily for the credibility of the apostolic testimony to the four major themes of the *kerygmas* (Jesus' Crucifixion and death, Resurrection in glory, gift of the Holy Spirit, and miraculous power), what can be said about the historicity of the rest of the Gospel—that is, about Jesus' sayings, disciples and friends, love of sinners and the poor, and his relationship to religious authorities? What can we say about His claim to be the eschatological judge ("the Son of man") and the exclusive Son of God the Father? What about His claim that God is unconditional love, and that He desires to bring us together with Him in His eternal Kingdom? What about the details of His Passion, death, and burial? Do these claims about Jesus also stand up against historical scrutiny? Can they be tested for historicity in the same way as the facts of His Crucifixion, miracle working, Resurrection in glory, and gift of the Holy Spirit? They can.

In Chapters 4 and 5, we will discuss several historical criteria that have been used to test the veracity of the major claims in the New Testament, such as the criteria of multiple attestation, embarrassment and discontinuity, sufficient and necessary explanation, continuity, and literary/textual criteria. The application of these criteria to the four Gospels enables the majority of mainstream Scripture scholars to affirm the historicity of a large part of them.

Some readers may have heard that New Testament scholars are skeptical about the majority of New Testament texts. No doubt there are some scholars (a minority) who feel this way, and the "Jesus

Seminar" (most notably Dominic Crossan, Marcus Borg, and Robert Funk) represents the extreme edge of these scholars (who seem to receive an inordinate amount of publicity). However, the most comprehensive Scripture scholars (such as Raymond Brown, Joseph Fitzmyer, N. T. Wright, and John P. Meier) do not subscribe to these skeptical views and, in fact, vigorously oppose them.[19] Furthermore, Gary Habermas has done a large survey of exegetes (from very liberal to very conservative) and found that the vast majority do not share the Jesus Seminar's skeptical views of the Resurrection (see Chapter 4 for a summary).

The Jesus Seminar's extreme position arises out of two erroneous historical assumptions that have been discredited by mainstream scholarship—that Jesus was heavily influenced by Greco-Roman and Hellenistic thought, and the elimination of future eschatology from Jesus' message. John P. Meier summarizes the majority viewpoint as follows:

> The Jesus Seminar as a whole has faced severe criticism for its methods and conclusions. Both the Cynic and the Gnostic coloration of its portrait of Jesus are questionable on the grounds of dating of sources and historical context, and the wholesale elimination of future eschatology from Jesus' message flies in the face of its widespread attestation in many different gospel sources and literary forms. Despite the Seminar's protestations to the contrary, it has not avoided the temptation of projecting a modern American agenda onto a first-century Palestinian Jew.[20]

Today most scholars hold that Jesus was not heavily influenced by Greco-Roman thought, and in fact grounded His thinking in the categories of the culture through which He was formed: Palestinian Judaism. When this background is combined with His unique emphasis on apocalyptic eschatology, Jesus emerges as a completely

---

[19] See the debate between N. T. Wright and Dominic Crossan (one of the principle members of the Jesus Seminar) on the historicity of Jesus' Resurrection in Robert B. Stewart, ed., *The Resurrection of Jesus: John Dominic Crossan and N. T. Wright in Dialogue* (Minneapolis: Fortress Press, 2006), pp. 78–92.

[20] John P. Meier, "The Present State of the 'Third Quest' for the Historical Jesus: Loss and Gain", *Biblica* 80 (1999): 460.

different Person from the one portrayed by the Jesus Seminar. Jesus' combination of Palestinian Judaism with apocalyptic eschatology is not only attested to in multiple sources and literary forms, but also provides a unified explanation for many sayings, which would otherwise be difficult to explain. This broad context provides a fresh new approach to the historicity of Jesus' miracles,[21] deeds, and sayings. In Wright's view,

> the "Jesus Seminar" has rejected Jewish eschatology, particularly apocalyptic, as an appropriate context for understanding Jesus himself, and in order to do so has declared the Marcan narrative a fiction. The "Third Quest," without validating Mark in any simplistic way, has placed Jesus precisely within his Jewish eschatological context, and has found in consequence new avenues of secure historical investigation opening up before it.[22]

So who was Jesus according to mainstream Scripture scholars? John Meier presents him this way:

> the total *Gestalt*, the total configuration or pattern of this Jew who proclaimed the present yet future kingdom, who was also an itinerant prophet and miracle worker in the guise of Elijah, who was also a teacher and interpreter of the Mosaic Law, who was also a charismatic leader who called disciples to follow him at great price, who was also a religious personage whose perceived messianic claims wound up getting him crucified by the Roman prefect, in the end, a crucified religious figure who was soon proclaimed by his followers as risen from the dead and Lord of all. It is this total and astounding configuration of traits and claims that makes for the uniqueness of Jesus as a historical figure within 1st-century Judaism.[23]

---

[21] John P. Meier, for example, uses this context for his historical justification of a considerable number of Jesus' exorcisms, healings, and "raisings from the dead" in an exhaustive four-hundred-page analysis. See Meier, *Marginal Jew*, pp. 509–1038; see also Meier, "Present State of 'Third Quest'", pp. 482–83. A detailed synopsis of Meier's exhaustive study is given in Chapter 5 of this book.

[22] Wright, *Jesus and Victory of God*, p. 81; for an excellent summary of how the Third Quest came from the first two quests for the historical Jesus, see pp. 75–79, 82–124. See also Meier, "Present State of 'Third Quest'", pp. 459–87 (the entire article); and Stewart, *Resurrection of Jesus*, pp. 1–15.

[23] Meier, "Present State of 'Third Quest'", pp. 476–77.

When Jesus is seen in light of this very credible portrait, most of His sayings and deeds recorded in the Gospels appear not only plausible, but probable—His unique way of working miracles, His love of sinners, His identification with the poor, His preaching of the present and future Kingdom, His mission of defeating Satan, His parables, the elements of His great sermons, His tension with religious authorities, His conviction about His Father's unconditional love, His claim to be the exclusive Son of God the Father, the Jewish polemic against him, the charges brought against him by religious and Roman authorities, and even the manner of His death and burial. When we combine the likelihood of these dimensions of His life and ministry with that of the Resurrection and gift of the Spirit, we see a plausible historical portrait of a man who could reasonably qualify for Emmanuel, the unconditionally loving God with us. The remainder of this chapter, as well as Chapters 3–6, will be devoted to verifying this claim.

III. Jesus' Proclamation of God's Unconditional Love

Jesus taught His disciples and the crowds in His own familiar Semitic way. He did not speak in the logical and conceptual discourse of Greek culture. Unlike Paul, He did not use syllogistic arguments or formulate circumstantial cases. Rather, He used two devices that were familiar to Semitic culture (commandments and names) and one device peculiar to Himself (parables). His revelation of the unconditional love of His Father follows this pattern, and so we see three anchors of that revelation:

1. The revelation of God's highest commandment—"*agapē*" (Section III.A below)
2. The *name* of God—"Abba" (Section III.B below)
3. The Parable of the Prodigal Son (Section III.C below)

A. Love as the Highest Commandment

Perhaps the most explicit statement of Jesus' belief in love is found in His proclamation about the highest commandment:

[L]ove [*agapēseis*] the Lord your God with all your heart, and with all your soul, and with all your mind. This is the great and first commandment. And a second is like it, You shall love [*agapēseis*] your neighbor as yourself. On these two commandments depend all the law and the prophets. (Mt 22:37–40)[24]

In this remarkable passage, Jesus changed the history of religion in two unique and vital respects:

1. He proclaims love to be the highest commandment upon which all other commandments (and virtues) depend.
2. He connects the love of God with the love of neighbor.

With respect to the first point, Jesus' proclamation to "love the Lord your God" as the "great and first commandment" surpasses the typical rabbinical use of a "heavy" (important) commandment. According to McKenzie,

> The rabbis counted 613 distinct commandments in the Law, of which 248 were positive precepts and 365 were prohibitions. These commandments were distinguished as "light" and "heavy" according to the seriousness of the subject.[25]

Though love of God was considered to be heavy (important) in rabbinical interpretation, it was never elevated to the level of the "*great* and *first*" commandment upon which the whole of the Torah depended. Viviano notes: "The rabbis said that the word hangs on Torah, Temple service, and deeds of loving-kindness.... Matthew makes the law itself depend upon deeds of love."[26]

---

[24] This commandment is proclaimed in all three Synoptic Gospels, though the context in which it occurs varies. Mark presents the scribe favorably (see Mk 12:28–34), and Luke has the scribe give the commandment (see Lk 10:25–28). Matthew sees the scribe as hostile and attempting to test Jesus. Matthew alone recounts the final phrase: "On these two commandments depend all the law and the prophets." By indicating this, Matthew intends to reconfirm Jesus' proclamation of love as the first and *greatest* commandment.

[25] John L. McKenzie, "The Gospel according to Matthew", in *The Jerome Biblical Commentary*, eds. Raymond Brown, Joseph A. Fitzmyer, and Roland E. Murphy (Englewood Cliffs, N.J.: Prentice-Hall, 1968), 2:101.

[26] Benedict T. Viviano, O.P., "The Gospel according to Matthew", in *The New Jerome Biblical Commentary*, eds. Raymond E. Brown, Joseph A. Fitzmyer, and Roland E. Murphy (Englewood Cliffs, N.J.: Prentice-Hall, 1990), p. 666.

The second point, the connection between love of God and love of neighbor, is equally important in the history of religion. When Jesus connects the second commandment ("love your neighbor as yourself") to the first, He elevates the second commandment from a moderate prescription to the second heaviest, tying it to the heaviest commandment. According to McKenzie:

> The novelty consists in placing Lv 19:18 on the same level [as Deut 6:5], making it equally "heavy." To this arrangement of the two commandments so that they become effectively one there is no parallel in Jewish literature. The *T. Issachar* (5:2 [*APOT* 2, 327]), often quoted in this connection, does indeed urge the love of God and of the neighbor; but these are not stated as the two greatest commandments of the Law, nor are they so explicitly given equal weight.[27]

The unification of the two commandments to love implies that the love of God leads to the love of neighbor, and that the love of neighbor, in turn, leads to the love of God. The two loves interact with and build up one another. The First Letter of John views this complementarity in a "necessary reciprocal" way:

> If anyone says, "I love God," and hates his brother, he is a liar; for he who does not love his brother whom he has seen, cannot love God whom he has not seen. And this commandment we have from him, that he who loves God should love his brother also. (1 Jn 4:20–21)

Saint Paul confirms this in the Letter to the Romans:

> [H]e who loves his neighbor has fulfilled the law. The commandments ... are summed up in this sentence, "You shall love your neighbor as yourself." Love does no wrong to a neighbor; therefore love is the fulfilling of the law. (Rom 13:8–10)

We may now treat the key point of this section—namely, that Jesus' revelation of the greatest commandment of the law is simultaneously a revelation of the heart and core identity of God. The

---

[27]McKenzie, "Gospel according to Matthew", p. 101. See also R. H. Charles, *Apocrypha and Pseudepigrapha of the Old Testament* (Oxford: Oxford University Press, 1913).

identification of law with the inner disposition of God is common in Wisdom literature. According to McKenzie:

> The post-exilic scribes identify the law with Wisdom (BS 24; 39:1–11) and find in it all knowledge, human and divine.... The rabbis included the Torah among the beings which existed before creation.[28]

In the teaching of the postexilic rabbis (with which Jesus is familiar[29]), the Torah is a reflection of Wisdom, and Wisdom is a reflection of the core identity of God, so much so, that Wisdom was thought to be a perfect image of God, from whom it originates:

> For [Wisdom] is a breath of the power of God, and a pure emanation of the glory of the Almighty; therefore nothing defiled gains entrance into her. For she is a reflection of eternal light, a spotless mirror of the working of God, and an image of his goodness. (Wis 7:25–26)

Inasmuch as Wisdom is a perfect reflection of God, and the Torah is a perfect reflection of Wisdom, the *greatest* commandment of the law (upon which the *entire* law depends) must likewise be a reflection of the core identity, power, and glory of God. Inasmuch as Jesus inextricably connects the commandment to love our neighbor to the commandment to love God, He includes the love of neighbor in "the first and greatest" commandment upon which the *entire* law depends. Hence, God's core identity, power, and glory reside most purely and excellently in His love. We can see the full impact of Jesus' declaration of "love" as the first and greatest commandment by replacing the word "wisdom" with "love" in the above passage from the Book of Wisdom.

---

[28] John L. McKenzie, *Dictionary of the Bible* (New York: Macmillan, 1965), p. 499.

[29] Jesus' parables reflect His knowledge of Wisdom parables (which have a moral significance). We may infer from this that Jesus was acquainted with Wisdom literature beyond knowledge of the parables. See Terence Y. Mullins, "Jewish Wisdom Literature in the New Testament", *Journal of Biblical Literature* 68, no. 4 (1949): 335–39. The reverence for the law as the reflection of God is embraced by Ben Sira (the author of the Book of Sirach, a part of the Wisdom literature), who, in turn, is embraced by the Sadducees. Jesus was quite familiar with the Sadducees' viewpoint and so would have been acquainted with this reverence for the law. Jesus uses the term "wisdom" to refer to God's comprehensive wisdom in Matthew 11:19 ("wisdom is justified by her deeds"), Luke 7:35 ("wisdom is justified by all her children"), and Luke 21:15 ("I will give you a mouth and a wisdom").

For she [Love] is a breath of the power of God, and a pure emanation
of the glory of the Almighty; therefore nothing defiled gains entrance
into her [Love]. For she [Love] is a reflection of eternal light, a spotless mirror of the working of God, and an image of his goodness.
(Adapted from Wis 7:25–26)

There is another reason for believing that Jesus' proclamation of
"love as the greatest commandment" indicates that God is love. It
stems from the implausibility of Jesus asking us to become something
that He (and His Father) are not. It is unthinkable that Jesus, who
exemplified the height of authenticity, would be inauthentic (and
even hypocritical) in asking us to conduct ourselves in a way that He
does not conduct Himself. The Gospels of Matthew (Chapter 5) and
Luke (Chapter 6) bear this out, showing that *agapē* is the essence of
God's perfection.

The final passage in Matthew 5 concludes the first part of the Sermon on the Mount, in which Jesus arguably gives an extensive definition of *agapē*. We saw in the previous chapter that the Beatitudes
were the essential *positive* interior attitudes from which *agapē* springs:
humble-heartedness, gentle-heartedness, desire for holiness, compassion for the marginalized, forgiveness, purity of heart (authenticity),
and the desire to bring peace. After elucidating these *positive interior*
prescriptions (Mt 5:3–12), Jesus goes further to indicate the attitudes
and behaviors that are *contrary* to *agapē* (proscriptions of both interior attitudes and exterior actions; see Mt 5:13–48). Though these
teachings build upon the positive interior explanation of *agapē* (and
are in a sense secondary to them), they are nonetheless essential to
Jesus' explanation of it. He teaches that *agapē* does not grow angry
or hold another in contempt, that it is chaste and honors the spouse,
that it does not seek retribution but allows compassion and mercy
to supersede justice, and that it loves and prays for enemies. After
this discourse, Jesus says, "I say to you, Love your enemies and pray
for those who persecute you, so that you may be sons of your Father
who is in heaven.... You, therefore, must be perfect, as your heavenly Father is perfect" (Mt 5:44, 48). There can be little doubt that
this phrasing indicates that the perfection of God consists in His love
of enemies,[30] which is confirmed by Luke's rendition of the passage

---

[30] See McKenzie, "Gospel according to Matthew", p. 73.

(also following the admonition to love enemies) that says, "Be merciful [compassionate], even as your Father is merciful" (Lk 6:36).

Yet, is love of enemies the *only* attribute that characterizes God's perfection (*agapē*/compassion)? For Matthew and Luke, love of enemies is the *highest expression* of God's perfection/*agapē*, but all the other attributes of *agapē* given in Matthew 5 must also be included in it, because they are foundational for it. Being humble-hearted, gentle-hearted, compassionate, forgiving, and peacemaking, as well as refraining from anger, contempt, and retribution, are essential for taking the final and highest step of *agapē*: loving enemies.

This means that if God's *agapē*/perfection consists in love of enemies, it also consists in the attributes essential for this highest expression of love. Therefore, God must be perfectly humble-hearted, gentle-hearted, compassionate, and forgiving, and He must also be perfectly free from anger, contempt, and the need for retribution. Jesus not only tells us that love is the highest commandment, implying that God is perfect love (*agapē*); He teaches us what this perfect *agapē* is like from its interior positive core to its highest external expression.

B. Jesus' Address of God as "Abba"

"Abba" is the Aramaic emphatic form of '*ab*—"father" employed as a vocative (as an address). McKenzie notes that Aramaic epistles show that it was a familiar address used by children,[31] which could have the meaning of "my father", or even a more intimate address, such as "daddy". The implications of childlike trust and affection should not be written out of the term when Jesus uses it to address the Father. Moreover, Jesus taught His disciples to address God as "Abba". Paul is aware of this but needs the help of the Holy Spirit to use it of God because of its high degree of familiarity (see Rom 8:15; Gal 4:6). In addition to its explicit use in Mark's Gospel (14:36), Jeremias sees other implicit references to "Abba" in the New Testament: "We have every reason to suppose that an *Abba* underlies every instance of *pater* (*mou*) or *ho patēr* in his words of prayer."[32] Jesus' address of

---

[31] See McKenzie, *Dictionary of the Bible*, p. 1.

[32] Joachim Jeremias, *New Testament Theology* (New York: Charles Scribner's Sons, 1971), 1:65; emphasis mine.

God in this intimate way is exceedingly unusual, so much so that for several decades it was thought to be unique to Jesus Himself. As Jeremias notes:

> In the literature of Palestinian Judaism *no evidence has yet been found* of "my Father" being used by an individual as an address to God.... It is quite unusual that Jesus should have addressed God as "my Father"; it is even more so that he should have used the Aramaic form *Abba*.[33]

Quite recently some rare instances of rabbinical use of "Abba" have been found.[34] Though this use of "Abba" is not unique to Christianity (as Jeremias conjectured) it is exceedingly rare in Judaism by comparison to its prolific use in Christianity.[35] The probable reason for this is the presumptuousness that the Israelite elders must have felt in addressing God (who is the "Master of the universe" and the "Master of history") with a possessive (*my* Father) in a childlike manner.

What might we conclude abut Jesus' revelation about the heart of the Father from His highly unusual address of God as Abba? He must have viewed God at once as gentle and affectionate, trustworthy and patient, compassionate and forgiving, and completely concerned with the protection, welfare, and advancement (toward salvation) of all His children—just like a perfectly loving Father. But how can we be sure that Jesus *really* intended this? The Parable of the Prodigal Son makes this interpretation unmistakable (see below, Section III.C).

In Semitic culture, a name is not merely a linguistic label and designation of a particular person (as it frequently is in contemporary Western culture). It has meaning and frequently expresses the heart, mind, characteristics, identity, and nature of the person. According to Rabbi Paysach Krohn,

> In Judaism, a name is not merely a conglomeration of letters put together as a convenient way to refer to someone. Ideally, it is a definition of the individual—a description of his personality and an interpretation of his traits. It may even be a portent of the person's future,

[33] Ibid., p. 64.
[34] See Wright, *Jesus and Victory of God.*
[35] See ibid., p. 649.

or perhaps a prayer that the person bearing this particular name shall live up to the potential expressed in the name.[36]

For this reason, Jesus selects the name of Peter ("rock") for His first apostle Simon: "[Y]ou are Peter, and on this rock I will build my Church" (Mt 16:18). Jesus reveals that His name from the Father is the "Beloved Son" ("My Son, the Beloved One")[37] because it reflects His character, identity, and essence with the Father. His disciple John refers to himself as the beloved disciple because the love of Jesus is the most important and defining characteristic in his life.[38] Thus Jesus' name (and address) of God as "Daddy"—affectionate, wise, trustworthy, loving, and compassionate Father—describes the heart, mind, and essence of God.

C. The Parable of the Prodigal Son

Jesus concretizes His revelation of the Father's love in the well-known Parable of the Prodigal Son (Lk 15:11–32). This parable may be considered one of Jesus' primary revelations of God the Father's *unconditional* love.

In the *Parables of Jesus*, Joachim Jeremias identifies Jesus' motive for telling the Parable of the Prodigal Son (along with the Parable of the Lost Sheep [Lk 15:1–7] and the Parable of the Lost Coin [Lk 15:8–10]). He notes that some of Jesus' detractors were accusing Him of unjustifiably seeking fellowship with sinners. Jesus justifies His actions by noting that His conduct is completely commensurate with His Father's (Abba's), who is absolutely concerned for sinners and is capable of justifying even those who have abandoned and shamed their families, countrymen, the law, the covenant, and God:

---

[36] Paysach Krohn, *Bris Milah: Circumcision*, Artscroll Mesorah Series (Brooklyn: Mesorah, 1986), http://www.torah.org/features/par-kids/names.html.

[37] *Ho huios mou ho agapētos* ("My Son, the Beloved One"). See the revelation of the Father ("my beloved Son") at Jesus' Baptism (Mk 1:11; Mt 3:17; Lk 3:22) and Transfiguration (Mk 9:7; Mt 17:5).

[38] The phrase "the disciple whom Jesus loved" (Greek: ὁ μαθητὴς ὃν ἠγάπα ὁ Ἰησοῦς, *ho mathētēs hon ēgapā ho Iēsous*) is used implicitly in the Gospel of John to refer to the evangelist himself. It is also phrased as "the Beloved Disciple" (Greek: ὃν ἐφίλει ὁ Ἰησοῦς, *hon ephilei ho Iēsous*). It is used five times in the Gospel of John (Jn 13:23; 19:26; 20:2; 21:8; and 21:20).

The Parable of the Prodigal Son is therefore not primarily a proclamation of the Good News to the poor, but a vindication of the Good
News in reply to its critics. Jesus' justification lies in the boundless
love of God.[39]

Three preliminary considerations should be made before retelling the parable as a first-century audience would have understood it.
First, Jesus intends that the father in the story be a revelation of the
heart of God the Father. The parable would be more aptly named
the Parable of the *Father* of the Prodigal Son. Second, notice that the
younger son has committed just about every sin imaginable according
to the mindset of Second Temple Judaism (the religious context in
which Jesus was operating), and so he has absolutely no basis or merit
for asking the father to receive him back into the household, even as
one of the servants. Third, the older son in this story represents the
Pharisees and those who are trying to remain righteous according to
their understanding of the Jewish law, and so we can see that Jesus
has not abandoned them, but He desires to give them everything
He has—so long as they come back into the house.

Now we may proceed to a retelling of the parable. A father had
two sons, the youngest of whom asked for his share of the inheri-
tance. This would have been viewed as an insult to the father, which
would have shamed both father and family (because the son is asking
not only for the right of possession, but the right of disposal of the
property, which legally does not occur until the death of the father[40]).
Nevertheless, the father hears the son's request and acquiesces to it.
He divides his property and lets his son go. Remember, the father in
the story is Jesus' revelation of God the Father.

The son chooses to go to a foreign land, probably a Gentile land,
indicated by his living on a Gentile farm with pigs. Whether he started
there or simply ended there is of little consequence. His actions indicate a disregard for (if not a rejection of) his election and his people,
and a further shaming of the family from which he came.

Then the son adds further insult to injury by spending his father's
hard-earned fortune on dissolute living (violations of the Torah) in
the Gentile land. This shows the son's callous disregard for (if not

[39] Joachim Jeremias, *The Parables of Jesus* (London: SCM Press, 1972), p. 131.
[40] See ibid., pp. 128–29.

rejection of) God's law, God's revelation, and perhaps God Himself. Furthermore, he manifests his callous disregard for his people, the law, and God before the entire Gentile community—bringing shame upon them all.

Just when it seems that the son could not possibly sin any more egregiously, the foreign land finds itself in a famine. The son has little money left and is constrained to live with the pigs, which were considered to be highly unclean animals. The son incurs defilement not only from working with the pigs but actually living with them! He even longs to eat the food of the pigs, which would defile him both inside and outside. This reveals the son's wretched spiritual state, which would have engendered both disgust and revulsion from most members of Jesus' first-century audience.

The son experiences a "quasi-change" of heart, not so much because of what he's done to his family, country, people, election, law, religion, and God, but because of the harshness of his condition ("How many of my father's hired servants have bread enough and to spare, but I perish here with hunger!" [Lk 15:17]). He decides to take advantage of what he perceives to be his father's merciful nature by proffering an agreement to accept demotion from son to servant (even though it was the father's right to reject and even disown him altogether). The son then makes his way back home.

The father (who is the God-Abba figure in Jesus' parable) sees him coming while he is still on his way (possibly indicating that the father is looking for him) and is so completely overjoyed that he runs out to meet him (despite the fact that the son has so deeply injured and shamed both him and his family). When he meets his son, he throws his arms around him and kisses him. The kiss is not only an act of affection, but also a sign of forgiveness.[41] The son's list of insults, injuries, and sins is incapable of turning the father's heart away from him. The father is almost compelled to show unrestrained affection toward him. The son begins to utter his prepared speech of quasi-repentance/quasi-negotiation: "Father, I have sinned against heaven and before you; I am no longer worthy to be called your son" (Lk 15:18–19, 21). But before he can say, "[T]reat me as one of your hired servants" (Lk 15:19), the father tells the servants to get him a

[41] See ibid., p. 130.

robe, which not only takes care of his temporal needs, but is also a mark of high distinction.[42] He then asks that a ring be put on his hand. Jeremias indicates that this ring is very likely a signet ring,[43] having the seal of the family. This would indicate not only belonging to the family, but also the authority of the family (showing the son's readmission to the family in an unqualified way). He then gives him shoes, which again takes care of his obvious temporal need, and inasmuch as they are luxuries, signifies a free man who no longer has to go about barefoot like a servant or slave.[44] He then kills the fatted calf (reserved only for very special occasions) and holds a feast. This is a further indication of the son's readmission to the family by being received at the festal family table.[45]

Jesus' audience probably felt conflicted (if not angered) by the father's "ridiculously merciful" treatment of his son, because it ignored (and even undermined) the "proper" strictures of justice. The father's love and mercy seem to disregard the justice of the Torah. This does not deter Jesus, because He is convinced that God the Father treats sinners—even the most egregious sinners—in exactly the same fashion—that is, with a heart of unconditional love.

Jesus continues the story by turning His attention to the older son, who reflects a figure of righteousness according to the Old Covenant. He has stayed loyal to his father, family, election, country, religion, law, and God. Furthermore, he has been an incredibly hard worker and seems to accept patiently the father's frugality toward him, saying, "[Y]ou never gave me a kid [goat]" (Lk 15:29). Most of Jesus' audience probably sympathized with this older son's plight when the father demonstrated his extraordinary generosity to his younger son. By all rights, the father should have either rejected or disowned the younger son, and if not that, he certainly should have accepted the younger son's offer to become a servant, but an unqualified re-admittance to the family appeared to be an injustice (if not a slap in the face) to his loyal son.

The father understands the son's difficulty with his actions and goes outside to "entreat" (Lk 15:28) his son, virtually begging him to

<hr/>

[42] See ibid.
[43] See ibid.
[44] See ibid.
[45] See ibid.

come back into the house (an almost unthinkable humiliation for a father at that time). He begins by giving his older son all his property, addressing his older son's need for justice: "[Y]ou are always with me, and all that is mine is yours" (Lk 15:31). Then, he gives him an explanation that did not fall within the mainstream interpretation of the law: mercy must take precedence over justice and love take precedence over the law, for that is the only way that the negativity of sin and evil can be re-dressed and overcome: "[Y]our brother was dead, and is alive; he was lost, and is found" (Lk 15:32).

This parable coincides precisely with Jesus' address of God as Abba, and love as the highest commandment, because the only way in which they can make sense together is through the logic of unconditional love in the heart of an unconditionally loving God.

We may now consider more deeply the four main movements of this parable because they bring to light Jesus' understanding of God, His Father. The first movement of the parable is the younger son's heartless and shameful treatment of his father (who represents God the Father). He tells his father that he is as good as dead to him and is only interested in his money. He then proceeds to the land of the Gentiles, rejecting his people and election, further dishonoring his father and family. Jesus keeps building up the younger son's deficits to make sure that the audience knows that the younger son's heartlessness and dishonor have reached the ultimate level and that there is almost nothing objectively redeeming about him. So He says that the son squanders all the money on dissolute living—further dishonoring his father, his people, the Torah (the law), and God before the Gentiles. Jesus continues to increase the younger son's deficits by saying that the land experienced famine, and the boy was forced to live with the pigs, which are exceedingly unclean animals. The boy not only touches the pigs; he lives with them and longs to put pig food inside of him, rendering him impure both inside and outside. Jesus' audience would not only have been dismayed by the boy's heartless and evil conduct, but also disgusted by his impurity.

Once Jesus has finished describing the son's seemingly irredeemable character, He begins the second movement of the parable. He implies that the son is in such great pain that he would do just about anything to get some relief. The son probably thinks that the father has disowned him, but in order to get relief from his pain, he decides to take a chance that the father might accept him back in a qualified way. He devises a plan to ask the father to forgive him and take him back into the household as a servant (a demotion from son to slave); so he proceeds toward his homeland and the family farm.

Before proceeding to the third movement of the parable, we should examine what Jesus' audience probably thought about the son's plan. They probably would have believed that the end of the story would be the father justifiably sending out a delegation to inform the son that he had been disowned and had no further right to be on his property, possibly thinking, "If you wanted to live in the land of the Gentiles, and throw away everything I have given you, then go back to 'your' people—your way of life and your 'religion'."

But the story takes a completely unexpected turn. Remember, the father in this story is Jesus' revelation of Abba. The father sees the boy coming from afar, as if he has been looking for him, and when he catches sight of him, he runs out to meet him and is overwhelmed with love and joy. He shows no anger at the son for his heartlessness and dishonor. He has not stopped loving (unconditionally loving) his son for a single second, and that love has caused him to feel immense worry for his son's welfare. The mere sight of the boy causes the father's worry to dissipate, and he does not want to lose a single second in radically accepting his son back into the house.

Jesus then continues the story; the father's first action is to throw his arms around the boy and to kiss him. His affection for his son has not diminished at all. It is as if he had done nothing to humiliate and dishonor his father and family. (Rembrandt painted a remarkable portrayal of this scene [called *The Return of the Prodigal Son*]. In it the father has a look of tremendous relief, love, compassion, and joy. He also has both a masculine and feminine hand, with which he is embracing his boy.)

The son now takes out his rehearsed lines and says, "Father, I have sinned against heaven and before you; I am no longer worthy to be called your son" (Lk 15:18–19, 21). The son also intended to say, "[T]reat me as one of your hired servants" (Lk 15:19); however, the father is not interested in the rehearsed lines and certainly has no intention of treating the boy as a slave. He knows there is no time to be lost, so the first words out of his mouth are "Bring quickly" (Lk 15:22). He asks that the best cloak be brought out for him. Recall that cloaks were worn by only people of high rank, and so the father is asking that his son be treated, as it were, like royalty. He then asks that sandals be given to him to take care of his temporal needs and to show that he is no longer a slave, but a freed man. He then proceeds to give the son a signet ring (explained above), indicating that he belongs in the family 100 percent. He has not lost a scintilla of his former status as son. The father is so overjoyed that he kills the fatted calf (the very best animal he has) and begins to celebrate a feast. Remember, this is your God.

A fourth movement of the parable now begins. Jesus indicates that the older son (who has been faithful to his father and has worked hard on the farm without benefit of his brother's labor while his brother was squandering the family fortune in a foreign land) hears the music and merriment and asks one of the servants about it. The servant indicates that his brother is back, and that his father is overjoyed and has killed the fatted calf. The older son (who represents the Pharisees) is justifiably indignant and hurt. He feels as if he has received no reward for his fidelity and labors throughout his brother's absence, and even worse, that the father has shown his heartless and irresponsible little brother greater favor than himself: "[Y]ou never gave me a kid, that I might make merry with *my* friends" (Lk 15:29; emphasis mine).

At this juncture Jesus indicates that the father comes out to meet his older boy. He says that the father implores him. The Greek word here is *parakaleō*, which has a multifaceted meaning. It means first to call to one's side in order to give comfort or consolation to someone who is intimate, and it also carries the meaning of begging, pleading, beseeching, or entreating, which puts the person making the request in a humble, weak, or even servile position. Why did Jesus use a word in Aramaic that would be translated by this Greek word? He wants to establish how God the Father feels toward the Pharisees who have been loyal to the Torah (and the Old Covenant) for many years. So how does God feel toward them? He feels like they are intimates, and that He can call them to His side in order to give them consolation. He is not beneath making the humble gesture of begging or pleading with them to come back into the house, because He loves them deeply and appreciates their loyalty. To demonstrate this, He makes an absolute pledge to them: "You have been with me always, and everything I have is yours. Now, come back into the house, for these sinners were lost and are found; they were dead and have come back to life" (adapted from Lk 15:31–32). The Father is willing to give these loyal servants everything He has, to demonstrate His love and gratitude to them.

Though Jesus has confronted the Pharisees with their hypocrisy and self-righteousness, particularly when they imply that sinners are not welcome in God's Kingdom, He wants to assure them that His Father loves them unconditionally and will bestow His Kingdom upon them. Interestingly, Jesus does not give an ending to this part of the parable; He does not say whether the older son goes back into the house, because He does not know how each Pharisee will react to His invitation to the Kingdom. Nevertheless, the invitation to God's Kingdom remains unconditionally open to their acceptance of it.

IV. Conclusion

Jesus' proclamation of the Father's unconditional love (*agapē*) is central not only to His teaching, but also to the writings of Saint John and Saint Paul. The Gospel of John can be considered an elaboration of the love of God and Jesus. Early in the Gospel, John teaches:

> For God so loved the world that he gave his only-begotten Son, that whoever believes in him should not perish but have eternal life. (Jn 3:16)

As if this were not enough, Jesus proclaims (through His prayer to the Father) that the Father's love for Jesus' disciples is the *same* as His love for His own Son:

> [T]he world may know that you have sent me and have loved them even as you have loved me. (Jn 17:23)

In his first Epistle, John clearly states the central doctrine of Jesus' teaching:

> Beloved, let us love one another; for love is of God, and he who loves is born of God and knows God. He who does not love does not know God; for God is love. In this the love of God was made manifest

among us, that God sent his only-begotten Son into the world, so that we might live through him. In this is love, not that we loved God but that he loved us and sent his Son to be the expiation for our sins. (1 Jn 4:7–10)

Saint Paul also recognizes the unconditional love of God in Jesus' words and actions:

If God is for us, who is against us? He who did not spare his own Son but gave him up for us all, will he not also give us all things with him? ... Who shall separate us from the love of Christ? Shall tribulation, or distress, or persecution, or famine, or nakedness, or peril, or sword? ... No, in all these things we are more than conquerors through him who loved us. For I am sure that neither death, nor life, nor angels, nor principalities, nor things present, nor things to come, nor powers, nor height, nor depth, nor anything else in all creation, will be able to separate us from the love of God in Christ Jesus our Lord. (Rom 8:31–32, 35, 37–39)

Saint Paul tries to express the superabundance of God's love for us in the Letter to the Ephesians, praying,

that you, being rooted and grounded in love, may have power to comprehend with all the saints what is the breadth and length and height and depth, and to know the love of Christ which surpasses knowledge, that you may be filled with all the *fulness of God*. (Eph 3:17–19; emphasis mine)

The New Testament writings on love are by no means limited to the passages cited above from the teachings of Jesus, Saint John, and Saint Paul; however, the above passages are sufficient to show that Jesus intended to proclaim that God's love has absolutely no conditions or imperfections. Though God's love has no conditions, there is one important condition to our receiving it from Him: we must want it enough to make it our own.

If we truly want this life of love, then we will enter into it, which means putting our trust in Him, forgiving others as we have been forgiven, and having compassion on those in need. We may fail again and again in our attempts to follow Jesus, but we can always continue to return without limit[46] until we reach the end of our journey with Him. Jesus does not leave us with this simple command; He gives us several gifts to help us—the gift of His Spirit, His Word, His Church, and His body and blood (the Eucharist). When we combine His teachings with His gifts, we can see five dimensions of His path to salvation: genuine repentance for our transgressions, entering into a relationship with His Father, joining a church community (for which He lays the foundation), being faithful to His Word, and following the Holy Spirit (see Chapter 7, Section IV).

As the reader has probably already surmised, Jesus' teaching on love does not stop at the love of His Father; it includes His own love, not only expressed in words but in action, particularly the consummate gift of Himself in complete self-sacrifice. This two-pronged teaching on love establishes His identity and relationship with His Divine Father—they are *both* unconditionally loving. This is the subject of the next chapter.

---

[46]When Jesus says in Matthew 18:22, "I do not say to you seven times, but seventy times seven", He is referring to a perfect prime number times ten times a perfect prime number, which is virtually *endless* in Jewish numeric symbolism. If Jesus asks this of us, we can be sure that this is central to His heart and the heart of His Father.

Chapter Three

The Unconditional Love of Jesus

Introduction

Jesus' love was manifest daily in His healings, exorcisms, friendship with sinners, and care for the poor, as well as in His relationship with His disciples. The four Gospels make clear that Jesus exhibited great affection, understanding, compassion, and self-sacrifice for His friends and disciples. But He went far beyond His circle of friends, and even beyond the wider circle of those who are easily loved—even beyond the much wider circle of those who are acceptable. He sought out the poor, outcasts, and even the most egregious sinners. Jesus wanted to be a healing, reconciling, and compassionate force for those who were in greatest need of His and the Father's love. Before examining the manifestations of Jesus' love in His ministry we will want to consider the centrality of love in His personal identity.

I. Jesus' Love and the Challenge of Suffering

In the Gospel of Matthew, we read:

> Come to me, all who labor and are heavy laden, and I will give you rest. Take my yoke upon you, and learn from me; for I am gentle and lowly [humble] in heart, and you will find rest for your souls. For my yoke is easy, and my burden is light. (Mt 11:28–30)

Jesus describes Himself as "gentle and lowly [humble] in heart", calling to mind the first and third Beatitudes, which set the tone for the Sermon on the Mount: "Blessed are the poor in spirit [the humble-hearted]" (Mt 5:3) and "[b]lessed are the meek [the gentle-hearted]"

(Mt 5:5).[1] Recall that humble-heartedness means genuinely *identi-fying* with the lowly (the opposite of being "puffed up" or "feeling superior") and that "gentle-hearted" means patience, forgiveness, and compassion for people in all their weaknesses. Recall from the defi-nition of *agapē* (Chapter 1) that these two interior attitudes underlie the possibility of *agapē*, which is the purest form of love. Jesus is not satisfied with associating with us and saving us; His empathy is so perfect that He *identifies* with us in our weaknesses: "[A]s you did it to one of the least of these my brethren, you did it to me" (Mt 25:40). He does not disdain weakness, but sees it as the "call to compassion"—that is, the vulnerability in each of us that needs and elicits compassion from others, and the vulnerability in others that elicits compassion from us.

Ironically, weakness and suffering provide opportunities for compassion (*agapē*), which has the effect of making the world more civil, gentle, understanding, and self-giving. What would the world be like if there were no weakness to produce vulnerability, humil-ity, and compassion? What would it be like to live in a world where no one needs anyone, and everyone is perfectly self-sufficient? Would it really be a perfect world? Or would we find ways to use our perfect power and our perfect self-sufficiency to raise ourselves above perfect mediocrity? One might ask, "How can mediocrity be perfect?" If everyone is perfect, then perfection is mediocre. We will have to find other ways to prove ourselves more than that. Think about a world of perfectly self-sufficient people trying to find a way out of mediocrity by any means available to them. The ancient Greeks considered this in the myth of the Titans, quasi-perfect deities who spent their existence battling each other to rule the universe.

For Jesus and the Christian Church, weakness and suffering are opportunities for humility, compassion, gentleness of spirit, and respect and empathy for others. Jesus takes on our finitude and weak-nesses to show us how to use our own weakness and vulnerability to grow in these vital areas of love—that is, to become more and more like Him who is perfectly humble and gentle of heart (perfect *agapē*).

---

[1] Notice that the same Greek root is used for the third Beatitude ("meek") and for Jesus' self-description ("gentle and lowly in heart")—namely, *praus*.

This parallels Jesus' revelation of the unconditional love of the Father (in the Parable of the Prodigal Son), who is perfectly humble and gentle toward both the younger (prodigal) son and his older brother (see Chapter 2). He does this quite consciously to show that the single underlying and unifying characteristic between Him and the Father is perfect *agapē*.

Jesus' self-revelation ("gentle and humble in heart") provides the basis for His promise to redeem suffering. In the above passage, Jesus gives an open invitation to everyone who is in need—the poor, the infirm, and the suffering—"*all* you who are weary and burdened". His heart goes out to all who suffer. Yet, we must ask how Jesus can promise to refresh every suffering person. Obviously he cannot help all of them; He is limited to a ministry within Israel—and to a fairly small region of it. He must mean that the alleviation of our suffering will occur, not just in this life, but in the next. Jesus' mission is not to take away our suffering in this life, but to help us *use* our suffering as a vehicle for eternal life—not only for ourselves, but for others. What does this mean? How can we use our suffering to help ourselves and others into eternal life? To answer this question we must take a look at Jesus' and the early Church's interpretation of suffering.

In Volume IV, I give an extensive discussion of Jesus' and the early Church's interpretation of suffering. I will here briefly summarize that discussion for the purpose of explaining how Jesus reconciled His and the Father's unconditional love with suffering in the world. There are five integral dimensions to Jesus' view of suffering:

1. Jesus supersedes the Old Testament view that suffering is God's punishment for sin.
2. Jesus preaches the certainty of the resurrection for all who believe (put their trust in Him and try to follow His way of love).
3. In light of Jesus' preaching, the early Church believes that suffering can provide an important preparation for the Kingdom of God.
4. Suffering can be offered up as "self-sacrifice" for the life, love, and light of the world.
5. Suffering can give witness to and spread the gospel message.

As we shall see, these five dimensions of suffering are connected with "giving ourselves definition and identity" during this lifetime, and we will carry this identity with us into the eternal life to come. Thus, the way we deal with suffering will determine who we will become for all eternity. Let us now turn to a discussion of each of these five dimensions.

With respect to the first dimension, Jesus rejects the well-known view from the Torah that suffering is a punishment from God that can be visited upon one's children down to the fourth generation (Ex 20:5; 34:7; Deut 5:9).[2] He takes the contrary position that God allows suffering to happen to the just, and that God allows blessing to happen to the unjust. God even *loves* His enemies (Mt 5:44–47). In so doing, Jesus must give an alternative interpretation of suffering.

This alternative interpretation takes a decidedly different turn from the interpretations given in the Book of Job (see Volume IV). He first establishes that man was created and redeemed to inherit eternal life with the God of unconditional love. He not only preaches this message, but gives evidence of His authority and power to do so by His Resurrection and glory, raising the dead in His ministry, and His gift of the Holy Spirit. This truth is so central to the preaching of Jesus and the early Church that Paul proclaims unequivocally:

> [I]f there is no resurrection of the dead, then Christ has not been raised; if Christ has not been raised, then our preaching is in vain and your faith is in vain. We are even found to be misrepresenting God, because we testified of God that he raised Christ, whom he did not raise if it is true that the dead are not raised. For if the dead are not raised, then Christ has not been raised. If Christ has not been raised, your faith is futile and you are still in your sins. Then those also who have fallen asleep in Christ have perished. If for this life only we have hoped in Christ, we are of all men most to be pitied. (1 Cor 15:13–19)[3]

---

[2] There is a "softening" of divine retribution in one passage of Deuteronomy (24:16) and in Ezekiel (18:20) that indicates that God's punishment rests only on the person committing a sin. This interpretation is by no means universal in Jesus' time, indicated by the apostles' question to Jesus concerning the blind man: "Rabbi, who sinned, this man or his parents, that he was born blind?" (Jn 9:2).

[3] The full significance of this passage is explained in Chapter 4, Section III.

Given an eternal life of unconditional love (for those who put their faith in God and try to follow the way of love), suffering cannot be viewed as ultimately tragic. It is only momentary and will be completely redeemed by God's unconditional love and joy in His eternal Kingdom. In light of this, did Jesus and the early Church believe that suffering can have any value? This is addressed by the third, fourth, and fifth dimensions of suffering listed above.

Reflecting on Jesus' teaching about *agape* and the efficacy of suffering, Saints Peter and Paul conclude that suffering is an invaluable preparation for the Kingdom of God (see 2 Cor 12:7–10). For them, suffering is vital to freedom *from* egocentricity, pride, hard-heartedness, and dominion of others, and so it is vital *for* humble-heartedness, gentle-heartedness, compassion, and respect (explained below).

Jesus also views suffering as a spiritual vehicle for bringing grace, light, and love to others and the body of Christ (the Church). As explained below and in Volume IV, Jesus uses Isaiah 52:13–53:12 (the Fourth Suffering Servant Song) and Psalm 22 (His dying words) to interpret suffering as a self-sacrifice or as an offering of self for others. He sees this self-offering as an act of love ("Greater love has no man than this, that a man lay down his life for his friends" [Jn 15:13]). This act of love is like a spiritual or mystical reality that can bring light and love to individuals in need as well as the body of Christ (the Church). Saint Paul encourages us to follow Jesus in making our suffering a self-offering in order to bring healing, light, and love to others (Col 1:24–25).

Finally, Jesus believes that suffering can manifest God's power and glory (Jn 9, 11, and 17). In light of this, Saint Paul views suffering as an opportunity to give witness to the gospel. When we remain faithful to God and the gospel message in the face of opposition to the gospel, we give a perfect witness to it, because people will see our conviction about its truth—not only in words, but in actions. When we combine this interpretation of suffering with the previous four, we can formulate a general Christian theology of suffering.

Let us begin with Jesus' central teaching on eternal life. For Jesus, eternal life is unconditional love, and entrance into a life of unconditional love requires freedom from egocentricity, inauthenticity, and the desire to dominate others. As will be explained in Volume IV, suffering can be extraordinarily helpful (and even vital) in gaining this freedom to love. Virtually every spiritual writer in every religious tradition affirms the benefits of suffering in our movement toward humility, compassion, forgiveness, authenticity, and gentleness of spirit. This movement toward *agapē* defines who we are; it literally "etches" *agapē* into our very nature and being, so that we can take this identity into the eternal life to come.

It is impossible to understand Jesus' perspective on the alleviation of suffering without considering His conviction about eternal life as unconditional love (with Him and the Father). Jesus does not believe that *any* kind of suffering in this life is *ultimately* tragic. He knows that if we believe His promise in the resurrection, and follow His example about how to suffer well, we will inherit eternal life with Him and the Father, and our suffering will be an indispensable vehicle for preparing us for a life of unconditional love—completely free from our egocentricity, pride, arrogance, and dominance.

So what does it mean to follow His example of suffering to take His "yoke upon" our shoulders "and learn from [Him]" (Mt 11:29)?

Jesus does not wish pain or suffering on anyone. Indeed, He would rather take our place in suffering than allow us to go through it, and He shows this by His complete self-sacrifice for us in his Passion and death. Nevertheless, He does not believe that suffering is completely negative and realizes that there is much to be derived from it—as a preparation for the unconditional love of the Kingdom, as a means of offering ourselves for the sake of others, and as a witness to the gospel. He gives us His Holy Spirit to help us actualize these benefits of suffering through His providential plan (described below).

Given that one of the major benefits of suffering is growth in *agapē* (humble-heartedness, gentle-heartedness, and compassion), we cannot succumb to the fallacy of stoicism. Jesus does not want us to develop a granite face toward the world and others (like the imperious and distant strength of Seneca; see Chapter 1, Section I). He does not view strength as "toughness" or "an impervious exterior", but rather as *agapē*—"a gentle and humble heart". He wants to convert hardness of heart into *softness* of heart capable of gentleness and humility: "A new heart I will give you, and a new spirit I will put within you; and I will take out of your flesh the heart of stone and give you a heart of flesh" (Ezek 36:26).

If this is what Jesus and the Father want for us, then it must be the way they are as well; they must have unconditionally soft hearts capable of gentleness and humility (as Jesus says of Himself in the above passage). What can we infer from this? We must presume that Jesus and the Father do *not* want anyone to suffer. Indeed they feel great sympathy and compassion for us in our suffering. Yet, they cannot extricate us completely from it, for they know well that it will provide us with a vital path to unconditional love by helping us to detach from egocentricity, arrogance, and dominion.

Jesus and the Father are like parents who are confronted with the predicament of sending their child to school for the first time. They know there will be challenges and sufferings with which their children will be confronted—ridicule from playmates, difficulties with learning particular subjects, accidents on the playground, and even the possibility of poor grades. Nevertheless they send their children to school, knowing that they will benefit greatly from socialization, learning, and their challenges. They know they have to take the risk of allowing their children to become their own persons. They are ready to help their children when they are challenged or suffering, but they know they cannot prevent them from suffering. If their children are to become independent, efficacious, virtuous, and wise, they will have to let them encounter the imperfect world while helping them to learn independence, wisdom, and virtue from it. Clearly these parents are not "heartless", but rather filled with love and hope for their children, ready to make the sacrifices necessary to help them transform their challenges into independence, maturity, and virtue. Jesus and the Father are in an identical position and are prepared to help us through the Holy Spirit and one another to transform our challenges and sufferings into freedom and love.

A. Why Would God Create an Imperfect World?

The reader may be wondering, "Why did God create us in an imperfect world, if He does not want us to suffer and will have to help us through it?" Though this question will be answered in considerable detail in Volume IV of the Quartet, we will need to look at it briefly here so that it does not become a stumbling block to understanding

Jesus' view of suffering. First, it should be noted that all suffering does not come from being born into an imperfect world. Though the imperfect world causes considerable deprivation, pain, and challenge, human evil also causes a great deal of suffering. The latter kind of suffering is not the fault of God, but the fault of individuals, who have been given the freedom to choose evil by God. He gives us this freedom, so that our choices to love and do good will come not from Him, but from *us*. If we did not have the option to choose evil, then our choice to do good would not be our own, but merely the result of a robotic program designed by the Creator. If God is to avoid making the decision for us, He will have to give us an option to do something other than the good. The same holds true for love—if we have no ability to choose "unlove", then our choice to love would not be our own, but again, merely a program designed by God.

With this distinction in mind, we can proceed to the question of why God *would* create an imperfect world that would cause deprivation, pain, and challenge. If we examine closely the above words of Jesus, Paul, and Matthew, we can infer God's rationale for creating an imperfect world. Once again, God's rationale concerns *freedom*—specifically the freedom to choose and define who we are and who we will become, the ability to determine our self-definition and identity. God has given us an awesome power not so much to determine *what* we are, but far more importantly, *who* we are. This ability is premised on the *free decisions and choices* we make—not only about ourselves, but also our relationships with others, particularly our relationships in the face of weakness, deprivation, pain, and challenge.

The imperfect world presents us with a gigantic "field" on which to make choices that will affect our lives, and the lives of others—in the face of *imperfection*. Will we be compassionate or hard-hearted? Will we be concerned only with ourselves, or will we make room for somebody else? Will we learn patience and humility from our challenges or only react with bitterness and resentment? Will we help others in their weakness or take advantage of their weakness? Will we bring hope and consolation to the deprived, or will we exploit them in their need? Will we want to make the world a better place for everyone, or will we only make the world a better place for us? Will we define ourselves in terms of love and faith or only in terms of worldly power and glory? Will we want to recognize the transcendent and eternal mystery in every person or merely look at material beauty and worldly productivity? Will we try to show people the way to transcendence through suffering or take away their hope by proclaiming the meaninglessness of suffering? Will we build a civilization of love or a civilization of arrogant egocentricity?

The vast majority of the above questions come from an *imperfect* world—a world that presents us with weakness, need, deprivation, pain, and challenge. If we are to help one another through this imperfect world, we will have to make choices in favor of love and compassion, justice and ethical responsibility, self-sacrifice, courage, humility, altruism, and self-transcendence—and we will have to move away from our proclivity toward egocentricity, arrogance, selfishness, disedification, abusiveness, greed, and other forms of darkness. Each time we make a choice—either toward love and compassion or toward egocentricity and darkness—a little dimension of that choice rubs off on us and "etches itself" into our identity and being. As we move along the road of life, our choices begin to form not only a pattern, but a momentum, and so we tend to make a greater number of choices in either one direction or the other—which continues to "etch itself" ever deeper into our identity and being. After a while, our choices become *us*. The longer we continue along a particular trajectory, the stronger our identity becomes, and as a consequence, it becomes more difficult to break with it and change it.

This is not to say that our identity will be completely solidified before we leave this world. As Jesus informs us (e.g., in the Parable of the Prodigal Son) we can change our minds—even with the most entrenched identity and even at the last moment. God will continually help us to transition out of even the darkest identity to help us make a free act of repentance (*metanoia*, change of heart), so that we will *not* continue on a trajectory into darkness forever. This act of repentance will have to consist of positive choices over a period of time—to create a new identity in the image of God's love. The more we make choices in one direction or the other, the more our identity is solidified in that direction, and the easier it is for us to continue in that direction.

Let us return to the question about the imperfect world. The reader might legitimately ask, "Is the imperfect world the *only* way that God could have presented us with the 'field of freedom' on which to solidify our identity?" It is difficult to see how God would have presented us with the choices of compassion versus hard-heartedness, humility versus arrogance, selfishness versus generosity, egocentricity versus altruism, and love versus narcissism in a *perfect* world, which has no need for compassion, courage, self-sacrifice, and altruism.

What about the angels? God did not create them in an imperfect world—and yet they made their choice between love and goodness versus egocentricity and evil. True enough—but there is an import-ant difference between the angels and us. The angels had the capacity to make an instantaneous and perfect self-reflective choice toward the extremes of pure love or pure evil. God has not created us in this way. We do not have perfect foreknowledge of our future or perfect awareness of how our choices and actions will affect others, or even perfect knowledge of *ourselves*. We are imperfect in our knowledge and self-consciousness, and so we must *gradually* learn within the context of our choices who we are, how we affect other people, how the mistakes we have made cause regret, and so forth. What better way to be presented with these choices than in a context of need, weakness, vulnerability, and interdependence—that is, in the context of an *imperfect* world?

Our imperfection is not a pure negative, for the gradual way in which we come to our identity allows us *many* chances to solidify a good identity and *many* chances to turn away from a dark one, and here is the best news of all: God loves us so much that He intended from the very moment of our creation to enter into our imperfect reality, not only to show us the way to love, but also to give us His Spirit, Word, Church community, and grace to help us. From the moment of our creation, God had already decided to give Himself to us in an unconditional act of love that would free us from the spell and darkness of evil and help us to use our freedom to enter into His Kingdom of unconditional love. When He created us in an imperfect world, He knew that we were not ready for that Kingdom of uncon-ditional love, because we would have to *choose* it—choose to embrace compassion, justice, service, humble-heartedness, gentle-heartedness, and goodness. We would have to recognize these qualities as the road to true happiness and make them our hearts' desire. In order to allow us the choice to live with Him in unconditional love, he also had to give us the option to choose the contrary: a life of egocentricity, arrogance, selfishness, and domination of others. God had no choice but to give us this choice—and so He not only gave us freedom, but also an *imperfect world* in which to make the fundamental choices determining "who we are" and how to live our eternity.

God never viewed this imperfect world to be anything more than a temporary "staging ground" in which to make our free choices so that we could proceed to the eternity we truly desire. From the moment of creation He intended to come to us both through prophets and sages, and then to come to us personally and ultimately—to love us and help us toward His Kingdom of perfect love, which is perfect joy, the joy of perfect relationship with one another (see Chapter 7, Section II). God fully intends to use the sufferings of this world—not only to present us with our essential identity choices, but also to help us out of our egocentricity and narcissism. As we shall see, pain, deprivation, and weakness are some of the "best" ways to shock us out of egocentricity, narcissism, superficiality, and darkness—so that we might see beyond that world to the world of our highest purpose and destiny, the world of unconditional goodness and love.

Jesus came to tell us about the power of freedom, the call to unconditional love, the destructiveness of egocentricity, and the importance and efficacy of suffering. When He did so, He fully intended to suffer Himself—to show us the way to the full efficacy of suffering. He knew that His Father would fully redeem that suffering in His Kingdom and wanted us to take literally His promise that "[b]lessed are those who mourn, for they shall be comforted" (Mt 5:4). He knew that no suffering in this world would be ultimately tragic, and that every bit of it would be transformed into love and joy in His Father's eternal Kingdom. He knew that suffering is essential to our freedom and identity, and that it is efficacious in bringing us out of darkness into light, out of arrogance into humility, and out of egocentricity into love. He knew the importance of the *imperfect* world, and the gift it is to all of us who are transcendentally self-conscious—not like the angels, but in our own unique way, capable of loving and being loved in his eternal Kingdom.

B. The Efficacy of Suffering for Jesus and the Apostolic Church

Jesus' intention is to transform all suffering into unconditional love in His eternal Kingdom. If we do not believe in His intention to do this, then the positivity of suffering will be nonsensical. Jesus is not trying to make sense of suffering in *this world alone* or to bring good out of suffering in *this life alone*. He works through the Holy Spirit to transform our suffering into freedom, wisdom, compassion, and virtue on our path to unconditional love. If we do not believe in Jesus' interpretation of suffering as the short-term vehicle to eternal unconditional love, we will be left only with the viewpoint of atheistic existentialism—namely, that suffering is meaningless, implying that life is absurd, and leaving us only with despair. However, if we do believe in Jesus' teaching about eternal life and suffering, and we put our trust in Him, then we can learn, mature, and develop optimally through our suffering.

The Christian interpretation of suffering is not restricted to gaining the freedom to love; it also includes a dimension of self-offering or self-gift for the sake of others and the Church. Saints Peter and Paul encourage us to follow Jesus in making suffering an offering of ourselves. As explained in Volume IV, Jesus interprets His Passion as a sacrificial offering in line with the Fourth Suffering Servant Song in Isaiah:

> Behold, my servant shall prosper, he shall be exalted and lifted up, and shall be very high. As many were astonished at him—his appearance was so marred, beyond human semblance, and his form beyond that of the sons of men—so shall he startle many nations; kings shall shut their mouths because of him; for that which has not been told them they shall see, and that which they have not heard they shall understand.... He was despised and rejected by men; a man of sorrows, and acquainted with grief; and as one from whom men hide their faces he was despised, and we esteemed him not. Surely he has borne our griefs and carried our sorrows; yet we esteemed him stricken, struck down by God, and afflicted. But he was wounded for our transgressions, he was bruised for our iniquities; upon him was the chastisement that made us whole, and with his stripes we are healed. All we like sheep have gone astray; we have turned every one to his own way; and the LORD has laid on him the iniquity of us all.... When he makes himself an offering for sin, he shall see his offspring, he shall prolong his days; the will of the LORD shall prosper in his hand; he shall see the fruit of the travail of his soul and be satisfied; by his knowledge shall the righteous one, my servant, make many to be accounted righteous; and he

shall bear their iniquities. Therefore I will divide him a portion with the great, and he shall divide the spoil with the strong; because he *poured out his soul to death*, and was numbered with the transgressors; *yet he bore the sin of many*, and made intercession for the transgressors. (Is 52:13–15; 53:3–6, 10–12; emphasis mine)[4]

In Section IV below (concerned with Jesus' Eucharistic words) we will show that Jesus used this Song of Isaiah and Psalm 22 to interpret His suffering as an act of complete self-sacrifice. He viewed self-sacrifice as a *gift* of Himself, which He took to be an unconditional act of *love*.[5] By sacrificing Himself, Jesus believed that He had brought unconditional love into the world—which He interpreted as a spiritual reality that He could give to the Father for the healing and redemption of individuals throughout the world who wanted to come out of darkness into His light.

Jesus believed that the unconditional love He had created could really affect the hearts of individual people and the collective heart of the Church. This mystical or spiritual reality brings light into our darkness and healing into our brokenness, and so His suffering produced a positive spiritual transformative power, which has remarkable efficacy.

It may be difficult to understand this interpretation of suffering through a contemporary lens with its overtone of materialism, but for Jesus (as well as for Isaiah and the Psalmist), this is not problematic. They did not see a huge divide between the material and spiritual world, nor between negative and positive outcomes. In their worldview, terrible suffering could be transformed into a gift of self (an act of love), which could have remarkably powerful spiritual effects in both the temporal and spiritual world. Saints Peter and Paul

[4]Lucien Cerfaux first made the strong case not only for the parallelism between the Fourth Suffering Servant Song of Isaiah and the Christological Hymn in Paul's Letter to the Philippians (Phil 2:6–11), but also the likelihood of this Fourth Song of Isaiah being in the mind of *Jesus Himself*. Jesus' Eucharistic words "poured out for many" (Mt 26:28; Mk 14:24) repeat the end of that song, showing that He had it in mind prior to His Passion and perhaps in His ministry. See Lucien Cerfaux, "L hymne au Christ-Serviteur de Dieu (Phil., II, 6–11 - Is., LII, 13, LIII, 12)", in *Miscellanea historica in honorem Alberti de Meyer Universitatis Catholicae in oppido Lovaniensi iam annos XXV professoris* (Louvain: Bibliothèque de l'Université, 1946), 1:117–30.

[5]"Greater *love* has no man than this, that a man *lay down* his *life* for his friends" (Jn 15:13; emphasis mine).

recognized this and encouraged all Christians to make their sufferings a self-offering (an act of love) in imitation of Jesus.[6] Paul captures it well in the Letter to the Colossians:

> Now I rejoice in my sufferings for your sake, and in my flesh I complete what is lacking in Christ's afflictions for the sake of his body, that is, the Church. (Col 1:24)

Notice that Paul believes he is entering into the same redemptive mystery as Jesus and that his suffering creates a spiritual power that will *benefit* the Church. When we follow Jesus and Paul, we too create a positive spiritual-loving force to overcome the darkness, evil, and hard-heartedness within the world. If we do not make our suffering a self-offering (producing a loving, spiritual power), we waste a perfect opportunity to do tremendous good for others and the Church.

Jesus also anticipates that we may have to suffer for the gospel—people may ridicule us, marginalize us, or even persecute us. For Jesus, Peter, and Paul, this is again an *opportunity* to bring something *positive* into the world—namely, the truth of the gospel message. If we remain trusting and undaunted by opposition to the gospel, we cannot help ourselves; we give witness to its truth by our determination to suffer for it. Ironically, the history of martyrdom in the Christian Church has almost always been followed by large numbers of conversions to Jesus. While the persecutors of Christians were ridiculing their willingness to suffer for the gospel, people of goodwill were being convinced of its veracity and turning to Jesus. Though it is difficult to be the one "in the line of fire", Saint Paul shows us that our courage, our conviction about the truth of the gospel, and our trust in Jesus will almost inevitably lead to a prolific spread of the gospel message, which will be the crowning glory of our lives:

> For I am already on the point of being sacrificed; the time of my departure has come. I have fought the good fight, I have finished the race, I have kept the faith. From now on there is laid up for me the crown of righteousness, which the Lord, the righteous judge, will award to me on that Day, and not only to me but also to all who have loved his appearing. (2 Tim 4:6–8)

---

[6]See 1 Pet 2:20–21; Rom 12:1.

Jesus does not leave us alone in our suffering. He sends the Holy Spirit to help us—sometimes to protect us, sometimes to alleviate suffering's negative effects, and sometimes to guide us. In all cases, the Holy Spirit brings us peace and inspiration so that we might have the calm and the "mind of Christ" (1 Cor 2:16) to deal positively with our suffering, to look for opportunities to change our lives for the better, to abandon superficiality and egocentricity, and to grow in humble-heartedness, gentle-heartedness, and compassion. The Spirit also provides opportunities to move away from negative and destructive paths, and to seek new ways to serve others and the Church, to bring light, love, and hope to the world, and to help others discover the path to their highest dignity and destiny. Furthermore, the Spirit opens the way to make our sufferings a self-offering (an act of love), to spiritually enhance others and the Church, and creates opportunities to give witness to the gospel. In Volume IV, we will discuss these opportunities in detail as well as how best to follow the guidance and inspiration of the Holy Spirit.

You have probably heard the adage "When one door slams, another door of opportunity opens." Christianity takes this idea to its height by advocating that the Holy Spirit creates a "conspiracy of Providence" within the complex intersection of all of our lives (see Volume I, Chapter 8). In 1 Corinthians 12, Saint Paul connects "the body of Christ" (v. 27) with the unifying and efficacious power of the Holy Spirit. He indicates that the same Spirit works through every person in different ways to bring about an optimal result, not just for individuals, but for everyone within the body of Christ.

When we suffer, the Holy Spirit works with us individually and through other people. He opens doors of grace by inspiring people to create opportunities for us, to share wisdom with us, to act on our behalf with other people, and to protect us from harm. He can inspire others (or groups of others) to bring us patience, consolation, suggestions, wisdom, compassion, and assistance. If we are not to let these providential opportunities pass us by, we must be confident that the Holy Spirit is working on our behalf, and stay on the lookout for such opportunities, pursuing the ones that are interesting, desirable, energizing, and even fascinating.[7]

---

[7] See Volume I, Chapter 8, and Volume IV.

In conclusion, the Christian Church's view of suffering is neither negative nor antithetical to love; indeed, it is precisely the opposite. For Jesus, all suffering will be completely redeemed in the unconditional love of His eternal Kingdom. For Christians, suffering offers the opportunity to detach from superficiality, darkness, egocentricity, and self-destruction by opening the path to true freedom—to *agapē* (particularly humble-heartedness, gentle-heartedness, and compassion). It also offers the opportunity to make an offering of ourselves, and so create a positive loving spiritual power to bring light and love to others and the Church. It also enables Christians to give witness to their faith and spread the gospel. These benefits of suffering do not occur in a vacuum, but through a Church community and the power of the Holy Spirit, who gives us the peace and inspiration to see and follow God's providential "conspiracy of grace". For Christians, suffering, though painful and difficult, can bring about tremendous love in the heart as well as spiritual and temporal goodness. It does not do this on its own; it needs the eyes of faith, the power of the Holy Spirit, and the support of the Christian community. When these are present, suffering becomes inextricably intertwined with freedom, love, goodness, transcendence, and God's Kingdom. In this way, the *irony* of "good and loving suffering" fades away and is replaced by the Kingdom of the unconditionally loving God.

We may now return to the passage with which we began:

> Come to me, all who labor and are heavy laden, and I will give you rest. Take my yoke upon you, and learn from me; for I am gentle and lowly in heart, and you will find rest for your souls. For my yoke is easy, and my burden is light. (Mt 11: 28–30)

We can now see what Jesus means by "my yoke is easy, and my burden is light." Through the eyes of faith, the power of the Holy Spirit, and the support of the Christian Church, the yoke of even tremendous suffering can be eased, and if we continue to trust in God's loving intention and Providence (through the peace and inspiration of the Holy Spirit), we shall find our suffering completely transformed into eternal and unconditional love with God and the blessed in His Kingdom.

Jesus truly is gentle and humble of heart, and He truly does give rest to anyone who comes to Him, so long as we see through the eyes of faith, trust in His promise, and work through the power of His Holy Spirit.

Jesus' promise to redeem all suffering extends to *everyone*—Christians and non-Christians—because as His Eucharistic words ("poured out for many" [Mt 26:28; Mk 14:24]) and dying words (Psalm 22) indicate, His offer of salvation is *universal* (see Chapter 7, Section I). Jesus does not ignore those who explicitly reject Him. He follows His Father's example and "makes his sun rise on the evil and on the good" (Mt 5:45). Furthermore, He instructs the Christian community to serve *all* mankind and identifies with the sufferings of *everyone*:

> [F]or I was hungry and you gave me food, I was thirsty and you gave me drink, I was a stranger and you welcomed me, I was naked and you clothed me, I was sick and you visited me, I was in prison and you came to me.... Truly, I say to you, as you did it to one of the least of these my brethren, you did it to me. (Mt 25:35–36, 40)

Jesus not only enters into our condition to suffer with us and for us; He continues to be present in every person who suffers, until He has brought everyone who desires His salvation into the Kingdom of his unconditional love.

II. Jesus' Love of the Poor, Sick, and Sinners

Jesus was greatly concerned for the suffering and the weak—not only those who were suffering physically (the sick and the poor), but also those who were suffering spiritually. He wanted to show them a way to make their suffering positive (for themselves and others), but also to assure them of redemption in His Kingdom of unconditional love. Beyond this, He wanted to be personally present to them, to identify with their suffering, and to give them the Holy Spirit to help them interpret and benefit from it.

A. Jesus' Love of the Poor

Jesus makes it a point to be with the poor and give alms to them,[8] and to ask His followers to care for the poor as if they were caring

---

[8] "Some thought that, because Judas had the money box, Jesus was telling him, 'Buy what we need for the feast'; or, that he should give something to the poor" (Jn 13:29).

for him: "Truly, I say to you, as you did it to one of the least of these my brethren, you did it to me" (Mt 25:40). Care for the poor is not simply central to His ministry and teaching; it is integral to bringing the Kingdom of God to the world. He proclaims this as the first Beatitude in the Gospel of Luke (6:20) and makes it the culminating moment of the end time (the definitive coming of the Kingdom) in His message to John the Baptist:

> Go and tell John what you hear and see: the blind receive their sight and the lame walk, lepers are cleansed and the deaf hear, and the dead are raised up, and the poor have good news preached to them. (Mt 11:4–5)

Jesus moves the good news for the poor from first place in the prophesy of Isaiah (61:1) to last place in His message to John (Mt 11:5) to indicate to him that the culminating act of the coming of the Kingdom will be the consolation of the poor. John P. Meier writes in this regard:

> The climactic action of Jesus in bringing in the end time, the action Jesus keeps to last in his list, is not any healing but rather the proclamation of good news to the poor—the good news spoken of in Is. 61:1, the good news Jesus quite literally proclaims to the "poor" in his first Beatitude in the great Q Sermon (Matt 5:3/Luke 6:20).[9]

Jesus had more than a "soft spot in His heart" for the poor, more than feelings of empathy and compassion for them; He felt that their salvation and the alleviation of their suffering was integral to the Kingdom of God, and he promised that the consolation of the poor will come when the Kingdom of God is fully realized. Apparently, Jesus did not expect the suffering of the poor to be completely alleviated until His Kingdom is fully actualized.

Furthermore, Jesus encourages His disciples to imitate His example and help the poor in their midst, particularly by giving alms to them. He praised Zacchaeus for doing so (Lk 19:8–10). In carrying out this key responsibility, Christians actualize His Kingdom in the present

---

[9] John P. Meier, *A Marginal Jew: Rethinking the Historical Jesus*, vol. 2, *Mentor, Message, and Miracles* (New York: Doubleday, 1994), p. 401.

moment. Those who help the hungry, thirsty, stranger, naked, sick, and imprisoned will also "inherit the kingdom prepared for [them] from the foundation of the world" (Mt 25:34).

Jesus also thought that heartlessness toward the poor put people in grave spiritual danger. He states that callousness toward the needy will be the basis for separating the righteous (sheep) from the unrighteous (goats) in Matthew 25:31–41. He attributes the chasm between Lazarus and the rich man to the callousness of the rich man's heart in Luke 16:23–31. For this reason, he makes the cultivation of a compassionate heart central to Christian spiritual life (in the central commandment, the fifth Beatitude, the Good Samaritan, and many other texts).

It might be thought that Jesus' concern for the poor was not as intense as implied above, because He tells His disciples who are criticizing a woman for anointing His head with expensive ointment, "Why do you trouble the woman? For she has done a beautiful thing to me. For you always have the poor with you, but you will not always have me" (Mt 26:10–11). Jesus here is not telling His disciples to be less concerned about the poor, but rather to appreciate the act of compassion done by the woman.[10] Indeed, if concern for the poor had not been central to Jesus, the apostles would never have protested that the perfume could have been sold and the proceeds given to the *poor*. For Jesus, concern for the poor is always central, but in different situations it may not be the highest priority.

Jesus' concern for the poor is not "clinical", and it does not arise out of a mere sense of obligation or duty. It comes from a deep empathy for all individuals, which is grounded in their intrinsic goodness and lovability. When the needs of these "beloveds" are not met, and they are impoverished or marginalized, Jesus' *heart* goes out to them in precisely the same way as the Good Samaritan's.

B. Jesus' Love of the Sick and Possessed

Jesus' exorcisms and healing miracles were not performed primarily to show His divine power and authority. This is only a consequence

---

[10] "In pouring this ointment on my body she has done it to prepare me for burial. Truly, I say to you, wherever this gospel is preached in the whole world, what she has done will be told in memory of her" (Mt 26:12–13).

of His main purpose: to usher the Kingdom of God into the world. An integral part of bringing God's Kingdom is the banishing of Satan and liberating the world from his dominant dark power (see Chapter 6, Section II). Jesus thought of His many ministerial activities as carrying out this purpose, including preaching the Word, exorcizing the possessed, healing the sick, caring for the poor, healing sinners, and most especially, His self-sacrificial death. These activities not only bring about God's Kingdom and break the power of Satan, but also express God's love (*agapē*). For Jesus, the recognition of the unique goodness, lovability, and transcendent mystery of each individual that leads to genuine care for them is the power that breaks Satan's grip on the world and establishes God's Kingdom. This leads Jesus to fill His ministerial day not only with preaching, but with a considerable number of exorcisms and healings.[11] When He is not actively involved in these "works of God", He befriends and ministers to sinners (see below, Section II.C).

Jesus' miracle working is quite unique in the ancient Jewish and Hellenistic world. Three major features distinguish His ministry from that of other so-called miracle workers: His genuine concern for the sick person, both physically and spiritually; His desire that there be faith in the petitioners; and His desire that the healing miracle point beyond itself—to God's love, God's Kingdom, and the banishing of evil.[12] For the moment, we will focus only on the dimensions of love and faith in these miracle stories. This is best accomplished by taking two concrete examples from Jesus' unique ministry:

---

[11] There can be little doubt that Jesus performed many exorcisms and healing miracles. Even His opponents did not dispute this; instead they tried to explain His prolific ministry as a consequence of magic or demonic possession. As Wright notes: "We must be clear that Jesus' contemporaries, both those who became his followers and those who were determined not to become his followers, certainly regarded him as possessed of remarkable powers. The church did not invent the charge that Jesus was in league with Beelzebul; but charges like that are not advanced unless they are needed as an explanation for some quite remarkable phenomena." N. T. Wright, *Jesus and the Victory of God* (Minneapolis: Fortress Press, 1996), 2:187. Furthermore, Jesus' ministry of exorcism and healing is attested by non-Christian sources (see Chapter 5, footnote 3, for a list of non-Gospel sources of Jesus' miraculous healing power by Raymond Brown, John P. Meier, and Luke Timothy Johnson as well as virtually all New Testament sources).

[12] See Chapter 5, footnote 3, for a list of non-Gospel sources of Jesus' miraculous healing power by Raymond Brown, John P. Meier, and Luke Timothy Johnson.

1. The healing of the blind beggar Bartimaeus
2. The raising of the only son of the widow of Nain

Let's begin with the healing of Bartimaeus:

> And they came to Jericho; and as [Jesus] was leaving Jericho with his disciples and a great multitude, Bartimaeus, a blind beggar, the son of Timaeus, was sitting by the roadside. And when he heard that it was Jesus of Nazareth, he began to cry out and say, "Jesus, Son of David, have mercy on me!" And many rebuked him, telling him to be silent; but he cried out all the more, "Son of David, have mercy on me!" And Jesus stopped and said, "Call him." And they called the blind man, saying to him, "Take heart; rise, he is calling you." And throwing off his cloak he sprang up and came to Jesus. And Jesus said to him, "What do you want me to do for you?" And the blind man said to him, "Master, let me receive my sight." And Jesus said to him, "Go your way; your faith has made you well." And immediately he received his sight and followed him on the way. (Mk 10:46–52)

The geographical and chronological specificity, as well as Bartimaeus' use of pre-Resurrection Semitic titles for Jesus, indicates that the details in the story are probably historically accurate.[13] We are presented with a scene in which Jesus attracts a large crowd as He enters into Jericho. A blind man on the side of the road, Bartimaeus, who few respect because of his infirmity, discovers that Jesus is passing by. He has heard about Jesus' healing power and uses an ancient Jewish term of respect, "Son of David", to cry out to Jesus, asking Him to have pity on him. People in the crowd rebuke him and tell him to be quiet while others barely notice him—*but Jesus hears his pleading*, which causes him to stop. Much to the surprise of the crowd, Jesus asks that this seemingly insignificant invalid be given special attention—and be brought to Him. The crowd changes their "tune" and tells him to "[t]ake heart; rise, he is calling you." Jesus asks Bartimaeus what He can do for him, and using another Jewish term of respect, he says, "Master, let me receive my sight." When Jesus sees Bartimaeus' belief, He has compassion on him and heals him with these words: "Go your way; *your* faith has made you well"

---

[13] See Chapter 5, Section I.B, for an explanation of the criteria of historicity.

(emphasis mine). Bartimaeus cannot help himself; he follows Jesus and His disciples.

Jesus' compassion is evident in this passage. He seems to be the only one who doesn't ignore Bartimaeus or treat him like a "second-class citizen". Instead, Bartimaeus' pleading attracts His attention and compels Him to stop and do something for him. In Jesus' view, Bartimaeus is in the grip of the power of evil, but not because he has committed a sin (as explained above, Jesus supersedes this Old Testament interpretation of suffering). He is already moved with compassion before healing him, but He first wants to see Bartimaeus' faith (his trust in the mercy of God). When Bartimaeus responds, "Master, let me receive my sight," Jesus knows that Bartimaeus not only trusts in the mercy of God, but believes that Jesus is the instrument of that mercy—or better, that Jesus *is* the mercy of God. Once the healing has occurred, Jesus gives Bartimaeus the credit: "Go your way; *your* faith has made you well."

Though this healing miracle attests to Jesus' divine power and authority, it is by no means the central point. Jesus is not interested in calling attention to *Himself*, or astonishing anyone with apparent magic or supernatural power. He is interested in healing *Bartimaeus*— the one who is gripped by the power of evil. Jesus cannot help Himself; Bartimaeus' pleading captures His attention and causes Him to move toward freeing Bartimaeus from the darkness that grips him. Jesus does not pray to God to heal Bartimaeus, but rather cures him by *His own* healing power[14] (the power of God's mercy) and, interestingly, uses Bartimaeus' trust in God's mercy to actualize the healing. Jesus sees Himself as "the compassion or mercy of God", and if anyone trusts in His divine compassion, he is healed from the power of evil. Notice that the attention is not fixed on "Jesus wielding power", but rather on "Bartimaeus trusting in Jesus as the mercy of

---

[14] As will be discussed in Chapter 5 (Section I.A), this action of Jesus is decidedly different from the Old Testament prophets, who do not heal by "their own" authority and word. They pray to God to intercede *through them* to heal a sick person. This is particularly important with respect to the only two Old Testament prophets who raised the dead—Elijah and Elisha. Again we see that these two prophets pray to God to use them as intermediaries—as instruments of His power to raise the dead. As will be seen in the next miracle story, Jesus raises the widow's son by *His own* word alone: "Young man, *I* say to you, arise" (Lk 7:14; emphasis mine). This is true for all the New Testament stories where Jesus raises the dead.

God". The whole dynamic is one of compassion, compassion for Bartimaeus (as a result of his pleading and infirmity) and Bartimaeus' trust in Jesus as "the compassion of God".

Let us now turn to another miracle, the raising of the son of the widow of Nain:

> Soon afterward [Jesus] went to a city called Nain, and his disciples and a great crowd went with him. As he drew near to the gate of the city, behold, a man who had died was being carried out, the only son of his mother, and she was a widow; and a large crowd from the city was with her. And when the Lord saw her, he had compassion on her and said to her, "Do not weep." And he came and touched the bier, and the bearers stood still. And he said, "Young man, I say to you, arise." And the dead man sat up, and began to speak. And he gave him to his mother. (Lk 7:11–15)

As with the Bartimaeus story, the geographical and chronological specificity of this story indicates that the details are likely to be historically accurate.[15] We are here presented with Jesus coming into a very small (and insignificant) town with a large group of disciples. Coming out of the town gate is a funeral party with a young man on a bier who is the only son of his widowed mother. Jesus sees the scene and intuits the tragic turn of events in this woman's life. He recognizes her anguish at the loss of her son, and realizes that without the support of her son she is probably destined for a life of abject poverty. The woman is weeping—and once again, Jesus cannot help Himself. The story specifies that Jesus is moved by a visceral sense of compassion (*esplagchnisthē*, the same word used by Jesus in the Parable of the Good Samaritan). He asks the woman to stop weeping because He intends to put an end to her pain by raising her son to life. This is very uncharacteristic for Jesus, who normally waits for a person to ask Him for a miracle—that is, to trust that He is "the mercy of God". Jesus knows that no one would ask for such a miracle, because "raising the dead" would not have been thought possible, even by a great prophet. So Jesus touches the bier, and the bearers stop. Jesus does not touch

---

[15] The town of Nain was so insignificant that many scholars doubted its existence until recent archaeological findings confirmed it. Why mention such an insignificant town unless this remarkable event had actually taken place *there*?

the young man, but instead raises him by His authoritative word: "Young man, *I say* to you, arise" (emphasis mine). Once again, Jesus does not pray to *God* to raise the young man, but rather raises him by *His own word*.[16] Jesus then gives the young man back to his mother.

Though Jesus clearly manifests divine power and authority in raising the dead by His own word, the emphasis is on His compassion (*esplagchnisthē*). Inasmuch as God alone has power over life and death,[17] Jesus manifests divine power; however, this power is inextricably connected to His deep compassion, showing that the power of God is unmitigated compassion for the needy. Jesus' care and compassion for this widow (a stranger) is what causes the dead to be raised through Him. He shows Himself to be the Son of the *loving* God by revealing at once that He possesses God's power, and that His power arises out of *compassion*.

In sum, Jesus' unique ministry of healing shows His empathy, sympathy, and compassion for those in need. He cannot resist the pleading of Bartimaeus or the sadness of the widow of Nain. Their obvious need for help moves His whole being with compassion (*esplagchnisthē*), and so His loving compassion becomes the power through which the needy are healed. In the case of Bartimaeus, Jesus waits until Bartimaeus expresses his trust in Him as "the mercy of God" (which typifies the majority of Jesus' healing miracles). Jesus' compassion overrules sickness and death, and breaks the grip of Satan over the world, establishing God's Kingdom.

C. Jesus' Acceptance and Love of Sinners

Joachim Jeremias indicates that many of the original followers of Jesus were sinners. Jesus associates them with "the poor" and orients His mission to alleviating their poverty:

> If we are to gain a clear picture of the people to whom Jesus brought
> the good news, our starting point must be the fact that, when we look

---

[16]See above, note 14.

[17]In Genesis 1, it is clear that God provides the "breath" of all living things, and that God creates man in His own image (Gen 1:27). In Genesis 2, God creates man by His own breath (spirit); see Gen 2:7.

at the various designations of the followers of Jesus as they are given in the gospels, we come to know these people from a double perspective. They are repeatedly called "publicans and sinners" (Mark 2.16 par.; Matt. 11.19 par.; Luke 15.1), "publicans and prostitutes" (Matt. 21.32), or simply "sinners" (Mark 2.17; Luke 7.37, 39; 15.2; 19.7). The deep contempt expressed in such designations shows that these phrases were coined by *Jesus' opponents*; Matt. 11.19 par. Luke 7.34 confirms that explicitly.[18]

To whom does the term "sinner" refer? Wright notes that it could refer to a large group of people ranging from non-Pharisaic Jews ("light sinners" whom the Pharisees held to be technically sinners because they did not agree with their interpretation of the Torah) to the wicked who deliberately flouted the law, like prostitutes (who would be considered "heavy sinners").[19] Tax collectors were considered to be particularly egregious sinners because they were collaborators with Rome, dishonest, and rapacious. Wright calls them "the moral equivalent of lepers".[20] It is clear from the Gospels that Jesus associates with all of these individuals and groups and enjoys table fellowship with them.

Recall from Chapter 2 that Jesus associated the father of the prodigal son with His Father (Abba) and that the prodigal son represents both individual sinners and perhaps also Israel (conceived as a sinful nation). Jesus reveals that His Father not only forgives the sins of the egregiously sinful son, but also restores him back to his former dignity and condition, and even reopens the family (the Kingdom) to him. Yet, Jesus does far more than *preach* the forgiveness and salvation of repentant sinners; He also associates with them, welcomes them into His company, and even eats with them. Dining (particularly table fellowship at a banquet) indicates not only friendship, but also familiarity and kinship.

---

[18] Joachim Jeremias, *New Testament Theology* (New York: Charles Scribner's Sons, 1971), 1:109; emphasis in original. See also John L. McKenzie, "The Gospel according to Matthew", in *The Jerome Biblical Commentary*, eds. Raymond Brown, Joseph A. Fitzmyer, and Roland E. Murphy (Englewood Cliffs, N.J.: Prentice-Hall, 1968), 2:83–84. See also E. P. Sanders, *Jesus and Judaism* (Philadelphia: Fortress, 1985), pp. 174–209.

[19] See Wright, *Jesus and Victory of God*, p. 266.

[20] Ibid.

Jesus' welcoming of and table fellowship with sinners incites the scribes and Pharisees to criticism and disdain:

> And as he sat at table in [Levi's] house, many tax collectors and sinners were sitting with Jesus and his disciples; for there were many who followed him. And the scribes of the Pharisees, when they saw that he was eating with sinners and tax collectors, said to his disciples, "Why does he eat with tax collectors and sinners?" (Mk 2:15–16)

The Pharisees' contempt is clearly manifest when they simultaneously accuse Jesus of being "a glutton and a drunkard, a friend of tax collectors and sinners!" (Mt 11:19). It may also be seen in the attitude of the Pharisee who upon observing a woman washing Jesus' feet with her tears and wiping them with her hair thought, "If this man were a prophet, he would have known who and what sort of woman this is who is touching him, for she is a sinner" (Lk 7:39). We hear this familiar refrain of the Pharisees once again when Jesus asks Zacchaeus if He might stay at his house: "He has gone in to be the guest of a man who is a sinner" (Lk 19:7).

Thus, Jesus endures not only ostracization by the official religious leaders, but also their contempt, insult, and disdain. This could not have been a comfortable religious or social position for Jesus. So why did He put Himself in this position? Because He could not resist any sinner who turned to Him.

The rationale for His peculiar sacrificial behavior is quite clear: "Those who are well have no need of a physician; only those who are sick. I came not to call the righteous, but sinners" (Mk 2:17). Jesus manifests a deep sympathy and affection for sinners when He explains why He receives and eats with them:

> What man of you, having a hundred sheep, if he has lost one of them, does not leave the ninety-nine in the wilderness, and go after the one which is lost, until he finds it? And when he has found it, he lays it on his shoulders, rejoicing. (Lk 15:4–5)

Jesus also acknowledges the love that sinners can manifest when they have been respected and loved. He believes that this love is tantamount to a "righteousness [that] exceeds that of the scribes and

Pharisees" (Mt 5:20). In response to the Pharisees' criticism of the woman who has washed Jesus' feet with her tears and dried them with her hair, Jesus says to Simon, the Pharisee:

> "Therefore I tell you, her sins, which are many, are forgiven, for she loved much; but he who is forgiven little, loves little." And he said to her, "Your sins are forgiven." (Lk 7:47–48)

Jesus forgives sinners and promises them righteousness and salvation. This is evident in the above passage, and is even more clearly manifest in a passage that suggests that sinners will enter the Kingdom of Heaven before even the strictly observant Pharisees:

> Truly, I say to you, the tax collectors and the harlots go into the kingdom of God before you [Pharisees]. For John came to you in the way of righteousness, and you did not believe him, but the tax collectors and the harlots believed him. (Mt 21:31–32)

Jesus clearly reveals the forgiveness and salvation of sinners in the story about the Pharisee and the tax collector praying in the Temple. He asserts that the tax collector is justified (made right before God and destined for salvation), but the Pharisee is not. Why? Because the tax collector humbly begs for the mercy of God, but the Pharisee tells God that he has done everything right, implying that he has made *himself* righteous:

> Two men went up into the temple to pray, one a Pharisee and the other a tax collector. The Pharisee stood and prayed thus *with himself*, "God, I thank you that I am not like other men, extortioners, unjust, adulterers, or even like this tax collector. I fast twice a week, I give tithes of all that I get." But the tax collector, standing far off, would not even lift up his eyes to heaven, but beat his breast, saying, "God, be merciful to me a sinner!" I tell you, this man went down to his house justified rather than the other; for every one who exalts himself will be humbled, but he who humbles himself will be exalted. (Lk 18:10–14; emphasis mine)

Jesus not only associates with and befriends sinners; He believes in them and defends them. He shows Himself to be *honored* in going to the house of Zacchaeus (a tax collector), and when Zacchaeus welcomes Him, and reforms his life because of Him, Jesus calls him "a son of Abraham" (Lk 19:9) (a member of the chosen people), even though he is an outcast in the eyes of the Pharisees. Jesus calls the tax collector Matthew to be one of His disciples. This is an extraordinary honor, and as if this were not enough, He goes to Matthew's house to enjoy table fellowship with him and his friends (many of whom were tax collectors and sinners). When challenged by the Pharisees about this, Jesus defends them by saying:

> Those who are well have no need of a physician, but those who are sick. Go and learn what this means: "I desire mercy, and not sacrifice." For I came not to call the righteous, but sinners. (Mt 9:12–13)

Jesus honors the sinful woman who washes His feet with her tears in a similar way. Simon the Pharisee is thinking to himself that Jesus could not be a prophet if He allows a sinful woman to touch Him, but Jesus responds that the woman has conducted herself in a better manner than Simon because of her great love, and Jesus reveals here a central truth: "I tell you, her sins, which are many, are forgiven, for she loved much" (Lk 7:47).

We can now see how Jesus thinks and feels about sinners. Instead of *excluding* them from the religious community and the Kingdom of God, He wants to *include* them—in everything. He believes in them and sees their dignity, amid the many problems in their lives. He invites them to repentance and recognizes this repentance in a variety of ways—in Matthew's decision to follow Him, in Zacchaeus' decision to reform his ways, and in the tax collector's simple prayer, "God, be merciful to me a sinner!" (Lk 18:13).

Jesus' strategy is to love and honor these sinners. When they see that He is "a prophet and more, beyond any prophet—the messiah", they believe His promise that God loves them and includes them in the Kingdom, and that God rejoices in their return, like the father of the prodigal son or a shepherd finding his lost sheep. This gives them hope, a sense of their own dignity and lovability, and a belief in their inclusion in the Kingdom of Heaven (counteracting the negative effects of the Pharisees). He believes that many of them will respond in gratitude and love to God, which will provide the conviction and spiritual power to begin the process of reforming their lives.

Jesus also *defends* sinners, both directly and indirectly. Sometimes He will tell the Pharisees that a particular sinner is justified in the eyes of God, such as the woman who washes Jesus' feet with her tears (Lk 7), Matthew the tax collector (Mt 9:10–13), the woman caught in adultery (Jn 8:1–11), and Zacchaeus (Lk 19:1–10). Sometimes He defends sinners indirectly by means of parables, sayings, and polemic. For example, the Parable of the Prodigal Son (Lk 15:11–32), the Parable of the Lost Sheep (Lk 15:1–7), the Parable of the Two Sons (Mt 21:28–32), and the story of the Pharisee and the tax collector praying in the Temple (Lk 18:9–14). Some of His sayings include His forgiveness of the woman caught in adultery, "Neither do I condemn you" (Jn 8:11), and his promise of salvation to the good thief on the cross: "Truly, I say to you, today you will be with me in Paradise" (Lk 23:43). His polemic in defense of sinners is extensive: He claims that tax collectors and prostitutes are entering the Kingdom before the Pharisees (Mt 21:31), that the Pharisees place heavy burdens on people's shoulders that they do not lift a finger to budge (Mt 23:4), and his most telling polemic:

> [W]oe to you, scribes and Pharisees, hypocrites! because you shut the kingdom of heaven against men; for you neither enter yourselves, nor allow those who would enter to go in. (Mt 23:13)

Here we see the opposition between Jesus' and the Pharisees approach to the Kingdom of God. The Pharisees attempt to exclude everyone who is "undeserving", while Jesus tries to include everyone who is willing to turn to God in trust.

Given the disagreements between Jesus and the Pharisees, and His rough rhetoric toward them when He defends sinners, one might legitimately ask whether He loved the Pharisees. Jeremias indicates that in fact He did and was very concerned about their salvation, and so He oriented the last part of the Prodigal Son Parable toward them (represented by the older son).[21] Furthermore, Jesus seeks out the Pharisees who do not reject Him out of hand. He dines at the house of Simon the Pharisee (Mt 26:6–13), speaks with Nicodemus at great length (Jn 3:1–21), and was befriended by Joseph of

---

[21] See Joachim Jeremias, *The Parables of Jesus* (London: SCM Press, 1972), pp. 129–31, and Chapter 2 of this book.

Arimathea, a member of the Sanhedrin who asked Pilate for Jesus' body and gave him his own prepared tomb (see Mk 15:43 and Jn 19:38). Jesus patiently endures the insults and disdain of the Pharisees, and reserves His harsh rhetoric to those who are preventing sinners from entering the Kingdom. Furthermore, many early converts to Christianity were Jewish scribes (very likely including Matthew the evangelist). Matthew writes his Gospel to attract Jewish religious leaders to Christianity. We must assume that some of this impetus came from Jesus Himself. In view of this, it seems evident that Jesus loved and was concerned for the Pharisees, and that His harsh rhetoric was directed at their salvation as well as the defense of sinners unjustifiably harmed by their exclusionary interpretation of the Torah.

In sum, Jesus was drawn to sinners because He recognized their goodness and dignity, their potential for salvation, and their "need of a physician" (Mt 9:12). He respected them, believed in them, and loved them—in the same way that the father of the prodigal son loved *both* of his sons. He not only cared for sinners; He felt affection for them and attributed that same care and affection to His Father.

III. Jesus' Love of Disciples and Friends

The Gospel of John is most explicit about Jesus' love of disciples and friends. Though John uses some of his own special words and concepts to describe this love, he does so to emphasize and nuance what he considers to be the most important truth in his Gospel: his experience of Jesus' deep and unconditional love. Jesus' new commandment in John's Gospel sums up the apostles' experience of Jesus during His ministry: "[L]ove one another as I have loved you" (Jn 15:12; see Jn 13:34). This commandment would scarcely be intelligible if all the disciples had not had a profound experience of Jesus' love. The *unconditional* nature of that love is specified after this new commandment: "Greater love has no one than this, that a man lay down his life for his friends" (Jn 15:13). When Jesus does in fact lay down His life for His friends, His unconditional love for them becomes not only a present reality, but one that will endure throughout history, and indeed, throughout God's eternity.

John refers to himself five times as the disciple whom Jesus loved (Jn 13:23; 19:26; 20:2; 21:7; 21:20). John here does not mean this phrase in an exclusive way (i.e., that Jesus did not love the other disciples), but rather as a reference to his core identity. Names in the Semitic world commonly referred to the core or heart of a person (e.g., Simon being called "Peter", which means "rock"). Thus, when John refers to himself as the disciple whom Jesus loved, he reveals his core reality—his very essence—namely, having been loved and being loved by Jesus. This reveals John's profound experience of Jesus' friendship and compassionate love.

We see other references to Jesus' love of disciples and friends, love that is recounted with empathy, depth, and affection. This is particularly manifest in the story of the raising of Lazarus: "Now Jesus loved Martha and her sister and Lazarus" (Jn 11:5). Again in the same story the evangelist tells us:

> When Jesus saw her weeping, and the Jews who came with her also weeping, he was deeply moved in spirit and troubled; and he said, "Where have you laid him?" They said to him, "Lord, come and see." Jesus wept. So the Jews said, "See how he loved him!" (Jn 11:33–36)

Perhaps the most profound reference to Jesus' love of disciples occurs with respect to Peter, though in a somewhat inverted way. On the shore of the sea of Tiberius (after the Resurrection), Jesus asks Peter:

> "Simon, son of John, do you love me more than these?" He said to him, "Yes, Lord; you know that I love you." He said to him, "Feed my lambs." A second time he said to him, "Simon, son of John, do you love me?" He said to him, "Yes, Lord; you know that I love you." He said to him, "Tend my sheep." He said to him the third time, "Simon, son of John, do you love me?" Peter was grieved because he said to him the third time, "Do you love me?" And he said to him, "Lord, you know everything; you know that I love you." Jesus said to him, "Feed my sheep." (Jn 21:15–17)

Though there is clearly redactional material in this section, Raymond Brown reports that even German theologian Rudolf Bultmann agrees that this passage goes back to a primary strand of tradition.[22] Most exegetes believe that this passage indicates Jesus' forgiveness and rehabilitation of Peter after his three denials.[23] The word "love" is used within the forgiveness/rehabilitation scene to convey the power through which Peter is rehabilitated and empowered as shepherd in the post-Resurrection Church.

How does this reflect *Jesus'* love for Peter (instead of only Peter's love for Jesus)? A hint is provided by Brown:

> Peter's repentance would be implicit in his pathetic insistence on his love and in the anguish that the thrice-repeated question causes him (vs. 17). Instead of boasting that he loves Jesus more than others (15), a chastened Peter rests his case on Jesus' knowledge of what is in his heart ["Lord, you know everything; you know that I love you"] (vs. 17).[24]

Though Peter is contrite, he relies on Jesus' heart to know his heart, and in so doing manifests the love that Jesus has for him.

Jesus' love for His disciples and friends is summed up in a narrative comment prior to His Passion:

> Now before the feast of the Passover, when Jesus knew that his hour had come to depart out of this world to the Father, *having loved* his own who were in the world, he loved them to the end. (Jn 13:1; emphasis mine)

The *unconditional nature* of Jesus' love (*agapē*) for His disciples ("his own") is revealed in the saying, "[H]e loved them to the end." Here, "the end" refers to both the end of Jesus' life and the absolute extent to which Jesus was willing to go in order to bring His love into the world. For the evangelist, this summary statement that begins the second part of the Gospel (the Book of Glory, Jn 13–20) explains Jesus'

---

[22] "It is interesting to note that while for different reasons neither Bultmann nor Grass thinks that the connection of [verses] 15–17 to [verses] 1–14 is original, both agree that 15–17 reproduces traditional material and is not the creation of the redactor." Raymond Brown, *The Gospel according to John XIII-XXI*, vol. 2, in *The Anchor Bible*, vol. 29A (New York: Doubleday, 1970), p. 1110.

[23] See ibid., pp. 1110–12.

[24] Ibid., p. 1111.

understanding of both Himself and His mission. We may infer from this that Jesus' love for His disciples was not only empathetic, affectionate, forgiving, compassionate and self-sacrificial, but also unconditional. The implication is that Jesus will extend the same unconditional empathy, affection, forgiveness, compassion, and self-sacrifice to all who desire to be His disciples—no matter what century, country, culture, or situation they live in. Thus, being a disciple of Jesus brings us into His life of unconditional love.

IV. Jesus' Unconditional Love in the Eucharist and Passion

Jesus set His face resolutely toward Jerusalem in the midst of His disciples' warning about impending persecution because He had a plan, a plan to give away His unconditionally healing and reconciling love to the world for all generations. The first step of the plan would unfold at the Last Supper. The second part would bring the plan to completion in His suffering and death. As noted above (Section I), Jesus interpreted this self-sacrificial act through the Fourth Suffering Servant Song of Isaiah:

> [W]hen he makes himself an offering for sin,
> he shall see his offspring, he shall prolong his days,
> the will of the Lord shall prosper in his hand;
> he shall see the fruit of the travail of his soul and be satisfied;
> by his knowledge shall the righteous one, my servant, make many to
> be accounted righteous; and he shall bear their iniquities. Therefore I
> will divide him a portion with the great, and he shall divide the spoil
> with the strong; because he poured out his soul to death, and was
> numbered with the transgressors; yet he bore the sin of many, and
> made intercession for the transgressors. (Is 53:10–12)

Jesus interpreted His self-sacrificial death as a gift or libation for sinners and transgressors. He wanted to take the darkness and negation of all their sins upon Himself, and to make reparation for it by the gift of His unblemished life. His plan was to make traditional sin offerings and the Paschal sacrifice into an offering of Himself by replacing the sacrificial animals with His own body and blood. He would do this at the celebration of the Passover with His disciples. After the supper, he would allow Himself to be taken captive by the Jewish authorities and be persecuted by the Roman authorities—actualizing the symbolic sacrifice of the night before. When the sacrifice was completed, He would have given Himself completely to mankind, which He interpreted as an act of *unconditional* love.[25]

A. The First Part of the Plan: The Last Supper

Jesus' Eucharistic words explain the first part of His plan to love the world into redemption.[26] Jeremias attempted a reconstruction of the original tradition of Jesus' Eucharistic words from the four New Testament traditions: 1 Corinthians 11:23–26; Mark 14:22–25; Matthew 26:26–29; and Luke 22:17–20. Notice that there are two distinct strands of tradition: the Mark-Matthew strand (constructed for liturgical purposes) and the Paul-Luke strand (constructed for a Gentile audience). Jeremias prefers the Mark-Matthew strand for the rite over the bread (body) and the Paul-Luke strand for the rite of the wine (blood). Using literary constructions and Semitisms as clues to resolve other differences within each strand, Jeremias concludes that the rite of the Last Supper probably took the following form.[27]

Jesus gathered with His disciples before the feast of the Passover and indicated to them that He longed to celebrate this Passover with

[25] See John 15:13: "Greater love has no man than this, that a man lay down his life for his friends." Saint Paul also understands this when he says in Romans 8:32–35: "He who did not spare his own Son but *gave* him up for *us all*, will he not also give us all things with him? Who shall bring any charge against God's elect? It is God who justifies; who is to condemn? Is it Christ Jesus, who died, yes, who was raised from the dead, who is at the right hand of God, who indeed intercedes for us? *Who* shall separate us from the love of Christ?" (emphasis mine).

[26] This thesis and the contents of this section are explained in great detail in Joachim Jeremias' work *The Eucharistic Words of Jesus* (London: SCM Press, 1966). It is also explained in an excellent essay by Johannes Betz; see "Eucharist", in *Sacramentum Mundi*, ed. Karl Rahner (London: Burns and Oates, 1968), 2:257.

[27] See Jeremias, *Eucharistic Words of Jesus*, pp. 171–73, 208–9, 223–24, and 238–43. See also John P. Meier, *A Marginal Jew: Rethinking the Historical Jesus*, vol. 1, *The Roots of the Problem and the Person* (New York: Doubleday, 1991), pp. 334–37.

them, but instead of doing so, fasted while the other disciples cel-
ebrated.[28] After drinking one of the four Passover cups while they
were eating the Passover meal (or an adapted Passover ritual),[29] Jesus
initiated the ritual of the bread, identifying it with His body: "Jesus
took bread, and blessed, and broke it, and gave it to the disciples and
said, 'Take, eat; this is my body'" (Mt 26:26; see Mk 14:22; Lk 22:19;
1 Cor 11:23–24). Then, after the completion of the Passover meal,
Jesus initiated the ritual of the wine that He identifies with the covenant in His blood. He took a cup of red wine, gave thanks, and gave
it to His disciples, saying, "[T]his [cup] is my blood of the covenant,[30]
which is poured out for [the] many"[31] (Mt 26:28; Mk 14:24; see Lk
22:20; 1 Cor 11:25). Sometime either prior to or after this (perhaps
both), Jesus gives a command to repeat the ritual: "Do this in remembrance of me" (Lk 22:19; 1 Cor 11:24).

When He says, "This is my body which is given for you" (Lk
22:19; see 1 Cor 11:24), the Greek word used to translate His Hebrew
(*zeh baśari*) or Aramaic (*den bisri*) was *sōma* instead of *sarx*. *Sarx* means
"flesh" and would certainly refer to Jesus' *corporeal* body given on
the Cross, while *sōma* is much broader and refers to the *whole* person
(mind, soul, and will, as well as corporeal body). Thus, *sōma* is much
like the word "body" in "everybody" or "somebody" in English. It
might, therefore, be roughly translated as "person" or "self". If we

---

[28] See Jeremias' convincing argument in *Eucharistic Words of Jesus*, pp. 208–9.

[29] See the discussion of this topic in the introduction to Section IV above.

[30] Though Jesus identifies the red wine with His "blood of the covenant", it is clear from
the red wine, the parallelism with the bread, and the use of "this cup" that Jesus is identifying the red wine with both His *blood* and the covenant in His blood. Jeremias notes that the
color of the wine is significant here: "The *tertium comparationis* in the case of the bread is
the fact that it was broken, and in the case of the wine the red colour. We have already seen
... that it was customary to drink red wine at the Passover.... The comparison between *red
wine* and blood was common in the Old Testament (Gen. 49.11; Deut. 32.14; Isa. 63.3,6),
further Eccl. 39.26; 50.15; I Macc. 6.34; Rev. 14.20; Sanh. 70a, etc." Jeremias, *Eucharistic
Words of Jesus*, pp. 223–24.

[31] Mark and Matthew report "poured out for many", but Luke reports "poured out for
you" (emphasis mine). Jeremias holds that "for the many" is the more original on the basis
of linguistic grounds; namely, "for the many" is a Semitism while "you" is not. Jeremias
attributes the replacement of "the many" by "you" as having a liturgical purpose where each
worshipper feels himself to be individually addressed (by "you"), which would not happen
with the indefinite "the many" (see ibid., p. 172). The Greek *to pollōn* (the many) is an unusual
expression and is probably an attempt to translate a common Semitic expression referring to
"all". This is explained below in this section (see IV.B).

substitute the word "self" for "body" in the Eucharistic words, we obtain "This is myself which is given for you." This is remarkably similar to Jesus' definition of unconditional love in John's Gospel, the gift of one's whole self ("[g]reater love has no man than this, that a man lay down his life for his friends" [Jn 15:13]). Thus, in the Eucharist, Jesus is not only giving us His whole self—that is, His whole person; He is also giving us His love, indeed, His *unconditional* love—that is, a love that cannot be surpassed.

This unconditional love is corroborated by the gift of His blood (which, according to Jewish custom, is separated from the body of the sacrificial offering). When Jesus offered His blood separately from His body, He showed Himself to be making an intentional self-sacrifice.

Blood (the principle of life for the Israelites) was the vehicle through which atonement occurred in sin or guilt offerings. Jesus' reference to His sacrificial blood would almost inevitably be seen as the blood of a sin offering, with the notable exception that the sin offering is no longer an animal, but rather, Jesus Himself, "the Beloved One of the Father". Jesus humbled Himself (taking the place of an animal, a sacrificial sin offering) to absolve the sin of the world forever.

Jesus goes beyond this by associating Himself with the Paschal lamb. He intentionally coordinates His arrival in Jerusalem with the Passover feast so that His sacrifice will be associated with that of the Paschal lamb. He loved us so much that He desired to become the new Passover sacrifice, replacing an unblemished lamb with His own divine presence.

The blood of the Passover lamb (put on the doorposts of every Israelite household) was the instrument through which the Israelite people were protected from death (the angel of death passing over those houses), which enabled them to move out of slavery into freedom (from Egypt into the Promised Land). When Jesus took the place of a sacrificial animal, He replaced the worldly freedom offered by the Passover—freedom from slavery in Egypt—with an unconditional and eternal freedom from sin and death. Thus, He made His self-sacrifice the new vehicle for protection from *every* form of sin and death for all eternity by outshining sin and darkness with His unconditionally loving eternal light.

There is yet a third dimension of Jesus' use of blood that He explicitly states as the "blood of the covenant". A covenant was a solemn promise that bound parties to a guaranteed agreement. When Jesus associates His blood with the covenant, He is *guaranteeing* the absolution from sin, freedom from slavery and darkness, and eternal life given through His unconditional love. By referencing the blood of the *covenant*, Jesus makes a solemn and unconditionally guaranteed promise to give us eternal life and love. If we put our faith in Him, trust in His promise, and try to remain in His teachings, His unconditional love will save us.

Jesus intended His sacrifice on the Cross to be universal (see below, Section IV.B, and Chapter 7, Section I), and to be the power of love and salvation for all mankind; but He did not stop there. He also provided a way for us to receive His unconditionally loving presence (body, mind, and soul) throughout the rest of history. He intended to make His loving presence within us a power of peace, reconciliation, healing, and transformation. He did this by making the actions and words of His Last Supper into a ritual, using the simple phrase "Do this in remembrance of me." This phrase requires explanation.

We need to understand the first-century Jewish view of time and memory to grasp the significance of Jesus' ritual (now known as the "Eucharistic celebration"). In this view, time is not an unalterable physical property (as in the "space-time continuum" of the theory of relativity). Rather, time was seen as a surmountable and controllable dimension of *sacred* history.[32] As Mircea Eliade notes, sacred history was seen as superseding profane history (physical history), and through ritual and myth, prophets and priests could return to the sacred time of history as if profane time were not relevant.[33] First-century Judaism was no exception to this. Religious authorities believed that the celebration of the Passover Supper was a return to the sacred events of the

---

[32] Mircea Eliade phrases it this way: "In *imitating* the exemplary acts of a god or of a mythical hero, or simply by recounting their adventures, the man of an archaic society detaches himself from profane time and magically re-enters the Great Time, the sacred time." Mircea Eliade, *Myths, Dreams, and Mysteries* (New York: Harper and Row, 1975), emphasis mine. First-century Jewish views of time follow Eliade's general form.

[33] Mircea Eliade, *The Myth of the Eternal Return: Or, Cosmos and History* (Princeton, N.J.: Princeton University Press, 1971).

Exodus, and that reliving this sacred moment would bring them close to the sacred reality (God/Yahweh), which would, in turn, sacralize them—that is, make them holy.[34]

As Jesus enters into the sacrificial meal with His disciples, He brings this view of time and history with Him.[35] When He says, "Do this in *remembrance* of me", He does not mean, "Call it to mind." His view of "remembrance" (translated by the Greek term *anamnesis*) did not separate "mind" from "heart", or separate a "mental remembrance" from a "ritual reliving".[36] For Him, the instruction to "[do] this in remembrance of me" meant "reengage in this ritual and relive the reality of me in it". To relive Jesus' ritual is to return to it—with Him *really* there. Johannes Betz summarizes this as follows:

> *Anamnesis* in the biblical sense means not only the subjective representation of something in the consciousness and as an act of the remembering mind. It is also the objective effectiveness and presence of one reality in another, especially the effectiveness and presence of the salvific actions of God, in the liturgical worship. Even in the Old Testament, the liturgy is the privileged medium in which the covenant attains *actuality*. The meaning of the logion ["Do this in remembrance of me"] may perhaps be paraphrased as follows: "do this (what I have done) in order *to bring about my presence*, to make really present the salvation wrought in me."[37]

It is difficult for us, as twenty-first-century scientifically oriented people, to enter into Jesus' perspective, because we really have to think about it since it is so dissimilar from the way we conceive time and reality. Nevertheless, if we are going to understand what He was doing, we will have to make the effort; otherwise, His words and actions will be completely masked by our inapplicable worldview.

---

[34]Jeremias quotes O. Michel, noting, "God's remembrance is, namely (this is an important fact to which O. Michel called attention), never a simple remembering of something, but always and without exception 'an *effecting and creating* event.' When Luke 1.72 says that God remembers his covenant, this means that he is *now fulfilling* the eschatological covenant promise." Jeremias, *Eucharistic Words of Jesus*, p. 348; emphasis mine. See also Betz, "Eucharist", pp. 260–61.

[35]See Betz, "Eucharist", pp. 258–62.

[36]See Jeremias, *Eucharistic Words of Jesus*, p. 348, and Betz, "Eucharist", pp. 260–61.

[37]Betz, "Eucharist", p. 260; emphasis mine.

The best historical research indicates that Jesus believed He would be *really* present to us in *every* reliving of His Last Supper ritual until the end of time. This intention not only stems from His view of history, time, and ritual, but also from His conviction that He would be raised from the dead[38] and would be present to us in His risen form throughout the rest of human history. Betz characterizes it in this way:

> *The bodily person of Jesus is present in the supper,* not however in the static manner of being a *thing*, but as the Servant of God who in his sacrificial death affects the salvation of us all and more precisely as the sacrificial offering of the Servant who delivers himself up on the cross. The *real presence* of the *person* is there to actualize the presence of the sacrificial deed and is united with this in an organic whole. The Eucharist becomes, then, the abiding presence in the meal of the sacrificially constituted salvific event "Jesus", in whom person and work form an inseparable unity.[39]

When Jesus approached Jerusalem knowing that He faced persecution and death, He had a plan to save all mankind throughout history by His act of total self-offering (unconditional love). His plan went further: He intended to initiate a ritual to be relived by His disciples throughout the rest of history. He would be really present in His self-sacrifice (body and blood), as well as in His risen form, and would convey through this presence His healing, forgiving, and transforming love to anyone who received His body and blood in this ritual.

---

[38] Jesus had a strong conviction in the resurrection, following Second Temple Judaism. In this regard He sided with the Pharisees and not the Sadducees (who did not believe in a resurrection, accepting only the Torah—the first five books of the Old Testament). Jesus makes clear His belief in a personal resurrection, which supersedes that of Second Temple Judaism (a merely bodily resurrection), which is evident in His Passion predictions, which include the phrase "on the third day be raised" (Mt 16:21; Lk 9:22; see Mk 8:31; Lk 18:33) as well as His assertion that He would rebuild the Temple in three days (found in two independent sources: Mt 26:61; 27:40; Jn 2:13–22). If Wright's interpretation of Jesus' trial before the Sanhedrin is correct, then Jesus must have said something to warrant the charge of blasphemy, which probably included His belief in being the eschatological judge who would return to judge the world: "[Y]ou will see the Son of man sitting at the right hand of Power, and coming with the clouds of heaven" (Mk 14:62). This presumes His Resurrection as more than a "resuscitated corpse". See Chapter 6 (Introduction).

[39] Betz, "Eucharist", p. 260; emphasis mine.

He would convey the love of complete self-gift; the forgiveness and healing of the ultimate sin offering; the liberation from darkness, evil, slavery, and death in the ultimate Passover sacrifice; and the eternal life of love in the blood of the New Covenant. His plan was to love us unconditionally, both universally (in His complete self-offering in death) and situationally (in the celebration of His Last Supper). After His Resurrection in glory, the early Church believed that He was the unconditional love of God with us—who is still with us until the end of time.

B. The Second Part of the Plan: Suffering, Death, and Resurrection

There is very strong evidence in favor not only of Jesus' Passion and death, but also for most of the details in the Passion narratives. Aside from the fact that the Roman historian Cornelius Tacitus and the Jewish historian Flavius Josephus assert the fact and time of Jesus' Crucifixion without qualification (see Chapter 2, Section II.A), the application of historical criteria to the Passion narratives indicates considerable concern for history.[40] In response to contentions that the apostles abandoned Jesus (and knew little about His trial, manner of execution, and burial), Raymond Brown explains:

> Yet as we move back from the Gospel narratives to Jesus himself, ultimately there were eyewitnesses and earwitnesses who were in a position to know the broad lines of Jesus' passion. He was accompanied in his ministry by a group of disciples known as the Twelve, and there is no reason whatsoever to doubt that the arrest of Jesus was the occasion of his being separated from them. It is inconceivable that they showed no concern about what happened to Jesus after the arrest. True, there is no Christian claim that they were present during the legal proceedings against him, Jewish or Roman; but it is absurd to think that some information was not available to them about why Jesus was hanged on a cross. The whole purpose of crucifixion, after all, was to publicize that certain crimes would be severely punished

[40] See, for example, Raymond Brown, *The Death of the Messiah: From Gethsemane to the Grave; A Commentary on the Passion Narratives in the Four Gospels* (New York: Doubleday, 1994), pp. 10–16.

(That is the sense in which I include "earwitness": hearing what was publicly said about the condemnation of Jesus). The crucifixion itself was public, and nothing suggests that the burial was secret.[41]

In addition to the above historical evidence, there is another remarkable "testimony" to the historicity of Jesus' Passion: the Shroud of Turin. Some readers may think that the Shroud was discredited as a medieval forgery by the 1988 carbon 14 dating, but Appendix I of this volume (on the Shroud), shows that the 1988 carbon 14 test was seriously flawed and in error by a significant factor, around thirteen hundred years.[42] Furthermore, four new testing procedures have been developed and used to date the Shroud since 2000, and they show (within a 95 percent confidence level) that the Shroud originated in about A.D. 50, very near to the time of Jesus' Crucifixion. Furthermore, there are three additional indicators of the Shroud's age that place it in first-century Palestine.[43] The combination of the above tests and evidence is quite overwhelming and supports the Shroud's authenticity as the burial cloth of Jesus.[44] As will be seen in the following chapter, the Shroud not only provides remarkable evidence for Jesus' Crucifixion and burial, but also His Resurrection.[45] The evidence for a resurrection also helps reveal the identity of the man who was wrapped in the Shroud.

[41] Ibid., p. 14.

[42] Appendix I (Section II.A) presents the evidence of Dr. Raymond Rogers and others that the samples from the Shroud were decidedly *not* from the original Shroud, but were later additions to it used for mending after the fire of Chambery. The presence of dye in the test fibers (that did not become available in Europe before 1250) makes this clear. Furthermore, the test fibers were not properly cleaned to account for microbic deposits of carbon, and the test results were not adjusted to account for carbon absorption during the fire of Chambery. If original fibers had been used and properly cleaned and adjusted, the carbon 14 test would have been drastically different.

[43] The carbon 14 dating of the Shroud conflicts with four other dating methods (Roger's Vanillin test, Fanti's infrared spectroscopy, Fanti's Raman laser spectroscopy, and Fanti's mechanical compressibility and breaking strength test). It also conflicts with three other reliable methods of dating the Shroud (Frei's pollen evidence, Whanger's polarized photographic overlay analysis of the coins, and the evidence for the Sudarium having touched the same face as the Shroud from the analysis of Heras, Villalain, and Rodriguez). All seven of these other dating techniques point to an origin of the Shroud in the first century, and two of them (the pollen grains and the coins on the man's eyes) point to a Palestinian origin. See Appendix I (Sections II.B and II.C).

[44] See Appendix I (Section IV).

[45] See Appendix I (Section III.D).

Inasmuch as the Shroud is the burial cloth of Jesus, it corroborates the historicity of the unusual parts of Jesus' Crucifixion: the crowning with thorns, the flogging, and the piercing with a roman pilium. It also gives poignant testimony to the sufferings He endured, which are elucidated in detail by the famous French surgeon Pierre Barbet in his work *A Doctor at Calvary: The Passion of Our Lord Jesus Christ as Described by a Surgeon*.[46] Barbet also shows that the bloodstains on the cloth are precisely what they ought to be if Jesus was crucified and buried in the way described in the four Gospel Passion narratives. Given the accuracy of the above tests and analyses, the historicity of the basic outline of Jesus' sufferings, Passion, death, and burial (as described by the Gospel narratives) is very probable, if not certain.

Does this strong historicity also apply to Jesus' dying words recounted in Mark's Gospel (Mk 15:34)? It is difficult to deny, because the lamentation ("My God, my God, why have you forsaken me?") could have been very apologetically unappealing, and difficult to explain to a Gentile audience. Why would Mark include it unless it was historically accurate? Furthermore, Mark's version of the dying words is a northern Galilean dialect of Aramaic (*"Elōi, Elōi, lama sabachthani"*).[47] This would have been the dialect in which Jesus learned the Psalms from His Mother when he was a child, which connects the recounted words to Jesus—not to Mark.

Jesus gives us the interpretation of His Passion through these dying words. The Marcan version of the final words is to be preferred over the Matthean one, because it is probable that Matthew tried to "clean up" Mark's Aramaic citation of the divine name (*Elōi*)[48] with the more proper Hebrew version of it (*'Ēlî*), which would have been recited in the synagogue.[49]

---

[46] Pierre Barbet, *A Doctor at Calvary: The Passion of Our Lord Jesus Christ as Described by a Surgeon* (New York: P.J. Kennedy, 1953).

[47] See Brown's linguistic analysis of the likely dialect of Jesus' dying words (in Mark) in Brown, *Death of the Messiah*, pp. 1051–52. Notice that Matthew, who was writing for a sophisticated Jewish audience, renders Jesus' Aramaic version in correct Hebrew.

[48] The Aramaic version is "*'Ēlāhî, 'Ēlāhî, lěmā šĕbaqtanî.*" Mark's *Elōi* is a common Greek transliteration of the Aramaic *'Ēlāhî*. See ibid., p. 1052. Thus, Mark's rendition is very probably his Greek transliteration of an *Aramaic* version of the Psalm.

[49] Recall that Matthew is writing for a well-educated Jewish audience, and was trying to convince them of the Messiahship of Jesus. He knew the appropriate Hebrew form of the Psalm and changed Mark's Aramaic *Elōi* to the Hebrew *'Ēlî*. See ibid., pp. 1051–52.

These dying words must be seen within the context of the Psalm from which Jesus derived them. They are the first line of Psalm 22, which refers to the *whole* Psalm (like a cantor who, by giving the first line of a Psalm, informs the congregation of the *whole* Psalm they are to recite). Brown points to a well-known hermeneutical principle in this regard:

> A New Testament citation of a specific Old Testament passage supposes that the readers will be familiar with the context of that passage and so understand implied references to that context.[50]

In the case of Psalm 22, the context speaks of trust in God, vindication, and salvation for the world.

So if we consider *"Elōi, Elōi, lama sabachthani"* to be the dying words of the historical Jesus, and if we apply Brown's hermeneutical principle to Jesus Himself (implying that Jesus expected informed listeners to be familiar with the context of that passage and understand implied references to that context), then it seems likely that the dying Jesus was praying the whole of Psalm 22 to His Father while giving His listeners an insight into how He interpreted His sacrificial death through that prayer. Edward Mally notes in this regard:

> As a quotation of an Old Testament Psalm, it can hardly be taken literally as an expression of real despair or dereliction. Rather, Jesus applies to himself an Old Testament passage that sums up the suffering of the upright individual who turns to his God in the stress of hostile opposition and its ensuing depression. In using the Psalm, Jesus does not express the feeling that his life's work has failed and that God has therefore abandoned him; he identifies himself with a biblical precedent, the persecuted upright man *who has trusted in Yahweh*, and found in him *the source of his consolation and ultimate triumph.*[51]

Thus, Jesus' reference to Psalm 22 is an expression of trust and confidence in the Father that His suffering will result in the triumph of His mission. As noted in the previous section, that mission is actualized for all future generations through the gift of His presence and unconditional redeeming love in the Eucharist.

[50] Ibid., p. 1050.

[51] Edward J. Mally, "The Gospel according to Mark", in *The Jerome Biblical Commentary*, ed. Raymond Brown, Joseph A. Fitmyer, and Roland E. Murphy (Englewood Cliffs, N.J.: Prentice-Hall, 1968), 2:58; emphasis mine.

A closer look at the Psalm may give a deep insight into Jesus' thoughts and feelings at the time of His Crucifixion. According to Roland E. Murphy, the Psalm may be divided into three parts:

1. "2–22, the complaint, with repeated requests, descriptions of suffering, and expressions of confidence (4–6; 10–11)",[52]
2. "23–32, thanksgiving, in which the community is invited to share (23–27)",[53] and
3. "the worldwide redemption and worship of Yahweh (28–32)."[54]

Each part will be presented in turn. Recall that *Jesus* is praying every part of this Psalm, and so when we reference "the Psalmist" below, we are also referencing Jesus' intention.

(1) Complaint, repeated requests, descriptions of suffering, and expressions of confidence.

> My God, my God, why have you forsaken me?
> Why are you so far from helping me,
> from the words of my groaning?
> O my God, I cry by day, but you do not answer;
> and by night, but find no rest. (vv. 1–2)

Then, the Psalmist shifts perspective, as he does several times throughout the Psalm, and introduces the theme of God's holiness and grandeur, worthy of praise and *trust*. Remember that this is also Jesus' intention as He is praying the entire Psalm:

> *Yet* you are holy,
> enthroned on the praises of Israel.
> In you our fathers trusted;
> *they trusted, and you delivered them.*
> *To you they cried, and were saved;*
> in you they trusted, and were not disappointed.
>   (vv. 3–5; emphasis mine)

[52] Roland E. Murphy, "Psalms", in *The Jerome Biblical Commentary*, eds. Raymond Brown, Joseph A. Fitmyer, and Roland E. Murphy (Englewood Cliffs, N.J.: Prentice-Hall, 1968), 1:579.
[53] Ibid.
[54] Ibid.

The Psalmist then turns back to the deplorable nature of his condition:

> But I am a worm, and no man;
> scorned by men, and despised by the people.
> All who see me mock at me,
> they make mouths at me, they wag their heads;
> "He committed his cause to the LORD;
> let him deliver him,
> let him rescue him,
> for he delights in him!" (vv. 6–8)

The uncanny resemblance between the Psalmist's words and the events taking place around Jesus give one pause. After describing the insulting words of the crowd (who believe that the Lord will not fulfill the trust of the Psalmist), the Psalmist shifts back to his fervent trust in the Lord:

> Yet you are he who took me from the womb;
> you kept me safe upon my mother's breasts.
> Upon you was I cast from my birth,
> and since my mother bore me you have been my God.
>   (vv. 9–10)

Having renewed his trust in the Lord, the Psalmist makes an earnest petition for help:

> Be not far from me,
> for trouble is near
> and there is none to help.
> Many bulls encompass me,
> strong bulls of Bashan surround me;
> they open wide their mouths at me,
> like a ravening and roaring lion. (vv. 11–13)

Then the Psalmist uses the same words seen in the Suffering Servant Song (Is 52:13–53:12) and Jesus' Eucharistic words ("poured out" [Mt 26:28; Mk 14:24]):

> I am *poured out* like water,
> and all my bones are out of joint;
> my heart is like wax,
> it is melted within my breast;
> my strength is dried up like a potsherd,
> and my tongue cleaves to my jaws;
> you lay me in the dust of death. (vv. 14–15; emphasis mine)

In continuing his description of his suffering to Yahweh, the Psalmist again describes events uncannily similar to Jesus' Crucifixion:

> Yes, dogs are round about me;
> a company of evildoers encircle me;
> they have pierced my hands and feet—
> I can count all my bones—
> they stare and gloat over me;
> they divide my garments among them,
> and for my clothing they cast lots. (vv. 16–18)

The Psalmist makes another earnest petition for God's help and consolation:

> But you, O LORD, be not far off!
> O my help, hasten to my aid!
> Deliver my soul from the sword,
> my life from the power of the dog!
> Save me from the mouth of the lion,
> my afflicted soul from the horns of the wild oxen! (vv. 19–21)

(2) Thanksgiving, in which the community is invited to share.

The Psalmist (and Jesus) then reaffirms his trust and confidence in the Lord, as if to say that he will *live beyond* his current persecution to bring the praise of the Lord's name to all who fear him:

> I will tell of your name to my brethren;
> in the midst of the congregation I will praise you:
> You who fear the LORD, praise him!
> All you sons of Jacob, glorify him,
> and stand in awe of him, all you sons of Israel! (vv. 22–23)

The Psalmist then gives his reason for his confidence in God, and his belief in his future:

> For he has not despised or abhorred
> the affliction of the afflicted;
> and he has not hidden his face from him,
> but has heard, when he cried to him.
> From you comes my praise in the great congregation;
> my vows I will pay before those who fear him. (vv. 24–25)

The Psalmist then moves into a prophetic, and even messianic, tone, speaking of signs of the new Jerusalem—messianic signs that Jesus says when quoting the prophet Isaiah are being fulfilled in Himself:[55]

> The afflicted shall eat and be satisfied;
> those who seek him shall praise the LORD!
> May your hearts live for ever! (v. 26)

(3) The worldwide redemption and worship of Yahweh.

The Psalmist (and Jesus) then confidently suggests *universality* of salvation arising out of Yahweh's mercy:

> *All* the ends of the earth
> shall remember and turn to the LORD;
> and *all* the families of the nations
> shall worship before him.
> For dominion belongs to the LORD,
> and he rules over the nations. (vv. 27–28; emphasis mine)

The Psalmist then suggests that Yahweh's salvation will extend to all those who are raised on high, and those who are in the grave (people of the past), as well as to all future generations:

> Yes, to him shall all the proud of the earth bow down;
> before him shall bow all who go down to the dust,
> and he who cannot keep himself alive.

---

[55] See Mt 11:5ff. and Lk 4:18ff., referring to Is 61:1ff.

Posterity shall serve him;
men shall tell of the Lord to the coming generation,
and proclaim his deliverance
to a people yet unborn,
that he has wrought it. (vv. 29–31)

This Psalm on the dying lips of Jesus is quite remarkable. In the midst of recounting events quite similar to His Crucifixion, the Psalm expresses His mind and heart as He cries out for help, as He is overwhelmingly confident in that help, and as He sees the ultimate result of that help in a salvation that will not only reach to the ends of the earth, but to all future generations on the earth, and even to those who have died in the past. Thus, the Psalm connects Jesus' torment with His *confidence* in the Father as He looks beyond His suffering, beyond Jerusalem, beyond the present age, and beyond earthly existence, to a redemption that will take hold in the life of God Himself.

Jesus' Eucharistic words are not only consonant with those of the Psalm—they give the Psalm's words ultimate meaning and reality; for they provide the vehicle through which Jesus' person and love will save *universally and eternally*.

Notice the parallels between the Fourth Suffering Servant Song (Isaiah 52:13–53:12; see above, Section I), the Eucharistic words of Jesus (see above, Section IV.A), and the dying words of Jesus (Psalm 22). Each one of them speaks of the persecution and death of a good and just person who does not deserve to be punished or killed. Each figure (the suffering servant, the Psalmist, and Jesus) believes that this undeserved persecution and death can be made into a self-offering (self-sacrifice) that acts as a perfect "sin offering" (the sacrifice of an animal for the remission of sins; see above, Section IV.A). The fact that the sin offering is no longer an unblemished animal, but an unblemished and innocent person, makes it a perfect offering—so much so that the Psalmist, Isaiah, and Jesus see it as initiating *universal* salvation. In His Eucharistic words Jesus uses Isaiah's Fourth Suffering Servant Song to describe His sacrificial action: "poured out his soul to death" for "he bore the sin of many" (Is 53:12).

We must pause for a moment to discuss the *universal* implications of Jesus' Eucharistic words—"poured out for *many*".

Recall from Section IV.A above Jeremias' justification for preferring the Mark-Matthew tradition ("poured out for many") to the Paul-Luke tradition ("poured out for you"). If he is correct, then Jesus very likely said "poured out for the many". In Jesus' Aramaic, this phrase probably means "poured out for *all*". Jeremias has done an exhaustive study on the Septuagint Greek translation of the Hebrew text of Isaiah 53:12 and has concluded as follows:

> While "many" in Greek (as in English) stands in opposition to "all", and therefore has the exclusive sense ("*many, but not all*"), Hebrew *rabbim* can have the inclusive sense ("*the whole, comprising many individuals*"). This inclusive use is connected with the fact that Hebrew and Aramaic possess no word for "all."[56]

When *rabbim* is accompanied by the definite article, it almost always means "all". Though Greek, unlike Aramaic and Hebrew, has a distinct word for "all", *panton*, many Greek translators did not use this word but chose instead to translate the Hebrew literally with its definite article—*to pollon* (*the* many). *To pollon* is a very unusual expression in Greek, and its use to translate Jesus' Eucharistic words very probably reflects the Greek translator's use of a Semitism—translating a Hebrew phrase into a very unusual Greek phrase. Hence, the use of *to pollon* in Mark and Matthew very probably referred to Jesus' use of *rabbim* with a definite article, meaning that Jesus said "poured out for *all*".

This is further corroborated by a phrase in 1 Timothy 2:6 that hearkens back to Isaiah 53:12 ("he bore the sin of many"), which Paul uses as a background for "who gave himself as a ransom for *all*", using the Greek word *panton* (all). Mark translates the same phrase as Paul: "to give his life as a ransom for many" (10:45). Jeremias does not see this as problematic; rather, he thinks that Mark is using the inclusive sense of "many", which Paul translates directly into "all" (*panton*):

> Of especial importance for our passage is Mark 10.45 par., *lutron anti pollon* "a ransom for many". That *polloi* has here the inclusive meaning "all" is shown by the reference in Mark 10.45 to Isa. 53.10–12, as

---

[56] Jeremias, *Eucharistic Words of Jesus*, p. 179.

well as by the parallel in I Tim. 2.6: *antilutron huper panton*, "a ransom for all". Just as Mark 10.45, so also our passage Mark 14.24 [Jesus' Eucharistic words] is to be interpreted in the inclusive sense. *Pollon* is therefore a Semitism.[57]

The evidence appears to be overwhelming. When Jesus uttered the Aramaic expression hearkening back to Isaiah 53:12, He said it in an inclusive way—meaning "poured out for *all*". Jesus intended that His sacrificial death be for *everyone* for all time—which is precisely what He envisioned when reciting the last part of Psalm 22 as His dying words:

> *All the ends of the earth*
> shall remember and turn to the LORD;
> and *all the families of the nations*
> shall worship before him.
> For dominion belongs to the LORD,
> and he rules over the nations.
> Yes, to him shall all the proud of the earth bow down;
> before him shall bow all who go down to the dust,
> and he who cannot keep himself alive.
> Posterity shall serve him;
> men shall tell of the LORD to the coming generation,
> and proclaim his deliverance
> to a people *yet unborn*,
> that he has wrought it. (vv. 27–31; emphasis mine)

Jesus also utters his Eucharistic words in a *prophetic* way at the Last Supper. In so doing, His words reach out to the historical events of His persecution and death, which will fulfill them. We can now understand the extent to which Jesus saw His love as redemptive. It would lead to *universal* redemption and would allow generations of people to reenter the mystery of His "whole self" poured out in unconditional love. Johannes Betz summarizes the significance of Jesus' words and actions as follows:

Taking on alien guilt [the guilt of other people] meant taking on also the necessity of death. As his life went on, Jesus thought more frequently of his death and spoke more frequently of it to his disciples....

57 Ibid., pp. 181–82.

It was for Jesus not something that merely happened to him, but a conscious and willed deed to which he assented as a necessity in the history of salvation, and on which he freely decided (Lk 12:50). His total readiness for the death which was the mission of the Servant of the Lord is also expressed in the logion of the ransom (Mk 10:45), and the prophecies of the passion (Mk 8:31; 9:31; 10:32ff).... His death is total dedication and the deepest fulfillment of his being.... Unlike the *cultic* sacrifices, there is no separate *gift* which stands for the offerer and symbolizes his dedication to God. Here the offerer himself functions as *gift* in his own person and accomplishes the sacrificial dedication by the real shedding of his blood. Jesus must have been sure that God would accept this sacrifice, his body, and hence that God would fill it with new life. Thus the death of Jesus brings with it the resurrection as an inner consequence, as an essential part of it, regardless of the difference in time between the two events.[58]

C. A Reflection on Jesus' Passion and Death

The Passion narratives open upon a virtually limitless depth of love, which can best be appreciated through contemplation. Jesus views His Passion as the culmination of His mission, the concretization of His unconditional love in history, and His gift of unconditional love to the world for all eternity. The reader's time will be well spent on considering His loving intention, attitude, and feeling in His gift of self in the events of the Passion.[59]

One successful method of entering into contemplation is recommended by Saint Ignatius of Loyola in his *Spiritual Exercises*.[60] It entails entering into the scene, considering the personalities and dispositions of people in the scene, and focusing on the heart of Jesus manifest through the people and events in it.

In light of the above, one may want to use the following structure to contemplate the Passion. After reading a particular passage at least twice, first consider various physical aspects of the scene, then

---

[58] Betz, "Eucharist", p. 258; emphasis mine.

[59] I have written about contemplation in a broader context in Robert J. Spitzer, *Five Pillars of the Spiritual Life: A Practical Guide to Prayer for Active People* (San Francisco: Ignatius Press, 2008); see Chapters 6–8.

[60] Ignatius of Loyola, *The Spiritual Exercises of St. Ignatius*, trans. Louis J. Puhl, S.J. (Chicago: Loyola University Press, 1951).

- the persons in the scene along with Jesus;
- Jesus' attitude toward the people in the scene (recalling that Jesus' attitudes are reflected in the Beatitudes—humble-hearted, gentle-hearted, merciful, peacemaking, etc.);
- Jesus' relationship to the Father (applying Psalm 22, the Suffering Servant Song in Isaiah 52:13–53:12, and Jesus' Prayer in the Garden);
- Jesus' universal salvific intent (applying the symbol of the Paschal lamb and the words "this is my body", "the blood of the covenant", "poured out for all" and "do this in remembrance of me"); and
- Jesus' love for the people in the scene (including His persecutors), His love of the Father, and His love of mankind.

You might then look at Jesus' acceptance of anguish for the sake of love. In light of this, you might consider Jesus' love, as well as His hopes and aspirations, for you and others. Accept that love, accept His wanting to be your Paschal lamb, sin offering, and blood of the covenant (to guarantee eternal life with Him and the Father).

V. Conclusion

In the previous chapter, we asked six questions regarding the primacy of love and the possibility of God coming to us in a *personal* and perfectly present way. We began by asking whether love is the most positive, creative, and meaningful capacity within us, and if so, whether the Creator could be devoid of love, or whether love would be a natural part of His creativity. We then went on to ask whether our desire was for only "some love" or "perfect and unconditional love", and if the latter, whether the Creator would have to have created this desire within us. Using the argument (from Volume II, Chapter 4, Section I.B) that the unique unrestricted act of thinking is the only reality capable of being perfectly loving, we concluded that the unique, unrestricted Creator must be the source of our awareness of and desire for unconditional love. We then asked whether an unconditionally loving Creator would *want* to be personally and perfectly present to us—coming to us as we are—so that He could be in perfect empathy with us, allowing us to appreciate His personal love face-to-face and peer-to-peer. Would an unconditionally loving God want to be incarnate ("God with us")? In light of the definition of "*agapē*" (given in Chapter 1) we concluded that an unconditionally loving God would want to be "God with us". This left us with one final question—whether *Jesus* is the perfect presence of the unconditionally loving God with us.

In the previous two chapters, we have seen many manifestations of Jesus' love and the revelation of His Father's love—in His revelation of the divine name ("Abba"—"affectionate, understanding Father"), His association of this affectionate Father with the prodigal son's father, His elevation of love to the highest commandment, and His definition of love as *agapē* (humble-heartedness, gentle-heartedness, compassion—for the sake of the other alone).

We then examined Jesus' view of Himself ("for I am gentle and lowly [humble] in heart" [Mt 11:29]) and looked at His view of suffering in light of this self-revelation. We saw how suffering can be an invaluable means for deepening our own love, serving others with compassion, making ourselves a self-offering, and spreading the gospel—all of which are oriented toward helping us and others into His Kingdom of unconditional love. We saw Jesus' love of the poor, which caused Him to identify completely with them ("[As] you did it to one of the least of these my brethren, you did it to me" [Mt 25:40]). We saw His compassion for the sick and possessed, and how He used His healing power not only to restore people physically, but also spiritually. Above all we saw His love of sinners—even the worst of them: prostitutes, tax collectors, criminals, and His persecutors. Finally, we saw His plan to make Himself a sin offering and Pascal lamb by accepting Crucifixion and death within the context of His Last Supper. We saw His desire to save all of us, and to be intimately and transformatively present to all who receive His body and blood poured out for us in an unconditional act of love.

Is Jesus *the One*? Is Jesus the perfect presence of the unconditionally loving God with us? From the vantage point of love's logic, He appears to be at least a *very* strong candidate. It is difficult to deny that Jesus is more than a candidate. After all, He gave us the criteria by which to judge His claims. If He had not defined *agapē*, would we have even known the depth of compassion, humble-heartedness, and gentle-heartedness with which to judge not only His love, but the love of everyone? If He had not given us the Parables of the Good Samaritan and the Prodigal Son as well as the Beatitudes, the highest commandment, and His example of loving enemies, would we have known enough to make a judgment about the perfection of His love? Inasmuch as Jesus established the criteria of love at its highest level, and exceeded it in His life and Person, we have good grounds for believing that He exemplified unconditional love.

Yet, the question lingers: Is He really divine? Is there some other sign besides His unconditional love that shows He is really "God with us"? It seems so, and it is to be found in His Resurrection (Chapter 4) in glory, the gift of His Holy Spirit (Chapter 5), His miracles (Chapter 5), and His proclamation of His divine Sonship (Chapter 6). When we combine the signs of His divinity, with the signs of His unconditional love, a conclusion begins to emerge: that He could really be Emmanuel—"God with us".

Yet, such a conclusion cannot be achieved through the "mind's reasons" alone. All the evidence of Jesus' unconditional love and divine status will not *prove* that Jesus is the Son of God. If we do not appreciate the truth of His teaching about love—even the hard truth about self-sacrifice, compassion, suffering, humility, and freedom from egocentricity—we will never be convinced by the evidence. If we do not recognize the genuineness and potential of *agapē* as Jesus preached and lived it, and if we are not in some sense attracted to His revelation of love, we will never be convinced—even if Jesus were to come to us as He did to Saint Paul. We would find some reason to believe that He is *not* Emmanuel.

Jesus anticipated this in the story about the rich man and Lazarus; the rich man asks Abraham to let Lazarus appear to his brothers so that they will know that there is a life after death. Abraham responds that they have Moses and the prophets, but the rich man insists that they would *really* believe if someone were to come back from the dead, to which Abraham responds, "If they do not hear Moses and the prophets, neither will they be convinced if someone should rise from the dead" (Lk 16:31).

Unless we are drawn to the truth of love (*agapē*) within our hearts, and see some *need* for this in our lives, we will not see a *need* to have this love brought to completion by Jesus or God. As a consequence, we will not be able to understand the reason for Jesus' revelation or for His Incarnation and self-sacrifice, and we will see no need for Him in our lives. We will view the whole of Christian revelation as an interesting, but unlikely, story. Furthermore, if we disdain and reject love as weak and worthless, we will likewise reject Jesus, who associated Himself so closely with it.

We began this volume with a definition of love; we also began our six questions concerning Emmanuel with the question about the significance of love in our personal lives. This was done to alert readers to the necessity of using "the heart's reasons" to understand the significance and need for Jesus. If we believe in our hearts that love (*agapē*) is significant, and that we need this love in our lives and we are attracted to Jesus' definition of love, then the rest of this volume will be meaningful. If readers see no significance or need for this love in their lives, they will not want to proceed any further.

If at this juncture readers are still positively engaged and want to proceed further, I would ask, as you examine the evidence for the Resurrection, the Holy Spirit, Jesus' miracles, and self-revelation, that you let the heart's reasons and the mind's reasons have equal sway—then make your judgment on the basis of both.

Chapter Four

Resurrection and History

Introduction

We concluded the previous chapter by showing the need for a move-ment of the heart—to see the significance of love (*agapē*), our need for this love, our need for fulfillment through this love, and our need for Jesus and God to help us. We also saw that Jesus exceeded the highest standard of *agapē* (which He defined) and showed Him-self to be unconditionally loving—precisely as He preached the Father to be. If we are to affirm that He is truly Emmanuel (the presence of the unconditionally loving *God* with us), then we will need some sign of His divine authority and power, so that we can know through both our hearts and minds whether He is more than an unconditionally loving *man* and *is* really the unconditionally lov-ing *God* with us.

The doctrine of the resurrection[1] is central to Christianity, so much so that Saint Paul states:

> [I]f there is no resurrection of the dead, then Christ has not been raised; if Christ has not been raised, then our preaching is in vain and your faith is in vain. We are even found to be misrepresenting God, because we testified of God that he raised Christ, whom he did not raise if it is true that the dead are not raised.... Then those also who have fallen asleep in Christ have perished. If for this life only we have hoped in Christ, we are of all men most to be pitied. (1 Cor 15:13–15, 18–19)

---

[1] There are at least forty-five explicit references to eternal life in the New Testament, and literally hundreds of other implications of it, as well as forty-three explicit references to the resurrection, forty-five explicit references to "raised from the dead", and many other implicit references to the risen life.

It is truly extraordinary that Paul made the claim that if there is no resurrection from the dead, then the faith of believers is useless and that all who have died in Christ have died in their sins. Paul knows that if he is lying, he and the other disciples have jeopardized the salvation of the whole Christian community, and furthermore he emerges as a false witness (a perjurer) before God and is answerable to Him. The consequences of lying to (or even deceiving) believers about the resurrection cannot be overstated, because the resurrection is the foundation of Jesus' claim to be the exclusive Son of God, and the unconditional love of God with us.

Is there any way of verifying the claims made by the Christian Church about Jesus' Resurrection in glory? As a matter of fact, there is: through the use of historical criteria.[2] We will use some of these criteria to probe the historicity of Jesus' Resurrection in four areas:

1. The common elements in the Gospel narratives about Jesus' risen appearance to the apostles (Section II)
2. The historical evidence of the Resurrection in the writings of Saint Paul (Section III)
3. N. T. Wright's historical analysis of the Resurrection (Section IV)
4. The historical status of the empty tomb (Section V)

There are many other ways of probing the historicity of the Resurrection, but these four will be sufficient to give reasonable validation to the Christian claim that Jesus rose in a spiritual body (*pneumatikon soma*) and promised to bestow this Resurrection eternally on those who are willing to accept and abide by that love. Before investigating the above four historical sources, we will examine Gary Habermas' survey of contemporary scholarship on the Resurrection.

---

[2] I will not discuss all of these criteria in this book, but only the ones that are most relevant to the Resurrection appearances (and the New Testament narratives that describe them). Readers interested in a fuller explanation may want to consider the following outstanding studies: Joachim Jeremias, "The Problem of the Historical Jesus", in *In Search of the Historical Jesus*, edited by Harvey K. McArthur (London: Charles Scribner's Sons, 1969), pp. 125–30; René Latourelle, *Finding Jesus through the Gospels: History and Hermeneutics* (New York: Alba House, 1979); Harvey K. McArthur, ed., *In Search of the Historical Jesus* (London: Charles Scribner's Sons, 1969); John P. Meier, "The Present State of the 'Third Quest' for the Historical Jesus: Loss and Gain", *Biblica* 80 (1999): 459–87; N. T. Wright, *The Contemporary Quest for Jesus* (Minneapolis: Fortress Press, 2002).

I. Gary Habermas' Study of Recent Scholarship on the Resurrection

Gary R. Habermas has completed an extensive survey of contemporary exegetes and has made several interesting discoveries. He notes:

> The latest research on Jesus' resurrection appearances reveals several extraordinary developments. As firmly as ever, *most* contemporary scholars agree that, after Jesus' death, his early followers had *experiences* that they at least believed were appearances of their risen Lord. Further, this conviction was the chief motivation behind the early proclamation of the Christian gospel. These basics are rarely questioned, even by more radical scholars. They are among the most widely established details from the entire New Testament.[3]

Habermas goes on to explain that

> more skeptical scholars often still acknowledge the grounds for the appearances as well. Helmut Koester [notes]: "We are on much firmer ground with respect to the appearances of the risen Jesus and their effect.... That Jesus also appeared to others (Peter, Mary Magdalene, James) cannot very well be questioned."[4]

In view of this general agreement about the historicity of the Resurrection appearances, where do opinions diverge? Habermas again notes that "the *crux* of the issue, then, is not *whether* there were real experiences, but how *we explain the nature* of these early experiences."[5]

Habermas then inquires into what these exegetes consider to be the cause of the apostolic Church's early and widespread belief that Jesus rose from the dead. Was it a natural cause or a supernatural cause? The vast majority of exegetes believe that the cause was *supernatural*. Nevertheless, Habermas examines the minority

---

[3] Gary R. Habermas, "Mapping the Recent Trend toward the Bodily Resurrection Appearances of Jesus in Light of Other Prominent Critical Positions", in *The Resurrection of Jesus: John Dominic Crossan and N. T. Wright in Dialogue*, ed. Robert B. Stewart (Minneapolis: Fortress Press, 2006), p. 79; emphasis mine.

[4] Ibid., p. 80.

[5] Ibid.; emphasis mine

opinion—namely, natural causation. His investigation ranges from the subjective vision theory of Gerd Lüdemann (who grounds his hypothesis in "stimulus", "religious intoxication", and "enthusiasm"[6]), to the illumination theory of Willi Marxsen (who asserts that Peter had an internal experience that led him to convince the other apostles about Jesus' Resurrection).[7] These theories do not stand up well to historical and exegetical scrutiny (see below, Section III.B),[8] and so Habermas concludes, "In the twentieth century, critical scholarship has largely rejected wholesale the naturalistic approaches to the resurrection."[9]

He then examines *supernatural* causes for the early witnesses' experience of the risen Jesus. "Supernatural causation" means that something happened to *Jesus* rather than to His followers. What happened to Jesus must be supernatural because it effects a transition from death to new life. Variations among supernatural explanations are centered on the ways in which the risen Jesus appeared—that is, *the ways* in which His risen life was mediated in the physical world (in history) so that it could be collectively experienced by His followers. There are two major hypotheses in this regard: (1) a luminous appearance and (2) a transformed corporeal appearance.

The vast majority of scholars hold to the second explanation—namely, that Jesus rose in a transformed corporeal state (as a spiritual body)—and some scholars hold that this appearance also had luminescent features.

Given the large number of scholars interviewed by Habermas (from every point on the theological and exegetical spectrum) and given the deep scrutiny with which these scholars examined the historicity of the Resurrection, their overwhelming consensus lends considerable probative force to the contention that Jesus appeared

---

[6] Gerd Lüdemann, *The Resurrection of Jesus: History, Experience, Theology*, trans. John Bowden (Minneapolis: Fortress Press, 1994), pp. 106–7, 174–75, and 180.

[7] Willi Marxsen, *The Resurrection of Jesus of Nazareth*, trans. Margaret Kohl (Philadelphia: Fortress Press, 1970), pp. 88–97.

[8] See Habermas, "Mapping Recent Trend", pp. 84–86. Stephen T. Davis opines: "All of the alternative hypotheses with which I am familiar are historically weak; some are so weak that they collapse of their own weight once spelled out." Stephen T. Davis, "Is Belief in the Resurrection Rational?" *Philo* 2 (1999): 57–58.

[9] Habermas, "Mapping Recent Trend", p. 86.

to His apostles (and hundreds of other followers) in a supernaturally transformed state, manifesting continuity with His former embodiment as well as a spiritual (transphysical) transformation.

There are three major reasons why scholars agree so overwhelmingly about Jesus' transformed corporeality in His risen appearance:

1. It is the overwhelming consensus of the Gospel writers in describing Jesus' appearance to His apostles after the Resurrection (see Section II).
2. This Gospel view is in agreement with Saint Paul's description of the "spiritual body" in 1 Corinthians 15 (see Section III).
3. The Christian view of "spiritual body" explains many other differences between apostolic Christianity and Second Temple Judaism (see Section IV).[10]

I will briefly address each in turn.

II. The Gospel Accounts of Jesus' Risen Appearances to the Apostles

The Gospel accounts show substantial agreement about Jesus' transformed embodiment in His risen appearances. Though it is described in different ways, several characteristics are quite similar. Let us begin with Matthew's narrative of Jesus' risen appearance.

> [T]he eleven disciples went to Galilee, to the mountain to which Jesus had directed them. And when they saw him they worshiped him; but some doubted. And Jesus came and said to them, "All authority in heaven and on earth has been given to me." (Mt 28:16–18)

Matthew accentuates the transformation of Jesus' appearance, noting that the apostles bow down and worship Him. The term *proskynéō* is used to communicate "homage shown to men and beings

---

[10]Second Temple Judaism refers to the religion of Judaism during the Second Temple period, between the construction of the second Jewish temple in Jerusalem in 515 B.C., and its destruction by the Romans in A.D. 70.

of superior rank—to the Jewish high priests, to God, to Christ, to heavenly beings, to demons".[11] When the devil asks, "All these I will give you, if you will fall down and worship me," Jesus replies, "You shall worship the Lord your God and him only shall you serve" (Mt 4:9–10). It seems that Jesus has been transformed in a divine and spiritual way, so much so that it evokes worship (reserved for God alone) from the disciples. This interpretation is confirmed by Jesus' subsequent words: "All authority in heaven and on earth has been given to me [which belongs to God alone]" (Mt 28:18).

There is yet another confirmation of Jesus' divine and spiritual transformation—namely, that many of the disciples have difficulty recognizing Him ("some doubted" [Mt 28:17]). What did they doubt? They were not doubting that a divine appearance (a theophany) was occurring—they were all bowing down and worshipping It. Thus, they must have been doubting that *Jesus* was part of the theophany. They thought they were seeing God, but they were uncertain about *Jesus*. When this divine-spiritual Being communicates with and *missions* them, they apparently become aware of His identity— it is Jesus who is transformed into a spiritual-divine Being to which "[a]ll authority in heaven and on earth" has been given.

Luke communicates the same spiritually transformed appearance of Jesus in the narrative of Jesus' appearance to the Eleven (Lk 24:33ff.). He differs from Matthew in attempting to show continuity between Jesus' risen appearance and His former embodiment:

> As they were saying this, Jesus himself stood among them, and said to them, "Peace to you." But they were startled and frightened, and supposed that they saw a spirit. And he said to them, "Why are you troubled, and why do questionings rise in your hearts? See my hands and my feet, that it is I myself; handle me, and see; for a spirit has not flesh and bones as you see that I have." (Lk 24:36–39)

Luke implies here that Jesus is transformed in appearance, looking like a spirit (the word "spirit" is mentioned twice in three sentences). As in Matthew, Luke mentions the disciples' "doubts". They are

---

[11] BibleStudyTools, "proskuneo", www.biblestudytools.com/lexicons/greek/kjv/proskuneo .html.

certainly not doubting that a spirit is appearing (because they are "startled and frightened"), so presumably they are doubting the presence of Jesus in this *spiritual* appearance. Notice that Jesus resolves those doubts by showing them the wounds of His Crucifixion, and inviting them to touch Him—calling attention to His body.

Luke is more concerned than Matthew to show continuity with Jesus' former embodiment, amid His spiritually transformed appearance. Perhaps there was confusion in the Gentile churches about Jesus being *only* a spirit (having no continuity with His former embodiment). However, Luke's repeated insistence on Jesus' embodiment shows that Jesus revealed not only His spiritual but also his embodied self. Given the parallel with John 20, Jesus probably showed the disciples His wounds in addition to His embodiment.

John's Gospel communicates the same point in a slightly different way. Instead of asserting that Jesus has appeared in a divinelike way (as Matthew does) or in a spiritually transformed way (as Luke does), he says that Jesus appears through locked doors (Jn 20:19; 20:26), which would not be possible for a resuscitated corpse:

> On the evening of that day, the first day of the week, the doors being shut where the disciples were, for fear of the Jews, Jesus came and stood among them and said to them, "Peace be with you." (Jn 20:19)

He then shows them the wounds of the Crucifixion on His hands and side (Jn 20:20), as if He were intentionally identifying Himself. John focuses all of the doubts in the story on Thomas, and so the doubts of the disciples about who Jesus is in the appearance are somewhat obscured. However, in the appendix (John 21, which was added later), John makes very clear that the apostles have doubts about Jesus in the appearance when He says, "[N]one of the disciples dared ask him, 'Who are you?' They knew it was the Lord" (Jn 21:12).

The term "the Lord" (*ho Kurios*) is significant here, showing that the evangelist is pointing to Jesus' *divine* appearance (very much like Matthew's Gospel). *Kurios* (Lord) in Greek can mean anything from "sir" to "master", but *ho Kurios* (*the* Lord—with the definite article) is the Septuagint Greek translation of the Hebrew divine name (Yahweh). Prior to Jesus' Resurrection, John never uses *ho Kurios* of Jesus, but after the Resurrection this is the *only* term used to refer to Jesus in the minds and on the lips of the apostles.[12] It seems that they saw a divinely transformed Jesus, and that Jesus makes His embodiment known to them through the wounds of His Crucifixion.

Now let us return to the curious passage where it is said, no one dared to ask Him, "Who are you?" for they "knew it was the Lord" (Jn 21:12). If the apostles knew that it was the Lord (the Divine One) appearing to them, then why are they having doubts? Once again we see the apostles having difficulty identifying *Jesus* amid His transformed divine appearance. Jesus apparently makes His embodiment known to them through His communication with and missioning of them.

As can be seen, all three Gospel writers who describe Jesus' risen appearance to the apostles (Matthew, Luke, and John) indicate that He has been divinely and spiritually transformed and that this transformation outshines His former corporeality—so much so that the apostles at first have doubts about whether Jesus is in this divine-spiritual appearance. Jesus overcomes these doubts by revealing His identity (and continuity with His former embodiment) through the marks of His Crucifixion (Lk 24:40; Jn 20:27) and through His communication with and missioning of them (Mt 28:16–20; Jn 21).

Paul's account of how the dead will be raised in 1 Corinthians 15 shows remarkable similarities to all three Gospel accounts (Matthew, Luke, and John) with respect to Jesus' spiritually transformed body. He asserts that we will be raised in a way similar to Jesus' Resurrection— namely, as spiritual bodies (*pneumatikon soma*). His explanation of this adds theological interpretation to the Gospel accounts.

The pertinent passage from 1 Corinthians 15 can be broken down into three parts (all emphasis mine):

  1. "But some one will ask, 'How are the dead raised? With what kind of body do they come?' You foolish man! What you sow

---

[12] In the closed room, when Jesus appears, the apostles recognize "the Lord" (Jn 20:20). When Jesus appears to Thomas a week later, he says, "My Lord and my God!" ("Ho Kurios mou, Ho Theos mou" [Jn 20:28]). At the Sea of Tiberius, when John recognizes the appearance to be Jesus, He turns to Peter and says, "It is the Lord [*ho Kurios*]!" (Jn 21:7). Onshore, the apostles recognize that it is "the Lord" who is appearing, but they want to ask Him, "Who are you?" indicating that they are having trouble recognizing *Jesus* in the appearance (Jn 21:12). Notice that only the narrator of the story (not the apostles) refers to "Jesus" in both John 20 and 21, but the apostles only see "*the Lord*" (the Divine One).

does not come to life unless it dies. And what you sow is *not* the body which is to be, but a bare kernel [seed], perhaps of wheat or of some other grain" (vv. 35–37).

2. "So is it with the resurrection of the dead. What is sown is perishable, what is raised *imperishable*. It is sown in dishonor, it is raised in *glory*. It is sown in weakness, it is raised in *power*. It is sown a physical body, it is raised a *spiritual body*. If there is a physical body, there is also a *spiritual body*" (vv. 42–44).

3. "The first man was from the *earth*, a man of dust; the second man is from *heaven*. As was the man of dust, so are those who are of the dust; and as is the man of heaven, so are those who are of heaven. Just as we have borne the image of the man of dust, we *shall also* bear the image of the man of heaven" (vv. 47–49).

Perhaps it is best to begin with the last line of part number 3 above ("Just as we have borne the image of the man of dust, we shall also bear the image of the man of heaven"). When Paul says that we are going to be in "the image of the man of heaven" (the risen Jesus), he is saying that all the descriptions he has given of this risen state in 1 Corinthians 15 are similar to the way that Jesus appeared to His disciples after the Resurrection. Thus, if we want to know how Jesus appeared to the apostles, all we have to do is look at how Paul describes our future risen state (which will be like that of Jesus).

So, how might we infer that Jesus appeared from Paul's description of our risen state? In part number 1 above, Paul says that there will only be a seed of our former natural bodies, and that the rest will be transformed. There will be continuity with our earthly bodies, but also a marked transformation of those bodies. From this we might infer that Jesus maintained continuity with His former embodiment but that it was spiritually transformed, giving rise to something new, glorious, and imperishable. This resembles the Gospel accounts of Jesus' risen appearance to His disciples (see above in this section).

How was Jesus transformed? In part number 2 above, Paul says that this seed was transformed with imperishability, glory, power, and spirit. What would this look like? Paul gives only one explicit description—that it will be a "spiritual body". If we want to know how the imperishability, power, and glory of this "spiritual body" appeared, we will have to turn to the Gospel writers, who describe

His power and glory as divine, so much so that the apostles bow down and worship Him (Mt 28:17) and were convinced that it was God appearing (see the references to "the Lord" in John 20 and 21). Furthermore, this powerful, glorious, spiritual, divinelike appearance engenders fear and awe ("[T]hey were startled and frightened, and supposed that they saw a spirit. And he said to them, 'Why are you troubled?'" [Lk 24:37–38]).

Paul summarizes this transformed corporeality by twice calling it "a spiritual body" (a *pneumatikon soma*), which is a completely new concept in both the Jewish and the Greco-Roman worldviews.[13] What provoked the Christian Church to develop a completely unique view of the resurrection as "spiritual body"? Why did the early Church radically depart from the doctrine of Second Temple Judaism in this regard (when they were careful not to do so in other doctrinal matters)?[14] Such a large-scale, uniform transformation of the doctrines of Second Temple Judaism by the Christian Church is exceedingly difficult to explain if Jesus' embodiment did not appear as spiritually transformed as the early witnesses maintain (see below, Sections IV.A and IV.B). This points to the plausibility that Jesus appeared in a divinelike glory, power, and spirit in which He showed continuity with His former embodiment.

III. Paul's Testimony to the Resurrection of Jesus

Saint Paul's testimony about the Resurrection of Jesus in 1 Corinthians 15 gives scholars of all subsequent generations the opportunity to test the historicity of his and the other witnesses' claims. While writing within living memory of the Resurrection, he challenges his Corinthian audience to check out the facts (Section III.A). He then

---

[13] See Wright's exhaustive analysis of this in N. T. Wright, *The Resurrection of the Son of God* (Minneapolis: Fortress Press, 2003), pp. 32–128.

[14] The early Christian Church did not want to separate from the synagogue or mutate the established doctrine of Second Temple Judaism. They did so only when there were strong reasons given by Jesus Himself. As will be seen below (in Section IV.B), Wright shows that virtually every mutation of Second Temple Judaism's doctrine of the resurrection (as well as the end time and the messiah) is explained by the description of Jesus' risen appearance given in both the Gospels and Saint Paul. This is viewed by many exegetes as an extrinsic confirmation of the historical truth of His appearance as a transformed or spiritual body.

provides an argument to show the value of his and the other witnesses' testimony to the Resurrection through an insightful dilemma (Section III.B).

A. Witnesses to the Resurrection

The most famous *kerygma* (very early proclamation about Jesus by the apostolic Church) concerned with the Resurrection is found in 1 Corinthians 15:3–8. Here, Paul says he is repeating a tradition that he himself received (showing that it predates the writing of 1 Corinthians). It has an obvious formulaic character, relates the Resurrection to the death and burial, and gives a list of witnesses to these appearances. This primitive formula contains some additions by Paul (indicated below by my italics). The *kerygma* may be translated as follows:

> *For I delivered to you as of first importance what I also received,*
> that Christ died for our sins in accordance with the Scriptures,
> that he was buried,
> that he was raised on the third day in accordance with the Scriptures,
> and that he appeared to Cephas,
> then to the Twelve.
> Then he appeared to more than five hundred brethren at one time
> *most of whom are still alive, though some have fallen asleep.*
> Then he appeared to James,
> then to all the apostles.
> *Last of all, as to one untimely born, he appeared also to me.* (1 Cor 15:3–8)

Two parts of the *kerygma* are obviously Pauline additions (in italics). First, the passage beginning with "Last of all ... he appeared also to me" is Pauline in origin, for Paul does not need to refer to a *tradition* about himself. The passage "most of whom are still alive, though some have fallen asleep" is also Pauline in origin. This passage merits special attention, not only because it is a Pauline addition, but also because it has value in ascertaining the historicity of the events portrayed in the *kerygma*. By phrasing the passage in this way, Paul is virtually inviting his Corinthian audience to check out the facts with the living witnesses. The fact that Paul is writing within living memory of these extraordinary events and seems to be acquainted with many of the witnesses he lists, as well as that he is aware that these witnesses are still alive, and challenges the Corinthians to investigate them, gives evidential weight to the claims in the passage.[15]

There are varied interpretations of Paul's list of witnesses. Some exegetes believe that the list could be chronological, as Paul seems to suggest with his use of "first", "then", and "last". Others have suggested that the first part of the list establishes Church governance[16] (and may also be chronological), while the second part of the list establishes the missionary Church.[17] It is not inconceivable that both interpretations could be true, such that Jesus could have established Church governance and a missionary Church through the precise chronology elucidated by the *kerygma*.

So who were these witnesses? The first appearance to Peter and His second to the Twelve are probably linked and occurred in Galilee. Reginald H. Fuller notes in this regard:

> The appearances to Cephas and to the Twelve form a closely linked group. A single *ōphthē* ("he appeared") functions for both appearances, and the particle *eita* ("then"), used in verses 5–7 to join two items within a single group, connects these two appearances.... Even if we assume that the disciples remained hidden in Jerusalem until after the Sabbath, as Mark seems to suppose, yet according to the earliest available tradition (Mark) it was in Galilee that the first appearances took place.... We may conjecture that upon arriving back in Galilee, Peter proceeded to assemble the disciples for the second appearance. Luke contains a hint that this was the procedure: "When you [singular] have turned again, strengthen your brethren" (Luke 22:32).[18]

The third appearance (to the five hundred) probably took place after the Twelve returned to Jerusalem and gathered the community together. Fuller believes that this Jerusalem appearance may have

---

[15] See Section III.B below and also Joachim Jeremias, *New Testament Theology* (New York: Charles Scribner's Sons, 1971), 1:307–8.

[16] Reginald H. Fuller indicates "that the appearances to Peter and to the Twelve share a common function. In these appearances the Risen One initiates the foundation of the eschatological community: they are church-founding appearances." Reginald H. Fuller, *The Formation of the Resurrection Narratives* (New York: Macmillan, 1971), p. 35.

[17] "[The first two appearances] must be distinguished from the later appearances, whose function is the call and sending of apostles to fulfill a mission." Ibid.

[18] Ibid., pp. 34–35.

been the point at which the risen Jesus bestowed the Holy Spirit upon the large crowd gathered there.[19] Joachim Jeremias adds to this contention by noting:

> Paul's remark in I Cor. 15.6 that of the five hundred "most are still alive, but some have fallen asleep," which is meant to underline the reliability of the account, also contains an indirect reference to the place of the appearance. That it is possible to ascertain which of the eye-witnesses to this appearance are still alive a quarter of a century later makes one wonder whether at least the majority of the five hundred lived in one and the same place, and that would apply to Jerusalem. Since the days of the Tübingen school, therefore, the hypothesis that the appearance to the five hundred and Pentecost are two different traditions of one and the same event has found many supporters. A further point in favour of this combination is that in John 20.22 we find Christophany and the receiving of the spirit linked together.[20]

Some exegetes stress caution with this thesis, because the appearance to the five hundred is clearly a Christophany, while the gift of the Holy Spirit in Acts is a charismatic activity, including speaking in tongues (Acts 2:3–4). But there is no evidence from Scripture to preclude both of these from being combined (i.e., the risen Christ giving the Holy Spirit to the disciples at Jerusalem). Even if one separates the gift of the Holy Spirit from the appearance to the five hundred, the remainder of Fuller's thesis could still be true—namely, that "the +500 are the first-fruits of the church-founding function of Peter and the Twelve after their return from Galilee to Jerusalem."[21]

The fourth appearance to James would seem to be (like Paul's) a post-Pentecost event. Fuller notes that this "James" would almost certainly have to be James the brother (the relative/follower)[22] of Jesus, for James the Less is too insignificant, and James the Greater is

---

[19] Ibid., p. 36.

[20] Jeremias, *New Testament Theology*, pp. 307–8.

[21] Fuller, *Formation of the Resurrection Narratives*, p. 36.

[22] "In a wider use [brother] signifies a person of common ancestry and relationship; in particular, a member of the same clan or tribe (e.g., Nm 16:10). It is extended to members of the same race or nation (e.g., Dt 15:12) or of a kindred nation (e.g., Dt 23:7). In the NT Christians are called brothers about 160 times, and Jesus Himself said that one who does the will of the Father is His own brother (Mt 12:50; Mk 3:35; Lk 8:21)." John L. McKenzie, *Dictionary of the Bible* (New York: Macmillan, 1965), p. 108.

martyred very early on. The appearance to this James would explain why he experienced such a rapid rise in the post-Pentecost Church when he does not appear to be even a significant disciple of Jesus during the ministry. Fuller goes so far as to say:

> It might be said that if there were no record of an appearance to James the Lord's brother in the New Testament we should have to invent one in order to account for his post-resurrection conversion and rapid advance.[23]

There is ample evidence in the Acts of the Apostles to show that James serves a double role; he is at once the head of the Jerusalem Church and also appears to be head of all missionary activities stemming from Jerusalem.[24] If this is the case, then the post-Pentecost appearance to James both establishes Church governance and initiates the mission function of the Church.

The fifth appearance to "all the apostles" (1 Cor 15:7) refers to "apostles" in another sense than "the Twelve" (1 Cor 15:5). Paul commonly uses the term *apostolos* in a way similar to its common usage ("sent forth" or "those sent forth")[25]—that is, "missionaries". This meaning would certainly correspond to the theory that the second set of appearances (James, "all the apostles", and Paul) in the 1 Corinthians 15 *kerygma* are mission-initiating.

If "all the apostles" is meant in this missionary sense, then it refers to all the primary missionaries mentioned in the Acts of the Apostles. This would include both Aramaic-speaking Jewish Christians and Hellenistic Jewish Christians in the early Church (i.e., prior to the conversion of Paul).[26] Fuller conjectures further:

> Were these perhaps the missionaries referred to in Acts 11:19, who embarked upon a mission to Hellenistic Jews in Phoenicia, Cyprus and Antioch? Were the seven of Acts 6 originally part of the group consisting of "all the apostles?"[27]

[23] Fuller, *Formation of the Resurrection Narratives*, p. 37.

[24] Ibid., p. 38.

[25] McKenzie notes: "A similar use transferred to a religious sense seems to lie behind 2 Co 8:23, where the apostles mentioned are not apostles in the technical sense, but missionaries or messengers sent by particular churches." McKenzie, *Dictionary of the Bible*, p. 46.

[26] See Fuller, *Formation of the Resurrection Narratives*, pp. 40–41.

[27] Ibid., p. 40.

Whether or not they were, "all the apostles" seems to refer to a significant group of Aramaic-speaking and Hellenistic missionaries who enjoyed prominence in the pre-Pauline Church.

It seems that these missionaries may have witnessed Jesus' appearance in several different groupings after Pentecost. Why several? Because there is no specific reference to "at one time" as is noted in the passage about the five hundred (1 Cor 15:6). It seems that these appearances were shared by different *groups* because specific individuals are not named (as they are for Peter, James, and Paul). Furthermore, Jerusalem is a likely place for these appearances, because it follows upon the Church-founding and mission-initiating activities that had already occurred there. The final appearance to Paul will be taken up below.

If the above explanation of Paul's list of witnesses is correct, then the 1 Corinthians 15 *kerygma* refers to (1) an appearance to Peter (which probably took place in Galilee and was Church-founding and governance-establishing); (2) a subsequent appearance to the Twelve (which also probably took place in Galilee and was Church-founding and governance-establishing); (3) an appearance to the five hundred brethren, which may be a Christophany associated with the gift of the Holy Spirit in Jerusalem (which is both Church-founding and mission-establishing); (4) a *possible* post-Pentecost appearance to James, the "brother" of Christ, in Jerusalem (which was both governance-establishing and mission-initiating, given that James is both the head of the Jerusalem Church and the head of the mission activities originating in Jerusalem); and (5) multiple post-Pentecost appearances, probably in Jerusalem, to the primary Aramaic-speaking and Hellenistic missionaries in the early Church (prior to the conversion of Paul). Most of the witnesses (from the above five groupings) would have lived within Paul's writing of the 1 Corinthians 15 *kerygma* (as Paul himself notes). The above list of witnesses is probably incomplete, for it does not account for the appearances to the women,[28] or seemingly to minor disciples (such as those on the way to Emmaus).

---

[28] It is quite certain that the women discovered the empty tomb, but their absence from the list of witnesses in the 1 Corinthians 15 *kerygma* is puzzling. Many exegetes believe that the women were the first to receive an appearance of the risen Christ, but that their witness value in a creedal list was less significant because of Jewish practice and law. For according to Raymond Brown, "Their testimony would have less public authority." Raymond Brown, *The Virginal Conception and Bodily Resurrection of Jesus* (New York: Paulist Press, 1973), p. 122, n. 204.

B. Saint Paul's Witness Dilemma

Immediately after the 1 Corinthians 15 *kerygma* (with its list of witnesses), Paul presents an interesting dilemma that could apply to all the witnesses in that list. The first side of the dilemma is that

> if Christ has not been raised, then our preaching is in vain and your faith is in vain. We are even found to be misrepresenting God, because we testified of God that he raised Christ. (1 Cor 15:14–15)

The other side of the dilemma is that

> [i]f for this life only we have hoped in Christ, we are of all men most to be pitied.... Why am I in peril every hour? ... I die every day! What do I gain if, humanly speaking, I fought with beasts at Ephesus? If the dead are not raised, "Let us eat and drink, for tomorrow we die." (1 Cor 15:19, 30–32)

If we look at this passage carefully, we can see the makings of a classical dilemma that has the objective of verifying the witness value not only of Paul, but also of the Twelve, the five hundred, James, and the "other apostles". From a legal perspective, the most objective way of validating a witness' testimony is to show that the witness has "everything to lose, and nothing to gain". From the opposite perspective, a witness who has everything to gain and nothing to lose may be telling the truth, but there is no extrinsic way of validating this. Indeed, there is a haunting suspicion that the witness may be acting in his own self-interest. A better witness would be one who had nothing to gain or lose, for at least he would not be acting in his own self-interest. But the best witness would be one who had everything to lose (and nothing to gain) because this witness would be acting against his own self-interest, which is a disposition that most of us want desperately to avoid. I believe that Paul is trying to show that not only he but also the others in the list of witnesses are in this category and therefore deserve to be ranked among the best possible witnesses.

Paul sets out his test for witness validity in a dilemma with (of course) two opposed parts: (1) the assumption that the witnesses believed in

God, and (2) the assumption that the witnesses did *not* believe in God. Let us return to the passage above and insert these phrases:

> [If, on the one hand, we believe in God, and] if Christ has not been raised, then our preaching is in vain and your faith is in vain. We are even found to be misrepresenting God, because we testified of God that he raised Christ....
>
> [If on the other hand, we do *not* believe in God, and] if for this life only we have hoped in Christ, we are of all men most to be pit-ied.... If the dead are not raised, "Let us eat and drink, for tomorrow we die."

The first part of the dilemma assumes that Paul (and the other witnesses) believes in God. If Paul truly believes in God, he does not want to bear false witness before God, because this would not only disappoint the Lord whom he adores, but also might, in fact, jeopardize his salvation. This problem is compounded by the fact that his false testimony would be leading hundreds, if not thousands, of people astray, which would not only be a colossal waste of his ministry and time ("our preaching is in vain"), but also a colossal waste of the time and lives of the people he is affecting by his false testimony ("your faith is in vain"). If Paul really does believe in God, why would he waste his life, waste the faith of believers, lead them to apostasy, bear false witness, and risk his salvation? This does not seem to be com-mensurate with someone of genuine faith (or common sense).

The second part of the dilemma looks at the consequences of Paul and the other witnesses being unbelievers. Paul is saying that the cost of preaching a false resurrection (without any belief in a God who saves) is simply too high. He and the other witnesses are not only being challenged by Jewish and Roman authorities; they are being actively persecuted. As he puts it, he is dying every day and is being subject to trials with substantial risk of martyrdom.

Why suffer persecution for preaching the Resurrection of Jesus if that preaching is false and he does not believe in God? There would be no hope of a resurrection or being saved by God. He would be suffering persecution for *nothing*. As he puts it, he may as well "eat and drink", and be merry, "for tomorrow, [he] will die."

Paul uses this dilemma to show (in a legal fashion) that he and the other witnesses have everything to lose and nothing to gain by bearing false witness to the Resurrection of Christ. Could all of the witnesses within living memory of Christ's Resurrection have been so naïve? It seems to me that they could not. If the witnesses lacked authentic motives for preaching the Resurrection, they would have had self-interested ones. However, as Paul shows, they could not have had self-interested motives, because false preaching of the Resurrection would have led either to risking their salvation for undermining God's will (if they believed in God), or to persecution for nothing (if they did not believe in God and a resurrection). This dilemma supports the likelihood of the witnesses' testimony that they had seen the risen Jesus. In view of this we should give Paul the benefit of the doubt—that he was speaking truthfully and with authentic motivations.

Paul not only believes that he is speaking the truth, but that he is speaking the truth about the Lord he loves (that is, the Lord who has loved him first). He endures persecution not simply because he believes he has a *duty* to bear witness to the truth about the Resurrection, but also because he *loves* the One about whom he bears witness. If Paul's love is true, then it can hardly be thought that he is preaching a falsity about his Beloved. As one probes the depths of Paul's authenticity, integrity, and love, it is very hard to believe that he and others like him could deliberately falsify their claim about the Resurrection.

IV. N. T. Wright's Two Arguments for the Historicity of Jesus' Resurrection

New historical-exegetical evidence has recently emerged in a particularly probative way through the scholarship of N. T. Wright[29] and other exegetes. He presents two important arguments:

1. The growth of the Christian messianic movement after the public persecution of its Messiah[30]

---

[29] See Wright's *Resurrection of the Son of God* for a remarkably scholarly and comprehensive example of the recent application of historical-exegetical method applied to the Resurrection appearances of Jesus.

[30] See N. T. Wright, *Jesus and the Victory of God*, vol. 2 (Minneapolis: Fortress Press, 1996).

2. The Christian mutations of Second Temple Judaism's view of the Resurrection[31]

A. The Remarkable Rise of Christian Messianism

E. P. Sanders presents the key insight of the messianic argument as follows:

> What is unique [about Jesus' claim to bring the Kingdom of God] is the result. But, again, we cannot know that the result springs from the uniqueness of the historical Jesus. Without the resurrection, would his disciples have endured longer than did John the Baptist's? We can only guess, but I would guess not.[32]

Wright expands this insight by noting that it applies not only to the disciples of John the Baptist, but also to the followers of

> Judas the Galilean, Simon, Athronges, Eleazar ben Deinaus and Alexander, Menahem, Simon bar Giora, and bar-Kochba himself. Faced with the defeat of their leader, followers of such figures would either be rounded up as well or melt away into the undergrowth.[33]

This did not happen in the early Church. After the public humiliation, persecution, and execution of their Messiah, the disciples maintained their identity and did not replace Jesus as the true leader of their community. Instead, the early Church acknowledged that Jesus was raised from the dead, continued to be its leader, and was the fulfillment of the prophecies of Israel. Wright points out that no other messianic movement displayed this behavior:

> In not one case do we hear of any group, after the death of its leader, claiming that he was in any sense alive again, and that therefore Israel's expectation had in some strange way actually come true.[34]

---

[31] See Wright, *Resurrection of the Son of God.*

[32] E. P. Sanders, *Jesus and Judaism* (Philadelphia: Fortress, 1985), p. 240.

[33] Wright, *Jesus and the Victory of God*, p. 110. An extensive consideration of all these figures is given in N. T. Wright, *The New Testament and the People of God* (Minneapolis: Fortress Press, 1992), 1:170–81.

[34] Wright, *Jesus and the Victory of God*, p. 110.

This early community is even stranger still. It actually begins to *worship* Jesus as Lord, associate Him with divine status, and attribute to Him co-eternity with the Father.[35] This is not only historically unique, but also apologetically unappealing, so much so that the early Church had to pay the ultimate price for it (including separation from the synagogue and even persecution).[36]

Additionally, the early Church organized herself into a missionary community that not only went beyond the boundaries of Israel but also to the very frontiers of the Roman Empire, making her one of the most pluralistic religious organizations in the history of religions. With a crucified Messiah as her head, the early Church formed one of the most dynamically expansive communities in history.

We are now led to N. T. Wright's probative questions. Why didn't the Church follow the patterns of other groups whose leaders had been persecuted? Why did she (uniquely) consider Jesus as her continued leader? Why did she consider Jesus (after the Crucifixion) to be the fulfillment of Israel's destiny? Why did she organize herself so uniquely? Why did she worship Jesus as the Lord and endure persecution for that worship? How did she become one of the most inspired and dynamically expansive missionary organizations in the history of religions with a publicly humiliated and executed so-called Messiah as her sole leader?

The answers to these questions requires a cause capable of explaining why Christianity does not follow the pattern of other religions or messianic movements. Why does Christianity pick up momentum from a crucified leader when other messianic movements at the time quickly faded away? Why didn't Christianity pick out another leader in the face of its leader's Crucifixion, like other messianic movements whose leaders were executed? Above all, why did it become such a powerful messianic movement capable of threatening the Roman Empire within a few generations after that same empire executed its Messiah?

---

[35] See Chapter 6 (Section III) of this volume. See also the many indications of the community's worship of Jesus in Matthew's, Luke's, and John's Resurrection narratives (above in this chapter).

[36] See Chapter 2 (Section II.B) of this volume. See also Wright, *Jesus and the Victory of God*, pp. 110–12.

What kind of cause could explain so many unique phenomena? A powerful one, one capable of overcoming the Crucifixion of the movement's leader and communicating both imminent and transcendent hope (amid the death of its presumed Messiah); one capable of revealing that God's Kingdom had arrived in the world; and one capable of providing sufficient momentum to turn a little Jewish subcult into an empire-wide—indeed, worldwide—religion within a few generations. This powerful cause would seem to be the post-Resurrection appearances of Jesus in combination with Jesus' gift of the Holy Spirit that enabled the apostles (along with other missionaries) to perform miracles in the *name* of *Jesus*. John P. Meier summarizes this unique historical phenomenon as follows:

> There was a notable difference between the long-term impact of the Baptist and that of Jesus. After the Baptist's death, his followers did not continue to grow into a religious movement that in due time swept the Greco-Roman world. Followers remained, revering the Baptist's memory and practices. But by the early 2d century A.D. any cohesive group that could have claimed an organic connection with the historical Baptist seems to have passed from the scene. In contrast, the movement that had begun to sprout up around the historical Jesus continued to *grow*—amid many sea changes—throughout the 1st century and beyond. Not entirely by coincidence, the post-Easter "Jesus movement" claimed the same sort of ability to work miracles that Jesus had claimed for himself during his lifetime. This continued claim to work miracles may help to explain the continued growth, instead of a tapering off, of the group that emerged from Jesus' ministry.[37]

If the Resurrection appearances and the apostles' ability to work miracles are not the cause of this uniquely powerful messianic movement (after the humiliation, persecution, and execution of its Messiah), then what other cause would have the same explanatory power? History has left us with a void of realistic alternatives, suggesting that the Christian claim to have seen the risen Jesus is true, and that the early community's power to perform miracles in Jesus' name was derived from the risen Jesus Himself.

---

[37]John P. Meier, *A Marginal Jew: Rethinking the Historical Jesus*, vol. 2, *Mentor, Message, and Miracles* (New York: Doubleday, 1994), p. 623.

B. The Christian Mutation of Second Temple Judaism

Wright's second and more extensive argument for the historicity of the Resurrection appearances stems from several Christian mutations of the Jewish doctrine of resurrection prevalent at the time of Jesus (Second Temple Judaism). He shows through a study of the New Testament (particularly the Letters of Paul and the Gospel narratives of the Resurrection appearances) that Christianity changed the dominant Jewish view of the resurrection in five major ways:

1. The Jewish doctrine of the resurrection was a return to the same kind of bodily life as the one experienced before death (except in a new world with the righteous). Christian views always entailed *transformation* into a very different kind of life—incorruptible, glorious, and spiritual while still maintaining embodiment.[38] The Christian view is so different from the Jewish one that Paul has to develop a new term to speak about it: "spiritual body" (*pneumatikon soma*). In 1 Corinthians he makes every effort to distinguish the Christian doctrine from the Jewish one: "It is sown a physical body, it is raised a spiritual body. If there is a physical body, there is also a spiritual body.... But it is not the spiritual which is first but the physical, and then the spiritual" (15:44, 46).

2. In Second Temple Judaism, no one was expected to rise from the dead before the initiation of the final age by Yahweh; however, Christians claimed that this occurred with Jesus.[39]

3. No one connected the Messiah to the resurrection or the Jewish doctrine of resurrection to the Messiah prior to Christianity: "There are no traditions about a Messiah being raised to life: most Jews of this period hoped for resurrection, many Jews of this period hoped for a Messiah, but nobody put those two hopes together until the early Christians did so."[40]

4. For the Jewish people, the eschatological age was in the future; for Christians the eschatological age had already arrived (and would be *completed* in the future).[41]

[38] See Wright, *Resurrection of the Son of God*, p. 273.
[39] See ibid., pp. 200–206 (the conclusion to Chapter 4).
[40] Ibid., p. 205.
[41] See ibid., p. 272.

5. The doctrine of the resurrection is *central* to the earliest writings of Christianity (e.g., all nine of the early *kerygmas*), is central to the writings of Paul[42] and all the Gospel writers,[43] and is the interconnecting theme among early Christian doctrines. The doctrine of the resurrection grounds Christology, particularly the doctrine of Christ's glorification and, in part, the doctrine of Christ's divinity; it grounds the Christian doctrine of soteriology ("for if the dead are not raised, then Christ has not been raised" [1 Cor 15:16]); it shows God's vindication of Jesus' teaching; it grounds Christian eschatology; and it is, in every respect, central to all other doctrines. Saint Paul thinks it is so important that he proclaims:

> If Christ has not been raised, your faith is futile [useless] and you are still in your sins. Then those also who have fallen asleep in Christ have perished. If for this life only we have hoped in Christ, we are of all men most to be pitied. (1 Cor 15:17–19)

Second Temple Judaism does not place the resurrection in any such central role and does not use it as an interconnecting theme for its doctrines. It is almost secondary in importance to other doctrines concerned with the law and prayer.

Once again, Wright finds himself as historian in the position of having to ask for a necessary and sufficient explanation of these radical mutations in Second Temple Judaism's doctrine of the resurrection. A responsible historian cannot simply say that there was no reason for this universally accepted change within early Christianity, because this position runs counter to the fact that Christianity remained faithful to Judaism except for when Jesus (or some historical event connected with Jesus) changed it.

So what could explain this radical change? The preaching of Jesus? This is not tenable, because Jesus does not put the resurrection at the center of His doctrine, but rather the arrival of the Kingdom. Furthermore, He does not connect the resurrection to His Messiahship, and He certainly does not talk about the resurrection as being

---

[42] See ibid., p. 274. Paul makes it so central that he claims that if Jesus is not risen from the dead, "our preaching is in vain and your faith is in vain" (1 Cor 15:14).

[43] See Wright, *Resurrection of the Son of God*, pp. 401–584.

transformed embodiment (or spiritual embodiment, or glorified embodiment), which is evident in the early Christian doctrine. The obvious explanation would be that the many witnesses (e.g., Peter, the Twelve, the five hundred disciples, James, the early missionaries to the Gentile Church, and Paul himself) saw the risen Jesus in a transformed embodied state (manifesting at once a spiritual transformation that had the appearance of divine glory and power, *and* some form of embodiment that was continuous with Jesus' embodiment in His ministry). This would easily explain all five of the above-mentioned mutations.[44]

Rigorous historical method requires more than leaping to the obvious explanation. The historian must eliminate all other plausible explanations for the same phenomena. In order to do this, Wright sets out five other possible explanations for the above-mentioned mutations: (1) paganism, (2) early Christian interior visions or experiences, (3) the empty tomb alone, (4) cognitive dissonance, and (5) Schillebeeckx's conjecture of a new experience of grace.

1. *Paganism.* Paganism offers virtually no possibility of explaining the Christians' view of the resurrection, let alone the mutations of Second Temple Judaism. Paganism generally held that the soul would be separated from the body, that the body would die and never be restored, and that the soul was very likely destined to be in Hades, manifest as a mere shadow of its former self.[45] The contrast between paganism and early Christianity is so stark that the attempt to derive the latter from the former is not coherent.

2. *Early Christian interior visions.* Given that the unique, uniform, early Christian view of the resurrection did not come from either Second Temple Judaism or paganism, might it not have come from an interior vision of Jesus after His Crucifixion? Wouldn't a vision be *sufficient* to produce a whole new viewpoint on the resurrection that became the central integrating theme of Christian doctrine and missionary activity?

[44] See ibid., pp. 205, 272–74, and 401–584; and Robert J. Spitzer, *New Proofs for the Existence of God: Contributions of Contemporary Physics and Philosophy* (Grand Rapids, Mich.: William B. Eerdmans, 2010), Chapter 4, Section II.

[45] See Wright, *Resurrection of the Son of God,* Chapter 2, particularly pp. 78–82.

In response, Wright shows that visions of the dead in the ancient world were quite commonplace and that these visions were never interpreted to be a resurrection of the body:

> The more "normal" these "visions" were, the less chance there is that anyone, no matter how cognitively dissonant they may have been feeling, would have said what nobody had ever said about such a dead person before, that they had been *raised from* the dead.[46]

Recall that "raised from the dead" refers to a resurrection of the body, and that this occurred with respect to Jesus, and that this grounded the early Church's belief in the initiation of the final age. There is no reason to believe that a vision of Jesus after death would have had any more effect than the frequently occurring visions of other dead people.

There is another related objection to the sufficiency of the vision hypothesis. The Resurrection of Jesus had three verifiable effects: (a) it created a new, unique doctrine of the resurrection; (b) this doctrine became the central, integral theme of Christian doctrine; and (c) it provided the main force for the belief in Jesus' Messiahship and lordship. Given that visions of the dead were quite normal in the ancient world, it is highly unlikely that a vision would produce these unprecedented effects.

3. *The empty tomb alone.* Some exegetes have contended that the empty tomb alone was sufficient to motivate early Christian belief in a bodily resurrection. They believe that the stories about Jesus' post-Resurrection appearances were mere add-ons either to enhance the empty tomb story or to re-dress the polemic that Jesus' disciples had stolen the body. This hypothesis is also insufficient to explain the five Christian mutations for two reasons: (a) it suffers from the same problem as interior visions—namely, that empty tombs and grave robbery were quite normal in the ancient world; and (b) an empty tomb does not explain four out of five of the above Christian mutations. Let us take each in turn.

---

[46] Ibid., p. 690; emphasis in original.

Wright addresses the first point as follows:

An empty tomb without any meetings with Jesus would have been a distressing puzzle, but not a long-term problem. It would have proved nothing; it would have suggested nothing, except the fairly common practice of grave-robbery. It certainly would not have generated the phenomena we have studied in this book so far. Tombs were often robbed in the ancient world, adding to grief both insult and injury. Nobody in the pagan world would have interpreted an empty tomb as implying resurrection; everyone knew such a thing was out of the question. Nobody in the ancient Jewish world would have interpreted it like that either; "resurrection" was not something anyone expected to happen to a single individual while the world went on as normal.[47]

Wright addresses the second major problem by showing that an empty tomb alone would not be able to explain four of the Christian mutations:

Had the tomb been empty, with no other unusual occurrences, no one would have imagined that Jesus was the Messiah or the lord of the world. No one would have imagined that the kingdom had been inaugurated. No one, in particular, would have developed so quickly and consistently a radical and reshaped version of the Jewish hope for the resurrection of the body. The empty tomb is by itself insufficient to account for the subsequent evidence.[48]

4. *Cognitive dissonance.* The phenomenon of cognitive dissonance begins with an expectation (arising out of a deep longing or yearning) for some particular state of affairs that is followed by a disappointment of that expectation. The group cannot reconcile itself to the fact that its deepest yearning has been disappointed, and so it perpetuates a state of denial that then provokes it to reorganize its view of *reality* to conform to this denied state of affairs. The group attempts to increase its numbers in order to help justify its interpretation of the denied state of affairs.[49]

[47] Ibid., pp. 688–89.
[48] Ibid., p. 689.
[49] See ibid., pp. 697–98.

The application of this theory to the early Christian Church might at first glance provide an alternative explanation to that of Saint Paul and the Gospels. Suppose the early Christian Church experienced cognitive dissonance; that is, they *really* wanted Jesus to be the Messiah, and they were *very* disappointed when Jesus was crucified. Being unable to reconcile themselves to this fact, they reorganized their reality to resolve their dissonance and disappointment by projecting His Resurrection into their reality. They further reinforced their perspective by adding converts to their ranks.

There are several problems with this hypothesis. As the reader will by now surmise, this explanation does not explain four out of five of the above Christian mutations of Second Temple Judaism. Why would cognitive dissonance have caused the early Christians to believe in a completely unique notion of the resurrection (i.e., spiritual embodiment)? Why would it have led them to believe that the resurrection would begin with a single individual (and not a group)? Why would cognitive dissonance have caused the early Christians to believe in a completely unique view of the final age (while earthly life continued as quasi-normal)? Why would cognitive dissonance have caused early Christians to make their unique doctrine of the resurrection so central and integral to all other doctrines? Cognitive dissonance explains neither the need for nor the content of these mutations. Wright sums this up as follows:

> The real problem is something that any first-century historian should recognize: that whatever it was that the early Christians were expecting, wanting, hoping and praying for, this was *not* what they said, after Easter, had happened.[50]

The early Christians did not expect anything like spiritual embodiment, the initiation of the final age, the resurrection of a single individual, or the doctrinal centrality of the resurrection, and it is difficult to see how cognitive dissonance would have enabled them to change their expectations. So it seems that cognitive dissonance is not a sufficient explanation of the highly unusual facts.

5. *Schillebeeckx's new experience of grace.* Edward Schillebeeckx's proposal may be summarized as follows: Peter (and some other disciples,

---

[50] Ibid., p. 699.

apparently through his influence) had a wonderful experience of forgiveness and conversion that led him/them to believe that Jesus was still alive. This led to cultic practice that then began to develop stories about the empty tomb (perhaps in light of veneration of the tomb), and even stories about post-Resurrection narratives. Each evangelist approaches the stories differently (from the context of the faith community in which they were writing), which not only explains the origin of the stories, but also their seeming differences.

Aside from the fact that Schillebeeckx makes no less than eight significant errors in his exegesis of the Gospel texts,[51] his interpretation of the Resurrection fails to explain all five of the above Christian mutations of Second Temple Judaism. Peter's experience of forgiveness and conversion (no matter how graced) does not explain the uniform Christian view of resurrection as spiritual embodiment. Furthermore, it does not explain why the Church held that the final age had been initiated (when Rome still occupied Jerusalem). Schillebeeckx's explanation for this is no more efficacious than those of the visions and empty tomb (alone) mentioned above. The same holds true for the proclamation of Jesus as Messiah and Lord (with lordship having divine implications). How in the world did Peter's experience of forgiveness and conversion lead the early Church to proclaim Jesus to be what was, in Second Temple Judaism, unthinkable—namely, that Jesus is the Lord? Finally, how did Peter's experience of forgiveness and conversion cause the primitive Church to put the Resurrection at the integrating center of all her doctrine? The Schillebeeckx alternative proposal (like all the others) fails the test of sufficient explanation.

Aside from their failure to explain most Christian mutations of Second Temple Judaism, the above five alternative explanations of Jesus' Resurrection reveal inadequacies in their authors' knowledge

---

[51] Schillebeeckx's exegetical errors are so prolific that Wright ridicules him: "This view is ingenious and subtle, but demonstrably wrong on almost every count.... His invention of a supposed 'Jewish–biblical way of speaking', in comparison with which stories of the risen Jesus appear crude and naively realistic, stands the truth on its head. His picture of the cultic practice of visiting Jesus' tomb, upon which he bases his reading of Mark, is without foundation. He is right to say that Matthew tells stories which assume that 'resurrection' means bodies, but wrong to imply that this is an odd innovation in the tradition. His analysis of a 'rapture' tradition is unwarranted, and does not in any case apply to Luke (when Jesus disappears in Emmaus this hardly constitutes a 'rapture', since he reappears in Jerusalem shortly afterwards). His account of Paul is inaccurate in its reporting both of the Acts stories and of Paul's own evidence." Ibid., p. 703.

of first-century paganism, Second Temple Judaism, social and religious customs in first-century Palestine, and proper exegetical method.[52] For this reason, Wright legitimately eliminates them from the realm of plausibility and concludes that the only reasonable and responsible explanation is the one given by Saint Paul and the Gospel narratives—namely, that Jesus really appeared to multiple witnesses in a transformed corporeal state (manifesting at once spiritual transformation in the glory and power of God, and continuity with His former embodiment).

V. The Empty Tomb

The empty tomb does not give direct evidence of Jesus' Resurrection and spiritual transformation as do His risen appearances; however, it gives *indirect* corroboration of His Resurrection and an indication of His continuity with His former *embodiment*. Some scholars have suggested that the empty tomb is a tenuous datum because we cannot be sure about where Jesus' body was placed, and therefore whether the tomb was in fact empty. However, the majority of mainstream scholars do not share this skeptical opinion for the following reasons.

It is unthinkable that Matthew would have reported the unflattering and embarrassing accusation of the Jewish authorities (that Jesus' disciples had stolen His body) unless the accusation had in fact been made. Why call attention to an accusation capable of undermining faith in Jesus' Resurrection unless it was already widely known by Church members and required a response? Why did the Jewish authorities make this accusation? They must have needed an explanation for a *real* missing body. If Jesus' body had been present where they laid Him, the polemic would be ridiculous; that is, how could the apostles have stolen His body if it were still there?

Some contemporary scholars have speculated that Jesus was not placed in a tomb, but instead, a mass grave or, in the case of Crossan,

---

[52] See ibid., Chapter 2, particularly pp. 78–82 (with respect to paganism); pp. 689–90 (with respect to Christian interior visions); pp. 688–89 (with respect to the empty tomb alone); pp. 697–99 (with respect to cognitive dissonance of early Christians); and pp. 699 and 702–3 (with respect to Schillebeeckx's new experience of grace).

left in an unknown place.[53] Aside from the *un*likelihood that the
followers of Jesus would have lost track of His body, one must
return to the above argument: Why would the Jewish authorities
have charged the apostles with stealing His body unless there were a
provably missing body? If there were any ambiguity about where the
body lay (e.g., in a mass grave), then there would be no problem
about a missing body. They would not have had to explain why it
couldn't be found. But the fact is that the authorities feel compelled
to charge the apostles with stealing the body, which implies that
a body is gone from a *known* place, presumably a tomb (the most
identifiable burial place).[54]

We are now in a position to reconstruct the events surrounding
the Jewish authorities' accusation of the apostles' theft of Jesus' body.
The moment the apostles started preaching that Jesus had appeared
to them (and began making converts on the basis of that preaching), their adversaries would have likely made every attempt to produce a body that would disprove (or undermine) the apostolic claim.
Apparently, they could not do this. We might infer from this that

[53] Dominic Crossan has proposed this on the basis of his interpretation of the Gospel of
Peter. He holds the highly contested position that Matthew's Gospel is reliant on the Gnostic
Gospel of Peter rather than vice versa. John P. Meier responds to Crossan with a far more
plausible contention: "When it comes to who is dependent on whom, all the signs point to
Matthew's priority.... The clause [concerning the empty tomb in the Gospel of Peter] is a
tissue of Matthean vocabulary and style, a vocabulary and style almost totally absent from the
rest of the Gospel of Peter." John P. Meier, *A Marginal Jew: Rethinking the Historical Jesus*,
vol. 1, *The Roots of the Problem and the Person* (New York: Doubleday, 1991), p. 117.

See also Charles Quarles' response to Crossan's contention that the Gospel of Peter is the
source for the canonical Gospels in "The Gospel of Peter: Does It Contain a Precanonical
Resurrection Narrative?" in *The Resurrection of Jesus: John Dominic Crossan and N. T. Wright
in Dialogue*, ed. Robert B. Stewart (Minneapolis: Fortress Press, 2006), pp. 106–20. See also
Brown's response to Crossan's contention that the apostles didn't know much about Jesus'
Crucifixion and burial: "It is inconceivable that they showed no concern about what happened to Jesus after the arrest.... The crucifixion itself was public, and nothing suggests that
the burial was secret." Raymond Brown, *The Death of the Messiah: From Gethsemane to the
Grave; A Commentary on the Passion Narratives in the Four Gospels* (New York: Doubleday,
1994), p. 14. See the explanation in Chapter 3 (Section IV.B) of this volume.

[54] Recent archaeological evidence at the site of the Church of the Holy Sepulchre shows
details about the placement of the Crucifixion and *burial* of Jesus in the Gospel of John to
be remarkably accurate. See the research in the following: James H. Charlesworth, "Jesus
Research and Archaeology: A New Perspective", in *Jesus and Archaeology*, ed. James H.
Charlesworth (Grand Rapids, Mich.: William B. Eerdmans, 2006), pp. 30–50, and Urban C.
von Wahlde, "Archeology and John's Gospel", in ibid., pp. 523–60.

the authorities made every attempt to find out where the body was laid, located the site of the grave/tomb, and found the body gone. If the body had not been put into an identifiable place, the charge of theft would not have been necessary. Now, if the authorities could have identified where the body was, we must suppose that His followers could do the same. Given this, it is likely that the women and other apostles witnessed the empty tomb, and shortly thereafter, Jesus appeared to them transformed—spiritually transformed.

When we combine the *spiritual* dimensions of Jesus' risen appearances with the implications of His *corporeality* from the empty tomb (as well as His risen appearance), we see why Saint Paul was so careful to call Jesus' risen state "a spiritual body" (*pneumatikon soma*), and why the majority of scholars think that Jesus appeared as a spiritually transformed body (see Habermas' survey above in Section I).

VI. The Shroud of Turin and the Resurrection of Jesus

In the previous chapter we noted that the 1988 carbon 14 dating of the Shroud was seriously flawed, and that there is overwhelming evidence for its probable origin in early first-century Palestine (see Appendix I, Section II). We also noted that the Shroud gave considerable evidence not only for the unique dimensions of Jesus' Crucifixion, but also for His Resurrection. How can a burial cloth give evidence of a resurrection?

Of course there cannot be a scientific test for a resurrection, because science is restricted to the domain of natural causation, while a resurrection requires a *transphysical* cause. Nevertheless, the Shroud of Turin has left us with some clues to Jesus' Resurrection in the formation of its image. Appendix I (the Shroud of Turin) gives a detailed explanation of five major enigmas of the image on the Shroud:

1. The fact that the image is limited to the uppermost surface of the fibrils and does not penetrate to the medulla of the fibers implies that the image was not produced by chemicals or vapors of any kind.
2. The fact that the image is not a scorch (but rather discoloration coming from dehydration) implies that the image could

not have been produced by slowly dissipating radiation (which would have scorched it).

3. The image is a perfect photographic negative in which the image intensity is related to the distance of the cloth from the body. Thus, the image was present regardless of whether the cloth touched the body. This implies that radiation (and not chemicals) was the likely source of image formation.

4. There is a double image on the frontal part of the cloth—a more intense image on the front surface (nearest the body) and a less intense image on the back surface (farthest from the body) without any effects between the two surfaces. This implies that the radiation was surrounding both surfaces of the cloth, meaning that the cloth was able to collapse *into* the body, which was emitting light (vacuum ultraviolet radiation).

5. Parts of the frontal image, particularly the hands, show an image that is resolvable into three dimensions, in which the inside skeletal parts of the hands are proportionately related to the surrounding exterior flesh on the hands. This implies that the cloth collapsed into *and through* the body on the Shroud.

Many physicists have tried to explain the formation of the image, and the current consensus surrounds the hypothesis of Dr. John Jackson, who proposed a solution that could address all five enigmas. The solution has two parts:

1. The decomposing body emitted a short, very intense burst of vacuum ultraviolet radiation that dissipated very quickly, giving rise to a nonscorched discoloration on the frontal and dorsal parts of the cloth. This image is a perfect photographic negative image resolvable into three dimensions.

2. In order to explain the fourth and fifth enigmas (the double image on the frontal part of the cloth and the image of both the interior skeleton and exterior flesh of the hands), Jackson further proposed that the body became mechanically transparent (losing the mechanical quality of solidity), which caused the frontal part of the cloth to collapse in and through the body. During the time of the collapse, the body emitted its vacuum ultraviolet radiation evenly from every three-dimensional point within it.

This two-part explanation of the five enigmas is explained in detail in Appendix I (Section III). For the moment, suffice it to say that no other satisfactory explanation of all five enigmas of the Shroud's image has been proposed, leaving Jackson's hypothesis as the "sole candidate". In 2010, Dr. Paolo Di Lazzaro and his team from three research centers (Frascati Research Center, the University of Padua, and Casaccia Research Center) replicated the first part of Jackson's hypothesis under laboratory conditions (see Appendix I, Section III.C). He did this by irradiating a linen fabric having the same absolute spectral reflectance as the Shroud with pulsed deep-ultraviolet radiation emitted by an ArF excimer laser. This is the first time that an image like the Shroud has been replicated.

If the first part of Jackson's hypothesis (and its confirmation by Di Lazzaro and others) is substantially accurate, then something *transphysical* occurred within the decomposing body enveloped by the Shroud. There is no known natural explanation (from the laws of physics) for such an intense, specialized, quickly dissipating mode of radiation to come from a decomposing body. Furthermore, if the unreplicated part of Jackson's hypothesis (a mechanically transparent body evenly emitting radiation from all three-dimensional points within it) is also true, then it shows the need for an additional *transphysical* cause, because there is nothing in the known laws of physics to explain how a body can become mechanically transparent and emit light evenly from every three-dimensional point within it.

Does this give evidence of Jesus' Resurrection? If Jackson's hypothesis is accurate, and it can only be explained by a *transphysical* cause (because it cannot be explained by natural physical causation), then it points to an action of a *transphysical* cause (God) in the natural world.

Furthermore, the characteristics of the energy and the body emitting it have a striking resemblance to the characteristics of the risen body described by Saint Paul—a *spiritual* body transformed in power and glory. It is not difficult to imagine that the powerful burst of intense light evenly emitted from every three-dimensional part of a mechanically transparent body is tantamount to the beginning point of the transformation of the body from a physical one to a spiritual (transphysical) one.

If we assume that this powerful burst of light emitted from the body has a transphysical cause and is the beginning of the transformation of the body from a physical to a transphysical one, does it indicate that the body belongs specifically to *Jesus*? Recall from Section IV.B above that one of the principal Christian mutations of Second Temple Judaism's doctrine of the resurrection (according to N.T. Wright) was to advocate for a *spiritual* body instead of a resuscitation of a *material* body. Indeed, there is nothing in Second Temple Judaism suggesting that the risen body would be spiritual or transformed in any way. Furthermore, pagan views hold that the body after death will be ghostlike and ethereal, but say nothing about being transformed in spirit, power, and glory. If Wright is correct, then the spiritual, powerful, glorified, risen body is unique to Christianity, and first occurred in Jesus' body. If this is the case, then it is not a far stretch to believe that the Shroud of Turin has left us with a clue to the Resurrection of Jesus as uniquely reported by the early Christian Church, a clue to the transformation process of Jesus' material body into a spiritual body by an intense burst of vacuum ultraviolet radiation emitted evenly from every three-dimensional part of a mechanically transparent body. This is explained in detail in Appendix I (Sections III and IV).

VII. Correlations between the Resurrection of Jesus and Near-Death Experiences

The above evidence is sufficient to show the likelihood of Jesus' Resurrection in glory. The Gospel and Pauline accounts of this are sufficient to explain Wright's five historical mutations (see above, Section IV). Furthermore, Saint Paul claims that our resurrection will be like Jesus'—we will have a transformed spiritual, glorified body (1 Cor 15:42–46). This partially corresponds to the descriptions of near-death experiences (given in Volume II, Chapter 5). Recall that a significant percentage of people having a near-death experience described a transphysical dimension of their "new" form (outside of their physical bodies). This new transphysical form is not subject to physical laws and structures such as walls and gravity. Patients would hover above their physical bodies, pass through the walls of waiting rooms and hospitals, ascend multiple floors of the hospital, and frequently "go to the other side".

Though Jesus' appearance is *different* from those of near-death experiences in its *power and glory*, it does bear a resemblance to them in its transphysicality (e.g., Jesus appearing like a spirit [Lk 24:37] and passing through closed doors [Jn 20:19]). Recall that Jesus arose not only in spirit, but also in power and glory—the disciples worshipped him (see Mt 28:16–20); the use of *ho Kurios* (the Lord) in John 20–21; and Paul's testimony that Jesus' body is raised in power and glory (1 Cor 15:40–44). Though near-death experiences indicate a transphysical state, they do not by themselves indicate a further transformation in power and glory. Christian revelation, however, does indicate this, and Saint Paul promises it (1 Cor 15:40–44).

The new transphysical form of near-death experiences is not only transphysical; it also frequently has continuity with embodiment—patients can not only see and hear, but also frequently have a sense of being extended. When patients pass to the "other side" they see their relatives and friends as embodied, but in a transformed way. They are visible, extended, and recognizable (from their former physically embodied state), but they are also transformed, appearing spiritual, beautiful, and somewhat luminous. This correlates with Saint Paul's and the Gospel accounts of Jesus' continued embodiment (Lk 24:39–40; Jn 20:19–20; 1 Cor 15:42–46).

In sum, there is *partial* correlation between the new transphysical form of near-death experiences and Jesus' risen appearances. Jesus' risen appearance differs from near-death experiences in its powerful and glorious manifestation. Saint Paul states that we will one day undergo this transformation: "[W]e shall also bear the image of the man from heaven [the risen Jesus]" (1 Cor 15:49). However, there is no indication of this from near-death experiences.

There is yet another partial correlation between Jesus' revelation and the accounts of near-death experiences—namely, the overwhelming presence of love. When patients cross over to the other side, they frequently encounter an overwhelmingly *loving* white light. The adjective "loving" is almost always part of the spontaneous description of the light, as if it were integral to the light's being and nature. Its love is just as obvious as the light itself. Patients frequently go on to describe the love of the light—not just its affirming and affectionate quality, but also its compassion and its desire to fulfill us and to bring us to its own state of love. Patients frequently say that they are overwhelmed by this love. Yet, their identities are not taken away from them (absorbed by this love). Furthermore, many patients who see deceased relatives and friends notice that they are loving, unselfishly displaying goodness, concern, and care not only for the deceased, but also their families. The children who see Jesus almost always indicate that He loves them.[55]

We saw in Chapters 1–3 that the *central* revelation of Jesus about Himself and the Father is their unconditional love. Jesus manifests this in everything He does—from befriending sinners to performing miracles, to the Last Supper and His death on the Cross. He also reveals that this unconditional love expresses the essence of His Father, by calling Him "Abba" (Daddy), whom He identifies with the father of the Prodigal Son. This view of God's unconditional love is unique in the history of religions prior to Christianity.[56]

Once again we see a partial correlation between near-death experiences and the Christian revelation of God; both sources indicate that God and Heaven are loving, even overwhelmingly loving. However, near-death experiences do not indicate the unconditional love of God or how to understand "unconditional love" (*agapē*).

As can be seen, the evidence of near-death experiences corroborates part of the Christian account of Jesus' Resurrection, but

---

[55] Many children indicate that they have seen Jesus, and that He has expressed His love for them. In a recent popular account of a four-year-old boy's near-death experience, *Heaven Is for Real*, a father tells the story for his son, which has the prominent feature of Jesus' love for children. See Todd Burpo and Lynn Vincent, "Jesus *Really* Loves the Children", Chapter 19 in *Heaven Is for Real: A Little Boy's Astounding Story of His Trip to Heaven and Back* (Nashville: Thomas Nelson, 2010).

[56] There is no doubt that Judaism viewed God as loving (Deut 4:37; 7:7; Hos 11:1; 14:5; Is 66:13; Jer 31:3; Zeph 3:17), but not in the same way as Christianity—that is, as *unconditional agapē* manifest by the father of the prodigal son and in the name "Abba". Furthermore, God's love in Judaism is focused on the *people Israel*, but in Christianity God's love is focused on *individuals*—all individuals, particularly sinful and weak individuals (Lk 15:1–7, 8–10; Mt 9:13; 11:29; Jn 3:16–17; 15:11–12).

The Christians also qualitatively transformed the *idea* of "love"; as McKenzie notes, "Greek uses the word *Eros*, *Philia*, and *agapē* and their cognates to designate love. *Eros* signifies the passion of sexual desire and does not appear in the NT. *Philein* and *Philia* designate primarily the love of friendship. *Agapē* and *agapan*, less frequent in profane Greek, are possibly chosen for that reason to designate the unique and original Christian idea of love in the New Testament. In English also the word 'charity' is used to show the unique character of this love and is used in most English versions of the Bible to translate *agapē* and *agapan*." McKenzie, *Dictionary of the Bible*, p. 521. (This was explained in detail in Chapter 1 of this volume.)

Christianity goes further in revealing the power and glory of the spiritual body, the *unconditional* love of God, and the definition of love as *agapē*. There are two other areas in which Jesus' revelation goes beyond the evidence of near-death experiences: the *eternity* of the afterlife and God's *universal* salvific will.

With respect to the first area, near-death experiences show only that a transphysical body can survive clinical death, and in so doing, show that we are more than our physical embodiment. They do not and cannot reveal the eternity of that transphysical state. To know this would require knowing the will of the Creator, which requires, in turn, a revelation from that Creator. If we grant that Jesus Christ is "the unconditional love of God with us", then His revelation of God's will to give us eternal life is more than sufficient to do this. This theme is central in the writings of Paul, particularly 1 Corinthians 15, as well as Romans 5:21 and 6:23 and Galatians 6:8. It is also central to the Synoptic Gospels, in which there are eight distinct mentions of it (e.g., see Mk 8:35; 10:30; Mt 16:25; 18:8–9; Lk 9:24). The theme of eternal life is most prevalent in John's Gospel where there are eighteen mentions of "eternal life" (e.g., see 3:15–16; 5:24; 17:1–11) and another nineteen mentions of "life", which imply eternal life. If we affirm that God is unconditional love (as Jesus teaches), we can also infer His desire to bring us into eternal life because if God truly is unconditional love, and unconditional love entails a desire to be with us in *perfect* empathy, it implies God's desire to be with us eternally.

The second area in which Jesus' revelation goes beyond the evidence of near-death experiences concerns God's desire to save *every* individual who seeks Him with a sincere heart. We have already encountered this theme (in Chapter 3, Section IV.A) with respect to Jesus' Eucharistic words ("poured out for many" [Mt 26:28; Mk 14:24]) and Jesus' selection of Psalm 22 for His dying words (which addresses the universality of salvation). As will be explained in Chapter 7 (Section I), "Jesus' intention to save *everyone* who seeks God with a sincere heart" is supported by several passages of Scripture throughout the Synoptics, John, and Paul.[57] Though

---

[57] See, for example, Matthew 18:14: "[I]t is not the will of my Father who is in heaven that one of these little ones should perish"; Luke 3:6: "[A]ll flesh shall see the salvation of God"; John 12:32: "I, when I am lifted up from the earth, will draw *all* men to myself"; John 17:2 "[Y]ou have given him power over all flesh, to give eternal life to *all* whom you have given him"; and Romans 6:10: "The death [Jesus] died he died to sin once for *all*." (Emphasis mine.)

God's *desire* to save is universal, each person must seek that salvation with a sincere heart.

Since *God's* universal *desire* to save us may not correspond to *our desire* to accept and seek that salvation, we cannot say that everyone *is* or will be saved. We know only that God's *desire* is to save *every* person who sincerely wants to be saved.

In contrast to this, near-death experiences reveal only that God (represented by the loving white light) expresses a desire to bring certain individuals to Himself. They do not indicate why only 9 percent through 20 percent of clinically dead adults have near-death experiences (though 85 percent of children do),[58] and so God's universal salvific will is left ambiguous. It is only through the revelation of Jesus that we know the intention of God to save everyone who desires and seeks His salvation.

What do we know after combining the evidence of Christian revelation and near-death experiences?

1. We are not limited to a corporeal life or the physical world; we have a transphysical dimension that can survive bodily death (from both near-death experiences and Jesus' revelation).
2. Our transphysical dimension has continuity with embodiment— but is not limited by physical laws or structures (from both near-death experiences and Jesus' revelation).
3. The transcendent deity (and the "other side") are overwhelmingly loving (from both near-death experiences and Jesus' revelation).
4. Our transphysical embodiment will be transformed in power and glory, like Jesus' (from only the revelation of Jesus).

[58] These statistics are reported by the International Association for Near-Death Studies, which states that negative near-death experiences are rare: "In the four prospective studies conducted between 1984 and 2001 involving a total of 130 NDErs, none reported distressing experiences. This finding seems to confirm that the experience is relatively rare". "Distressing Near-Death Experiences", International Association for Near-Death Studies, last updated July 17, 2012, under "How Common Are Distressing NDEs?", http://iands.org/about-ndes /distressing-ndes.html#a. The 2014 study carried out by Sam Parnia at Southampton University reported that the 9 percent who had a near-death experience indicated that it was overwhelmingly positive. However, some of the 30 percent who maintained some postmortem consciousness, but did not have a full near-death experience, reported having some feelings of distress. See Sam Parnia et al., "AWARE—AWAreness during REsuscitation—A Prospective Study", *Resuscitation*, October 6, 2014, pp. 1799–1805, http://www.resuscitationjournal .com/article/S0300-9572%2814%2900739-4/fulltext.

5. Life after death is eternal (from only the revelation of Jesus).

6. God and Jesus' intention is to give eternal life to *all* who accept and seek it, still allowing for the possibility of some to reject love, a loving God, and loving people freely (from only the revelation of Jesus).

If this confluence of evidence indicates our destiny, it must also indicate our nature; we are loving beings whose purpose is to love and whose destiny is the fullness of love. Only the unconditionally loving God can satisfy us. As Saint Augustine said long ago, "For thou hast made us for thyself, and our hearts are restless until they rest in thee."[59]

VIII. Conclusion

The above historical analysis validates two conclusions:

1. There is significant reason to believe that Jesus appeared to the apostles (and other witnesses) after the women had discovered His empty tomb. He appeared spiritually transformed—possessing transphysical capacities, such as the ability to pass through closed doors (Jn 20:19–20), with spiritlike qualities, which caused the disciples to think He was a spirit (Lk 24:37). He was more than a spiritual presence, appearing transformed in power and glory as if He were clothed in the glory of God (1 Cor 15:50–56; Mt 28:16–20; and references to "the Lord" [*ho Kurios*] in Jn 20 and 21). Though transformed, He maintained continuity with His former embodiment, revealing the wounds of His Crucifixion (Jn 20:20–21; Lk 24:41). This interpretation explains all five of Wright's Christian mutations of Second Temple Judaism (see above, Section IV.B).

2. After Jesus' powerful transformed appearance to the witnesses, He imparts the Holy Spirit upon them, and they are able to perform the same miracles as He did (in *His* name).

---

[59] Augustine, *De Baptismo Contra Donatistas Libri Septem*, in *The Fundamentals of Catholic Dogma*, by Ludwig Ott, trans. Patrick Lynch (Rockford, Ill.: Tan Books, 1955), Bk. I, Chap. 1.

Jesus' risen glory and gift of the Spirit substantiated everything He said to His apostles about being the exclusive Son of the Father, and so the early Church declared Him to be the Lord and the Son of God (see Chapter 6, Section III). Recall that the proclamation of Jesus' divinity was apologetically unappealing and cost the Church dearly (separation from the synagogue, loss of social and financial status, and persecution). Jesus' Resurrection and glory explains why Church leaders brought persecution upon themselves when they could have avoided it by simply omitting mention of His divinity. It also explains why Christian messianism grew stronger after the public execution and humiliation of its Messiah, and why the Christian Church grew so rapidly in the midst of persecution.

In view of this, we can see why Paul and the other witnesses were so willing to risk everything in order to proclaim Jesus as risen Messiah and Lord. As Paul notes in his dilemma (see above, Section III.B), all these witnesses had everything to lose and nothing to gain by their proclamation. It also explains why the Jewish authorities and even the Roman Empire could not arrest the growth of this unique religion within its confines, and why that religion moved beyond Rome and became the most dynamic missionary church in history. When this historical evidence of Jesus' Resurrection is combined with the data of near-death experiences, it further corroborates the case for our ultimate spiritual destiny in Jesus: a destiny of eternal and unconditional love without suffering—transformed in the very image of the risen Savior.

The historical case for Jesus' Resurrection is significant and provides an essential part of the foundation for believing that He truly is the "unconditional love of God with us". In Chapter 5, we will examine two additional parts of this foundation: Jesus' miracles and his gift of the Holy Spirit. When these three pieces are combined with His unconditionally loving life and death (and His preaching of His Father's unconditional love), we see the solidity of His claim to be the exclusive Son of the Father.

We conclude with our introductory observation—namely, that reason alone will not bring us to faith in Jesus Christ. Reasonable evidence can mitigate barriers to faith while providing strong support for its foundations. However, faith requires that we recognize a need for God and His help to bring us out of darkness and alienation;

it requires a recognition that there is something incomplete within ourselves, a recognition that we cannot by ourselves (or even with other people) overcome this alienation and incompleteness, and a recognition that the word, actions, and way of Jesus Christ are the vehicle for doing this. When we see the evidence of the resurrection in light of Jesus' preaching about God's unconditional love, and acknowledge our *need* for that love, the assent of faith begins. The more grace works in our lives, the more we know that Jesus is "the way, and the truth, and the life" (Jn 14:6).

Chapter Five

Jesus' Miracles and Spirit

Introduction

We have discovered two significant clues thus far in our investigation of the evidence for Jesus as the unconditionally loving "God with us" (Emmanuel):

1. His unconditional love for everyone (and His preaching of His Father's unconditional love)
2. His Resurrection in a glorious spiritual body

These two clues give us a partial picture about how and why the apostolic Church was so certain that Jesus was not only a martyr, prophet, and the Messiah, but also the Lord and the Son of God. These enhanced claims cost the Church dearly because they were apologetically unappealing (repugnant to Jewish audiences and unintelligible to Gentile ones) and prompted the Jewish authorities to remove Christians from the synagogue, leading to a loss of religious community, social status, and financial status, and ultimately resulting in persecution.

There are three other significant clues that help us understand why the apostolic Church was certain that Jesus possessed divine power before His Resurrection, and even before His birth:

1. The exorcisms, healings, and raisings of the dead that Jesus did by His own authority (Section I)
2. Jesus' gift of the Holy Spirit, enabling His disciples to perform miracles in His name (Section II)
3. Jesus' claim to be the exclusive beloved Son of the Father and bringer of God's Kingdom (Chapter 6)

When all the clues are assembled in their complementary relationship, we will be able to understand better why the apostolic Church was so certain about Jesus' lordship and divinity that they sacrificed virtually everything to proclaim it. This chapter will first consider Jesus' unique ministry of miracles and then consider His gift of the Holy Spirit, enabling subsequent generations to perform those same miracles in His name.

I. Jesus' Miracles

For Jesus, miracles are not merely an indication of divine *power*, they are the initiation of God's Kingdom in the world. He performs miracles to vanquish evil and to bring the Kingdom so that we may be saved. In this respect, Jesus' ministry of exorcism, healing, and raising the dead is unique in the history of religions. In order to understand the significance of this unique ministry, we will consider four major areas of contemporary scholarship:

1. The Purpose and Distinctiveness of Jesus' Miracles (Section I.A)
2. A Brief Consideration of Historical Criteria (Section I.B)
3. The Historicity of Jesus' Exorcisms and Healings (Section I.C)
4. The Historicity of Jesus Raising the Dead (Section I.D)

Why be so concerned with the historicity of Jesus' miracles? As noted above, miracles ("deeds of power") are the initiation of God's Kingdom in the world, which entails vanquishing Satan and evil. This is clearly manifest in Jesus' response to His critics' accusations that "he casts out demons by Beelzebul, the prince of demons": "But if it is by the finger of God that I cast out demons, then the *kingdom of God* has come upon you" (Lk 11:15, 20; emphasis mine). The establishment of this Kingdom is not only the entryway, but the passageway to our salvation; and when our journey is complete, it is the fullness of eternal life with the unconditionally loving God. Inasmuch as Jesus' miracles initiate God's Kingdom in the world, they initiate the pathway to our salvation, and so their historicity is of immense importance.

Jesus differentiates Himself from all other Old Testament prophets by accomplishing His miracles through *His own* authority and power, meaning that He possesses this divine authority and power (see below, Section I.D.3). This possession of divine authority and power not only enables Him to initiate the Kingdom; it also validates His claim to be the exclusive beloved Son of the Father during the time of His ministry. This is precisely the question we are attempting to answer in this volume—making the historicity of the miracles integral to our quest to discover whether Jesus is Emmanuel.

Throughout the last century of New Testament scholarship, several objections have been raised against the historicity of Jesus' miracles.[1] Some of these objections are quite superficial, manifesting almost complete ignorance of the historical biblical scholarship throughout the last six decades (e.g., the objection that the miracles are just a bunch of stories that Jesus' friends and disciples invented). These objections fly in the face of ancient non-Christian testimony to Jesus' miracles, the Jewish polemic against His miracles ("he casts out demons by Beelzebul, the prince of demons"), and the basic application of historical criteria to the miracle narratives. The historical analysis given below will make this point abundantly clear.

Some objections focus on Jesus' raising of the dead, objecting that perhaps Jesus did some healings and exorcisms, but raising the dead sounds like an early Christian contrivance to prove Jesus' divinity during his ministry. John P. Meier has made a two-hundred-page rigorous investigation into the historicity of Jesus' raisings of the dead in the second volume of his series *A Marginal Jew.*[2] This evidence

---

[1] Extreme naturalistic positions ruling out the possibility of miracles (such as the one advanced by David Hume and appropriated by late nineteenth- and early twentieth-century liberal theologians) are unjustifiable, because natural laws are not inviolable in the sense that their violation implies logical impossibility. For example, a violation of $E = Mc^2$ is not logically impossible (an intrinsic contradiction); it is a logical possibility that we assume will not occur. Now, inasmuch as natural laws are not inviolable, and inasmuch as "miracle" is defined as a supernatural intervention in the natural order, and inasmuch as a supernatural power is neither governed nor conditioned by the natural order (and therefore the natural order cannot prevent a supernatural power from affecting it), then "miracle", as defined, is neither impossible in principle nor impossible in our natural order. Hence, any a priori denial of miracles must be a priori unjustified. Though first-century Jewish thought did not have a formal conception of miracles similar to the one given above, its view of miracles was commensurate with it. See N. T. Wright, *Jesus and the Victory of God* (Minneapolis: Fortress Press, 1996), 2:186, and Anthony Ernest Harvey, *Jesus and the Constraints of History: The Bampton Lectures, 1980* (London: Duckworth, 1982), pp. 101ff.

[2] John P. Meier, *A Marginal Jew: Rethinking the Historical Jesus*, vol. 2, *Mentor, Message, and Miracles* (New York: Doubleday, 1994), pp. 623–840.

is sufficiently strong to respond to the above objection (see below, Section I.D).

Other objections center on the conviction that ancient people were unable to identify a "real miracle" (violating a law of nature) because they were ignorant of both natural laws and natural science. This objection erroneously associates "recognition of miracle" with "understanding of natural science". As most historians recognize, the people of first-century Palestine were quite capable of recognizing the superordinary and supernatural when they saw instantaneous cures of leprosy, withered limbs, deafness, and lifetime blindness (see below, I.E).

In the forthcoming historical analysis, we will respond to these and other objections to the historicity of Jesus' miracles and, in so doing, show the strong likelihood that Jesus exorcised, healed, and raised the dead by His own authority and power, indicating not only that He had initiated God's Kingdom in the world, but that He had revealed Himself to be the exclusive beloved Son of the Father.

A. The Purpose and Distinctiveness of Jesus' Miracles

There is considerable evidence for the historicity of Jesus' miracles. They are mentioned in non-Christian polemical sources,[3] and by adversaries during His ministry (who did not challenge the fact that He worked miracles, but attributed them instead to the devil or sorcery[4]). N. T. Wright notes in this regard:

> We must be clear that Jesus' contemporaries, both those who became his followers and those who were determined not to become his

[3] As noted in Chapter 2 (Section II.A) there are three credible early non-Christian sources attesting to Jesus. Though Tacitus does not mention Jesus' miracles, Flavius Josephus and the Babylonian Talmud do. Most scholars agree that this external testimony is historically accurate and, in the case of the Babylonian Talmud, corresponds to the Jewish polemic against Jesus during His ministry that "he casts out demons by Beelzebul" (Lk 11:15). See Raymond Brown, *An Introduction to New Testament Christology* (New York: Paulist Press, 1994), pp. 62–63, 373–76; Luke Timothy Johnson, *The Gospel according to Luke*, Sacra Pagina Series, ed. Daniel J. Harrington, vol. 3 (Collegeville, Minn.: Liturgical Press, 1991), pp. 113–14; and Meier, *Marginal Jew*, pp. 592–93.

[4] As Brown notes: "[Jesus' enemies] attributed [His extraordinary deeds] to evil origins, either to the devil (Mark 3:22–30) or in 2d-century polemic to magic (Irenaeus, *Adversus Haereses* 2.32.3–5)." Brown, *Introduction to New Testament Christology*, pp. 62–63.

followers, certainly regarded him as possessed of remarkable powers. The church did not invent the charge that Jesus was in league
with Beelzebul; but charges like that are not advanced unless they
are needed as an explanation for some quite remarkable phenomena.[5]

The importance of this charge should not be underestimated,
because it cannot be imagined that Mark, or the other evangelists,
for that matter, would have dared to mention that Jesus was in league
with the devil or was doing miracles by the power of the devil unless
they believed it was absolutely necessary to respond to a charge that
was *really* being leveled against Jesus (see below, Section I.B, on the
criterion of embarrassment). It can hardly be thought that Jesus'
harshest critics would concede to His having supernatural power
unless there was wide contemporaneous acknowledgment that Jesus
was doing exorcisms and healings. Therefore, His "deeds of power"
are almost certainly historical.

Furthermore, miracles are an integral part of every stratum of the
New Testament. They are mentioned in the earliest *kerygmas* and
in the writings of Paul and John (1 Jn), and they are manifest in
every tradition constituting the Gospel narratives. Whatever one
might believe about the interpretation of miracles by the evangelists,
it seems unreasonable to suspect that Jesus did not perform a large
number of "extraordinary deeds of power" before multiple witnesses
in multiple places throughout the course of His ministry.

Jesus' gift of the Holy Spirit at Pentecost makes miracles almost
commonplace in the apostolic Church, so much so that they are
openly discussed in the writings by Paul as well as in Acts and the
Gospels without hesitation.[6] Though Jesus performed miracles by His
own power, His disciples did so through His name. The adversaries
of the Church do not dispute this fact and were therefore forced to
find other grounds to attack the apostles and the young Church.

Perhaps more interesting than the consistent documentation of
Jesus' miracles is the unique way in which they are presented. They
are *not* similar to the presentation of miracles in Hellenistic writings
or in the Old Testament and, as noted above, are not portrayed as
direct manifestations of Jesus' divine power but rather as the initiation
of the Kingdom of God and the vanquishing of Satan. Raymond

[5] Wright, *Jesus and the Victory of God*, p. 187.
[6] See below, Section II.

Brown describes five unique, consistent features in the presentation of Jesus' miracles in all four Gospels:[7]

1. Jesus does miracles by His own authority.
2. Jesus' miracles have the purpose not of showing His glory but of actualizing the coming of the Kingdom and the vanquishing of evil.
3. Jesus is not a wonder-worker or magician in either the pagan or Jewish sense.
4. Jesus combines teaching with His miracles.
5. The faith and freedom of the recipient is integral to the miraculous deed.

We will discuss each point in turn.

1. *Jesus does miracles by His own authority.* As will be seen below, Jesus exorcises, heals, and raises the dead by *His* own power and by *His* own word. The Old Testament prophets did not do anything like this, but believed themselves to be only *mediators* of *God's* power, and so they had to petition God to help them and work through them. Indeed, the greatest prophetic miracle workers of the Old Testament (Elijah and Elisha) would not have dared to make the claim that the power of God resided in *them.* As Brown notes:

> Granted that Jesus did perform acts of power, does that tell us more about him than that he was a prophet like Elijah or Elisha who were thought to have performed many of the same miracles? Yes, precisely because in the tradition Jesus connects them with the coming of the kingdom, a definitive eschatological context.... The lines of demarcation between Jesus and God ... are very vague. The kingdom comes both in and through Jesus. The power to do the healings and other miracles belongs to God *but also to Jesus.*[8]

2. *Jesus' miracles have the purpose not of showing His glory but of actualizing the coming of the Kingdom and the vanquishing of evil.* As noted above, Jesus' miracles actualized the Kingdom of God. They did so

---

[7]Brown, *Introduction to New Testament Christology*, pp. 60–70.
[8]Ibid., p. 65; emphasis in original.

by vanquishing the power of Satan in the world. This interpretation is not only integral to virtually every miracle story in the Gospels but also explicitly mentioned in the primitive Church's *kerygmas*: "God anointed Jesus of Nazareth with the Holy Spirit and with power; how he went about doing good and healing all that were oppressed by the devil, for God was with him" (Acts 10:38). As Brown notes, "Jesus is accomplishing something no one has ever done before since Adam's sin yielded to Satan's dominion over this world."[9] Inasmuch as Jesus is accomplishing something totally unique, the Gospel writers are totally unique in writing about it.

3. Jesus is not a wonder-worker or magician in either the pagan or Jewish sense. Rudolf Bultmann contended that Jesus' miracles were meant to show that Jesus was competitive with the so-called pagan miracle workers.[10] Brown responds to Bultmann by advancing two more probable contentions. First, though it is popularly believed that there were a large number of miracle workers at the time of Jesus, there is little evidence for this.[11] Second, among these few miracle workers, none resembles Jesus in either style or purpose. With respect to pagan miracle workers, Brown notes:

> The most popular pagan parallel offered for Jesus is Apollonius of Tyana (1st century A.D.) for whose activity we are largely dependent on a life written 200 years later by Philostratus, a life that some serious scholars regard as largely fictitious. The miracles attributed to that figure, some of which may be influenced by knowledge of the stories about Jesus, have the *purpose* of causing astonishment and bringing about adulation—quite unlike the Gospel presentation of Jesus' miracles.[12]

The Gospel writers not only avoid the portrayal of Jesus as a worker of "astonishing deeds"; Jesus Himself is portrayed as shunning such a purpose. Indeed, when Herod, the Pharisees, and the devil ask Jesus to work a miracle for no other purpose than to show off His power, He refuses to do so.

[9] Ibid., p. 66.
[10] See ibid., p. 64, n. 82.
[11] See ibid., p. 63.
[12] Ibid.; emphasis in original.

John P. Meier (in conjunction with David E. Aune) adds to this conclusion by noting that Jesus was not in any sense a magician (as conceived by His contemporary Jewish audience). He was not even accused of magic by His adversaries. The New Testament was aware of the notion of magic, designated by the term *magos* (Acts 13:6, 8), and the Jewish authorities were certainly aware of the charge of practicing magic, but as Meier notes, this term is never used to describe Jesus' activity by His disciples, the Jewish authorities, the early Church, Jesus' fiercest critics, or Jesus Himself.[13]

Some contemporary exegetes have suggested that the accusation of being in league with Beelzebul is similar to the charge of magic, but as Meier points out,

> that is a move made by modern scholars engaging in model-building at a high level of abstraction. It does not reflect the precise vocabulary and immediate reaction of Jesus' fellow Jews in his own day or in the decades immediately following his death.[14]

Furthermore, if Jesus were to have been accused of magic, it would have carried a very pejorative connotation within the Jewish culture of His time, and even after His death. However, the New Testament accounts militate against this interpretation by continuously noting that Jesus' miracles are greeted with amazement and praise by His Jewish audience (while magic would have been viewed quite negatively).[15]

Finally, Meier notes:

> An amoral or antinomian magician, unconnected with the eschatological fate and ethical concerns of Israel, is not the historical Jesus that emerges from the most reliable traditions of his words and deeds.[16]

As will be seen, the contrary is very much the case.

---

[13] Meier, *Marginal Jew*, p. 551. See also David E. Aune, "Magic in Early Christianity", in *Aufstieg und Niedergang der römischen*, ed. Wolfgang Haase (Berlin: Walter de Gruyter, 1980), II, 23.2, pp. 1523–24, nn. 67, 68, 69.

[14] Meier, *Marginal Jew*, p. 551.

[15] See ibid., p. 552.

[16] Ibid., p. 451.

4. *Jesus combines teaching with His miracles.* Unlike both the pagan and Jewish miracle workers of the time, Jesus integrated teaching into His miraculous deeds. He did not simply heal the sick (which is a good purpose in itself, and a vanquishing of Satan); He included lessons about faith, the forgiveness of sins, seeing through the eyes of faith, giving thanks, the Kingdom of God, salvation for the Gentiles, and even the Holy Eucharist. Jewish miracle workers, in contrast, were not portrayed this way. As Brown again notes:

> That combination [of miracle and teaching] may be unique. The two most frequently cited Jewish wonder-workers are Honi (Onias), the rain-maker (or circle-drawer) of the 1st century BC, and the Galilean Hanina of the 1st century AD. Almost all that is known of these men comes from much later rabbinic literature, and by that time legendary and theological developments had aggrandized the portrayal.... Almost certainly in the earliest tradition they were *not* rabbinical teachers.[17]

In contrast to the Jewish miracle workers, Jesus is not only a rabbinical teacher but also one who integrates His teaching with the deed of power. Thus, the first effect of Jesus' miracles is to vanquish Satan and simultaneously actualize the Kingdom of God; the second effect is *to teach* about faith, love, and the Kingdom of God. The last effect is to manifest His possession of divine power pointing to His divine authority and origin.

5. *The faith and freedom of the recipient is integral to the miraculous deed.* Unlike pagan and Jewish miracle workers of the time, Jesus used miracles to both teach about and call forth faith. The oft-repeated lines, "Your faith has saved you; go in peace" (see Lk 7:50), or, "Do you believe that I am able to do this?" (Mt 9:28) move the recipient of the miracle beyond a physical healing to faith and ultimately toward salvation. Notice that this call to faith involves the highest use of the recipient's freedom. Jesus wants the recipients in their freedom to enter into a *life* of salvation through the vehicle of His deed of power. The miracle workers of Jesus' time do not have this intention.

---

[17]Brown, *Introduction to New Testament Christology*, p. 63; emphasis mine.

These five unique aspects of Jesus' miracles reveal that the Gospel writers are not "competing" with other miracle workers or even trying to "show off" the astonishing power of Jesus. Rather, they were trying to convey Jesus' intentions in a remarkably restrained and humble way.

There is always a temptation when talking about a "deed of power" to emphasize power instead of the coming of the Kingdom, and the importance of the miracle worker instead of the importance of the recipient. The Gospel writers did not succumb to this temptation, but rather restricted themselves to certain sets of deeds that were well-known and attested, and presented them in subdued ways. They did not feel a need to multiply raisings of the dead, to add to or supplement the regular features of Jesus' miracles, or to exaggerate their narratives as did the later Gnostic writers.[18] This last point merits some discussion.

The New Testament miracles are almost free from frivolous elements, needless exaggerations, and punitive actions. In stark contrast to this, the Gnostic Gospels are full of them. With respect to frivolous miracles, for example, the Infancy Gospel of Thomas has the Child Jesus making clay sparrows fly to prove to His Father that He has the right to violate the Sabbath.[19] The Gnostic Gospel of Philip has Jesus going into the dye works of Levi and turning seventy-two different colors into white in order to show that "the Son of Man [has] come as a dyer."[20] We find in the Gospel of Peter (for which we have only

---

[18] The Gnostic Gospels are a set of apocryphal works attributed falsely to Jesus' disciples and friends. They were written several decades after the four canonical Gospels (Matthew, Mark, Luke, and John) during the second half of the second century to the fourth century. Their authors are not accepted authorities within the apostolic Church (as the four canonical Gospels), but rather spiritual writers who were heavily influenced by Gnostic philosophy, which attempts to achieve spiritual freedom through special knowledge or enlightenment. The so-called Christian Gnostics who wrote these texts departed from apostolic Christianity by advocating salvation not only through Jesus Christ, but through enlightenment proposed by its spiritual leaders. As can be seen from their miracle stories, their view of salvation and miracles was considerably different from that of Jesus, and in some cases, is ridiculous and fantastic.

[19] See Andrew Bernhard, trans., "The Infancy Gospel of Thomas", in *Other Early Christian Gospels: A Critical Edition of the Surviving Greek Manuscripts*, T&T Clark Library of Biblical Studies (London; New York: T&T Clark, 2006), Chapter 2, verses 1–7, http://gnosis.org /library/inftoma.htm.

[20] See Wesley W. Isenberg, trans., "The Gospel of Philip", in *The Nag Hammadi Library in English*, rev. ed., ed. James M. Robinson (San Francisco: HarperCollins, 1990), http://www .gnosis.org/naghamm/gop.html.

fragmentary evidence) a gratuitous elaboration of Matthew's reference to "darkness over all the land" (Mt 27:45); the sun had already set at the noon hour, causing people to stumble and take out lamps in order to see.[21]

With respect to punitive miracles, the Gnostic Gospels portray Jesus as punishing His critics. For example, in the Infancy Gospel of Thomas the Child Jesus curses a child to death who disperses water He has just collected, saying:

> You godless, brainless moron, what did the ponds and waters do to you? Watch this now: you are going to dry up like a tree and you will never produce leaves or roots or fruit.[22]

In another instance, He curses a child to death for accidentally bumping into Him, and strikes His neighbors blind when they complain.[23]

The four canonical Gospels (Matthew, Mark, Luke, and John) stand in stark contrast to this tendency. Aside from the discussion surrounding Matthew 17:24–27 (the coin in the fish's mouth) and Mark 11:12–14, 20–21 (Jesus cursing the fig tree), there is a virtual absence of frivolous and punitive miracles in the four canonical Gospels. Given the apologetical appeal and fascination intrinsic to wonder-working and blatant (but useless) displays of power, the almost total absence of such exaggerations in the four canonical Gospels is striking.

When we think of how the evangelists could have been tempted to put the emphasis on the deed of power (instead of the deed of compassion) in order to make Jesus look more powerful, glorious, and successful, and when one thinks about the temptation to appeal to the baser nature of an audience of potential converts, it seems remarkable that the evangelists resisted that temptation in almost every form and in every miracle story. Their light shines on the need of the petitioner and Jesus' compassionate response, the gentleness of the healing, and the admonition to tell no one. This approach is quite unique among miracle stories in the ancient world, and seems to put the need and

---

[21] See M. R. James, trans., "The Gospel of Peter", in *The Apocryphal New Testament* (Oxford: Clarendon Press, 1924), fragment I, V, 15–19, http://www.gnosis.org/library/gospete.htm.

[22] Bernhard, "Infancy Gospel of Thomas", Chapter 3, verse 2.

[23] See ibid., Chapters 4 and 5.

faith of the petitioner on the same plane as Jesus' power to vanquish evil and bring the Kingdom.

The four evangelists assiduously avoid aggrandizement, frivolousness, retribution, and virtually anything that does not fulfill a need of a suffering or grieving person. This editorial restraint points to the thought and care used to respect the words and actions of their Lord—an implicit indication of their historical accuracy.

B. A Brief Consideration of Historical Criteria

Before proceeding to an examination of the historicity of Jesus' miracles, we should briefly show how historical scholars assess historicity. We have already used some of these historical criteria in our earlier assessment of the historicity of Jesus' miracles:

1. The presence of Jesus' miracles in all independent sources of the Gospels, exemplifying the criterion of multiple attestation
2. The Jewish polemic against Jesus' miracles ("he casts out demons by Beelzebul" [Lk 11:15]), exemplifying the criterion of embarrassment
3. The uniqueness of Jesus' miracles, exemplifying the criterion of coherence with the unique style of Jesus

We also noticed the considerable editorial restraint on the part of the Gospel writers, which differentiates them from those of the apocryphal Gnostic Gospels.

We will now formally consider these three historical criteria along with three others used by contemporary exegetes to assess the historicity of the miracle narratives:

1. The presence of Semitisms
2. The presence of identifiable names and places that can be checked by readers and hearers within living memory of Jesus
3. Coherence with Palestinian customs during the time of Jesus

A brief description of each criterion will be helpful in examining the historicity of Jesus' exorcisms, healings, and raisings of the dead.

The Criterion of Multiple Attestation. Multiple attestation refers to the principle that the more often a story or saying appears in *independent* traditions, the more probable its historicity. Note that the converse statement cannot be deduced from the former ("the less often a story or saying appears in independent traditions, the less probable its historicity"). This is the logical fallacy of negating the antecedent.[24] Appearance in a multiplicity of independent traditions strongly suggests that those traditions go back to a common source, which would presumably be either the early Palestinian community or Jesus Himself. However, an absence of multiple attestation does not *necessitate* nonhistoricity, because sometimes the author(s) of particular traditions may not have heard about a particular story or saying or may have chosen to ignore it (for theological or apologetical reasons).

Prior to the extensive use of literary, form, and redaction criticism, it was commonly thought that each Gospel represented a separate tradition, and therefore multiple attestation consisted merely in repetition in the four Gospels. However, since the time of literary criticism (leading to form and redaction criticism), this simplistic view could no longer be sustained. These methods showed that Mark was very likely the first Gospel, and that Matthew and Luke relied very heavily upon it. Furthermore, it was also shown that Matthew and Luke shared a common source (which Mark did not use or know)—namely, Q (referring to *Quelle*, meaning "source" in German). Q is an early collection of Jesus' sayings translated into Greek.[25] Luke and Matthew had their own special sources that are not found in either Mark or Q. We know that these sources are not mere inventions of the evangelists because many of them have the characteristics of an oral tradition developed prior to *any* literary tradition, and many of them do not follow the literary proclivities of the evangelists (e.g., some of Luke's sources write in a far less sophisticated and stylized way than Luke himself, and the fact that Luke does not correct them

---

[24]Since the time of Aristotle, it has been widely known that negating the antecedent is fallacious. It takes the following form: "If A, then B. Not A. Therefore, not B." This applies to the following syllogism: "If multiple attestation, then historically probable. Not multiple attestation. Therefore, not historically probable." This conclusion is fallacious, because it negates the antecedent.

[25]Most scholars believe that Q is a single written source, though some hold that it is a plurality of sources. We do not know who the editor or editors were.

indicates that he is being respectful of his sources). The Johannine source has long been recognized to be independent of the Synoptics (Matthew, Mark, and Luke). Thus, contemporary biblical criticism has been able to identify five *independent* traditions for the four Gospels—namely, Mark, Q, M (Matthew special), L (Luke special), and J (the independent Johannine tradition). We may now retranslate our principle to read, "The more often a story appears in the five *independent* Gospel traditions, the more probable its historicity." Thus, if a story appears in all five traditions, it is very probable that it originated with a very early common Palestinian oral tradition or Jesus' ministry itself. If it appears in three or four independent traditions, it is still quite probable. Recall that if a story appears in only one or two traditions, it does *not* indicate nonhistoricity.[26]

The Criterion of Embarrassment. This refers to actions or sayings that the early Church would have found embarrassing, apologetically unappealing, disrespectful to Jesus, or disrespectful to the apostles. Evidently, no evangelist would want to include such statements in the Gospels (which are written to instruct and edify the community and potential converts), because they undermine the Gospels' purpose. Therefore, we assume that they are included in the Gospel only because they are true. For example, in the previous chapter (with respect to the empty tomb), Matthew reports the accusation of the religious authorities that the disciples of Jesus stole His body. Why would Matthew have reported such an accusation, with all of its severely negative implications, unless it were true? Again, as we saw above, the Gospels report that the Pharisees accused Jesus of casting out demons through the power of Beelzebul. Why would they do this unless the charge had really been leveled against Jesus, was known by many in the general public, and required a response?

Coherence with the Environment of Palestine at the Time of Jesus. Béda Rigaux in 1958[27] recognized that the evangelists' accounts conform almost perfectly with the Palestinian and Jewish milieu of the period

---

[26] See Harvey K. McArthur, "Basic Issues: A Survey of Recent Gospel Research", in *In Search of the Historical Jesus*, ed. H.K. McArthur (London: Charles Scribner's Sons, 1969), pp. 139–40.

[27] Béda Rigaux, "L'historicité de Jésus devant l'exégese récente", *Revue Biblique* 68 (1958): 481–522.

of Jesus, as confirmed by history, archeology, and literature. René Latourelle summarizes several of Rigaux's examples as follows:

> The evangelical description of the human environment (work, habitation, professions), of the linguistic and cultural environment (patterns of thought, Aramaic substratum), of the social, economic, political and juridical environment, of the religious environment especially (with its rivalries between Pharisees and Sadducees, its religious preoccupations concerning the clean and the unclean, the law and the Sabbath, demons and angels, the poor and the rich, the Kingdom of God and the end of time), the evangelical description of all this is remarkably *faithful* to the complex picture of Palestine at the time of Jesus.[28]

The environment of the early Church, with its post-Resurrection faith and extensive ministry to the Gentiles, became progressively detached from the ethos of Palestine at the time of Jesus, and by the writing of the Gospels, much of this ethos was obscure to many Christians. Remarkably, the Gospel narratives preserve not only the customs and actions of Palestinian Judaism, but also expressions (such as "Son of David"[29] or "Rabbi"[30] or "He is a prophet"[31]) that would have been superseded by other more suitable titles or expressions in the post-Resurrection Church. This speaks to the historicity not only of the Gospels in general, but of the specific narratives within the Gospels where these anachronisms occur.

Coherence with the Unique Style of Jesus. Some expressions, attitudes, and actions of Jesus depart significantly from those of the milieu in which He lived, and constitute a style that is distinctive or unique to Him. For example, the way in which Jesus worked miracles is completely different from that of Jewish or Hellenistic miracle workers (see above, Section I.A). This unique style of miracle working is present in all five independent sources, which leads to the following

---

[28] René Latourelle, *Finding Jesus through the Gospels: History and Hermeneutics* (New York: Alba House, 1979), p. 227; emphasis mine.

[29] "Son of David": see, for example, Matthew 1:1; 1:20; 9:27; 12:3; 12:23; 15:22; 20:30; 20:31; 21:9; 21:15; 22:42; Mark 10:47; 12:35; Luke 3:31; 18:38; 18:39; 20:41.

[30] "Rabbi": see, for example, Matthew 25:25; 26:49; Mark 9:5; 10:51; 11:21; 14:45; John 1:38; 1:49; 3:2; 3:26; 4:31; 6:25; 9:2; 11:8.

[31] "He is a prophet": see, for example, Matthew 14:5; 16:14; 21:11; 21:46; Mark 6:4; 6:15; 8:28; Luke 13:33; 24:19; John 4:19; 4:44; 6:14; 7:40; 7:52; 9:17.

question: If the evangelists did not derive this *unique* style from the teachings, expressions, and actions of an original common tradition about *Jesus*, how could it occur so consistently in every independent tradition? This leads to the inference of a common source for this common tradition, the most probable of which is Jesus Himself.

Criteria of Semitisms. The New Testament Gospels were written in Greek; however, the oral and written traditions underlying their many narratives were formulated in Aramaic. If these traditions can be identified from the Greek text, it shows a probable origin within a Palestinian community near the time of Jesus. Aramaic does not translate perfectly into Greek, so when linguists identify strange or awkward Greek expressions, they look for possible underlying Aramaic traditions. Much of the time, a *strange Greek* expression reveals a very *common Aramaic* expression of Palestinian origin.

Additionally, there are Palestinian expressions that are virtually unknown to Gentile audiences, and so their occurrence in, say, a Gospel written by a Gentile for Gentile audiences (e.g., Luke) shows an earlier Palestinian origin.

Specific Identifiable Names and Places. Many Gospel narratives, including miracle narratives, follow what is termed "a standard form". These forms are general and tend to avoid specific details about people, places, and times. When these details (going beyond the standard form) are present in a narrative, they are probably retained from an earlier tradition, because details are frequently lost during a tradition's transmission, and so their inclusion indicates a retention of them (from a previous source) instead of a subsequent addition of them. Moreover, many of these details can be checked by individuals within living memory of Jesus, because the people mentioned are known within the community. Furthermore, a spectacular event such as raising the dead or curing blindness or a paralytic would certainly be known and remembered by people in a particular small town or village. This too can be verified within living memory of Jesus.

C. The Historicity of Jesus' Exorcisms and Healings

Exorcisms and healings may be viewed as two extremes on a single continuum. For Jesus, healing was a form of dispelling evil (even though a demon is not driven out). Likewise, exorcisms are a form of healing, because when demons leave, people regain their sanity, capacity for speech, relief from convulsions, etc. Both actions result in the Kingdom of God being actualized in the world. The key distinction between exorcisms and healings is the explicit presence of a possessing demon in the former and the presence of God's redemptive love in the latter. Thus, exorcisms accentuate the vanquishing of evil, while healings accentuate the presence of God's redeeming love, both of which actualize God's Kingdom in the world.

For Jesus, the Kingdom of God is both present and future. He follows Jewish eschatology in announcing the future Kingdom, the Kingdom in its fullness and completion. However, He departs from Jewish eschatology by announcing the arrival of the Kingdom "here and now" in His Person. He saw Himself as bringing not only an entryway into the future Kingdom of Heaven, but a passageway that connected the present Kingdom to the future Kingdom (see Chapter 6, Section II). His exorcisms, healings, and raising the dead are part of the establishment of that Kingdom, but these actions alone do not fully establish it; they anticipate Jesus' Eucharist, Passion, death, Resurrection, and gift of the Spirit, which complete Jesus' mission to build the "conduit" between earth and Heaven. Since exorcisms, healings, and raising the dead represent the initial actualization of the Kingdom, we will want to be sure of their historicity, and so we will discuss each in turn.

Below in this section and in Section I.D, I rely closely on John P. Meier's thorough historical study of Jesus' miracles in *A Marginal Jew: Rethinking the Historical Jesus*, volume two, *Mentor, Message, and Miracles*.[32] Since Meier's work is the most comprehensive exegetical analysis of the miracle narratives currently available, I have summarized some of its high points to show readers how extensive and probative the historical evidence is for Jesus' miracles and the individual accounts of them.

1. The Exorcisms

According to Meier, there are seven nonoverlapping accounts of exorcisms in the Synoptic Gospels (John recounts no exorcisms, but this is his theological proclivity):

[32] Meier, *Marginal Jew*, pp. 650–870.

1. The possessed boy (Mk 9:14–29)
2. A passing reference to the exorcism of Mary Magdalene (Lk 8:2)
3. The Gerasene demoniac (Mk 5:1–20)
4. The demoniac in the Capernaum synagogue (Mk 1:23–28)
5. The mute and blind demoniac in the Q tradition (Mt 12:24; Lk 11:14–15)
6. The mute demoniac (Mt 9:32–33)
7. The Syrophoenician woman (Mk 7:24–30; Mt 15:21–28)

Meier concludes as follows about the historicity of Jesus' exorcisms: "That there should be seven individual 'specimens' of a very specific type of miracle, namely, exorcism, supports the view that exorcisms loomed large in Jesus' ministry."[33]

These seven distinct instances are complemented by many *sayings* (about exorcisms) as well as references to exorcisms within *summary texts*.

There is multiple attestation of sources, though Mark is responsible for most of the extended exorcism narratives (which are used by Matthew and Luke).

- L (special Luke) gives a passing reference to the exorcism of Mary Magdalene: "some women who had been healed of evil spirits and infirmities: Mary, called Magdalene, from whom seven demons had gone out" (Lk 8:2).
- Q has one narrative: the mute and blind demoniac (Mt 12:22–24; Lk 11:14–15).
- M (special Matthew) recounts one narrative: Jesus exorcises a mute demoniac (Mt 9:32–33).

When we combine the Marcan narratives and the Q *sayings* with the above three other sources, we see a strong confluence of attestation, which Meier summarizes as follows: "Q sayings join Marcan sayings and Marcan narratives in providing multiple attestation for the existence of exorcisms in the ministry of the historical Jesus."[34]

In addition to multiple attestation, the criterion of embarrassment (narratives or sayings that undermine the reputation of Jesus or His

[33] Ibid., p. 648.
[34] Ibid.

teaching) also plays a significant role for ascertaining the historicity of exorcisms. We have already mentioned the Pharisees' accusation of Jesus' association with the devil ("he casts out demons by Beelzebul, the prince of demons" [Lk 11:15]), which reveals His adversaries' belief in His power to exorcise evil spirits.

The criterion of coherence (continuity with the unique style of Jesus) also comes into play because exorcisms are integral to the proclamation of the Kingdom. Inasmuch as the Kingdom is central to Jesus' *unique* mission, and exorcisms are integral to the actualization of the Kingdom, exorcisms are likely to be as historical as Jesus' proclamation of the Kingdom.

Moreover, Jesus does not cast out demons by invoking the name of God or by asking God to work *through* Him. Recall that Jesus distinguishes Himself from other Jewish miracle workers by acting through His command and word alone. See, for example, the following:

- "You mute and deaf spirit," He said, "*I command* you, come out of him, and never enter him again" (Mk 9:25; emphasis mine).
- The demons *begged Jesus*, "Send us to the swine, let us enter them" (Mk 5:12–13). *He gave* them permission.
- "Be silent, and come out of him!" *said Jesus sternly*. The impure spirit shook the man violently and "came out of him" with a shriek (Mk 1:25–26).

In conclusion, there is more than ample evidence to support a belief in the historicity of Jesus' exorcisms. Indeed, the evidence suggests that they played a frequent and prominent role in His ministry, particularly in the region of Galilee.

2. The Healings

The evidence for Jesus' healing miracles is even stronger than the evidence for His exorcisms, and this is reflected in the fact that the early Church remembered Jesus more as a healer than as an exorcist.[35] As noted above, Jesus' healings have a connection to His exorcisms, because they were thought to be an overcoming of evil. Recall that physical infirmity was associated with evil or sin

[35] See ibid., p. 679.

in the Judaism of Jesus' time. However, healings do not have an element of direct struggle with spirits or Satan. Instead, they focus on the *need* of particular persons and the *plea* of those persons or a concerned petitioner. Jesus sees faith (trust in His desire and power to heal) in these cries for help and is moved by compassion to heal the sick person.

As with exorcisms, Jesus accomplishes healings by His own authority and power (without making recourse to God or prayer), and in so doing initiates the Kingdom and reveals His possession of divine authority and power. Inasmuch as Jesus was aware of possessing divine authority and power, and aware that *possession* of this power was categorically different from *all* the Old Testament prophets, He must have also been aware of His divine status (signified by calling Himself "Son") that made His possession of divine power possible (see below, Section I.D.3 and Chapter 6, Section III).

What can be said about the historicity of healings? First, with respect to multiple attestation, there is a large number of healing miracles in four out of five independent sources: Mark, Q, special Luke, and John. Special Matthew alone lacks an independent healing narrative. There are fifteen distinct (nonoverlapping) accounts of healing miracles in the Gospels, plus the general Q list in Matthew 11:2–6 and Luke 7:18–23. This totals sixteen nonoverlapping references to healing miracles in the Gospels. The breakdown is as follows:

- Mark relates *eight* miracle accounts: two concerned with cures of paralytics (2:1–12 and 3:1–6), two concerned with cures of blindness (10:46–52 and 8:22–26), one concerned with the cure of leprosy (1:40–45), and three concerned with various diseases mentioned only once (fever of Peter's mother-in-law in 1:29–31, the woman with a hemorrhage in 5:24–34, and the deaf-mute in 7:31–37).[36]
- Q relates only *one* account of a healing miracle, which is the cure of a centurion's servant (at a distance). Matthew calls this a cure of a paralytic, but Luke calls it a cure of someone with a grave illness. Curiously, John agrees with Luke instead of Matthew, meaning

---

[36] This reflects Meier's list given in ibid., p. 678.

that Matthew has probably changed the Q source (instead of Luke). The presence of this miracle in both Q and John indicates multiple attestation of sources for a single healing account. Q also has a list of miracles (Mt 11:2–6; Lk 7:18–23) that include healing of the blind, the lame, lepers, and the deaf.

- L (special Luke) relates *four* healings: one paralytic (13:10–17), one concerned with leprosy (17:11–19), and two cures of various ailments mentioned only once (the man with dropsy in 14:1–6 and the ear of the slave of the high priest in 22:49–51).
- John relates *two* healings: one concerned with the cure of a paralytic (5:1–9) and one concerned with the man born blind (9:1–41).[37]

Evidently, healings enjoy wide multiple attestation. Furthermore, healings of paralytics, the blind, and lepers also enjoy independent multiple attestation.

Healings are mentioned in a variety of other contexts outside of narratives. For example,

- allusions to miracles that are not narrated in full (e.g., Mk 6:56: "And wherever he came, in villages, cities, or country, they laid the sick in the market places, and begged him that they might touch even the fringe of his garment; and as many as touched it were made well");
- in sayings implying his fulfillment of prophetic expectation (Lk 4:17–18: "He opened the book and found the place where it was written, 'The Spirit of the Lord is upon me, because he has anointed me ... to proclaim recovering of sight to the blind'");
- the disciples performing or failing to perform miracles (Lk 9:6; 10:17–20; Mk 3:15; 9:18, 28, 38);
- various sayings in which Jesus refers to His miracles;
- the scribes' accusations that He performed miracles by the power of Beelzebul;
- giving the power to heal to the disciples (Mt 10:1; Mk 6:7; Lk 9:1); and
- several summary statements.

[37] See ibid.

When these are combined with the disciples' power to heal through the Holy Spirit *in the name of Jesus* (after the Resurrection), it becomes evident that healings were a common and central part of Jesus' ministry.

This strong conclusion is corroborated further by applying additional historical criteria (see above, I.B) to seven *particular* miracle stories:

- The cure of the centurion's servant (Mt 8:5–13; Lk 7:1–10); the cure of the royal official's son (Jn 4:46–54)
- The blind Bartimaeus (Mk 10:46–52)
- The paralyzed man let down through the roof (Mk 2:1–12)
- The paralyzed man by the pool of Bethesda (Jn 5:1–9)
- The blind man of Bethsaida (Mk 8:22–26)
- The man born blind (Jn 9:1–41)
- A cure of a deaf-mute (Mk 7:31–37)

In order to use additional historical criteria, we must first identify the typical form of a healing story so that we will be able to recognize departures from that form and details added to it. The standard form is as follows:

1. A sick or infirm person (or a concerned friend or relative) approaches Jesus and begs for a cure (sometimes Jesus notices the sick person and is moved to heal without being asked).
2. There is an indication of the faith of the petitioner (generally in the way they ask for a cure).
3. Jesus is moved by the person's need or faith.
4. He heals by touching or by His command alone.
5. The immediate cure is noted and confirmed.
6. The crowd is amazed and spreads word about Him.

We are now ready to apply historical criteria to the above seven healing stories, summarizing Meier's extensive analysis of these narratives.[38]

The cure of the centurion's servant (Mt 8:5–13; Lk 7:1–10) and the official's son (Jn 4:46–54). There is here multiple attestation of a single

[38] See ibid., pp. 680–700.

miracle story (Q and John). Despite the fact that Q (represented by Luke) speaks of a *centurion's* servant (which Matthew changes to "son"), while John speaks of an *official's* son, the similarities among the stories are too great to be explained by any means other than a common primitive tradition. Meier ridicules the alternative explanation of John redacting Q by noting:

> We would have to imagine the Fourth Evangelist spreading out copies of Mark, Matthew, and Luke in front of him on his desk and proceeding to pick out a verse here and a verse there from each of the Synoptics, at times without any discernible reason or pattern.[39]

Though Q and John received different oral traditions, those traditions undoubtedly refer back to a common earlier tradition that was probably grounded in a single historical incident. This is corroborated by a considerable number of underlying Semitisms detected by Uwe Wegner,[40] and the placement of the incident (in both Q and John) at Capernaum. Furthermore, the miracle has a very unusual characteristic: Jesus cures the sick boy *at a distance*. The convergence of this evidence makes a primitive tradition linked to a source incident quite probable.

The blind Bartimaeus (Mk 10:46–52). This story presents one of the most unique convergences of historical data in the Gospels. It is full of Semitisms: two Aramaic words (*Bar Tim'ai* and *Rabbouni*) and a very ancient reference to Jesus: "Son of David" (Mk 10:47–48), a Jewish rather than a Christian title for Jesus. This title would certainly have had no place in the earliest Church community, and undoubtedly dates back to Jesus' ministry where very probably Bartimaeus uses it to refer to the one whom he thinks is merely a miracle worker in the image of "Solomon the miracle-worker".[41] It is most unlikely that a Christian interpreter would have invented these details and outmoded expressions as a way of reflecting on the risen Christ.

The story is also filled with details that fall outside the standard form and have no apparent apologetical or catechetical purpose. As Meier notes, it possesses

[39] Ibid., p. 724.
[40] See ibid., p. 725.
[41] See ibid., p. 690.

the naming of the direct recipient of a miracle performed by Jesus; the tying of this named individual to a precise place (the road outside Jericho leading up to Jerusalem), to a precise time of year (shortly before Passover), and to a precise period of Jesus' ministry (his final journey up to Jerusalem along with other Passover pilgrims).[42]

These details indicate a report from an eyewitness, for how else could they have come to light? This might suggest that the conveyors of the tradition had some acquaintance with the eyewitness himself. Could the eyewitness have been Bartimaeus? Meier notes:

> If Bartimaeus was a resident of Jericho, and especially if he did actually follow Jesus up to Jerusalem, it is hardly surprising that the earliest Christian communities in Jerusalem and Judea would have preserved this story from one of their earliest members and most notable witnesses.[43]

The combination of historical indicators gives us a veritable treasure chest of evidence of historicity: (1) an independent verification of Jesus' healing power, (2) His well-known reputation as a healer in the district of Jericho and Jerusalem (beyond His home district of Galilee) that causes Bartimaeus to recognize Him as a healer and cry out for His help, and (3) a possible link between the eyewitness source of this story and the recipient of the miracle, Bartimaeus himself.

The paralyzed man let down through the roof (Mk 2:1–12). This narrative is very lengthy and indicates several decades of development in its oral tradition. This implies that the core story is quite ancient and may go back to the time of Jesus. There are also several details in the story falling outside the standard form that have no apologetical, catechetical, or instructional purpose. These details also indicate the reminiscence of an eyewitness (e.g., four individuals going up to a roof, digging out a hole in the roof, and lowering the man down to the amazement of Jesus). This story also manifests coherence with the unique style of Jesus; Jesus heals the man by His own authority and power and uses the occasion to forgive his sins.

The paralyzed man by the pool (Jn 5:1–9). Though the final form of this story was completed several decades after the actual incident, it

[42] Ibid.
[43] Ibid.

appears to be faithful to its historical circumstances. Recent archeological findings concerning the portico and the pool reveal that the description in the story is accurate to great precision.[44] Such accurate geographical detail does not have apologetical, catechetical, or instructional relevance and indicates the presence of a witness. Moreover, there are a considerable number of details falling outside the standard form that have no apologetical, catechetical, or instructional purpose (and would seem to require an eyewitness), such as the paralyzed man's ambivalence about being healed, his lack of gratitude, and his reporting of Jesus to the authorities.[45] Finally, as Meier notes, the evangelist has to "tack on" the themes of Sabbath and sin, because they are absent from the core of the story, indicating that that core was more primitive and had to be woven into the Gospel.[46]

The blind man of Bethsaida (Mk 8:22–26). There are a considerable number of unusual facts in this story that fall outside the standard form and have no apparent apologetical, catechetical, or instructional purpose. Moreover, they do not further Mark's redactional agenda, and they have no christological significance—Jesus spits directly into a blind man's eye; seems to have only partial success in curing the blindness (which is quite distinct from any other miracle He worked except the cure of a deaf-mute in Mark 7:31–37); has to ask the blind man what he can see; and finally achieves success on a second try.

The criterion of embarrassment applies to these highly unusual facts because Jesus' partial success and His technique's similarity to that of a Hellenistic wonder-worker (i.e., spitting in the man's eye) would have been difficult to explain from both an apologetical and catechetical perspective. These difficulties provoked Matthew and Luke to omit the narrative completely. Inasmuch as Mark would not have invented such a story, we can infer a primitive underlying tradition that Mark left unaltered. Given that this story would not have been invented by either Mark or the formulators of its oral tradition, it probably reflects a real (though unusual) way in which Jesus performed miracles in His Galilean ministry.

The man born blind (Jn 9:1–41). This story mentions specific identifiable places. For example, Siloam is mentioned, which was

---

[44] See ibid., p. 681.
[45] See ibid.
[46] See ibid.

destroyed by the Romans in A.D. 70. In light of the story's geographical accuracy, it suggests a time of writing prior to A.D. 70 (before the writing of John's Gospel). Additionally, Jesus makes a paste out of His saliva mixed with mud. This is the only miracle story that recounts such a paste (although two Marcan miracles do attest to Jesus' use of saliva). Furthermore, the miracle does not occur instantly, but only after the blind man obeys Jesus' request to wash in the pool of Siloam. These unusual features do not seem to serve an apologetical purpose or an obvious catechetical purpose. For these and other reasons, Meier believes that the historicity of the core story can be reasonably affirmed.[47]

The healing of the deaf-mute (Mk 7:31–37). This story contains evidence of historicity in three areas. There are several elements falling outside the standard form (and which may be considered unique among all healing stories in the Gospels): Jesus puts His fingers into the man's ears, puts His saliva on the man's tongue, looks up to Heaven, and groans inwardly. These elements do not have apologetical, catechetical, or instructional purpose, and therefore are not likely to be either additions to the oral tradition or Marcan redactions. This is confirmed by the fact that one of the special features (saliva on the tongue) could be interpreted as magic, which is an embarrassment to the early Church. Matthew and Luke deliberately leave it out of their Gospels for this reason. Finally, there is an obvious Semitism: the Aramaic word for "be opened" (*ephphatha*). Notice that it is accompanied by the Greek translation instead of being replaced by it. The combination of these factors supports the very likely historicity of the core story, particularly the way in which Jesus carries out His cure.

In conclusion, there is ample evidence to support reasonable belief in the historicity of Jesus' healing miracles. Multiple attestation abounds—not only for healings in general, but even for the particular story of the centurion's son. Furthermore, the criterion of embarrassment applies to several stories; Semitisms, place names, personal names, and unusual details are prevalent in most of these stories; and there is even the possibility of seeing a link between the recipient of a miracle and its transmission to the Jerusalem Church (Bartimaeus).

[47] See ibid., pp. 697–98.

There are very few facts of ancient history that are better attested than the healing miracles of Jesus.

Recall that the purpose of healings in Jesus' ministry was to initiate the Kingdom of God in the world (and in so doing to vanquish Satan and evil). He performs these acts in a unique way—not to demonstrate his supernatural power, but rather to respond in compassion to the needs of petitioners.[48] He works miracles through the faith (trust) of the petitioner, and links them to a spiritual teaching that is relevant for both the petitioner and bystanders. He performs healing miracles by His own command (by his own authority and power), and does not pray to God for the power to perform them. Each miracle puts an end to evil and brings the Kingdom ever more deeply into the world. These same unique characteristics are even more manifest in Jesus' raising of the dead.

D. The Historicity of Jesus Raising the Dead

Unlike healing miracles (of which there are fifteen full nonoverlapping stories and dozens of other references in lists, summary statements, etc.), there are only three nonoverlapping stories about raising the dead, and fewer nonnarrative references than the healing miracles. However, these three stories all come from *different* traditions that can be traced to their very probable early Palestinian origins.

The three traditions of "raising the dead" are the Marcan tradition (the raising of Jairus' daughter [Mk 5:21–43]), the special Luke tradition (the raising of the son of the widow of Nain [Lk 7:11–17]), and the Johannine tradition (the raising of Lazarus [Jn 11:1–44]). To these three narratives we should add a saying from a list in Q: "The blind receive their sight and the lame walk, lepers are cleansed and the deaf hear, and *the dead are raised up*, and the poor have good news preached to them" (Mt 11:5; emphasis mine). Thus, raising the dead

---

[48] The blind beggar Bartimaeus cries out "mercy" (*Eleos* [Mk 10:47–48]), which is a near-perfect explanation of Jesus' interior disposition in His ministry of healing. In His radical openness to the petitioner, Jesus manifests not only His saving heart for that petitioner, but His saving will for the world. The same word is used to describe the compassion of the Good Samaritan (Lk 10:37), who exemplifies Jesus' state of mind when He sees the sick, poor, and sinners.

is mentioned in four out of five nonoverlapping traditions. Special Matthew is the only source that does not specifically make mention of it. Though raising the dead is infrequent, it enjoys almost complete multiple attestation.

Curiously, despite the spectacular character of the "raisings", none of the Gospel writers felt a need to multiply them. Mark, Matthew, and John limit themselves to one, and Luke limits himself to two. The fact that the evangelists do not multiply these stories indicates a mature editorial restraint and respect for the truth.

The three stories about *raising* the dead must be distinguished from Jesus' *Resurrection*. All three stories about raising the dead are really a restoration of a person to his former *corporeal* existence. However, Jesus' Resurrection is not a restoration to former corporeal existence, but rather is a transformation of former embodiment to a spiritual and divinelike (glorious) form (see Chapter 4). Moreover, raising the dead is not permanent, but spiritual resurrection is eternal. Despite the important differences between a temporary raising of the body and an eternal spiritual resurrection, we should not diminish the importance of Jesus raising the dead. These miracles indicate that Jesus has within Himself power over life and death (a power reserved to Yahweh), which strongly testifies to the coming of God's Kingdom through Jesus. We may now examine each distinct tradition of Jesus raising the dead.

1. The Raising of Jairus' Daughter (Mk 5:21–43)

There is good reason to believe that the original story of the raising of Jairus' daughter (Mk 5:21–43) was written in Aramaic, but that story cannot be reconstructed today. Nevertheless, we can uncover a primitive tradition even if we cannot know its original Aramaic words. Meier believes that this primitive tradition follows the three-part standard form of a story about raising the dead with multiple additions to the first part:[49]

> 1. Jairus, a synagogue leader, petitions Jesus to come and heal his sick daughter. Jesus agrees to come with him, but on the way

[49] See Meier, *Marginal Jew*, pp. 780–81.

there, news comes that the daughter has died. And yet, Jesus persuades him to continue on. Thus, a story of healing becomes a story of raising the dead.

2. The miracle proper—Jesus touches the little girl and utters the Aramaic expression, "Talitha koum"—"Little girl, get up" (Mk 5:41), which causes the little girl to get up and walk around.

3. The reaction of the bystanders is great astonishment.

The first part takes on new material going beyond the standard form. Jesus hears the weeping and lamenting and asks the crowd why they are weeping and says, "The child is not dead but sleeping" (Mk 5:39). This leads to ridicule and scorn, which in turn provokes Jesus to literally throw the mourners out.

In the second part, there are *two* confirmations of the miracle: the little girl gets up *and* Jesus asks that she be given something to eat. Though somewhat unusual, Meier believes that this probably belongs to the original tradition because it may have been a way of staving off the thought that the girl might be a spirit.[50]

Meier and others believe that there is a strong basis for the historicity of this narrative for six reasons:

1. As noted above, personal names are quite unusual in the New Testament. Jairus and Bartimaeus are the only named petitioners for miracles; and Bartimaeus seems to have had continued influence in the Church. The presence of the name throughout the lengthy development of the oral tradition situates it and makes it "checkable". The fact that Jairus is named as a synagogue official, giving him a position of high status within the region of Galilee, situates the story in Galilee's history even more, making it easier to be checked within living memory of Jesus.[51]

2. The identification of Jairus as a synagogue ruler was objectionable to many early Christians living in Jerusalem and its environs, because they experienced ostracization and considerable pressure from the synagogue and its leaders. Matthew (who was preaching to a Jewish church) found this so personally and

---

[50] See ibid., p. 781.
[51] See ibid., pp. 784–85.

apologetically unappealing that he not only drops the reference to the synagogue, but also the reference to Jairus, who is subsequently reduced to "a ruler" (Mt 9:18). This is an excellent example of the criterion of embarrassment, meaning that it would be highly unlikely that the name of Jairus and his profession would have been added by early Christians to the oral tradition prior to the Marcan narrative. Why would the authors of the oral tradition and the Marcan Gospel mention it when it was so apologetically unappealing? If it weren't true, it would be inexplicable.[52]

3. There is another example of embarrassment in the Marcan narrative that manifests a very early tradition—namely, the mourners laughing Jesus to scorn and then Jesus literally throwing the mourners out of the house (the Greek: *autos de ekbalōn pantas*). The idea of Jesus being laughed to scorn would have been disturbing to members of the early Church, and the portrayal of Jesus literally throwing grieving people out of the house would have been embarrassing. One can scarcely imagine the author of the oral tradition or Mark himself adding this disturbing incident to the narrative. Therefore, it seems likely that the entire incident of the mourners was part of a primitive story probably dating back to the ministry of Jesus.[53]

4. The story also contains a rather unique Semitism—namely, *talitha koum*. As noted above, Semitisms reveal an early Palestinian origin of the stories in which they are contained. In the case of the Jairus story, the Semitism is *popular* Aramaic (*talitha koum*), as distinct from formal or written Aramaic (*talitha koumi*). It is highly unlikely that a scribe or author of the oral tradition would have preserved this incorrect way of speaking (like "ain't") without a good reason, such as the expression's origin being Jesus Himself.[54]

5. In addition to the direct Aramaic expression, *talitha koum*, the Marcan version of the narrative manifests six other Semitisms underlying the unusual construction of the Greek text. Gérard Rochais has identified these six candidates that reveal highly

[52] See ibid., p. 785.
[53] See ibid., p. 787.
[54] See ibid., p. 785.

unusual or impossible constructions in Greek, but are regular constructions when Aramaic is translated into Greek.[55] Once again, we can see an early Palestinian origin for the story.

6. Meier notes the very unusual absence of a christological title in a story that portrays Jesus as having the power over life and death. This kind of story should be a perfect candidate for demonstrating Jesus' divinity, and therefore for adding a post-Resurrection christological title (such as "the Lord"). However, the title used to refer to Jesus is quite ordinary—"teacher" (in Mark and Matthew). Luke appears to have been concerned about the ordinariness of the title and so elevates it to "Master" (*epistata*).[56] This indicates Mark's and Matthew's fidelity to an earlier Palestinian tradition, and a decision not to embellish it.

In sum, the historicity of the Jairus story[57] is well-founded, including the highly unusual naming of Jairus (who is a person of high position probably known to many in the Galilean region, a detail that can be checked within living memory of Jesus); the retention of embarrassing and disturbing elements of the narrative, including the reference to the synagogue leader, the mourners laughing Jesus to scorn, and Jesus throwing them out of the house; the abundance of Semitisms (indicating a Palestinian origin of the story), including a popular (incorrect) use of *talitha koum*; and the complete absence of a christological title within a narrative that would be a perfect candidate for it. The combination of these unusual factors attests to the likelihood that this narrative not only has an early Palestinian origin, but retains elements dating back to the public ministry of Jesus Himself. The historical basis of the Palestinian narrative is further strengthened by the spectacular nature of the story, the large number of mourners, and its early circulation among Christians that made it falsifiable at the time of its initial circulation. It does not seem to have been falsified because it was kept in its original state and included in the Marcan Gospel.

[55] Meier cites and summarizes Gérard Rochais' six candidates in ibid., p. 849, n. 57. See also Gérard Rochais, *Les Recits De Resurrection Des Morts Dans Le Nouveau Testament* (Cambridge: Cambridge University Press, 1981), pp. 54–73, 104–12.

[56] See Meier, *Marginal Jew*, p. 786.

[57] See ibid., pp. 780–88.

In view of the above, we may conclude that this narrative, standing by itself, provides significant evidence that Jesus did raise people from the dead. When it is combined with the Lucan narrative (the raising of the son of the widow of Nain) and the Johannine narrative (the raising of Lazarus), the case for Jesus raising the dead becomes quite strong.

2. The Raising of the Son of the Widow of Nain (Lk 7:11–17)

The story of the raising of the son of the widow of Nain (Lk 7:11–17) comes from the special Lucan source and so does not overlap with the Marcan or Johannine sources. The story has relatively simple lines for which there is significant evidence of a primitive source, and it follows the basic three-part standard form of a narrative of raising the dead:

1. It begins with Jesus moving toward the gate of a small town a few miles south of Nazareth in Galilee. As Jesus approaches, He notices a dead man being carried on a bier who was the only son of a widow. She was weeping. When Jesus sees her, He feels a very visceral compassion for her (*esplagchnisthē*), and in a very uncharacteristic move (falling outside the standard form of this kind of story), He does not await a request. Indeed, He does not seem to expect one because a request for a "raising to life" would have been quite beyond the imagination of His audience. Instead, He asks the mother not to weep and then touches the bier, which incites the bearers to come to a halt.

2. The miracle proper: The commissioning of the miracle recounts another uncharacteristic feature. Jesus does not touch the man. Instead, He works the miracle by His word alone. The words are important here: "Young man, *I say* to you, arise" (Lk 7:14; emphasis mine).[58] And immediately, the dead man sits up and begins to speak, and Jesus gives him to his mother.

---

[58] The emphasis on Jesus calling attention to Himself saying the command "arise" will become important in the forthcoming comparisons to the Elijah and Elisha stories, and will also demonstrate the distinctiveness of Jesus' way of healing and raising the dead—that is, by His own authority.

3. Conclusion: Fear grips the crowd and they glorify God. The exclamation of the crowd is interesting. First they call Jesus "a great prophet" (Lk 7:16)[59] and then say that God has visited His people. The story concludes with a notation that word "spread through the whole of Judea and all the surrounding country" (Lk 7:17), which is unusual because it goes beyond the Galilean locale.

Meier discusses four major indications of a primitive Palestinian story upon which the Lucan narrative is built. First, Luke's mention of the town of Nain is inexplicable if he is not being faithful to the tradition given to him. As Meier notes, this town is very small and remote, and is never mentioned in the Old Testament, the New Testament (beyond this unique reference), the pre-Christian pseudepigrapha, Philo, Josephus, or the Mishna.[60] Considering that Luke did not have a good grasp of the geography of Israel, we might ask how he had an intimate knowledge of this remote village, how he knew it had a gate (a fact that has only recently been confirmed by archeology[61]), and why he would have selected it for one of the greatest of Jesus' miracles. Answer: he didn't *select* Nain; it was really the place at which Jesus' miracle occurred. The possibility of Luke inventing this town out of thin air is so remote that we should have confidence that he inherited it from a tradition whose author might have known where the town was.

We would then want to ask the following further question: Why would any formulator of an oral tradition choose this remote town as the site for one of Jesus' greatest miracles if that miracle had not in fact occurred there? If one were going to make up a miracle of this magnitude, why not place it in a better known Galilean town, say, Capernaum? Indeed, why get so specific? After all, if you choose a really small, remote town, just about everyone in that village is going

---

[59] Though this may have been an accolade to Jesus during His ministry, it certainly does not represent the status of Jesus in the post-Resurrection Church, and so Luke very subtly introduces the high christological title "the Lord" just three verses before; but interestingly, he does not change the title "great prophet", which he undoubtedly inherited from an earlier narrative.

[60] See Meier, *Marginal Jew*, p. 795.

[61] See ibid.

to know that that miracle either occurred or did not occur in the locality. It does not make any sense from the vantage point of apologetics or falsifiability to select a small, remote town as the location for a spectacular miracle, if that miracle had not really occurred there. The fraud could be easily exposed.

Meier's second indication concerns Semitisms. He relies on Gérard Rochais' analysis of Semitisms underlying the Greek text.[62] The most obvious Semitism is the presence of parataxis (stringing together multiple simple sentences with "and") throughout the narrative. Luke, as a very fine Greek stylist, probably abhorred the style and certainly tried to eliminate it when appropriate. It can scarcely be imagined that he would have introduced this intentionally into his own free-standing work. Secondly, the clause *kai autē ēn chēra* ("and she was a widow" [Lk 17:12]) corresponds closely to a circumstantial clause in Aramaic,[63] but much less so in Greek. Thirdly, the Greek verb *exerchomai* (which means literally "to go out") is not used to refer to a report spreading; the only way of making sense of this is to see *exerchomai* used as a translation of the Hebrew verb *yāsā* or the Aramaic verb *něpaq* (which occurs in the Septuagint).[64] As Meier notes, none of these Semitisms by themselves can be considered definitive of an Aramaic substratum; however, when all of them are combined (along with other minor Semitisms), the Aramaic backdrop is almost undeniable. It seems likely, therefore, that Luke inherited a tradition that had a very old Palestinian background, and that referred to the town of Nain, which very probably went back to the ministry of Jesus (for the reasons mentioned above).

Meier's third indication of an older pre-Lucan narrative concerns the title used for Jesus after the miracle is complete: "He is a great prophet."[65] This expression would have been quite appropriate for a Jewish audience during Jesus' ministry that had little knowledge of Jesus beyond this spectacular miracle. They may well have seen Him in light of Elijah or Elisha, who were designated as great prophets. However, this designation is completely surpassed two years

---

[62] See ibid., pp. 795 and 857, n. 94; and Rochais, *Les Recits De Resurrection*, pp. 21–30.

[63] See Meier, *Marginal Jew*, p. 857, n. 94; and also Rochais, *Les Recits De Resurrection*, pp. 21–30.

[64] See Meier, *Marginal Jew*, p. 795; and also Rochais, *Les Recits De Resurrection*, pp. 21–30.

[65] See Meier, *Marginal Jew*, p. 796.

later after Jesus' Resurrection and gift of the Spirit, the formation of the Church, and the Church's proclamation of Him as "the Lord". "Great prophet" doesn't come anywhere near what the early Church thought of Jesus. Nevertheless, Luke leaves it on the lips of the audience, indicating his respect for and fidelity to the underlying Palestinian tradition.

Meier's fourth indication of a pre-Lucan narrative concerns Luke's avoidance of literary doublets. This proclivity is shown by his refusal to use both of Mark's stories for the feeding of the four thousand and the feeding of the five thousand, preferring to keep only the second. It is also shown by the fact that he does not add his special narrative of the anointing of Jesus' feet to Mark's narrative, but instead replaces Mark's narrative with his own narrative.[66] This proclivity is carried out in other ways throughout the Lucan Gospel, which provokes the following question: Why would Luke have added this "raising of the dead" narrative to his Gospel when he intended also to include the Marcan narrative of the raising of Jairus' daughter one chapter later? Given his proclivity to avoid doublets, why would Luke have created a doublet when in virtually all other circumstances he eliminates them? The answer very likely is that he felt that the narrative tradition he inherited was true, he noticed the differences between it and the Jairus narrative, and he felt that these differences warranted a doublet.

When one considers the totality of the evidence for a pre-Lucan narrative, particularly the naming of the remote small village of Nain, the multiplicity of Semitisms, the use of the outmoded title "great prophet" for Jesus, and the addition of a doublet (rather than the elimination of one), it seems highly unlikely that Luke invented this narrative. It can hardly be thought that Luke would have known about the town of Nain (or its gate), that he would have used parataxis and other awkward Greek expressions instead of his elegant Greek style, that he would have invented a completely inadequate christological title, and that he would have added a doublet simply to repeat a "raising the dead" narrative of his own making.

The above evidence does not stop at indicating a pre-Lucan narrative. It proceeds further back to the public ministry of Jesus Himself.

[66] See ibid., p. 797.

This is indicated first by the naming of the town of Nain, which no Christian author (of an oral tradition) would have invented as the place for one of Jesus' greatest miracles (because of the town's smallness, remoteness, obscurity, and capacity to produce falsifiability), and second, by the use of a completely inadequate christological title for Jesus (which only makes sense on the lips of a Jewish audience at the time of Jesus' public ministry). These reasons alone are sufficient to build a strong circumstantial case in favor of the historicity of this miracle.

Before proceeding to the raising of Lazarus, we will want to revisit an important point made above with respect to exorcisms and healings—namely, that Jesus performs the miracle by His own command (through His own authority and power). When Jesus raises the dead, He does not pray to God for power; He simply makes a command—in the Lucan narrative, He says, "Young man, I say to you, arise." This stands in stark contrast to all Old Testament prophets, even the two greatest miracle workers: Elijah and Elisha. Both prophets raised the dead (Elijah in 1 Kings 17:17–22; Elisha in 2 Kings 4:18–37). Notice that Elijah and Elisha spend considerable time praying and even pleading to God for help. They then put themselves into a position to mediate *God's* power by making bodily contact with the corpse, including lying on it. Jesus neither prays to God for help nor makes bodily contact with the corpse; His word alone is sufficient to raise the young man to life.

In the Lucan narrative, there is an additional interesting feature: the use of the emphatic *egō*. In Greek it is not necessary to use the pronoun *egō* with a verb because it is implicit in the verb's conjugation. Thus Jesus could have said to the boy, "Legō" ("I say"), and it would have been sufficient. The addition of the extra *egō* is emphatic and calls attention to the person making the command, particularly His authority. Jeremias discovered that this is a very distinctive (if not unique) characteristic of Jesus' commands—not only when exorcising, healing, and raising the dead, but also when modifying or fulfilling the Torah, missioning His disciples, and creating new doctrines.[67] It is probably derived from Jesus' Hebrew and Aramaic "Amen I say

---

[67]Joachim Jeremias, *New Testament Theology* (New York: Charles Scribner's Sons, 1971), 1:253, 35–36.

to you." The fact that Luke uses this distinctive expression indicates a likelihood that it originated with Jesus. Even without the emphatic *egō*, Jesus' raising the dead by His command (without the need for prayer to God or mediation of God's power by touching) indicates that Jesus' word is God's power over life and death, and that He possesses this power in Himself. It is hard to imagine that Jesus was not aware of His possession and command of divine authority and power when exorcising, healing, and raising the dead by His own command. As such, He probably saw Himself as sharing in His Father's power and life.[68]

We may now proceed to the third narrative of raising the dead—namely, the Johannine account of the raising of Lazarus.

3. The Raising of Lazarus (Jn 11:1–44)

John's Gospel contains several layers of tradition as well as favored Johannine teachings and redactions. The Lazarus story is no exception, detailing everything from Jesus' love for Lazarus and his family, to the Johannine theology of Jesus as the resurrection and the life. After twenty pages of assiduous exegesis (peeling back redactions and accretions to the oral tradition), Meier proposes a probable pre-Johannine narrative about the raising of Lazarus. His textual and exegetical rationale for this early narrative may be found in volume two of *A Marginal Jew*.[69] We may begin with the primitive tradition as Meier has uncovered it (square brackets indicate Meier's uncertainty about whether particular words or phrases belong to that tradition):

> Once there was a sick man, Lazarus of Bethany, the town [in which] Mary his sister [also lived]. His sister sent [a message] to Jesus, saying: "Lord, behold, he whom you love is sick." When Jesus heard that he was sick, He then remained in the place where He was for

---

[68] From Jesus' vantage point, sharing in power is similar to sharing in life (implying divine Sonship). John L. McKenzie notes that the Old Testament does not distinguish between life as a principle or power of vitality and life as living (the concrete *experience* of vitality), and so he states, "Its language is concrete rather than abstract, and life is viewed as the *fullness of power*". John L. McKenzie, *Dictionary of the Bible* (New York: Macmillan, 1965), p. 507; emphasis mine.

[69] See Meier, *Marginal Jew*, pp. 798–818, for the methodology and exegesis leading to Meier's rendition of the pre-Johannine narrative.

two days.... When Jesus came [to Bethany], He found him already four days in the tomb. Many of the Jews had come to Mary to comfort her over her brother. [Mary was sitting at home.] When she heard [that Jesus had come], she arose quickly and came to Him. [Jesus had not yet come into the town.] When the Jews who were with her in the house and were comforting her saw that Mary had quickly arisen and went out, they followed her, thinking that she was going to the tomb to weep there.... When Mary came to the place where Jesus was, seeing Him she fell at His feet, saying to Him: "Lord, if you had been here, my brother would not have died." When He saw her weeping and the Jews who had come with her weeping, Jesus groaned in spirit. And He said: "Where have you laid him?" They said to Him: "Lord, come and see ..." Jesus came to the tomb. It was a cave, and a stone lay over its entrance. Jesus said: "Take the stone away." They therefore took the stone away. In a loud voice Jesus shouted: "Lazarus, come forth." The dead man came forth [with his feet and hands bound with burial cloths, and his face wrapped in a handkerchief.] Jesus said to them: "Untie him and let him go." Now many of the Jews who had come to Mary and had seen what He had done believed in Him.

There are four major indications of historicity. First, it is evident from Meier's exegetical work that the Johannine story (Jn 11:1–44) has undergone a very lengthy development. Many of these developments were made by the evangelist, but, as Meier makes clear, many were also part of the development of the pre-Johannine tradition.[70] This multilayered complex development must have taken place over a considerable number of years, and so it is reasonable to assume that the above primitive narrative was formulated close to the time of Jesus.

Second, as far back as the tradition can be reconstructed, it seems to have been firmly anchored in Bethany.[71] Such a historical detail seems quite gratuitous (if it is not true) because it falls outside the standard form and does not advance any apologetical, catechetical, or instructional purpose. Its preservation seems to be dependent on the belief of the early formulators of the tradition that it was true.

[70] See ibid.
[71] See ibid, p. 831.

Third, and perhaps most important, the early formulation of the tradition includes the names of Lazarus and Mary. When one considers that John (and the Synoptics) do not generally preserve the names of the recipients of miracles (with the exception of Jairus and Bartimaeus in Mark and Luke, respectively), it is quite striking that not one, but two names are preserved. The preservation of Mary's name is truly unusual, because she is not the recipient of a miracle, but only the sister of Lazarus and a friend of Jesus. Again, these personal names fall outside the standard form of the story and do not advance any apologetical, catechetical, or instructional purpose. Therefore, it seems very unlikely that they would have been added during the lengthy development of the Lazarus tradition. So, why were both names preserved? Because they were historically accurate, and more importantly, Lazarus and his sister Mary were probably disciples of Jesus and known in the early Church. If this were not the case, it would be difficult to explain Mary's extended presence in the early narrative. If this is the case, then the tradition would be linked back to the recipient of the miracle (Lazarus) and his sister Mary (an eyewitness). Meier notes in this regard: "I think it likely that John 11:1–45 goes back ultimately to some event involving Lazarus, a disciple of Jesus, and that this event was believed by Jesus' disciples even during his lifetime to be a miracle of raising the dead."[72]

The silence of the Synoptics about the Lazarus tradition may seem somewhat perplexing, but if one remembers that the Synoptics did not have access to many of the Johannine sources, it would not be surprising if they had not even heard of it. Furthermore, even if the Synoptics had heard about it, they were not in need of another narrative about raising the dead because they already had the Jairus account, and it was not their proclivity to multiply miracles of this kind.

In view of all this, it is reasonable to conclude that Jesus raised His disciple Lazarus from the dead in Bethany, and that Lazarus' sister Mary was an eyewitness, and that this miracle was well-known in the region of Bethany, and rapidly became a story that experienced a very lengthy development leading to the above-mentioned pre-Johannine narrative, and finally, to the fully expanded Johannine narrative.

[72] Ibid.

One final point should be made. In the earliest constructible pre-Johannine narrative, we see once again that Jesus gives the command to raise the dead by His own authority.[73] We saw this in the previous two narratives: Jesus commands, "Talitha koum"—"Little girl, get up" (Mk 5:41), and, "Young man, I say to you, arise", using the emphatic *egō* (special Luke, Lk 7:14). Now we see Jesus giving a command for the dead Lazarus to come out of the tomb after the stone had been rolled away. Unlike Elijah and Elisha, He does not make recourse to prayers and does not act as an intermediary for the working of *God's* power. Rather, He manifests divine power and authority (the power of life and death) in Himself.

It is difficult to imagine an early formulator of the tradition making such a radical claim without some grounding in history. Most impressive is the fact that this radical claim enjoys multiple attestation not only through three sources (Mark, special Luke, and John), but also through the primitive traditions standing behind these three sources.

It should be noted that the three *primitive* traditions of Jesus raising the dead were formulated by three *different* authors grounding their stories in three *different* historical incidents originating in three *different* locations. All of them reveal the same important difference from the prophetic tradition of the Old Testament—namely, that Jesus raises the dead by His own command (authority and power). The probability of this significant difference occurring in three Gospel sources derived from three different traditions with three authors from three locations by pure chance is quite miniscule. Reason dictates that there must be a common source—but what could that common source be except Jesus or the apostles who witnessed Jesus on all three occasions? The datum that reveals most lucidly Jesus' divine power and authority contains within itself the validation of its historicity.

---

[73] Note that in the fully expanded version of the Lazarus narrative, the Johannine author has added the passage that Jesus prayed to the Father: "Father, I thank you that you have heard me. I knew that you always hear me, but I said this on account of the people standing by, that they may believe that you sent me" (Jn 11:41–42). This Johannine addition concerns verification of one of his favorite themes—that the Father has *sent* Jesus. It should not be interpreted to mean that Jesus had to pray for the power to raise the dead. As is clear from the primitive tradition (uncovered by Meier), Jesus makes the command for Lazarus to "come out" (Jn 11:43) by *His own* authority and word.

E. Conclusion to Section I

Some skeptics have contended that Jesus' healings may have been nothing more than alleviation of psychosomatic problems, that His exorcisms were nothing more than the healing of epilepsy and grand mal seizures, and that His raisings of the dead were nothing more than alleviation of suspended animation. Though there were no medical experts with appropriate equipment on the scene to make scientific diagnoses, it is safe to assume that the apostles' testimony about the blind, the lame, the lepers, the mute, and so forth was accurate, because most blind people are physically blind, and the same with deaf people, mute people, people with atrophied limbs, and lepers. Furthermore, most dead people are really dead; they are not cases of extended suspended animation without signs of respiration. The signs of death, blindness, deafness, leprosy, and so on were able to be detected by ancient people, not just modern ones. Semitic people at the time of Jesus could also surmise that when individuals were *instantaneously* cured of physical maladies that either lasted a lifetime or took years to cure, something was "out of the ordinary"—even superordinary.

Exorcisms are a different case, because there is no physical test for spiritual possession. All scientific tests are devised to detect physical causes (not spiritual ones). Thus, cases of demonic possession (and exorcism, which rectifies it) can only be judged to have occurred by someone who believes in demons and demonic possession (as Jesus certainly did). Even if we concede that every exorcism was a cure of epilepsy or grand mal seizures (or some other physical malady), we have simply shifted the categorization of the *miracle* (i.e., from exorcism to healing). Though this may be satisfying to materialists, I do not think it is accurate. There is a long history of demonic haunting and possession that continues to this day.[74] Most Christian churches acknowledge the existence of evil spirits and Satan (the leader of the

---

[74] There is an interesting book by the psychiatrist M. Scott Peck that gives a detailed analysis of the distinction between severe mental illness and demonic possession in two well-documented cases. See his *Glimpses of the Devil: A Psychiatrist's Personal Accounts of Possession, Exorcism, and Redemption* (New York: Simon and Schuster, 2005). According to the Vatican guidelines issued in 1999, "the person who claims to be possessed must be evaluated by doctors to rule out a mental or physical illness" (*Rite De Exorcismis et Supplicationibus Quibusdam* [Vatican City: Libreria Editrice Vaticana, 1999]).

evil kingdom), and the Catholic Church has exorcists assigned to most dioceses throughout the world. As will be discussed in Chapter 6, the vanquishing of Satan is central to Jesus' mission of bringing the Kingdom to the world.

We now arrive at our conclusion. There is considerable evidence for the historicity of Jesus' miracles, including the following:

1. Testimony in two non-Christian sources written near the time of Jesus (e.g., Flavius Josephus and the Babylonian Talmud)
2. The Jewish polemic against Jesus ("he casts out demons by Beelzebul" [Lk 11:15]), implying that His adversaries acknowledged His miraculous power
3. Attestation in many apostolic *kerygmas*
4. Multiple attestation of exorcisms and healings in all five independent sources (Mark, Q, special Luke, special Matthew, and John), and attestation to raising the dead in three independent sources (Mark, special Luke, and John)
5. Jesus' unique style of performing miracles, which is unlike any other miracle worker in the ancient world and unlike the performance of miracles in the apocryphal Gnostic Gospels.
6. Mention of particular places and people in miracle narratives, which could have been checked within living memory of Jesus, particularly true for the narratives concerned with raising the dead
7. The presence of Semitisms in narratives concerning exorcisms, healings, and particularly, raising the dead, indicating reliance on an early Palestinian tradition
8. Coherence with Palestinian titles, expressions, and phrasing that would have been used in Israel at the time of Jesus' ministry, but would be anachronistic after His Resurrection and gift of the Spirit

In view of the above, it is reasonable and responsible to hold not only that Jesus performed exorcisms, healings, and raisings of the dead, but did so by His own authority and power, showing that He possessed God's authority and power in Himself. The apostolic Church saw in this a confirmation of Jesus' divine Sonship during His ministry.

If we accept this, then we also must accept that Jesus knew about His divine Sonship during His ministry, for raising the dead by His own command requires it. If He really did not possess the power and authority of God (power over life and death) within Himself, He would have suffered the terrible embarrassment of saying, "Young man, I say to you, arise," only to find that the young man remained dead.

As we shall see in the next chapter, Jesus not only knew that He possessed divine power and authority in Himself through His ministry of miracles; He used that power and authority to bring the Kingdom of God, to vanquish evil, to modify and fulfill the law, to initiate the New Jerusalem, and in doing all this, to complete the mission reserved to Yahweh alone.

II. The Holy Spirit in the Apostolic Church

In the last chapter we investigated what differentiated the Christian messianic movement from those of John the Baptist and other proclaimed messiahs between the first century B.C. and the first century A.D. (such as Judas the Galilean, Simon, Athronges, Eleazar ben Deinaus and Alexander, Menahem, Simon bar Giora, and bar-Kochba). We concluded with N. T. Wright and E. P. Sanders that Christianity's remarkable success and growth, by comparison to the failure of all the other messianic movements, required some sufficient cause. This extraordinary and unprecedented success and growth could not be attributed only to the strength of Jesus' preaching or even Jesus' miracles, because Jesus had suffered public humiliation and public execution after these events. Not just any cause was required, but a powerful one, and this very probably was Jesus' Resurrection in glory.

Though this would explain how the Christian messianic movement received its remarkable jumpstart—with its certainty, exuberance, hopefulness, strong proclamation, uniform doctrinal proclivities, and large number of missionaries (who, as we saw, were very likely recipients of Resurrection appearances among the five hundred and the apostles)—it does not completely explain how this Christian messianic movement accelerated and received such an open reception among both Jewish and Gentile communities (many of whom had not even heard about Jesus or the Jewish background from which He came). This seems to require another sufficient cause that John P. Meier identifies as the apostles' power to perform healings and miracles in a similar fashion to Jesus (with the important exception that Jesus performed miracles by His own authority while the apostles performed them in *His name*):

> There was a notable difference between the long-term impact of the Baptist and that of Jesus. After the Baptist's death, his followers did not continue to grow into a religious movement that in due time swept the Greco-Roman world. Followers remained, revering the Baptist's memory and practices. But by the early 2d century A.D. any cohesive group that could have claimed an organic connection with the historical Baptist seems to have passed from the scene. In contrast, the movement that had begun to sprout up around the historical Jesus continued to grow—amid many sea changes—throughout the 1st century and beyond. Not entirely by coincidence, *the post-Easter "Jesus movement" claimed the same sort of ability to work miracles that Jesus had claimed for himself during his lifetime.* This continued claim to work miracles may help to explain the continued growth, instead of a tapering off, of the group that emerged from Jesus' ministry.[75]

Though these miracles are performed in the name of Jesus, the power that is used to perform them (in His name) is attributed to the Holy Spirit, who works through individuals and the Church to bring about the salvation of the world.

A. Jesus' Gift of the Holy Spirit

The early Christians characterized the Holy Spirit as "the power of God" (*dunamis tou Theou*), which was uniquely possessed by Jesus during His ministry and continued to flow from Him in the life of the Church. As their understanding of the Holy Spirit developed through experience, they became progressively aware of Its *personal* presence flowing through Jesus. John L. McKenzie succinctly describes this more developed theology as follows:

[75] Meier, *Marginal Jew*, p. 623.

The spirit is basically the divine and heavenly dynamic force; it is conceived as peculiarly existing in Jesus (and specifically in the risen Jesus), as pervading the body of Jesus which is the Church, and as apportioned to the members of the Church. Jesus is the son of David in the flesh but the son of God in power according to the spirit (Rm 1:3); the unique possession of the spirit by Jesus and the unique power which flows from this possession reveal His true reality, which is the reality of the spiritual sphere, i.e., the divine and heavenly sphere.[76]

We can trace the development of the early Church's experiential understanding of the Spirit through its exposition in Luke and Acts (Section II.A.1), and later exposition in Saint Paul (Section II.A.2).[77] Let us begin with the earlier exposition.

1. The Visible Manifestation of the Spirit in the Acts of the Apostles

In the Acts of the Apostles, Luke recounts three kinds of powerful experiences that the early Church community attributes to God, or more specifically, to "the Spirit of God" or "the power of God": (1) healings and miracles, (2) prophesy, and (3) ecstatic experiences (such as glossolalia and visions).

Though all three of these areas merit consideration, an overview of the first will be sufficient to show (1) that the early Church saw the charisms as explicit manifestations of God's power and God's Spirit, and (2) that the risen Jesus is seen to be the source of this power and Spirit (because the Spirit works through His name).

Luke recounts a large range of healings and miracles performed by Peter, Paul, and others in the Acts of the Apostles:[78]

- The healing of the lame man at the Temple (Acts 3:1–10)
- Healings and exorcisms performed by Philip in Samaria (Acts 8:4–8)
- Paul's healing from blindness (Acts 9:18)
- The healing of Aeneas' paralysis (Acts 9:32–35)

---

[76] McKenzie, Dictionary of the Bible, p. 843.

[77] I am indebted to the following work by James Dunn, from which I have derived the majority of the following materials on early apostolic miracles and charisms: Jesus and the Spirit: A Study of the Religious and Charismatic Experience of Jesus and the First Christians as Reflected in the New Testament (Philadelphia: Westminster Press, 1975).

[78] See the more complete list in ibid., pp. 163ff.

- The raising of Tabitha from the dead by Peter (Acts 9:36–41)
- The healing of a cripple in Lystra (Acts 14:8–10)
- Paul's restoration of Eutychus (Acts 20:9–12)
- The healings performed by Paul in Malta (Acts 28:8–9)

There are some unconventional healings and miracles also recounted in Acts:

- Healings through Peter's shadow (Acts 5:15)
- Healings through cloths touched by Paul (Acts 19:11)
- Peter's liberation from prison (Acts 5:19–24; 12:6–11)
- Paul's liberation from prison (Acts 16:26)

There can be little doubt that such healings and miracles occurred in the earliest Church communities, as they are recounted not only by Luke, but also by Paul[79] (who is writing to the actual witnesses of the events) and the author of the Letter to the Hebrews. With respect to the first category of healings (those worked through the personal intercession of the apostles), few scholars doubt that Luke had either firsthand experience of these miracles (the "we" passages) or reliable firsthand sources. James Dunn notes even with respect to the raising of Tabitha by Peter: "It is quite likely that the tradition goes back to a genuine episode in the ministry of Peter."[80]

If one accepts that such healings and miracles were quite frequent within the early Church community, and that the members of that community viewed them as extraordinary and powerful (in contemporary terminology, falling outside normal boundaries of natural causation), then it will not be difficult to understand why they thought that "the power of God" / "the Spirit of God" was in their midst. When this is combined with Luke's contention that the Spirit's power arises out of the name of *Jesus* (or the disciples' ministry on behalf of Jesus), it seems reasonable to conclude that the primitive Church experienced the *risen Jesus* as the ongoing source of the Holy Spirit (the power of God) in the world.[81] Dunn notes in this regard:

---

[79] See Rom 15:19; 1 Cor 12:10, 28; 2 Cor 12:12; Gal 3:5; Heb 2:4. See also Dunn, *Jesus and the Spirit*, p. 163.

[80] Dunn, *Jesus and the Spirit*, p. 165.

[81] This key insight is justified in a detailed way in ibid., pp. 163–65.

Where Jesus healed in his own right, by the immediate power and authority of God (cf. Acts 2:22; 10:38), his disciples healed in the name of Jesus. It would appear that from the first they recognized that their power to heal was somehow dependent on Jesus and derivative from him (cf. Luke 10:17). Whereas he had been the direct representative of God in his healing ministry, they saw themselves primarily as representatives of Jesus. They healed by the same power, but that power was now linked with the name of Jesus.[82]

The frequent occurrence of the charismatic manifestation of the Spirit arising out of the name of Jesus provides an *experiential* ground (within the early Church) for the association of Jesus with the source of divine power.

2. Visible and Interior Manifestations of the Spirit in Paul

Though Saint Paul's letters were written before the Acts of the Apostles, Luke saves and recounts traditions about "the power of the Spirit and the name of Jesus" that *predate* Paul's theology of the Spirit. An exploration of Paul's theology of the Spirit reveals his awareness of these earlier traditions and his *personal experience* of the visible and tangible manifestations of the Spirit emphasized by Luke.

Paul's experience of the Spirit, as Fitzmyer notes, is "God's gift of his creative, prophetic, or renovative *presence* to human beings or the world" (emphasis mine).[83] This "presence of God" is more than merely "the power of God" viewed as a blind supernatural force; it has a subjective (indeed, intersubjective) quality. The Spirit not only searches our hearts, but also searches the depths of God the Father, having a comprehensive knowledge of Him: "For the Spirit searches everything, even the depths of God" (1 Cor 2:10).

When Paul refers to the visible gifts of the Spirit, he generally uses the term *charismata* (a specific instance of *charis*, a gratuitous gift for the well-being of another, which, in this case, is God's gratuitous gift of salvation). When Paul looks at the *charismata* from the vantage point of agency, he refers to them either as *phanerōsis tou pneumatos*

---

[82] Ibid., p. 164.

[83] Joseph A. Fitzmyer, "Pauline Theology", in *The New Jerome Biblical Commentary*, eds. Raymond E. Brown, Joseph A. Fitzmyer, and Roland E. Murphy (Englewood Cliffs, N.J.: Prentice Hall, 1990), p. 1396 (82:65).

(manifestation of the Spirit, e.g., 1 Cor 12:7), or as *dunamis tou Theou* (the power of God, e.g., 1 Cor 1:24), or as *onomati tou kuriou* (what is given in the name of the Lord/Christ, e.g., 1 Cor 6:11). As Dunn, referring to H. Gunkel's longstanding work, notes:

> So far as Paul was concerned charismata are the manifestation of supernatural power. Charisma is *always* God acting, *always* the Spirit manifesting himself.... For Paul, *every* charisma was supernatural. *The character of transcendent otherness lies at the heart of the Pauline concept of charisma*.... The "infinite qualitative distinction" (Kierkegaard) between divine and human means that every expression of grace is always something *more* than human.[84]

We may now explore the vast array of Paul's and others' experience of the supernatural power of the Spirit, beginning with the public charismatic gifts and concluding with the interior gifts (in the next Section II.A.3).

It is noteworthy that Paul is writing to communities and individuals who have witnessed the powerful visible manifestations of the Spirit multiple times. It is therefore reasonable to assume that these gifts were virtually commonplace in the early community as Luke indicates in the Acts of the Apostles. Dunn mentions further:

> It is worth pointing out that in 1 Cor. 12.9, 28, 30 we have firsthand testimony to the fact that there were cures and healings experienced in the Pauline communities for which no natural or rational explanation would suffice—they could only be put down to the action of God.[85]

So what do the visible gifts consist in? From the list given in 1 Corinthians 12:8–10, three may be easily identified:

1. Healings (*charismata iamatōn*—gifts of cures)
2. Miracles (*energēmata dunameōn*—workings of power)
3. Speaking in tongues (*genē glōssōn*—kinds of tongues)

---

[84] Dunn, *Jesus and the Spirit*, p. 255. See also H. Gunkel, *Die Wirkungen des heiligen Geistes nach der populären Anschauung der apostolischen Zeit und nach der Lehre des Apostels Paulus* (Göttingen, 1888), pp. 82f; emphasis mine.

[85] Dunn, *Jesus and the Spirit*, p. 210.

There are two other gifts that the community thought to be supernatural and public (as distinct from interior)—namely, prophesy
and revelation. As Paul recognizes, there are false prophets who can
lead the Church astray, and so there is need to discern the quality
of prophesy within the early community. I will give a brief description of the first three gifts as an illustration of why the community
believed that the Holy Spirit was the power of God, that Jesus was
the ongoing source of that Spirit, and therefore that "Jesus is Lord"
(Rom 10:9; see Rom 14:9; Phil 2:11).

1. *Healings.* Paul uses the plural *charismata* (in contrast to using the
singular in referring to the other gifts) because he probably believed
that there was a special charisma for every kind of illness.[86] From
this, we may infer that Paul witnessed different kinds of healings,
and that those healings probably resembled those recounted by Luke
in Acts, and in the Gospels with respect to Jesus' ministry. There
can be little doubt that Paul views these as arising solely out of the
power of God (that is, not occurring in nature, but only through
supernatural power).

2. *Miracles.* Paul's distinct listing of miracles next to healings would
seem to indicate that they included supernatural acts other than cures.
Exegetes suspect that these would be of two sorts: exorcisms[87] and
nature miracles.[88] Clearly, Paul was familiar with Jesus' exorcisms,
and even though they do not figure as prominently in Paul's ministry
as in Jesus', Paul certainly was involved in exorcisms.[89] Paul may also
have in mind nature miracles, such as cures taking place through his
handkerchief (Acts 19:18) or other "signs and wonders" (*en dunamei
sēmeiōn kai teratōn*—by power of signs and wonders; Rom 18:19),
which he evidently worked from Jerusalem to Illyricum.
    The working of miracles (*energōn dunameis*) factored prominently
into Paul's ministry in new communities, and in encouraging converts

---

[86] Dunn, *Jesus and the Spirit*, pp. 210–11.

[87] See ibid., p. 210.

[88] See ibid.

[89] See Acts 16:18: "Paul ... turned and said to the spirit, 'I charge you in the name of Jesus
Christ to come out of her.' And it came out that very hour." See also Acts 19:12: "[A]nd
diseases left them and the evil spirits came out of them."

among people who had not yet heard the Word. In Galatians 3:4–5, Paul uses the history of miracles worked in the community through the Holy Spirit as a proof of why the Galatians should remain faithful to him:

> Did you experience so many things in vain?—if it really is in vain. Does he who supplies the Spirit to you and *works miracles* among you do so by works of the law, or by hearing with faith?[90] (Emphasis mine.)

Given that Paul is writing to those who have directly experienced *dunameis*, it can hardly be doubted that the experience of these persuasive outward signs is not only common to Paul's ministry, but continues after Paul has left (presumably through people with that charism), and is sufficiently powerful within the community to persuade it of the veracity of Paul's words years after his departure.

The power to heal and to work miracles does not belong to the human agent working them. The power is distinctly that of God (the Spirit of God) done through the name of "the Lord Jesus Christ" (e.g., 1 Cor 6:11). That power is meant not for the benefit of the healer or miracle worker, but for the benefit of one *in need*, or for the good of the *community*. The healer/miracle worker is purely the instrument of God.

Despite the incredible persuasiveness of healing and miracles in the early community, Paul believes that they must be put in perspective to allow for the prominence of gifts that produce deep conversion of the heart. In this respect, Paul is distinct from Luke, who gives clear prominence to powerful visible gifts of the Spirit.

3. *Speaking in Tongues.* Paul views this ecstatic charism as a proof of the Spirit, an aspect of his ministry of initial conversion, a spiritual benefit to individual believers,[91] and an occasional benefit to the community (when there is an authentic interpreter of the tongues).[92]

---

[90] Though *dunameis* here may include healings, it certainly should not be restricted to them, for Paul would have used the more appropriate term *charismata iamatōn* if he meant it in the restricted sense. Therefore, he probably meant it to include exorcisms and possibly even nature miracles.

[91] See Dunn, *Jesus and the Spirit*, pp. 230–31.

[92] As Paul notes in 1 Corinthians 14:18: "I thank God that I speak in tongues more than you all."

However, Paul views speaking in tongues as the lowest of the "deeds of power", because it does not directly serve either to deepen conversion, or to build up the community's understanding of God, Jesus, or even itself. Hence, in 1 Corinthians 14:6, Paul warns the community not to seek speaking in tongues as an end in itself, and to prefer prophesy (which builds up the community and leads to its deeper conversion) over glossolalia:

> Now, brethren, if I come to you speaking in tongues, how shall I benefit you unless I bring you some revelation or knowledge or prophecy or teaching? If even lifeless instruments, such as the flute or the harp, do not give distinct notes, how will any one know what is played? ... So with yourselves; since you are eager for manifestations of the Spirit, strive to excel in building up the Church.... I thank God that I speak in tongues more than you all; nevertheless, in church I would rather speak five words with my mind, in order to instruct others [prophesy or revelation], than ten thousand words in a tongue. (1 Cor 14:6–7, 12, 18–19)

I will not discuss prophecy and revelation here because the above points on healing, miracles, and speaking in tongues are sufficient to establish my central conclusion, which is explained below.

3. Conclusion to Section II.A

The conclusion may be set out in three parts:

1. There were frequent "deeds of healing and power" in the early Church (as there are today) that are difficult, if not impossible, to explain by natural causation.
2. These extraordinary occurrences were reasonably interpreted by the early Church to be the power (Spirit) of God.
3. The ongoing source of this spiritual power was attributed to Jesus, for it came through the use of His name.

The frequent occurrence of these healings and miracles through the power of the Holy Spirit and the name of Jesus allowed the Church to engage in a remarkably expansive missionary effort, because it substantiated the apostles' claim that Jesus was raised in glory and is the exclusive beloved Son of the Father. This gave rise to the post-Easter churches' titles for Him—"the Lord" and "the Son of God" (see Chapter 6, Section III).

In many respects, the Holy Spirit is just as active today as in apostolic times. One does not have to look far to see the millions of testimonies to the charismatic manifestation of the Spirit (with literally millions of Internet search results devoted to the Holy Spirit, healings, miracles, prophesy, and tongues) that resemble those recounted by Luke and Paul almost two thousand years ago.[93] Additionally, several scholars have chronicled hundreds of modern, medically documented miracles occurring through the power of the Holy Spirit in Jesus' name.[94] With so many accounts of visible manifestations of the Holy Spirit (i.e., modern miracles) in the *United States*, how much greater would be the accounts of the *interior* gifts of the Holy Spirit, and how much greater still when both the charismatic and interior gifts of the Spirit are seen throughout the entire world? It seems evident that the Holy Spirit is truly alive and well in any individual or culture that wants the Spirit's help, guidance, inspiration, peace, and above all, love.

B. *The Interior Gifts of the Spirit according to Saint Paul*

Though Paul saw the importance of the powerful visible manifestations of the Spirit in initial conversion and in initiating and sustaining communities, he prefers to address the *interior* gifts of the Spirit. The reason for his preference for the interior over the exterior gifts arises out of his belief that the interior gifts have a more profound and lasting effect on the believer and the community. The interior gifts not only lead to initial conversion (as do the powerful visible gifts) but also to a deeper conversion of the heart in imitation of Christ.

---

[93] A simple Google search on the Internet for "Holy Spirit healing" currently yields 11,200,000 results; for "Holy Spirit Miracles" there are 7,220,000 results; for "Holy Spirit prophecy" there are 5,480,000 results; and for "Holy Spirit tongues" there are 3,490,000 results.

[94] For example, see Craig Keener, *Miracles: The Credibility of the New Testament*, 2 vols. (Grand Rapids, Mich.: Baker Academic, 2011).

It was noted above that Paul did not believe the Holy Spirit to be a blind force, but rather a conscious and sensitive power capable of knowing the heart of the Father. This conclusion was grounded in Paul's (and others') *experience* of these interior gifts, which include prayer, hope, trust, love, zeal, peace, and joy.[95] Though these gifts may not be immediately recognized as supernatural power or be manifest in a group or public setting (as powerful visible gifts), they do lead to the buildup of the Church through the deepening conversion arising out of them. Since these gifts are more subtle and difficult to recognize as divine, Paul takes pains not only to exhort his communities to them, but also to point to their origin in the Holy Spirit and the risen Christ.

A proper exposition of these themes would require another book beyond the scope of this one, and so I will not address it here. However, I have addressed several of these themes in Volume 1 of this Quartet: *Finding True Happiness: Satisfying Our Restless Hearts*:

- Inspiration of the Holy Spirit (Chapter 8, Section I)
- Discernment of spirits (Chapter 8, Section II)
- Guidance by the Holy Spirit (Chapter 8, Section III)
- The Holy Spirit in the Church community (Chapter 6)
- The Holy Spirit in contemplative prayer (Chapter 7)
- The Holy Spirit in deepening faith, hope, and love (Chapter 9)

III. Conclusion

Thus far, we have encountered four significant clues in our investigation of the evidence for Jesus as the unconditionally loving "God with us" (Emmanuel):

1. His unconditional love, which we studied in three parts:
   a. His special definition of love—*agapē* (Chapter 1)

---

[95] Paul gives one list of interior gifts as the "fruit of the Spirit" in Galatians 5:22–23: "But the fruit of the Spirit is love, joy, peace, patience, kindness, goodness, faithfulness, gentleness, self-control". He includes many of these gifts under the general gift of love in 1 Corinthians 13:1–5.

    b. His preaching of the unconditional love of God—His Father, Abba (Chapter 2)

    c. His unconditional love for all mankind, particularly the poor, the sick, and sinners and His willingness to sacrifice Himself totally to give us that love (Chapter 3)

2. His Resurrection in a glorious spiritual body (Chapter 4)

3. Exorcisms, healings, and raising the dead by His own authority and power (Section I above)

4. The gift of the Holy Spirit, enabling the apostolic Church to perform miracles in His name (Section II above)

The complementarity of this evidence is so strong that we could almost infer from it that Jesus is the unconditionally loving Emmanuel; yet, at the same time, it begs the final question, the final clue: Did Jesus really say that He was "God with us"? We will discuss this in the next chapter.

Chapter Six

Jesus' Identity and Mission

Introduction

We concluded the previous chapter with the following question: Did Jesus really claim to be "God with us"? The short answer is yes, but He did so explicitly only with His disciples and closest friends. When He is with the crowds and religious authorities, He speaks implicitly and cryptically.

Some readers familiar with New Testament scholarship will know that Jesus did not proclaim to general audiences that He was "the Son of God"[1] or "the Lord"[2] or "God with us" in an explicit way. These were titles given to Him by the apostolic Church shortly after His Resurrection and gift of the Spirit.[3] Why didn't Jesus come out to the crowds and clearly state "I am the Lord" or "I am the Son of God"? As the reader may already know, such a proclamation would have brought opprobrium upon Him, putting a premature end to

[1] "The New Testament use of ['Son of God'] does not reflect a Hellenistic background. Neither does it reflect the Old Testament background; Son of God is not a messianic title in Judaism. The title becomes a means by which the early Church expressed its faith in the absolutely unique character of Jesus. The use of the term reflects the developed faith of Easter and Pentecost." John L. McKenzie, *Dictionary of the Bible* (New York: Macmillan, 1965), p. 830.

[2] McKenzie concisely summarizes the above data from the early Jewish Christians, Paul, and John as follows: "The title [*Kyrios*] is relevant to Paul's conception of the divinity of Jesus. There can be no doubt that it is intended to raise Jesus above the level of common humanity; the very fact that it is associated with the resurrection and with the second coming is sufficient for this.... The Lord Jesus Christ has powers which are *divine* in any sense of the word. The concept of the divinity of Jesus in Paul cannot be determined on the basis of this word alone. Nevertheless, it is not without significance that the use of the word Kyrios in the LXX [Septuagint] is the usual divine name." Ibid., p. 518.

[3] The development of the titles "the Lord" and "the Son of God" *after* Jesus' Resurrection and gift of the Spirit is acknowledged by virtually every critical New Testament scholar. As McKenzie notes, "The use of [the title 'the Son of God'] term reflects the developed faith of Easter and Pentecost." Ibid., p. 830; for a summary of this, see pp. 517–18 and 830–31.

His ministry and mission. The crowds would have been shocked (and probably repulsed), because they were looking for a Messiah (the anointed one of God), but had no expectation that the Lord Himself (the Son of God) would be the Messiah. Without Jesus' Crucifixion, Resurrection in glory, and gift of the Spirit, the extraordinary nature of the "good news" would not have been easily understood. The shocked reaction of Jesus' general audience would have been considerably less than that of the religious authorities. They would have found His blasphemous claim to deserve not only contempt and ostracization (undermining His ministry), but also condemnation and possibly death. Since Jesus did not want to bring His ministry to a premature end, He waited until the appointed time to openly expose His relationship to God the Father.

Jesus chose the "appointed time" to be at His trial, where He expressed the significance of His impending self-sacrifice. At this point, no part of His ministry would come to a premature end, because He knew He was about to be executed, and so He had nothing to lose by announcing that He is the preexistent judge of the world sent by God to initiate the new age. This announcement conveyed His conviction that He would fulfill the mission reserved by Israel to Yahweh alone, revealing not only His Messiahship, but His exclusive Sonship with God (see below, Section II). When the high priest asks, "Are you the Christ, the Son of the Blessed?" He responds with an unambiguous, "I am; and you will see the Son of man sitting at the right hand of Power, and coming with the clouds of heaven" (Mk 14:62).

Wright believes that this unambiguous declaration is essentially historical. Jesus' response to the questions of the interrogators led them to believe that He not only had messianic but *divine* "pretensions", worthy of a charge of blasphemy. This charge in Jewish legal proceedings seems to have been wholly original and was apparently formulated specifically to address Jesus' response to His interrogators. According to N. T. Wright: "Since we have no evidence of anyone before or after Jesus ever saying such a thing of himself, it is not surprising that we have no evidence of anyone framing a blasphemy law to prevent them doing so."[4] It seems that Jesus chose His trial to

---

[4] N. T. Wright, *Jesus and the Victory of God* (Minneapolis: Fortress Press, 1996), 2:551.

declare His divine Sonship to His adversaries, which provided them with more than enough judicial warrant to persecute and condemn Him. As Wright suggests:

> [After bringing witnesses and charges against Jesus], all that remained was to extract some sort of confession of guilt in relation both to the Temple and to the charge of false prophecy.... That was what the nocturnal hearing succeeded in doing. Succeeded, indeed, beyond their hopes. The prisoner, in agreeing to the charge of being a would-be Messiah, "prophesied" his own vindication in such a way that a plausible charge of "blasphemy" could be added to the list ... in such a way as to prophesy that he, as Messiah, would sit on a throne beside the god of Israel. "You will see 'the son of man' 'sitting at the right hand of Power', and 'coming on the clouds of heaven.' [Mk 14:62]"[5]

Jesus chose the trial to be the appointed time for the definitive revelation of His divine Sonship. This showed that it was not just a man who was sacrificing himself out of love for the world, but the Son of God Himself. He really did show that "God so loved the world that he gave his only-begotten Son, that whoever believes in him should not perish but have eternal life" (Jn 3:16).

At the beginning of His ministry, Jesus decided to keep His divine Sonship (and even to some extent His Messiahship) partially veiled from the crowds, though He gradually revealed it to His disciples and close friends (see below, Section I.B). In the latter part of His ministry (prior to His cleansing of the Temple), He reveals to His friends that He is the exclusive Son of the Father (in the well-known Q logion: "no one knows the Father except the Son" [Mt 11:27]; see below, Section I.B.1), but chooses the path of indirect references (through parables and allegories) for the crowds and religious authorities. He comes very close to declaring His divine Sonship explicitly to the religious authorities in the allegory of the Wicked Tenants ([Mk 12:1–12]; see below, Section I.B.2), but does not identify Himself with the "beloved Son" (Mk 12:6) in the allegory. Nevertheless, if the authorities had listened closely to Him, they would have recognized what He was saying about Himself.

---

[5] Ibid.

For general audiences, Jesus uses the title "Son of man". This title refers to the "son of man" in Daniel 7:13, which in an apocalyptic context portrays a divine figure of "*preexistent* origin who is glorified by God and made a judge".[6] He also signals His divine authority by speaking of Himself as the bringer of the Kingdom and the vanquisher of evil. We have already seen, in the previous chapter, that these are two complementary parts of the same mission; when Jesus brings God's Kingdom into the world—to bring an entranceway leading here and now into His actual Kingdom—He simultaneously vanquishes evil, because all who enter and progress into the Kingdom become more protected from and resistant to evil and its dark master.[7] When Jesus proclaims, after a healing or exorcism, that "the kingdom of God has come upon you",[8] the religious authorities (and some of the crowds) cannot help but see the messianic implications—and if they had "eyes to see" they would see Jesus' divine power manifest by His own authority, making them wonder, "Is this man saying that He is bringing the New Jerusalem, the final age, the reign of Yahweh by His own authority? Who does He think He is?" The combination of Jesus working the miracle by His own authority and claiming that this action is bringing the Kingdom of God into the world (by His own authority) indicates not only His Messiahship but His possession of divine power, which provokes the following question: Who has the authority to bring the Kingdom of God? This question will only be fully answered after Jesus' Crucifixion, Resurrection, and gift of the Spirit.

Some scholars have suggested that Jesus could not have known that He was the exclusive Son of the Father (the only Divine Son who

---

[6] Raymond Brown, *An Introduction to New Testament Christology* (New York: Paulist Press, 1994), pp. 95–96; emphasis mine.

[7] This does not mean that people who enter into the Kingdom are completely safe from evil. As Jesus says again and again, we must remain vigilant and persevere in His Word and works so that the evil one will not prevail over us, for if this should happen after conversion, it can be quite severe, causing incredible harm to the individual as well as many victims: "When the unclean spirit has gone out of a man, he passes through waterless places seeking rest, but he finds none. Then he says, 'I will return to my house from which I came.' And when he comes he finds it empty, swept, and put in order. Then he goes and brings with him seven other spirits more evil than himself, and they enter and dwell there; and the last state of that man becomes worse than the first" (Mt 12:43–45).

[8] "But if it is by the finger of God that I cast out demons, then the kingdom of God has come upon you" (Lk 11:20).

shared in the Father's divine life and power), because it would have been too outlandish for a prophet even of Jesus' stature (a prophet greater than Moses, Elijah, and John the Baptist). Does the evidence support this skeptical position? Readers must ask themselves, "Would Jesus really have exorcised, healed, and raised the dead by His own authority and power, if He did not have some sense that He possessed God's power, that it belonged to Him?" As noted in the last chapter, if He did not really possess God's power, He would have inevitably suffered the terrible embarrassment of saying, "Young man, *I say to you*, arise" (Lk 7:14; emphasis mine), and the young man would have remained dead. The same would have happened with His exorcisms and healings by His own authority and power: "Come out of the man, you impure spirit" (see Mk 1:25–26), and the man would have remained possessed.

Still more questions arise: Would Jesus have really proclaimed the coming of the Kingdom and the vanquishing of evil by His own authority and power if He did not have some cognizance of sharing in the Father's divine power and life?[9] Would Jesus really have declared to His disciples, "All things have been delivered to me by my Father; and no one knows the Son except the Father, and no one knows the Father except the Son and any one to whom the Son chooses to reveal him",[10] unless He believed Himself to be the exclusive Son of the Father? As we shall see, Jesus said and did many other things that would not make sense if He did not believe Himself to be the exclusive Son of the Father—changing and enhancing the Torah by His own authority, declaring the good of individuals to be more important than the law and the Sabbath by His own authority, being the definitive judge of Israel and the initiator of the new age by His own authority, and so on. These prerogatives were thought to be reserved to Yahweh alone by the religious authorities at the time of Jesus.[11] If Jesus had no sense of His divine Sonship, would He have claimed these divine prerogatives?

Well then, who did Jesus think that He was during His ministry? He thought He was a prophet in the line of Elijah, and much

---

[9] As noted in the last chapter, McKenzie shows that the Old Testament associates "life" with "the fullness of power". See McKenzie, *Dictionary of the Bible*, p. 507.

[10] Mt 11:27; cf. Lk 10:22.

[11] Wright, *Jesus and Victory of God*, pp. 649–51.

more—the final prophet and definitive judge of Israel, the bringer of the Kingdom of God, the vanquisher of evil, the preexistent Son of Man, the final interpreter of the law, the unconditional lover and Savior of mankind, and the exclusive beloved Son of the Father, who shared in the fullness of divine life. In short, Jesus thought of Himself as the unconditionally loving God with us. If He did not, the majority of His sayings and actions would be, at best, enigmatic. The above contention is in need of considerable explanation, for how can we be sure that the above claims are historical and how can we know their meaning (at least in part) for Jesus? Research of contemporary scholars has shed considerable light on each of these points, and I am indebted particularly to N. T. Wright for elucidating them so clearly. I will present these findings in two steps:

1. Jesus' identity: the exclusive beloved Son of the Father (Section I)
2. Jesus' mission: bringer of the Kingdom of God (Section II)

I. Jesus' Identity:
The Exclusive Beloved Son of the Father

Some readers may be asking why we are discussing Jesus' identity before His mission since His mission is so integral to His identity. Though this is true, I thought it would be helpful to have a clear insight on how Jesus saw Himself (as the preexistent Son of Man sent in power to be judge of the world and as the exclusive beloved Son of the Father) before considering His claim to bring the Kingdom of God to the world. If we know what Jesus believed to be the source of His divine authority and power (i.e., His preexistent Sonship with the Father), it makes His claims to possess God's Kingdom and to vanquish evil more meaningful and inspiring. It is not just a prophet, not even the greatest of prophets, who claimed to bring the Kingdom and vanquish evil through supernatural intervention—it is the only beloved Son of the Father, who did so by His own divine authority and power. This is the full extent of the good news of Jesus Christ.

There are three major Synoptic texts revealing how Jesus understood His identity (which have stood the test of rigorous historical scrutiny):[12]

1. The Son of Man (Section I.A)
2. "No one knows the Father except the Son" ([Mt 11:27] Section I.B.1)
3. The Parable of the Wicked Tenants (Section I.B.2)

A. The Son of Man

Raymond Brown, among many other scholars, attests to the likelihood that Jesus used the title "Son of Man" for Himself. Two reasons are generally offered for this. First, "Son of Man" is used eighty times in the Gospels by comparison with relatively few uses of titles like "Messiah", "the Lord", or "Son of God". As Brown asks: "Why was this title so massively retrojected, being placed on Jesus' lips on a scale far outdistancing the retrojection of 'the Messiah,' 'the Son of God,' and 'the Lord'?"[13] Such massive retrojection makes little sense if Jesus did not use the title favorably of Himself. Second, there are only four non-Gospel New Testament uses of "Son of Man" by comparison with the eighty Gospel uses. Brown again asks: "If this title was first fashioned by the early church, why has it left almost no traces in nonGospel NT literature, something not true of the other titles?"[14]

The answer almost certainly has to be that "Son of Man" was no longer useful in the post-Resurrection Church. The theology of the New Testament (outside of the Gospel references to Jesus) had evolved because the disciples had witnessed the lordship of Jesus in the Resurrection, His gift of the Holy Spirit, and His miracles

---

[12] There are many other mentions of Jesus' divine Sonship in the New Testament. I have chosen these three, because there is significant agreement among mainstream historical Scripture scholars about the likelihood of their origin in Jesus and their significance for revealing His view of Himself. These texts are sufficient to ground the historicity of Jesus' view of Himself as the preexistent, exclusive beloved Son of the Father. Other texts may enhance these three, but for our purposes, they would only "gild the lily".

[13] Brown, *Introduction to New Testament Christology*, p. 90.

[14] Ibid.

(particularly raising the dead). They had already concluded, as Jesus had told them, that He was the exclusive Son of the Father. In light of all this, it would have made little sense to refer to Jesus (anachronistically) as the "Son of Man". They needed titles that better reflected His Resurrection in glory and gift of the Spirit, such as "the Son of God" and "the Lord".[15] Perhaps the more difficult question is, how did Jesus intend the title "Son of Man" when He used it of Himself during His ministry?

It should first be noted that "Son of Man" can have rather mundane meanings (e.g., "human being", as in the ninety addresses to Ezekiel that mean "O human being"). But this is not the way that Jesus used it of Himself, because He intimates that it has an apocalyptic meaning that hearkens back to "the son of man" in Daniel 7:13–14:

> [T]here came one like a son of man, and he came to the Ancient of Days and was presented before him. And to him was given dominion and glory and kingdom, that all peoples, nations, and languages should serve him; his dominion is an everlasting dominion, which shall not pass away, and his kingdom one that shall not be destroyed.

As noted above, Jesus' most straightforward use of "Son of Man" in this apocalyptic way occurs in Mark's Gospel where Jesus responds to the interrogation of the high priest with an almost verbatim recitation of the passage from Daniel:

> [T]he high priest asked him, "Are you the Christ, the Son of the Blessed?" And Jesus said, "I am; and you will see the Son of man sitting at the right hand of Power, and coming with the clouds of heaven." (Mk 14:61–62)

The parallels between Daniel 7:13–14 and Mark 14:61–62 (which is very likely historical[16]) shows the strong likelihood that Jesus used "Son of Man" in an apocalyptic way, signifying that He is the emissary sent by God to judge the world at the end of the age. It is

---

[15] See above notes 1 and 2.

[16] As noted above, Wright believes that this text is probably historical, because it explains why the authorities had to invent the legal charge of "blasphemy" during Jesus' trial. See Wright, *Jesus and Victory of God*, p. 551.

irrelevant whether the author of Daniel actually intended such a meaning, because subsequent interpreters of it did. Jesus and some of His followers were well aware of these apocalyptic interpretations. These interpretations continued after Jesus' lifetime (see, for example, I Enoch, A.D. 50, and IV Ezra, A.D. 100+).[17]

Brown notes that Michael Stone sees "*pre-existent* Messianic indications" in the four Ezra passages concerned with Daniel 7: "Man is interpreted as the Messiah, precreated and prepared in advance, who will deliver creation and direct those who are left."[18] From this, Brown concludes:

> All this evidence suggests that in apocalyptic Jewish circles of the 1st cent. AD, the portrayal in Dan 7 had given rise to the picture of a messianic human figure of heavenly *preexistent* origin who is glorified by God and made a judge.... Jesus, if he was familiar with apocalyptic thought, could have used "Son of Man" terminology. He need not have read the Parables of *I Enoch*, but only have been aware of some of the burgeoning reflection on Dan 7 that gave or would give rise to the presentation of the Son of Man in the Parables and of the man in *IV Ezra*.[19]

Recent scholarship on the historical Jesus shows that Jesus was aware of and moved by a Jewish apocalyptic mindset, and that He applied this to Himself—not only in His use of the title "Son of man", but also in His belief that He was the final judge of Israel and the final judge of the world itself.[20]

If recent scholarship is correct, then Jesus used the term "Son of man" to refer not only to His present Messiahship, but also to His

---

[17] See Brown, *Introduction to New Testament Christology*, p. 95.

[18] Ibid., referring to Michael E. Stone, *Fourth Ezra* (Minneapolis, Minn.: Fortress, 1990), p. 397.

[19] Brown, *Introduction to New Testament Christology*, pp. 95–96; emphasis mine.

[20] As Wright notes, "The 'Jesus Seminar' has rejected Jewish eschatology, particularly apocalyptic, as an appropriate context for understanding Jesus himself, and in order to do so has declared the Marcan narrative a fiction. The 'Third Quest,' without validating Mark in any simplistic way, has placed Jesus precisely within his Jewish eschatological context, and has found in consequence new avenues of secure historical investigation opening up before it." Wright, *Jesus and the Victory of God*, p. 81. For a summary of the rationale for Jesus' use of "apocalyptic", see ibid., and John P. Meier, "The Present State of the 'Third Quest' for the Historical Jesus: Loss and Gain", *Biblica* 80 (1999): 459–87.

preexistent Messiahship (as implied in the apocalyptic interpretations of the Daniel passage). He very likely thought of Himself as the pre-existent emissary of God sent into the world to be its final judge.

B. The Only Beloved Son

Jesus gave many *indirect* indications of His divine power and authority that implied His awareness of being the Father's only-begotten Son. For example,

1. exorcising, healing, and raising the dead by His own authority alone (see Chapter 5);
2. referring to Himself as the apocalyptic Son of Man, implying that He is the *preexistent* judge of the world (see above);
3. teaching His disciples to address God in the same way He did, as "Abba" (see Chapter 2, Section III.B); and
4. preaching that He was bringing the Kingdom of God and vanquishing Satan by His own power and authority (see below, Section II).

Jesus was undoubtedly aware of His divine power to exorcise, heal, and raise the dead. If He were not, He would never have attempted to use it in a public way in which He could have been easily exposed as a fraud (i.e., by failing in His attempts to exorcise and heal by His own word and authority).

Jesus believed that the source of His divine power was His relationship—that is, His Sonship—with His Divine Father (Abba). He viewed this relationship as a deep, loving communion that existed prior to His appearance in the world. Can this be historically validated? In addition to Jesus' apocalyptic use of "Son of Man" (implying "preexistence with God"), there are two passages from the Synoptic Gospels that have undergone substantial historical testing and validation by mainstream scholars:

1. Jesus' proclamation that "no one knows the Father except the Son" (Mt 11:27; cf. Lk 10:22)
2. The allegory of the Wicked Tenants (Mk 12:1–12)

There are many other references in the New Testament to Jesus' preexistent divine Sonship, but these two almost certainly originated with Jesus and are sufficient to show that He had an awareness of Himself as the only-begotten Son of His Divine Father (and saw this Sonship as the source of His divine power).

1. "No One Knows the Father except the Son"

In Matthew 11:25–27 and Luke 10:21–22, we encounter a Q logion,[21] which some have characterized as a "meteor from the Johannine heaven"[22] because of its direct reference to Jesus' exclusive Sonship:

> I thank you, Father, Lord of heaven and earth, that you have hidden these things from the wise and understanding and revealed them to infants; yes, Father, for such was your gracious will. All things have been delivered to me by my Father; and no one [fully] knows[23] the Son except the Father, and no one [fully] knows the Father except the Son and any one to whom the Son chooses to reveal him. (Mt 11:25–27; cf. Lk 10:21–22)

This prayer and proclamation is a Q logion that predates Matthew and Luke, and probably originated with Jesus. Joachim Jeremias provides evidence to support this. Recall from his study of "Abba" (Chapter 2, Section III.B) that "Abba" used in the context of prayer is virtually unique to Jesus, and that continued use of this address (and its Greek translation) indicates that Jesus is its probable source. Jeremias also specified that "we have every reason to suppose that an

---

[21] Recall that the Q source was a compilation of Jesus' sayings translated into Greek, which both Matthew and Luke used in their Gospels. It is a very early source of Jesus' sayings.

[22] John L. McKenzie, "The Gospel according to Matthew", in *The Jerome Biblical Commentary*, eds. Raymond Brown, Joseph A. Fitzmyer, and Roland E. Murphy (Englewood Cliffs, N.J.: Prentice-Hall, 1968), 2:83. The reason for this comment is that John has a developed Christology that speaks frequently about the exclusive relationship between the Father and the Son while the Synoptics do not. The occurrence of this passage as a Q logion (an early source of Jesus' sayings) indicates that it did not arise after a long period of theological reflection (as John's Gospel), and so it seems to have come from a time close to Jesus Himself. When one considers the number of "Abba" references in this passage, it can be traced back to Jesus and gives us an insight into what He thought about Himself (see the analysis below in this section).

[23] In Luke, *ginōskei* (knows); in Matthew, *epiginōskei* (fully knows).

Abba underlies every instance of *pater* (*mou*) or *ho patēr* in his *words of prayer*."[24]

This is precisely what we find in the above Q logion (the later part of which is *a prayer*),[25] where the Greek translation for "Abba" is used not only once, but twice: (1) in Matthew 11:25 (Lk 10:21), where *pater* is used without the definite article in a prayer context that is translated as a vocative "Abba",[26] and (2) in Matthew 11:26 (Lk 10:21), where *ho pater* is used as an articular nominative indicating a vocative "Abba".[27] The vocative use of the Semitism "Abba" in this logion points to Jesus as its source, because this address to God within prayer is virtually unique to Jesus and is used almost exclusively of Him.

This passage shows that Jesus believed Himself to be the *exclusive* Son of the Father because it uses three references to "*the* Son" (in which the definite article implies exclusivity): "ton huion ... ho huios ... ho huios".

Furthermore, Jesus claims within the prayer that all things have been given over to *Him*. As McKenzie notes, *panta* (all things) probably refers to all revelation, and "this is a direct contradiction of the Jewish claim to have the complete revelation of God in the Law and the Prophets."[28] Jesus claims to have greater revelation than the law (a divine prerogative), which implies that "the Son" in the next line (who fully knows the Father) refers to Him.

---

[24]Joachim Jeremias, *New Testament Theology* (New York: Charles Scribner's Sons, 1971), 1:65; emphasis mine.

[25]See Geoffrey Bromiley, *The International Standard Bible Encyclopedia* (Grand Rapids, Mich.: William B. Eerdmans, 1988), s.v. "Abba". See also Chapter 5, Section II.B, for a specific quotation of this confirmation with respect to Matthew 11:25 and Luke 10:22 (the Q logion under consideration).

[26]See the following in ibid.: "*pater* ('father'), the Greek vocative (Mt. 11:25 par. Lk 10:21a; Lk. 11:2; 22:42; 23:34, 46; Jn. 11:41; 12:27f.; 17:1, 5, 11, 21, 24f.)" See also Chapter 2, Section III.B., for the full quotation.

[27]See the following in ibid.: "'*ho pater*' ('the father'), the articular nominative used as a vocative (Mk. 14:36 [*Abba ho pater*; cf. Rom. 8:15; Gal. 4:6]—correct Greek form, since the second member of a compound address is always in the nominative [Robertson, p. 461]; Mt. 11:26 par. Lk. 10:21b—incorrect Greek usage, and therefore in all probability a Semitism, since the articular nominative constitutes the vocative in both Hebrew and Aramaic [Turner, p. 34])" (*The International Standard Bible Encyclopedia*, entry under "Abba"). Note that the use of *ho pater* is incorrect Greek usage in Luke 10:21 (which Luke intentionally preserves), indicating an underlying Semitism for the reasons mentioned above.

[28]McKenzie, "Gospel according to Matthew", p. 83.

Despite the textual indications that Jesus is the source of the logion, some scholars hesitate to ascribe it to Jesus because its claim to Sonship is uncharacteristically straightforward and developed. Jesus generally avoids straightforward references to Himself as "exclusive Son of the Father", except to His disciples. As noted above (Section I.A), He prefers to use the title "Son of man" for Himself, and only *indirectly* indicates His divine Sonship. If He had expressed this to the crowds and religious authorities, it would have resulted in a premature end to His mission.

We should not infer from Jesus' cryptic and implicit references to his divine Sonship that He did not know it. As noted previously, this would have made His ministry of miracles and His bringing the Kingdom inexplicable. Furthermore, Jesus took it upon Himself to complete the mission reserved by Scripture to Yahweh alone (see below, Section II.C). He would never have done this without recognizing His divine Sonship. As Wright notes:

> If it is true, as I have argued, that [Jesus] acted upon a vocation to do and be for Israel and the world what, according to scripture, only Israel's *God* can do and be, then we may legitimately enquire whether we have any clues as to what generated, sustained, or at least centrally characterized that vocation. When, asking that question, we discover that Jesus seems to have addressed Israel's God as "father" in a way which, even if not completely unique, is at least very remarkable, we may be near to an answer. And when we find a passage like [the Q logion—Mt 11:25–27; Lk 10:22]—then we may be confirmed in this deduction.[29]

The above Q logion indicates Jesus' awareness of being the exclusive Son of the Father and that this relationship, which brought with it divine authority and power, was the source of His ministry of exorcism, healing, and raising the dead that brought the Kingdom of God and the fulfillment of the mission reserved for Yahweh alone. If we had no record of this logion, it would present historical conundrum because everything about Jesus' ministry indicates that it should have been recounted in the Gospels and their sources.

---

[29] Wright, *Jesus and Victory of God*, pp. 649–50; emphasis mine.

What did Jesus mean by His prayer and proclamation? First, He says that He has special access to the Father and special knowledge of the Father, the access and knowledge that only a son could have— a familial access and knowledge that penetrates to the heart. We must understand the Semitic sense of "knowing" to appreciate this. McKenzie states:

> The Israelite *knew* with the *heart*, and Hebrew has no word which corresponds exactly to our "mind" or "intellect." ... In general it may be said that in Hebrew, to know is to experience; experience develops into acceptance or possession.[30]

Jesus had an intimate experiential knowledge of the Father that was so close that He could know the Father in His heart just as the Father knew Him. This claim suggests being in loving union with His Father, which in turn suggests a sharing in the divine *life*. As McKenzie notes, the idea of "life" also entails the idea of "fullness of power",[31] and so sharing in the divine life is also sharing in the fullness of power. One would be hard-pressed to find a clearer Semitic statement indicating "loving unity with the Father" and "sharing in the Father's life and fullness of power".

As the context of the logion indicates, the prayer is addressed to the Father while the proclamation is for the benefit of the disciples. It could not have been addressed to other audiences, because if it were overheard by the religious authorities, it may have resulted in a persecution of Jesus before His appointed time.

For Jesus (and His Semitic interpreters), "knowing the Father as the Father knows Him" implies union with the Father, which implies sharing in the life of the Father, which in turn implies sharing in the Father's "fullness of power". It is not a far stretch from there to the early christological hymns (which make use of Hellenistic philosophical concepts[32])—such as "in the form of God"

---

[30] McKenzie, *Dictionary of the Bible*, p. 485; emphasis mine.

[31] See ibid., p. 507.

[32] The early Church was aware of Hellenistic philosophical terminology through later Wisdom literature, particularly the hymns to Wisdom in Sirach and the Book of Wisdom. See, for example, Wisdom 7:25–27: "For [wisdom] is a breath of the power of God, and a pure emanation of the glory of the Almighty.... For she is a reflection of eternal light, a spotless

(Phil 2:6; "morphē Theou") and "being equal to God" (Phil 2:6 [D-R]; "to einai isa Theō")—and to identification with God (Jn 1:1: "and the Word was with God"; "kai Theos ēn ho Logos"). (These christological hymns and their references to Jesus' divinity are examined below in Section III.)

Did Jesus claim to be the exclusive Son of the Father? To His disciples, He did, and He interpreted this exclusive Sonship as sharing in the Father's life (and the fullness of His power). To the crowds, Jesus claims to be the preexistent Son of Man who comes from God to judge the world and initiate the new age. To his adversaries, Jesus claims to be the only-begotten beloved Son who comes as final prophet and judge of Israel (in the Allegory of the Wicked Tenants; see the following subsection). Jesus tailored each of these identity statements for His three audiences. Though the phrasing of each statement is different, they all imply exclusive Sonship and a sharing in God's life and power. Let us now turn to the allegory of the Wicked Tenants.

2. The Allegory of the Wicked Tenants (Mk 12:1–12)

The Allegory of the Wicked Tenants (Mk 12:1–12) portrays the history of Israel; the owner of a vineyard (symbolizing God) sends several servants (symbolizing the prophets) to the tenants of the vineyard to obtain his fair share of the produce. The tenants beat some of the servants and even kill some. Finally, the owner sends his "beloved son" (huion agapēton; Mk 12:6), whom they also kill. The implication is that the owner had only one son ("he had ... one"—ena eichen; Mk 12:6), which the allegory later describes as being "the heir" (ho klēronomos; Mk 12:7; emphasis mine). Wright believes that this allegory was not only spoken by Jesus, but was deliberately self-referential.[33]

Some exegetes have challenged the historicity of the story because it is more like an allegory (with many points of connection between symbol and reality; e.g., the owner = God, the servants = the prophets, the beloved son = Jesus) than a parable (which has a more general

---

mirror of the working of God, and an image of his goodness. Though she is but one, she can do all things, and while remaining in herself, she renews all things".

[33] See Wright, Jesus and the Victory of God, pp. 497–501. See the analysis given below in this subsection.

point of connection—frequently a single one). Jesus spoke mostly in parables and rarely in allegories.[34]

Just because Jesus uses parables *most* of the time does not mean He *has to* use parables *all* the time. Jesus was aware of many examples of allegory in Old Testament writings and was certainly capable of effectively using them in an appropriate context. His use of allegory here reflects an exception to His usual parabolic style. The allegory is not about the Kingdom of God (as with most parables), but rather, about the judgment of Israel.

So what does Jesus mean by this implied allegory? Wright and other Scripture scholars see it as an interpretation of His cleansing of the Temple (i.e., driving out the money changers and vendors from the Temple area), which initiates His prophetic and final judgment of Israel. The allegory symbolically represents the history of Israel's rejection of the prophets culminating in Jesus' rejection by the Jewish authorities, which will result in God's cleansing action (the destruction of the Temple).[35]

Jesus' prediction of the destruction of the Temple must be considered within the context of His prophetic mission. Jesus saw Himself as a prophet in the line of Elijah—and much more. In the allegory, He defines Himself as the *final* prophet who will render definitive judgment on Israel.

In Israel, prophets render judgment, issue warnings about impending disaster, call to conversion, and speak of the vindication of the just. Inasmuch as Jesus saw Himself as the *final* prophet (bringing the prophetic tradition to its completion and fulfillment), His

---

[34] The Parable of the Prodigal Son (Luke 15) also has allegorical features (e.g., the father = God, the older son = the righteous representative of the Old Covenant, the foreign land represents the Gentiles, etc.). Wright sees an even deeper allegorical base in this parable with various symbols representing the history of Israel (see Wright, *Jesus and the Victory of God*, pp. 125–31). Some exegetes have contended that the Parable of the Prodigal Son did not originate with Jesus because of its use of allegory and its single attestation (special Luke only). However, as Wright points out, the evidence for historicity is quite telling (ibid., p. 51), and Jeremias has identified several Semitisms and other features that would have to have come from a Jewish author who was writing to a Jewish audience (unlike Luke who was a Gentile, writing for Gentile audiences). See Joachim Jeremias, *The Parables of Jesus* (London: SCM Press, 1972), pp. 128–31. Even the Jesus Seminar's Dominic Crossan believes that it is historical (see Wright, *Jesus and the Victory of God*, p. 51).

[35] See Wright, *Jesus and the Victory of God*, pp. 497–501.

Temple-cleansing action called Israel to its *final* repentance, and predicted a *final* disaster if Israel did not repent. If this disaster were to befall Israel, it would lead to a New *Jerusalem*, and then to the salvation of the Gentiles through it.

Why did Jesus believe He was the final prophet and judge of Israel, the one to bring the Old Jerusalem to its close, and to initiate the New Jerusalem? He says it clearly in the allegory: He is the only-beloved Son of the Vineyard Owner (God the Father). His belief in His divine Sonship warrants His mission as final prophet and judge of Israel, which in turn justifies His cleansing of the Temple. The Temple cleansing was not an act of spontaneous rage, but rather a prophetic gesture to initiate the time of judgment and destruction that would open the way to the New Jerusalem. If Jesus did not believe in His divine Sonship (and Messiahship), He would not have considered Himself the final prophet and definitive judge of Israel, and if He did not believe this, He would not have cleansed the Temple.

If Wright has correctly interpreted this allegory, then it is likely that Jesus claimed to be God's only Son. His adversaries knew they were being judged and most likely understood the implications of Jesus' Temple cleansing. Though Jesus does not directly identify Himself as the only-beloved Son in the allegory, His use of the allegory to interpret His Temple cleansing made the identification clear for anyone who wanted to see it.

So who did Jesus think that He was? So far, we have seen four dimensions of His self-understanding:

1. The one who possesses divine authority and power within Himself (Chapter 5)
2. The preexistent Son of Man, who comes to judge Israel and the world (Section I.A)
3. The exclusive Son of the Father, who shares fully in the Father's life and power (Section I.B.1)
4. The final judge of Israel as the Father's beloved Son (Section I.B.2)

Is there any other indication of Jesus' claim to be the exclusive Divine Son besides these sayings and actions? There is, and it is integral to His mission: to bring the Kingdom of God, to vanquish evil, and to initiate the new age—the mission reserved by Scripture to Yahweh alone.[36]

II. Jesus' Mission: To Bring the Kingdom of God

Bringing the Kingdom of God is central to the mission of Jesus. It is mentioned over one hundred times in the New Testament, over seventy of which are in the Synoptic Gospels. If we are to understand Jesus' view of Himself and His mission, we will have to probe this deep, rich, mysterious, dialectical, immanent, and transcendent already-and-not-yet reality.

A. Jesus' Idea of the Kingdom

The "Kingdom of God" is the most synthetic concept in the Gospels. It is the reality that is thought to be the way, the means, and the end of humanity, and, as such, is identified with Jesus Himself. It is also identified with the divine life, and therefore, with the perfect, eternal condition of God to which all humanity is called. When Jesus says that "the kingdom of God is at hand" (Mk 1:15), He means at once that He is bringing the divine life of the Father (with its incredible dynamic to overcome evil) into our midst, which calls us to eternal life with the Father.

Jesus' proclamation of the reality of the Kingdom (coming in His Person) calls upon His audience's awareness of the Old Testament, particularly apocalyptic and prophetic literature.[37] According to McKenzie:

> The idea of the kingdom of God reflects the Old Testament conception of the kingship of *Yahweh*.... In Daniel 7:14, 18, 22, 27 the

---

[36]For Wright's analysis of "the mission reserved by Israel to Yahweh alone" and his Old Testament sources for this, see ibid., pp. 463–64 and 649–53. His conclusions are given below in Section II.C.

[37]See E. P. Sanders, *Jesus and Judaism* (Philadelphia: Fortress, 1985), pp. 123–41, and John P. Meier, *A Marginal Jew: Rethinking the Historical Jesus*, vol. 1, *The Roots of the Problem and the Person* (New York: Doubleday, 1991), pp. 125–27 and 174–77.

kingdom is given to the Son of Man and to the saints. In Daniel 4:3 the everlasting kingdom of God is mentioned. The throne of the reign of God appears in Daniel 3:54 (Greek). The kingdom of *Yahweh* is universal and everlasting, a kingdom of glory, power, and splendor (Psalms 103:19; 145:11–13).... These allusions show how Jesus could employ the term with no introductory explanation.[38]

Jesus adds to this Old Testament apocalyptic context the idea of an eternal, messianic banquet[39] and extends the notion to opening the Father's eternal life, love, and joy to all who have faith in Him.[40]

The Kingdom is not limited to its future perfect manifestation; it also causes a dynamic force (the goodness of God) to enter into the world here and now. This dynamic activity is best characterized by Jesus' many parables of the Kingdom (which Jeremias and other scholars believe to be the unedited voice of Jesus Himself[41]). The eight parables in Matthew 13[42] illustrate three dimensions of the Kingdom's presence in the world:

1. its dynamism and capacity to grow within individuals and the community,
2. the need for each person to choose it and remain faithful to it, and
3. the need to contend with evil that remains in the world.

The later parables in Matthew[43] emphasize three additional themes:

1. the interaction of God with His Kingdom in the world,
2. God's generosity and mercy, and
3. the need for us to be compassionate (as the Father is) and vigilant in remaining true to the Kingdom.

[38] McKenzie, *Dictionary of the Bible*, pp. 479–80.

[39] Mt 8:11f.; 22:1–10; 26:29; Mk 14:25; Lk 13:28f.; 14:16–24; 22:30.

[40] Mt 16:28; Jn 18:36; Mk 9:1, 47; Lk 1:33; 9:27; 23:42.

[41] See Jeremias, *Parables of Jesus*.

[42] The Parable of the Sower, the Parable of the Weeds, the Parable of the Mustard Seed, the Parable of the Yeast, the Parable of the Hidden Treasure, the Parable of the Pearl of Great Price, the Parable of the Catch of Good and Bad Fish, and the Parable of the Householder with Good and Bad Treasure.

[43] The Parable of the Wicked Servant (Mt 18:23–35), the Parable of the Generous Vineyard Owner (Mt 20:1–16); and the Parable of the Foolish Virgins (Mt 25:1–13).

Luke associates this dynamic force with the gifts of the Holy Spirit (Lk 17:20f.). McKenzie summarizes the above six themes as follows:

> The kingdom is the preaching of the word; it contains both good and bad; it grows to greatness from imperceptible beginnings; it is a treasure for which a man should trade all his possessions. It imposes obligations of love and forgiveness. It admits all comers. It demands an alert readiness. The emerging conception is of a single reality which is present and operative but which inevitably must reach a fulfillment of cosmic scope. It presents a challenge to each man which cannot be evaded: the challenge whether he accepts the sovereignty of God or not.[44]

In sum, Jesus views the Kingdom of God as the arrival of God's dynamic and perfect goodness and love in the world. He tells us we will have to look for it (amid many distractions and glories in the world), as well as choose it and remain faithful to it. If we do choose and remain faithful to the Kingdom, its power will affect us, making us "Kingdom builders". We will be confronted by evil (which remains in the world along with the Kingdom), but when we reach the perfection of the Kingdom (with God), there will be no evil. God's love is the power of the Kingdom, Jesus is its definitive bringer, and the Holy Spirit helps both individuals and the community. God will accept us anytime we want to enter, and will lavish His generosity upon us regardless of when we enter. We must remain vigilant about staying in the Kingdom, and we should use our talents to build it.

B. Jesus as Definitive Bringer of the Kingdom

Jesus viewed Himself as the definitive bringer of God's salvation[45] and Kingdom. As Jeremias notes:

> [Jesus] describes himself as the messenger of God who issues a call to the festal meal (Mark 2.17 par.), as the physician for the sick (*ibid.*),

---

[44] McKenzie, *Dictionary of the Bible*, p. 481.

[45] The name of Jesus (*yēsua*) means "Yahweh is salvation", and so designates Jesus as "Savior".

as the shepherd (Mark 14.27f. par.; John 10), as the master-builder of the Temple of God (Mark 14.58 par.; Matt. 16.18) and as the father of the house, who gathers the family of God at his table (Mt10.24f.; Lk 22.29f). These pictures describe in symbolic language the bringer of salvation, and all have an eschatological ring.[46]

Jesus not only speaks of the Kingdom; *He acts it out* and with each action further infuses it within the world. We have already seen this effect of the Kingdom in the previous chapter with respect to exorcisms, healings, and raising the dead. Brown confirms this by noting:

> The miracle was not primarily an external proof of the coming of the kingdom (i.e., the fact that Jesus worked miracles proved that the kingdom had come), *but one of the means by which the kingdom came.* The acts of power were weapons Jesus used to reclaim people and the world from the domination of evil. When Jesus healed the sick or resuscitated the dead, he was breaking Satanic power that manifested itself in illness and death ... and those activities lock into the coming of the kingdom: "If it is by God's spirit that I cast out demons, then it follows that the kingdom of God has at last overtaken you" (Matt 12:28).[47]

It is not only through the miracles that Jesus allows the Kingdom to break through into the world; it is through many other consciously selected activities. Meier notes in this regard:

> In his exorcisms, in his other striking deeds judged miraculous by his contemporaries, in his formation of an inner circle of disciples, in his table fellowship with toll collectors and sinners, in his "cleansing" of the Jerusalem temple—in all these deeds he was "acting out" his message. Hence it is significant and hardly accidental that at least on some occasions Jesus chose to explain such striking actions in terms of the kingdom of God having already come to his audience.[48]

Jesus saw every exorcism, miracle, loving action (toward the poor, sinners, and His disciples), and every proclamation of the good news

[46] Jeremias, *New Testament Theology*, p. 251.
[47] Brown, *Introduction to New Testament Christology*, pp. 64–65.
[48] John P. Meier, *A Marginal Jew: Rethinking the Historical Jesus*, vol. 2, *Mentor, Message, and Miracles* (New York: Doubleday, 1994), p. 425.

as building and strengthening His Kingdom in the world. He saw His impending self-sacrifice as the unconditional love that would bring the Kingdom definitively and eternally. Bringing the Kingdom has two effects that are opposite sides of the same coin:

1. Making present the healing, protecting, sustaining, guiding, inspiring, and fulfilling love and goodness of God
2. Defeating the kingdom of evil in the world and vanquishing Satan (the leader of the evil kingdom)

When Jesus brings the Kingdom, He not only brings the dynamic healing and redeeming presence of *Yahweh*; He simultaneously brings the vanquishing of Satan. We have already discussed the first dimension of the Kingdom (the presence of God's dynamic love in the world) with respect to the Holy Spirit and the Church community in Volume I of this Quartet (Chapters 6 and 8). We will discuss the second dimension (the defeat of evil) in Volume IV of this Quartet. Readers may be unfamiliar with the second dimension of the Kingdom, particularly as Jesus saw it, and so it merits further consideration.

Jesus' awareness of His battle with Satan[49] comes from His privileged vision into the casting out of Satan from Heaven:

> The seventy returned with joy, saying, "Lord, even the demons are subject to us in your name!" And he said to them, "I saw Satan fall like lightning from heaven. Behold, I have given you authority to tread upon serpents and scorpions, and over all the power of the enemy; and nothing shall hurt you. (Lk 10:17–19, my translation)[50]

Jeremias contends:

> There is no analogy to these statements in contemporary Judaism; neither the synagogue nor Qumran knows anything of a vanquishing of Satan that is already beginning in the present.[51]

---

[49] Satan is called the "strong one" (Mt 12:29; Mk 3:27; Lk 11:21), "the evil one" (Mt 13:19), the "prince of this world" (Jn 12:31 [D-R]), and the source of the power of darkness (Lk 22:53; Acts 26:18).

[50] These statements may be found in a variety of non-Lucan texts, such as Mark 3:14; 6:7–13; and Matthew 7:22; 10:7.

[51] Jeremias, *New Testament Theology*, p. 95.

For Jesus, the battle is initiated when He successfully overcomes the temptations of Satan. Wright characterizes this as follows:

> Where did Jesus' victory over the powers of evil begin? All three synoptic gospels provide an answer: in a dramatic battle at the outset of Jesus' public career.... Some kind of experience, early in his career, in which Jesus believed himself to have won an initial decisive victory over the "real enemy," must be postulated if we are to explain what was said during the Beelzebul controversy.[52]

After the initiation of His battle with Satan (in successfully overcoming the temptations), Jesus begins His ministry of exorcisms, which continues (along with His healing miracles) until His final journey to Jerusalem. At this point, Jesus brings His battle with Satan and His initiation of the Kingdom to a whole new level—a definitive climax, in which He voluntarily sacrifices Himself in great suffering for all (see Chapter 3, Section IV). Jesus harkens back to a long-standing, deep tradition in Israel of redemption through suffering. We saw this with respect to the Fourth Suffering Servant Song (Is 52:13–53:12), in Jesus' Eucharistic words, and in Psalm 22 on the lips of the dying Jesus (see Chapter 3, Section IV). Wright sees an even deeper tradition with which Jesus was familiar:

> The symbol of suffering was itself a key ingredient within the Jewish expectation of the great deliverance, the great victory. If, then, Jesus was retelling a story which belonged genetically within this group of Jewish narratives [Daniel facing the lions, the Maccabaean martyrdom, the Son of man suffering at the hands of the beasts], as I have argued that he was, there is a strong probability that he envisaged for himself a similar fate of suffering and vindication. The language placed on his lips at various points of the passion narrative [particularly Psalm 22[53]] probably reflects an awareness of vocation that, historically, had preoccupied him for much longer. [This event of suffering would bring] to birth the reign of [Israel's] God.[54]

As implied in the three narratives of the Book of Daniel, as well as the Fourth Suffering Servant Song and Psalm 22, God vindicates

---

[52] Wright, *Jesus and the Victory of God*, p. 457.

[53] See the extensive explanation of Psalm 22 in Chapter 3, Section IV.B of this book.

[54] Wright, *Jesus and the Victory of God*, pp. 465–66.

the suffering of the innocent victim and uses it for the redemption of Israel. Jesus sees His mission in an even larger context. He sought not merely the redemption of Israel but the defeat of evil and the initiation of God's Kingdom in the *world*. Jesus anticipated His Resurrection and vindication, and so He believed that His act of total self-sacrifice would be a culminating act to bring the Kingdom into the world, which entails the ultimate defeat of Satan. When the apostles witnessed His Resurrection, they realized that the Kingdom had indeed been established, and that Jesus' gift of the Holy Spirit and the Church (for which they were now responsible) would be the means through which the Kingdom would be manifest until the end of the age, when it would be brought to its ultimate fulfillment in the eternal unconditional love of the Father.

We must still address the central question of this section. Is Jesus' Messiahship and divine Sonship implicit in His mission to bring God's Kingdom to the world? It is, and it blends well with the other clues we have encountered: His exorcisms, healings, and raisings of the dead by His own authority and power, as well as His claim to be the preexistent Son of Man, the only one who knows the Father, and the only beloved Son of the Vineyard Owner. This can be seen in three dimensions of His ministry:

1. His unique claim to vanquish evil,
2. His prohibition of fasting to His disciples, and
3. His appropriation of the mission reserved by Scripture to Yahweh alone.

We will discuss each in turn.

First, as we have seen, Jesus intended to vanquish Satan in the very act of bringing God's Kingdom, beginning with His successful overcoming of temptation, extending into His ministry of exorcism, and concluding in His complete self-sacrifice. No other figure in Jewish history ever saw himself as responsible for the defeat of evil, the defeat of Satan; no other figure thought he was responsible for replacing the dominion of Satan with the Kingdom of God; no other figure had a plan to accomplish this definitive eschatological task; no other figure had the power over Satan to initially effect it, and the vindication of the Resurrection and gift of the Holy Spirit to complete it. If Jesus did not think of Himself as the Messiah and *Divine* Savior, how could He have considered Himself to be worthy and capable of this *divine* eschatological mission?

Second, Jesus sees His mission of bringing God's Kingdom to be the time of joy in which Yahweh is present (initiating the renewal of Jerusalem). This is evident in His prohibition of fasting:

> Now John's disciples and the Pharisees were fasting; and people came and said to him, "Why do John's disciples and the disciples of the Pharisees fast, but your disciples do not fast?" And Jesus said to them, "Can the wedding guests fast while the bridegroom is with them? As long as they have the bridegroom with them, they cannot [*ou dunantai*—'impossible'] fast." (Mk 2:18–19)

Fasting was an important regular dimension of Jewish piety, and so prohibiting His disciples from fasting would have been considered an affront to both Jewish tradition and authority. Why would Jesus have made such a requirement of His disciples? After all, it would seem that fasting is spiritually beneficial. The answer is directly connected to Jesus' belief that He is bringing the salvation (Kingdom) of God, in its eschatological and eternal significance, to the world, indicating both the presence of Yahweh (in Jesus) and the time of joy that marks Yahweh's presence. Just as it would be absurd to think about fasting during a wedding feast, so also it is absurd to think about fasting during the time of joy when *Yahweh is present*. Meier notes in this regard that "*as a matter of principle* [Jesus] proclaims that it is *impossible* for his disciples to undertake voluntary fasts because of the joyful time of salvation he announces and brings (Mark 2:18–19a)."[55]

C. Jesus Accomplishes the Mission Reserved to Yahweh

Finally, when we put all the puzzle pieces together, we notice that Jesus' bringing of God's Kingdom into the world manifests all the characteristics of the mission reserved by Scripture to Yahweh alone. As we have seen above, Jesus' bringing of the Kingdom is the presence

---

[55] Meier, *Marginal Jew*, p. 449; emphasis in original.

of Yahweh (marked by His prohibition of fasting), the vanquishing of Satan (marked by His overcoming of temptation, ministry of
exorcism, and complete self-sacrifice), and the renewal of Jerusalem
(implicit in the Temple cleansing and the Allegory of the Wicked
Tenants). Wright notices that all three of these activities are reserved
by Scripture to Yahweh alone:

> The kingdom of YHWH was itself [Jesus'] proffered solution [to the
> impending cosmic battle], with its component elements of *the return*
> *of the true Israel from exile, the defeat of evil, and the return of YHWH to*
> *Zion.* ... But, if this is one obvious answer, the other one is "Jesus
> himself". He claimed that the kingdom had arrived where he was, and
> with his activity.... His own work—his kingdom-announcement, his
> prophetic praxis, his celebrations, his warnings, his symbolic activity—
> all of these were part of the movement through which Israel would be
> renewed, evil would be defeated, and YHWH would return to Zion
> at last.[56]

The Kingdom of God would bring Yahweh back to Israel, the
defeat of evil, and the renewal of Jerusalem, and this is precisely
what Jesus claims for Himself. Jesus *is* the presence of God's dynamic
Kingdom in the world; He is God's presence, power, and authority
defeating evil and renewing Israel—He is not only the preexistent
Son of Man; He shares directly in the presence, power, and authority
of Yahweh Himself. In view of this, Wright concludes:

> Jesus' prophetic vocation thus included within it the vocation to enact,
> symbolically, the return of YHWH to Zion. His messianic voca-
> tion included within it the vocation to attempt certain tasks which,
> according to scripture, YHWH had reserved for himself. He would
> take up himself the role of messianic shepherd, knowing that YHWH
> had claimed this role as his own. He would perform the saving task
> which YHWH had said he alone could achieve. He would do what
> no messenger, no angel, but only the "arm of YHWH", the presence
> of Israel's God, could accomplish.... He believed he had to do and
> be, for Israel and the world, that which according to scripture only
> YHWH himself could do and be.... I propose, as a matter of history,

[56]Wright, *Jesus and the Victory of God*, pp. 463–64; emphasis mine.

that Jesus of Nazareth was conscious of a vocation: a vocation, *given* him by the one he knew as "father", to enact *in himself* what, in Israel's scriptures, God had promised to accomplish all by himself.[57]

Did Jesus believe He was the Messiah? If He did not, how could He have endeavored, let alone accomplished, the mission reserved to Yahweh? Did Jesus believe that He was the exclusive Son of the Father? If He did not, how could He have authentically enacted "*in himself* what, in Israel's scriptures, God had promised to accomplish all by himself"? As Wright suggests, Jesus "believed he had to do and be, for Israel and the world, that which according to scripture only YHWH himself could do and be."

If Jesus truly is the Messiah, God's Son, and the unconditionally loving God with us, then the Kingdom He brought is no fiction; it is a reality second only to the triune God.

III. Jesus Is Emmanuel

In the introduction to this chapter, we gave an initial answer to the following question: Who did Jesus think he was? The foregoing analysis justifies the answer we gave there. He thought He was a prophet in the line of Elijah—and much more: the final prophet and definitive judge of Israel, the bringer of the Kingdom of God, the vanquisher of Satan, the preexistent Son of Man, the final interpreter of the law, the unconditional lover and Savior of the world, and the exclusive beloved Son of the Father, who shared in the fullness of His divine life and power.

His consciousness of this identity came from five sources:

- His intimate relationship with the Father (manifest in the Q logion—Mt 11:25–27 and Luke 10:22 discussed above—and His address of God as "Abba")
- His awareness of possessing the Spirit of God, His Father, within Himself (manifest in His proclamation of being the fulfillment of Isaiah 61:1–3)

---

[57] Ibid., p. 653; emphasis in original.

- His possession of the power of God within Himself (manifest in His exorcisms, healings, and raisings of the dead by His own authority and word)
- His awareness of being the *one* missioned to confront and defeat Satan (manifest in Satan's confrontation with Him during the temptations; discussed above in Section II.B)
- His understanding of these four divine prerogatives through the Scriptures of Israel

Jesus was so confident in His preexistent and exclusive Sonship with God His Father that He took on and completed the mission reserved by Israel to Yahweh alone, and proclaimed that He knew the Father as the Father knew Him. Everything He experienced about Himself—His intimate relationship with the Father, His possession of the Holy Spirit, the power of God working through His word and authority, and His victories over Satan—made Him aware of this exclusive Sonship. He could not avoid it, and so He turned to the Scriptures of Israel to interpret His identity and mission. He knew He was Emmanuel, the unconditionally loving God with us.

When the apostles and early witnesses saw His risen glory and received the gift of the Holy Spirit, they knew He was precisely who He claimed to be: the exclusive Son of His heavenly Father. As they proclaimed his divine Sonship and used His name in their ministry of healing and miracles, they formed the Church that would spread throughout the world, open to *all* who desire it and who believe that love is the meaning of life, and unconditional love, their redemption and fulfillment.

Shortly after Jesus' Resurrection (prior to the writing of Paul's Letter to the Philippians), scribes within the new Christian Church created a liturgical hymn to express their belief in Jesus as Emmanuel.[58]

---

[58] Though this hymn is presented in Paul's Letter to the Philippians, it predates the writing of that letter by several years and is not of Pauline origin. This is indicated by a probable Aramaic background for the hymn, which is later translated into technical (philosophical) Greek by early Christian scribes. See the work on the Aramaic background of the Philippians hymn in Ernst Lohmeyer, "Kyrios Jesus: Eine Untersuchung zu Phil 2:5–11", *Sitzungsberichte der Heidelberger Akademie der Wissenschaften*, Philosophisch-historische Klasse 1927-28/4 (Heidelberg: Winter, 1928), and Joseph A. Fitzmyer, "The Aramaic Background of Philippians 2:6–11", *The Catholic Biblical Quarterly* 50 (1988): 470–83.

They professed His divinity and equality with the Father as well as His unconditional love manifest in His coming to be with us, humbling Himself, and giving Himself to us in complete self-sacrifice:

> Though, being[59] in the *nature of God*,[60] [Jesus] did not count *equality with God* a thing to be grasped, but *emptied himself*, taking the *nature of a servant*, being born in the likeness of men. And being found in human form he *humbled himself* and became obedient unto death, even *death on a cross*. Therefore God has highly exalted him and bestowed on him the name which is above every name, that at the name of Jesus every knee should bow, in heaven and on earth and under the earth, and every tongue confess that Jesus Christ is *Lord*, to the glory of God the Father. (Phil 2:6–11, my translation)

The italicized terms in the above hymn ("nature of God", "equality with God", and "Lord") indicate the early Church's belief that Jesus shared in the Father's divine life and power from all eternity, and that this life-power is unconditional love (indicated by the italicized phrases—"emptied himself", "nature of a servant", "humbled himself", and "death on a cross"—which are all associated with Jesus' and the apostolic Church's use of *agapē*). This affirmation reveals the central belief of the Christian Church—that the God of power and creation (Yahweh) is also the God of affectionate, humble, and compassionate love (Abba). This profession of God's unconditional love explains why the Son of God would want to be with us in a perfect act of empathy, face-to-face and peer-to-peer. In view of this remarkable revelation, we no longer have to fear the strict justice

---

[59] The present participle, *Huparkōn*, is better translated "being" than "was". This term signifies "being in substance"—that is, "what something is". When combined with *morphē* (form), the combination is best rendered "nature". See the following note.

[60] The term *Morphē* in *classical* Greek frequently indicates substance or nature ("what a thing is"). However, in biblical Greek it generally indicates "fashion" ("outward appearance"). Though the New Testament usage should generally be preferred over the classical, an exception should probably be made in this case, because of the context. The previous note indicated that *Huparkōn* means "being" in the sense of "what a thing is". The hymn's author intends the two words *Huparkōn* and *Morphē* to be taken together, which probably indicates more than mere outward appearance. Does the combination indicate "nature"? There is reason to believe this because of the terms' proximity to "equality with God". The latter expression (literally, "to be equal to God") reinforces "Morphē Theou.... Huparkōn", indicating that the author intended something close to a classical rendition of *Morphē*—namely, "nature".

and retribution of the wrath of God;[61] we can look forward to the unconditionally loving God helping us to remain on the path to His heavenly Kingdom, where His unconditional love will be actualized with all those who seek Him with a sincere heart.

The evidence used to substantiate this claim, mostly from Jeremias, Brown, Meier, and Wright, represents the most contemporary historical study of the New Testament by mainstream scholars. It carefully applies historical criteria, situates Jesus within His first-century Palestinian milieu, and tries to understand comprehensively the Kingdom He believed Himself to have brought, not only through His ministry and self-sacrificial act, but also through the Resurrection and vindication He anticipated.[62] This should be sufficient to substantiate reasonably not only Jesus' belief in His divine Sonship, but also the reality of His identity as Emmanuel—"the unconditionally loving God with us".

Some readers may be wondering how God (with an infinite nature) could become incarnate in a finite nature (a man). The Christian Church long ago responded that the infinite *nature* of God did not become human (finite), for that would have been a contradiction. It asserted, instead, that the *Person of the Son*—the second Person of the Trinity—became human. This gives rise to the question about the distinction between the *nature of God* and the *Person of the Son*. "Nature" refers to the infinite being or power of God (of which there can be only one; see Lonergan's proof of only one infinite power in Volume II, Chapter 3, Sections III and IV). In contrast to this, "divine

---

[61] As Paul notes, Jesus saves us from "the wrath of God" (see Rom 5:9; 1 Thess 1:10; 5:9). Paul considers this Old Testament theme to be a corollary of "God's justice" (see Rom 2:4–5), and so he sees the compassion and mercy (*agapē*) intrinsic to Jesus' self-sacrificial act as overcoming strict justice, which enables us to be saved.

[62] At the Last Supper, Jesus anticipates his Resurrection in Heaven during the rite of the wine/blood: "Truly, I say to you, I shall not drink again of the fruit of the vine until that day when I drink it new in the kingdom of God" (Mk 14:25). This phrase appears in the Mark-Matthew tradition as well as the Lucan tradition, though the Lucan tradition has different phrasing: "I shall not drink of the fruit of the vine until the kingdom of God comes" (Lk 22:18). This amounts to a double attestation and has a very probable Semitic origin, indicating historicity. There are other indications of Jesus' anticipation of His Resurrection and vindication that can be historically corroborated, such as His selection of Psalm 22 as His dying words, His siding with the Pharisees against the Sadducees on belief in the resurrection, and His prediction about the Temple: "Destroy this temple, and in three days I will raise it up" (Jn 2:19 and partial parallel Mt 26:61).

person" (e.g., the Son) is like a "distinct self-consciousness" (self-awareness) that makes use of the *one* infinite power source (nature of God). The Son (the second self-consciousness making use of the one infinite nature) becomes man, but not the infinite nature of God. This is explained in detail in Appendix II of this volume.

IV. Conclusion

In the introduction to this volume, we noted that reason alone would not be sufficient to understand our transcendent nature and destiny. Though reason can establish the existence of a unique unrestricted act of thinking that creates everything else in reality (see Volume II, Chapter 3 and Appendix II) and the likelihood that this divine Being is also perfect love, justice or goodness, and beauty (see Volume II, Chapter 4), it leaves many questions unanswered, particularly about our relationship with this unique transcendent entity. Some of these questions are the following: What is His love and goodness like? How does He manifest it without undermining our freedom? Why would a perfectly loving God allow suffering? Why would a perfectly good God allow evil? What is God's purpose in suffering? How do we enter into the cosmic struggle between good and evil? How should we pray? Does God answer prayers? How does God inspire us and how can He guide us without undermining our freedom? What is our eternal destiny like? Is there any possibility of being separated from God, even eternally? How does God judge? Is God's Kingdom open to all?

We conjectured that if reason could not answer these questions, then God Himself would have to do so through self-revelation. We presumed that God would make this revelation available to all peoples and cultures (through a multiplicity of religions), and we showed that this expectation is fulfilled in Friedrich Heiler's seven common elements of world religions.[63] We then asked whether God would want to manifest Himself *personally* and *ultimately*, to be with us in a

[63] See Friedrich Heiler, "The History of Religions as a Preparation for the Cooperation of Religions", in *The History of Religions*, ed. Mircea Eliade and J. Kitagawa (Chicago: Chicago University Press, 1959), pp. 140–55.

perfect act of empathy, face-to-face and peer-to-peer. We reasoned that He would want to do this if He were *unconditional love*, which led to the obvious question: Is He?

To answer this question, we first reasoned that if love is our most positive power—capable of leading us to our highest purpose, fulfillment, and destiny—then it would be inconceivable that the Creator of our nature would not be loving. We reasoned further that if we have a desire for *unconditional* love, the only source of that desire would be an unconditionally loving entity, a perfect unity: God (see Chapter 2, Section I). Inasmuch as an unconditionally loving God would *want* to be with us in the most perfect way possible—in the most perfect empathetic relationship—then He would want to be with us *personally* and *ultimately*, face-to-face and peer-to-peer, not only to show us the way to love (*agapē*), but to give that love to us definitively.

This led to a final question: Is Jesus the unconditionally loving God with us? In Chapters 2–6 we laid out the evidence in favor of Jesus' divine Sonship, from the vantage point of His unconditional love, His revelation of the Father's unconditional love, His Resurrection in glory, His miracles by His own authority and power, His gift of the Holy Spirit, and His claim to be the exclusive Son of the Father.

This evidence has been historically corroborated to a high degree and is sufficient to ground the likelihood that Jesus is the unconditional love of God with us. However, as we have noted before, evidence is not enough to move us to faith, to turn to Jesus as our salvation and to seek the answers to life's ultimate questions from Him. Faith requires two additional movements of the heart:

1. A recognized *need* for His redemption and salvation, arising out of a perceived darkness, emptiness, self-alienation, and incompleteness within ourselves
2. An affinity of the heart for His proclamation of *agapē*, arising out of an interior conviction that selfless love is truth, goodness, and beauty itself

If we sense no darkness, emptiness, incompleteness, or self-alienation within ourselves (that is, if we believe that we are perfect light, perfect fullness, perfect love, and perfect authenticity), then we will have no need for redemption through Jesus' healing love and grace, and if we feel no need for Him or His love, the evidence for His divine Sonship will simply be interesting, but irrelevant. Furthermore, if we have no affinity for love as Jesus defined it (*agapē*), or we view love as negative, as mere sentimentality, weakness, or dependency, then Jesus' revelation of God as unconditional love (and His promise of a Kingdom of unconditional love) will be either irrelevant or repulsive. In either case, the evidence for Jesus as Emmanuel will be insufficient to move us to faith. However, if we do feel a need for His redemption and salvation, and an affinity for love as He defined it (*agapē*), then the evidence will become probative and will give us the freedom to move toward a relationship with Him that will confirm not only His divine Sonship, but the power of the Holy Spirit, who will lead us through suffering and evil to the fullness of life with His Father.

Consider the implications of this conclusion. If Jesus is Emmanuel, then God really is unconditional love, and His Son has come into our reality to be with us in a perfect act of empathy and to give Himself to us in a complete act of self-sacrifice. If Jesus is Emmanuel, then we can be sure of God's unconditional salvific intention—that His sole intention is to bring each of us into His kingdom of love, that if we turn to Him, even in our darkest hours of sin, He will forgive us and bring us back to Himself, just as the father of the prodigal son. We can be sure that the only way we could be separated from God in His eternity is if *we* freely choose it. Thus, if Jesus is Emmanuel, then we can be sure that we are on the way to the unconditionally loving God's salvation so long as we keep choosing that God as our Sovereign, keep returning to Him in our darkness, and try to follow the loving example of His beloved Son. If Jesus really is Emmanuel, then we can have unconditional hope in an eternity with the God of unconditional love and joy. As Saint Paul states: "[N]o eye has seen, nor ear heard, nor the heart of man conceived, what God has prepared for those who love him" (1 Cor 2:9).

No truth could be more important than this. If Jesus is Emmanuel, He is not only the fullness of revelation; He is the way, the truth, and the life that we must endeavor, no matter how imperfectly, to follow.

We are now in a position to answer the question with which this volume is primarily concerned: What is our transcendent *destiny*?

If Jesus truly is the unconditionally loving God with us, for which there is abundant evidence, then the answer to this question, which lies beyond the bounds of reason, can be answered. Throughout the previous chapters, we have discovered clues to the answer, and now they can be assembled by Emmanuel Himself. This is the topic of the next chapter.

Chapter Seven

Our Transcendent Destiny

Introduction

In the previous six chapters, we examined the evidence for God as unconditional love and for Jesus being Emmanuel. We concluded that there was significant evidence to substantiate that Jesus is the unconditionally loving God with us, and that this evidence could lead us to faith if we see a need for Jesus' redemption and believe that love (*agapē*) holds out the central meaning of life. If Jesus really is Emmanuel (for which there is abundant evidence), then God (His Father) is unconditional love, like the father in the Parable of the Prodigal Son.

This truth is absolutely central to Jesus' preaching and Christian doctrine, so much so that we cannot understand Christian doctrine properly without using "the Father of the Prodigal Son" (God) as our interpretative key. Thus, we cannot come to a proper understanding of God's will for us in our lives as well as an understanding of suffering, struggle against evil, and ultimate destiny unless we believe that God is unconditional love. Without this belief, we will not recognize His inspiration, providential guidance, and presence to us, even if He is trying to be obvious. Furthermore, we will not be able to understand properly Jesus' teaching on Heaven, Hell, and the path to salvation. Doctrinal understanding in the mind alone is not enough; we must see these doctrines through the heart of love—God's unconditional love.

Without this heart of love, Christian doctrine could become sterile or skewed toward the opposite of love—anger, contempt, retribution, and punishment. Imagine interpreting Christian doctrine through the lens, not of the Prodigal Son's Father, but of the indifferent, angry, and vengeful God; instead of seeing grace as God's providential assistance for salvation, we would see it as a series of tests from God to determine whether we are really deserving of salvation; instead of seeing suffering as a call to higher meaning, compassion, courage, and trust, we would see it as the punishment of an exacting, angry God; and instead of seeing God's intention as completely salvific, we would see it as either stoically indifferent or oriented toward Hell. Every Christian doctrine could be skewed in precisely the opposite direction from what Jesus intended. Thus, it is imperative from the outset that we use "Abba", "the Father of the Prodigal Son", and "Jesus' love of sinners" as our interpretive keys.

Before looking at the four central doctrines of salvation (God's universal offer of salvation, Heaven, Hell, and the path to salvation), we will want to be sure that our view of God corresponds to "the Father of the Prodigal Son". Some readers may be thinking that they already have this view of God's heart, and so they are ready to examine the Christian view of salvation, suffering, and the struggle with evil. Though this may in fact be the case, you may want to test yourself to make sure that your belief in the Father of the Prodigal Son is not only a belief of the *mind*, but also the *heart*. This can be done by examining a few popular false notions of God that come not from God, but from our enemy: the evil one.

Recall from Volume I, Chapter 8, where Saint Ignatius of Loyola makes recourse to the wisdom of Saint Paul: "[F]or even Satan disguises himself as an angel of light" (2 Cor 11:14); that is, the devil appears with suggestions that sound pious, good, and consistent with Christian doctrine. However, there is an exaggeration or skewing of some truth within those suggestions that leads a person to a *decrease* in faith, trust, hope, and love (instead of an increase in them). As Ignatius implies, this cannot be the work of the Holy Spirit, but only of the evil one, who wants us to distance ourselves from God, to despair, and to move away from *agapē*. The best place for the evil one to practice his art of deception is with the notion of "God" itself; so we must continually examine our hearts' notion of God to be certain that it is not straying down an errant path. The reader may recognize some of the following errant notions of God:

- *"The Payback God"*—"Spitzer, the reason you have an eye problem is because you deserve it. I've been waiting to punish you for your past sins for a long time, and the reason you must *feel* the pain is because *you* deserve it."

- *"The Disgusted God"*—"I'm sick and tired of you, Spitzer; you have made very little progress in your spiritual life throughout these many years, and I've run out of patience! Your sinfulness and lackadaisical pace disgust me!"
- *"The Stoic God"*—"Spitzer, I'm sick and tired of your whining every time a little suffering comes into your life; stop being a wimp. Why don't you show a little strength and character for once!"
- *"The Competitor God"*—"Spitzer, look at what I am capable of— never submitting to temptation, dying on the Cross for people who are completely unworthy, and bending over backwards to help sinners—and look at you. When are you going to measure up?"
- *"The Fearsome God"*—"Spitzer, I expect you to get and stay in your proper place. I am a God who judges harshly, and you had better bow down, grovel, and fear me, for that is what I want and deserve—your dread and terror."

Some people can believe in their *minds* that God is the Father of the Prodigal Son, but in their hearts, imaginations, and dreams, they believe that He is really the payback God, or the disgusted God, and so forth. Frequently we do not discover these errant views of God *directly* (by examining our daydreams, night dreams, or implicit assumptions), but sense their presence indirectly through a decrease in trust, hope, and love. So, for example, we might find ourselves avoiding prayer (indicating a decrease in trust), or falling into despondency or despair (indicating a decrease in hope), or increasing in irritability, unkindness, impatience, contempt, and anger (indicating a decrease in love). When we notice these symptoms, we will first want to look at what is happening in our lives; are we moving away from virtue toward vice? If we are not, we will want to look at our heart's notion of God (e.g., the payback God, the fearsome God, and so forth). If we find an indication of one or more of these false views of God in our hearts, then we will want to call to mind the Father of the Prodigal Son, and then call upon Him to reinforce in our hearts the revelation given us by His Son. We may want to repeat this prayer several times to counteract strong implicit beliefs. This will not only alleviate our downward cycle away from trust, hope, and love, but allow us to understand better the teachings of Jesus, and to develop our spiritual lives.

We may now turn to the four principle doctrines of salvation:

1. God's universal offer of salvation (Section I)
2. Heaven (Section II)
3. The rationale for why an unconditionally loving God would allow Hell (Section III)
4. The path to salvation (Section IV)

I. God's Universal Offer of Salvation

If God is truly *unconditional* love (*agapē*) as Jesus has revealed, then He would not condition or restrict that love to any particular group of people, but rather, would offer it universally to every individual. It would be a contradiction to assert at once that God is unconditional *agapē* (unconditional humble-heartedness, gentle-heartedness, compassion, forgiveness, authenticity, and peacemaking) *and* that God condemns people who do not recognize His Son for no other reason than a lack of opportunity to know Him meaningfully. If God is not to hold the blameless to blame, then His intention must be to offer salvation to everyone who seeks Him with a sincere heart.

Furthermore, if God is unconditional *agapē* (as Jesus defined it), then that love would be unconditionally compassionate and forgiving. This means that God would not reject a repentant sinner (someone who has strayed from the path of love, but is trying to get back onto it); rather, He would do everything possible to bring sinners back into His life and love.

Well then, did Jesus really believe that God offers salvation to everyone who seeks Him with a sincere heart? We will need to examine three sources of teaching from Jesus and the Christian Church:

1. New Testament passages in favor of God's universal offer of salvation (Section I.A)
2. New Testament passages that imply God's restricted offer of salvation (Section I.B)

3. Contemporary documents from the Christian Church concerning God's universal offer of salvation (Section I.C):
   • The Dogmatic Constitution on the Church, *Lumen Gentium*
   • The Pastoral Constitution on the Church in the Modern World, *Gaudium et Spes*

A. New Testament Passages in Favor of God's Universal Offer of Salvation

As noted in Chapter 3 (Section IV.A), Jesus' Eucharistic words provide an important insight into His intention to offer salvation to *all* people, because they can be traced back to Him (through His Aramaic phrasing). Recall that the more original tradition of Jesus' Eucharistic words comes from Mark-Matthew ("poured out for [the] many" [Mt 26:28; Mk 14:24]) instead of Luke ("poured out for you" [Lk 22:20]), because the former is a Semitism, and the latter has been altered for liturgical purposes.[1] Recall also that *to pollōn* (the many) is an unusual Greek expression that attempts to translate the Hebrew *rabbim*. In Hebrew, there is only one word for both "many" and "all"—namely, *rabbim*. The only way of distinguishing these meanings is the presence of the definite article. If the definite article is present, *rabbim* is translated "all", but if the definite article is absent, it is translated as "many".[2] In the case of Jesus' Eucharistic words, a definite article does precede *pollōn* (*to pollōn*) in the Mark-Matthew tradition. This means that it should be translated "poured out for *all*". This is confirmed by 1 Timothy 2:6, in which the phrase from Isaiah 53:12 is translated "gave himself as a ransom for *all* (*pantōn*)". In view of this, we should prefer an inclusive translation for Jesus' Aramaic Eucharistic words, "poured out for *all*".[3]

If this analysis (of Joachim Jeremias) is correct, then Jesus unambiguously stated His will to save everyone through His Passion and death. This is confirmed by Jesus' selection of Psalm 22 for His dying words. Recall from Chapter 3 (Section IV.B) that Mark recounts a

---

[1] See Joachim Jeremias, *The Eucharistic Words of Jesus* (London: SCM Press, 1966), p. 179.
[2] See ibid.
[3] See ibid.

very likely version of Jesus' last words: "*Elōi, Elōi, lama sabachthani*" ("My God, my God, why have you forsaken me" [Mk 15:34]). This rendition of the first line of Psalm 22 is probably a northern Galilean Aramaic dialect (the dialect in which Jesus probably learned this Psalm from His Mother as a child), and so it manifests not only what is in Jesus' mind, but His heart. Recall also that the first line of the Psalm represents the *whole* Psalm, and there is an expectation that Jesus' audience will recognize the Psalm upon hearing the first line (just as a cantor expects the congregation to recognize the Psalm from his recitation of the first line).

The parallels between Jesus' Crucifixion and the torments described by the Psalmist are uncanny (verses 6–8; 12–18), but that is not the only reason Jesus chooses this song for His dying words. He intends that His Father (and the bystanders) hear three other themes: His trust in His Father (verses 3–5), His belief that His Father will vindicate His death (verses 24–26), and that this vindication will lead to the salvation of the *whole* world (verses 27–31). Thus, Jesus' dying words are not a cry of forsakenness and despair, but a song of trust in God, a belief in His final vindication and an offer of salvation to the *whole* world.

Let us look more closely at the last point. The final part of the Psalm runs as follows:

> *All* the ends of the earth
> shall remember and turn to the LORD;
> and *all* the families of the nations
> shall worship before him.
> For dominion belongs to the LORD,
> and he rules over the nations.
> Yes, to him shall all the proud of the earth bow down;
> before him shall bow all who go down to the dust, and he
>   who cannot keep himself alive.
> Posterity shall serve him;
> men shall tell of the LORD to the coming generation, and
>   proclaim his deliverance
> to a *people yet unborn*,
> that he has wrought it. (Ps 22:27–31; emphasis added)

The Psalmist believes that God will not only vindicate his suffering, but that his suffering will be joined to God's final victory in which *all* the ends of the earth will turn to the Lord. The Psalmist goes even further; it is not just people of the time of vindication, but also those who are deceased since the beginning of the human race ("before him shall bow all who go down to the dust") and all the people of future generations ("men shall tell of the LORD to the coming generation, and proclaim his deliverance to a *people yet unborn*, that he has wrought it").

This Psalm is one of the clearest statements of God's universal offer of salvation in the Old Testament, and it would make no sense for Jesus to have selected it as His dying words unless He was in agreement with the Psalmist's belief in the universality of Yahweh's final vindication. In the previous chapter, we saw that Jesus' view of Himself as the preexistent Son of Man was to be the final judge of Israel (which He initiated through the cleansing of the Temple). Thus Jesus saw Himself as the vehicle through which Yahweh's final vindication would come, not just to Israel, but, as the Psalm indicates, to the *whole* world for *all* time. Jesus selected Psalm 22 precisely because it gave His suffering and death a *universal* eschatological significance. He was initiating the final age through His suffering and death, and He desired and intended that this final judgment not be condemnation, but salvation for the whole world for all time.

God's intention to save *everyone* who seeks Him with a sincere heart is also supported by several passages of Scripture in special Matthew (sources used by Matthew alone), special Luke, and John.

- *Matthew 18:14*—*"[I]t is not the will of my Father who is in heaven that one of these little ones should perish."* This passage, which occurs after the Parable of the Lost Sheep, is concerned with God's intent to save all sinners, but does not specifically address God's desire to save people of every time and nation. Yet, one must ask: If God's intention is to lose no one, even the greatest sinner, would that not extend to those who do not know Jesus (simply because of an accident of birth)? Sinners are culpable for what they have done, but people who do not know Jesus because they had no opportunity to hear or understand

Him are not culpable. If God's intention is to lose no one who is *culpable*, why wouldn't it extend to those who are not culpable?

- *Luke 3:6—"[A]ll flesh [people] shall see the salvation of God."* This phrase comes originally from the prophet Isaiah (Is 40:4–5) and is placed by Luke on the lips of John the Baptist announcing the coming of Jesus. Luke includes this passage from Isaiah in His Gospel precisely because it shows God's desire to reveal His glory to the *whole* world. As a Gentile, Luke is especially sensitive to this. What does "seeing God's glory" mean? For Luke, "God's glory" is manifest perfectly in Jesus, particularly His salvific self-sacrifice. Luke's belief in Jesus' offer of salvation extends beyond this passage throughout his whole Gospel; indeed, it is one of his key themes, beginning with the infancy narratives until the end of the Acts of Apostles.[4] Luke did not say how *all* people will be able to see Jesus' salvation, because he knew well that many people would not hear about Jesus before they passed from this world. Did Luke believe that everyone would be given a chance to see the salvation of Jesus, in this life or the next? If he did not, his belief in God's universal offer of salvation would be contradictory.

- *John 12:32—"I, when I am lifted up from the earth, will draw all people to myself."* In this passage Jesus is addressing the crowds about the meaning of His death—that it will be His and the Father's glorification. This glory has two dimensions: (1) the end of Satan's reign ("now shall the prince of this world be cast out" [Jn 12:31 (D-R)]), and (2) all people will be drawn to Jesus. This passage implies that Jesus will offer His salvation to everyone, by drawing everyone to Himself. Yet, John, like Luke, must have known that many people would die before hearing about Jesus. Is there some way in which John's rendition of Jesus' universal offer of salvation can come to pass? Evidently he thought so.

- *John 17:2—"[Y]ou have given him power over all flesh, to give eternal life to all whom you have given him."* In this passage from the Priestly Prayer of Christ, Jesus acknowledges that His Father has

---

[4]See Robert J. Karris, "The Gospel according to Luke", in *The New Jerome Biblical Commentary*, eds. Raymond E. Brown, Joseph A. Fitzmyer, and Roland E. Murphy (Englewood Cliffs, N.J.: Prentice Hall, 1990), p. 686.

given Him authority over everyone in the world so that He can give eternal life to *all* of them—that is, to *all* people. Again, John must have known that much of the world would not have heard of Jesus before dying. How could Jesus' authority to give eternal life to *all people* be brought to fruition under this circumstance? Jesus must have made some provision for those who had no possibility of hearing about Him during their lifetime; otherwise, the universal claim in this statement would be impossible.

In conclusion, there is considerable evidence for Jesus' offer of salvation to all people for all time. The Aramaic version of Jesus' Eucharistic words ("poured out for all") strongly supports this; so also does His selection of Psalm 22 for His dying words. Furthermore, there is multiple attestation of this theme in special Matthew, special Luke, and John, and Luke makes it central to his Gospel. If Jesus did not intend His offer of salvation to be universal, then these passages would be difficult to explain, if not unintelligible. Yet, there are also some passages that seem to go against this theme (see below, I.B). Is the New Testament contradictory, or can these seemingly non-universalistic passages be explained?

B. *New Testament Passages That Possibly May Imply a Restricted Offer of Salvation*

There are two particularly prominent passages that seem to contradict those in the forgoing section:

- Acts 4:12: "[T]here is salvation in no one else, for there is no other name under heaven given among men by which we must be saved."
- John 14:6: "[N]o one comes to the Father, but by me."

At first glance, one might think that these passages mean that if someone has not heard of the name of Jesus or acknowledged belief in Jesus, then that person will not be saved. However, we must ask whether these passages, like many others in the New Testament, have an inclusive or exclusive meaning. The exclusive meaning was given immediately above (i.e., if you have not heard of the name of Jesus, or do not believe *for any reason*, you are excluded from the Kingdom of Heaven).

However, there is another way of looking at the same passages—namely, that the *name* of Jesus (Acts 4:12) and Jesus Himself (Jn 14:6) constitute *the way* in which we *are* saved. It does not say *who* is saved or *not* saved by Jesus (or His name). Could Jesus (or Jesus' name) save someone who has not even heard of the name of Jesus? These passages do not answer these questions, but the seven passages listed and explained in Section I.A do (Mk 14:24 and Mt 26:28; Mk 15:34 and Psalm 22; Mt 18:14; Lk 3:6; Jn 12:32; 17:2; and 1 Tim 2:6).

When we see the above disputed passages in Acts 4:12 and John 14:6 in the context of these other passages, an inclusive interpretation appears more appropriate. Thus the passage from Acts would mean that Jesus has provided the way for all to come to the Father, but it does not restrict salvation only to those who profess the name of Jesus.[5] Similarly the passage from John should be read, "I am the only way to the Father", but it does not restrict Jesus' saving activity *only* to those who *profess* His name. When both passages are interpreted inclusively, they affirm that Jesus is the *one* and only *Savior* of the world, but they do not restrict that saving activity only to those who profess His name.

Another problematic passage in the Gospel of John is also open to an inclusive or exclusive interpretation:

> For God so loved the world that he gave his only-begotten Son, that whoever believes in him should not perish but have eternal life. For God sent the Son into the world, not to condemn [*krinē*] the world, but that the world might be saved through him. He who believes in him is not condemned; he who does not believe is condemned

[5] This passage can be misunderstood if we do not bear in mind the Semitic and Christian use of "name". A contemporary audience is likely to see "name" in a nominalistic way and so believe that someone must profess the name of Jesus in order to be saved. But this is not the Christian view, which sees the name of Jesus to represent His salvific action and power (see Chapter 5, Section II). Thus the passage in Acts should be interpreted as, "We are saved only by the power and salvific action of Jesus", but it does not specify whether someone must profess that name in order to be saved by it. See John L. McKenzie, *Dictionary of the Bible* (New York: Macmillan, 1965), pp. 604–5.

already, because he has not believed in the name of the only-begotten
Son of God. (Jn 3:16–18)

The exclusive interpretation is obvious: "not believing *for any reason
whatsoever* warrants condemnation." But does the Johannine author
really mean "for any reason whatsoever"? John's usage in other parts
of the Gospel indicates the contrary, where both belief *and unbelief*
require an act of the will. If this is the case, then "not believing", here,
would mean *refusal* to believe in Jesus' name[6] (but *not ignorance* of it).

This might seem unusual from the vantage point of contemporary
English usage, because nonbelief seems to denote the contrary of
belief, which could mean not believing because of ignorance (e.g.,
not having heard about Jesus because of being born before the time
of Jesus, or being born into a culture where missionaries had not
gone; or never having heard missionaries in a culture where they
had gone; or never having understood missionaries in a place where
one heard them, etc.). But it is very unlikely that the Johannine
author is using "nonbelief" in this sweeping sense, because this passage indicates that God's primary intention is to *save the world*.

This inclusive interpretation is confirmed later in the Gospel (Jn
12:47–48; emphasis mine):

> If any one hears my sayings and does not keep them, I do *not judge*
> [*krinō*] him; for I did not come to judge the world but to *save* the
> world. He who *rejects* [*athetōn*] me and does not receive my sayings has
> a judge; [*krinonta*—the one accusing]; the *word* that I have spoken will
> be his judge [*krinei*] on the last day.

This passage indicates that Jesus' *word* is the judge. Yet, how could
Jesus' word be the judge unless someone has heard it? Indeed, in this
passage, Jesus indicates that the condition for being judged *is hearing*
his word ("If any one hears my sayings"). We also see in this passage
that Jesus' intention is to *save* the world (not to condemn it), and
that condemnation comes only from *rejecting* His word ("He who
rejects me and does not receive my sayings has a judge; the word that
I have spoken will be his judge"). Condemnation clearly does not

---

[6]See the previous note on "name" as the "power and salvation of Jesus".

come from *not hearing* His word. Therefore, condemnation does not come through Jesus, but from *rejection* of the word that the listener has heard.

The two problematic passages in John (14:6 and 3:16–18) must be interpreted in an inclusive way if they are to be consistent with the above passage (Jn 12:47–48). If they are interpreted in an *exclusive* way, the blatant contradiction in the Gospel would be quite baffling. Furthermore, an exclusive interpretation would contradict the two affirmations of God's universal offer of salvation in John's Gospel (mentioned above in I.A, Jn 12:32; 17:2). If this interpretation is correct, then the Johannine author is not referring to "unbelief out of ignorance", but only "unbelief arising out of explicit rejection of the word heard and understood".

In John's Gospel, refusal to believe in the name of Jesus entails a refusal to renounce the world. As John McKenzie notes, "When the preaching is uttered, and in particular when Jesus presents Himself, one refuses to believe only because one refuses to renounce the world."[7] Thus, "unbelief" in John's Gospel has a very refined meaning, "a refusal to believe in the word of Jesus, which comes from a refusal to renounce the world". Therefore, the Johannine author is not saying that people who never heard of Jesus will be condemned ("a crass doctrine of predestination"[8]), but rather is warning that those who refuse to renounce the world will likely refuse to believe in the saving power and action of Jesus, and that this rejection of the Word can lead to the path to condemnation.

In sum, the above three disputed passages (Acts 4:12; Jn 3:16–18; 14:6) are best interpreted in an *inclusive* sense. They are not meant to exclude those, who through no fault of their own, have not heard the word of Jesus. This inclusive interpretation is consistent with the inclusivity of Jesus' Eucharistic words, His dying words, and the five passages on universal salvation mentioned above (Mt 18:14; Lk 3:6; Jn 12:32; 17:2; and 1 Tim 2:6). In light of this, it is reasonable to infer that Jesus' intention was to offer salvation to *every* person seeking God with a sincere heart. This interpretation is verified in subsequent Christian doctrine.

[7] McKenzie, *Dictionary of the Bible*, p. 271.
[8] Ibid.

C. Christian Doctrines of God's Universal Offer of Salvation

The universality of Christ's offer of salvation has been a part of Christian theology throughout the centuries, and explicitly surfaced in controversies surrounding the necessity of Baptism for salvation. This doctrine seemed to run contrary to the universality of Jesus' offer of salvation because all people prior to the time of Jesus could not have been baptized and all people who had not heard or understood the word of Jesus would likewise not be baptized. Saint Ambrose was one of the first Church Fathers to address this problem in his funeral oration for Emperor Valentinian II, who was assassinated before he was officially baptized: "Should he not acquire the grace for which he longed? Certainly: As he desired it, he has attained it. . . . His pious desire has absolved him."[9] This is further confirmed by Saint Augustine in his tractate *On Baptism against the Donatists*: "I find that not only suffering for the sake of Christ can replace that which is lacking in Baptism, but also *faith and conversion of the heart* (fidem conversionemque cordis)."[10]

Baptism by desire was implicitly acknowledged by the Church before Saints Ambrose and Augustine because it believed, in accordance with Jesus' teaching, that the Old Testament patriarchs, prophets, and holy men and women were with God in Heaven (as implied by Jesus' conversation with Moses and Elijah during the Transfiguration and implied by Jesus' Parable of Lazarus and the Rich Man in which Abraham is the representative of Heaven). Furthermore, Jesus uses the implicit resurrection of Abraham, Isaac, and Jacob to counter the Sadducees' refusal to believe in it: "And as for the resurrection of the dead, have you not read what was said to you by God, 'I am the God of Abraham, and the God of Isaac, and the God of Jacob'? He is not God of the dead, but of the living" (Mt 22:31–32). Evidently, an exception to "Baptism by water" had to be made for the holy men and women of the Old Testament, and this may have provided Saints Ambrose and Augustine with the rationale to formulate

---

[9] Ambrose, *De obitu Valent*, in *The Fundamentals of Catholic Dogma*, by Ludwig Ott, trans. Patrick Lynch (Rockford, Ill.: Tan Books, 1955), 51, 53.

[10] Saint Augustine, *De Baptismo Contra Donatistas Libri Septem*, in *The Fundamentals of Catholic Dogma*, by Ludwig Ott, trans. Patrick Lynch (Rockford, Ill.: Tan Books, 1955), IV 22, 29; emphasis mine.

"Baptism of desire". This was further formalized by Saint Thomas Aquinas[11] and the Council of Trent, which affirms that we are saved by "the washing unto regeneration or *the desire for the same*".[12] The Catholic Church formalized the universality of Jesus' offer of salvation in the Second Vatican Council and promulgated it in its Dogmatic Constitution on the Church (*Lumen Gentium*)[13] and its Pastoral Constitution on the Church in the Modern World (*Gaudium et Spes*). *Lumen Gentium* states:

> Those who, through no fault of their own, do not know the Gospel of Christ or his Church, but who nevertheless seek God with a sincere heart, and, moved by grace, try in their actions to do his will as they know it through the dictates of their conscience—those too may achieve eternal salvation.[14]

Gaudium et Spes reinforces and expands the understanding of Jesus' universal offer of salvation as follows:

> The Christian is certainly bound both by need and by duty to struggle with evil through many afflictions and to suffer death; but, as one who has been made a partner in the paschal mystery, and as one who has been configured to the death of Christ, he will go forward, strengthened by hope, to the resurrection. All this holds true not for the Christian only but also for all men of good will in whose hearts grace is active invisibly. For since *Christ died for all*, and since all men are in fact called to one and the same destiny, which is divine, we must hold that the Holy Spirit offers to all the possibility of being made partners, in a way known to God, in the paschal mystery.[15]

---

[11] "Some have received the invisible sanctification without visible sacraments, and to their profit; but though it is possible to have the visible sanctification, consisting in a visible sacrament, without the invisible sanctification, it will be to no profit. Since, therefore, the sacrament of Baptism pertains to the visible sanctification; it seems that a man *can obtain salvation* without the sacrament of Baptism, by means of the invisible sanctification". Thomas Aquinas, *The Summa Theologica of St. Thomas Aquinas*, trans. Fathers of the English Dominican Province (New York: Benziger Brothers, 1947), III, q. 68, a. 2 (emphasis mine).

[12] H. Denzinger and A. Schönmetzer, *Enchiridion Symbolorum* (New York: Herder, 1965), no. 796.

[13] A dogmatic constitution is the highest infallible document in the Catholic Church.

[14] *Lumen Gentium*, no. 16, in Austin Flannery, *Vatican Council II, Vol. 1: The Conciliar and Postconciliar Documents* (Northport, N.Y.: Costello, 1975), p. 376.

[15] *Gaudium et Spes*, no. 22, in Flannery, *Vatican Council II*, pp. 923–24; emphasis mine.

These teachings of the Second Vatican Council are reflected in the *Catechism of the Catholic Church*, which specifically affirms that "Christ died for all":

> "Since Christ died for all, and since all men are in fact called to one and the same destiny, which is divine, we must hold that the Holy Spirit offers to all the possibility of being made partakers, in a way known to God, of the Paschal mystery." Every man who is ignorant of the Gospel of Christ and of his Church, but seeks the truth and does the will of God in accordance with his understanding of it, can be saved. It may be supposed that such persons would have *desired Baptism explicitly* if they had known its necessity.[16] (Emphasis in original.)

In sum, the teachings of Jesus and the New Testament are consistent with what would be expected of an unconditionally loving God—namely, that God would not condemn anyone because of an accident of birth (being born prior to the time of Jesus, or being born in a culture that has not heard of or does not understand Jesus, and so forth). Rather, Jesus' (and God the Father's) intention is to save all people of good will—that is, those who "seek God with a sincere heart, and, moved by grace, try in their actions to do his will as they know it through the dictates of their conscience" (*Lumen Gentium*, no. 16). This is validated by the doctrines of many Christian churches and is an integral part of the dogma of the Catholic Church.

At this juncture, one might be tempted to ask, "Well, if everyone of good will can be saved, what is the point of Christian evangelization?"

D. Why Should Christians Evangelize?

Why should Christians evangelize? It is not to counteract a heartless god who would capriciously condemn someone for being born at the wrong place or time, but precisely for the opposite reason: because God *does* have a heart, and people deserve to know it; because God does *not* condemn people for an accident of birth, and people deserve

---

[16] *Catechism of the Catholic Church*, 2nd ed. (Washington, D.C.: Libreria Editrice Vaticana—United States Conference of Catholic Bishops, 2000), no. 1260; the internal quotation is from *Gaudium et Spes*, no. 22.

to know *that*; and because God *does* have a universal intention to save, and people deserve to know that. Everyone deserves to know that there is no ultimate tragedy in this world, because all suffering will be redeemed in God's unconditional love; that our destiny is to be with God and one another in perfect love and joy forever; that every person possesses a uniquely good, lovable, transcendent nature that deserves justice and compassion irrespective of social, economic, political, or educational status; and that every good work and act of love in which we participate will reverberate throughout the Kingdom in God's eternity. These truths can make the difference between a life of hope or a life of despair, a life of ultimate purpose or merely superficial purpose, a life devoted to *agapē* or indifferent to it, a life that builds up the common good and the Kingdom of God or one that undermines them.

This is not the only reason why Christians would want to share the good news about Jesus Christ. Jesus gave us tremendous gifts not only to help us on our journey to salvation, but also to build His Kingdom and to engage in the struggle against evil. Some of these gifts include the presence of the Holy Spirit within us,[17] the New Testament Scriptures, the Church community, the Holy Eucharist, and the teaching tradition of the Church (see below, Section IV). As noted above, non-Christians do not have to have these gifts in order to be saved. Nevertheless, these gifts help us freely appropriate a loving identity (in imitation of Jesus' *agapē*); be disciples of hope, love, and joy for the world; contend with the forces of evil; and build up the common good in the Kingdom of God, which adds countless layers of meaning to our lives. Well then, why should Christians evangelize? Not because they fear that God will condemn

---

[17] The Holy Spirit also works in and through non-Christians. As the above section of the Pastoral Constitution on the Church (*Gaudium et Spes*) clearly states: "We must hold that the Holy Spirit offers to all the possibility of being made partners, in a way known to God, in the paschal mystery" (no. 22). Christians have a special partnership with the Holy Spirit through Baptism, which is termed "indwelling" (see 1 Cor 3:16; 6:19; 2 Cor 6:16; 2 Tim 1:14; Acts 6:5; Eph 5:18; Rom 8:11; Gal 4:6; and Jn 16:13). This indwelling enables us to recognize in the depth of our hearts that God is "Abba" (see Gal 4:6), to know and desire God's heart of love (*agapē*; see 1 Cor 13), to abide in peace beyond all understanding (Phil 4:7), and to receive the inspiration and guidance to edify and build the Kingdom of God and the community (see Volume I, Chapter 8).

those who have not heard of Jesus, but because Jesus is their source of ultimate purpose, destiny, dignity, hope, love, and joy. If Christians really believe this, they will not be able to stop themselves from sharing Jesus' word, for it can change the contours and horizon of everything we do and strive for on our way to the Kingdom of unconditional love.

II. Heaven according to Jesus

The popular view of Heaven is frequently boring (e.g., people sitting atop clouds playing harps). We have the feeling that Heaven will be devoid of emotion and excitement, yet, Jesus had no such view of Heaven; indeed He thought it was precisely the opposite.

We have already seen one indication of the Kingdom manifest in Jesus' own Resurrection: the spiritual transformation and glorification of our bodies in the same way as Jesus' (see Chapter 4, Section II). Recall that Paul calls this new reality a *pneumatikon soma* (a spiritual body), which will be incorruptible and glorious, not subject to any imperfection, sickness, suffering, or physical law. It will be our embodied nature brought to perfection through Jesus' own glorification. As marvelous as this promise is, it is just the tip of the iceberg. Jesus goes far beyond this in His preaching of the Kingdom of Heaven, specifically in His allusion to the messianic banquet. In the previous chapter, we noted that Jesus' preaching of the Kingdom had two interrelated dimensions: the present Kingdom (brought to the world by Jesus) and the future Kingdom (which will be the eternal fulfillment of every person through the unconditional love and joy of the triune God). We explored the present Kingdom in some detail in the last chapter (Section II), and it now remains to explore the future Kingdom in the same detail.

So how does Jesus describe this future Kingdom of eternal love and joy? His central organizing image is the *messianic banquet*. Saint John and Saint Paul extend this image by implying that it is a Kingdom of unconditional love. We will first examine Jesus' image (Section II.A), then that of John and Paul (Section II.B), and then put the two together in a contemporary reflection on Heaven (Section II.C).

A. The Messianic Banquet

Jesus uses the image of the messianic banquet to describe the fundamental dynamic of the heavenly Kingdom—intimate friendship and love (*philia*) characterized by table fellowship brought to perfection. He indicates that it will be a universal reality (including people from north, south, east, and west—Gentiles and Jews), and a transtemporal reality (including the early patriarchs): "I tell you, many will come from east and west and sit at table with Abraham, Isaac, and Jacob in the kingdom of heaven" (Mt 8:11).[18] The messianic banquet was a familiar concept in first-century Judaism,[19] taking its most explicit form in the prophet Isaiah:

> On this mountain the LORD of hosts will make for all peoples a feast of fat things, a feast of choice wines—of fat things full of marrow, of choice wines well refined. And he will destroy on this mountain the covering that is cast over all peoples, the veil that is spread over all nations. He will swallow up death for ever, and the LORD God will wipe away tears from all faces, and the reproach of his people he will take away from all the earth, for the LORD has spoken. It will be said on that day, "Behold, this is our God; we have waited for him, that he might save us. (Is 25:6–9)

The mountaintop here implies an eschatological or heavenly event. The banquet is filled with foods that were considered delicious and beautiful, inciting joy. The banquet will have people from every nation, and the Gentiles will be brought to a similar status with the Jewish people ("And he will destroy on this mountain the covering that is cast over all peoples, the veil that is spread over all nations"). There will be no sadness at this heavenly banquet, and all suffering will be redeemed ("the LORD God will wipe away tears from all faces"). He will also put an end to death for all eternity ("He will swallow up death *forever*").

---

[18] The Lucan parallel states that "when you see Abraham and Isaac and Jacob and all the prophets in the kingdom of God and you yourselves thrust out. And men will come from east and west, and from north and south, and sit at table in the kingdom of God" (Lk 13:28–29).

[19] Brant Pitre, "Jesus, the Messianic Banquet, and the Kingdom of God", *Letter and Spirit* 5 (2009): 145–66.

The banquet image conveys several important points. First, inasmuch as banquets are for family and close friends, it implies that all in the Kingdom will be elevated to this familial status. The banquet is also a time to enjoy the abundance, joy, and beauty of creation. It relieves us of the concerns and sadness of the day and brings people together in a spirit of joy, and so we are able to enjoy friendship with people at their "joyful best". Thus, it can lead us to a deeper insight into and appreciation of others. In short, the banquet is not only a time of joy, but also a time of deep *familial* love, which can be so profound that we lose track of the passage of time.

Did Jesus really intend all of these themes by using this image? No doubt He did, because this is what the image conveyed to popular sentiment during His day. But Jesus intended much more than the conviviality, friendship, and familial love of the banquet. He wanted to show that this image applied to the eternal, universal, and transcendent Kingdom of God. John Meier notes in this regard:

> With the affirmation that the Gentiles will join the long-dead patriarchs of Israel at the banquet, Jesus indicates that this fully realized Kingdom of God is not only future but also in some way discontinuous with this present world.... In particular, the depiction of the three great patriarchs as alive and participating in a heavenly banquet implies both the transcendence of death and the regathering of the people of Israel not only from all places but also from all times.[20]

Brant Pitre and N. T. Wright see Jesus' Last Supper as a prefigurement of the eternal messianic banquet, in which love will be victorious over death, darkness, evil, and discord. Recall from Chapter 3 (Section IV.A) that the prophetic action reaches out to the future to bring its fulfillment into the present. For Jesus, the Last Supper is a prophetic action that reaches out not only to His Passion and death on Cavalry, but also to the eternal messianic banquet that will bring His prophetic action to fulfillment.[21]

In sum, Jesus sees the heavenly Kingdom to be an eternal state in which we will see and enjoy one another at our good, lovable,

[20]John P. Meier, *A Marginal Jew: Rethinking the Historical Jesus*, vol. 2, *Mentor, Message, and Miracles* (New York: Doubleday, 1994), p. 317.

[21]See N. T. Wright, *Jesus and the Victory of God* (Minneapolis: Fortress Press, 1996), 2:558.

and convivial best. This atmosphere of beauty, goodness, love, and joy is like a gigantic network of interpersonal relationships among people from every nation and time, brought together through the love and lavishness of his Father. For Jesus, the Kingdom of Heaven is the kingdom of love, the love of family, friends, and banquet fellowship, catalyzed by the love of the risen Messiah and the communion of those who have placed their trust in Him (the communion of saints).

B. The Kingdom of Love in John and Paul

The Kingdom of God is a reflection of the reality and fullness of God—what He is and who He is—and this fullness of reality is perfect love. We have already seen this revelation in the preaching of Jesus in His address of Yahweh (all powerful one) as Abba (the affectionate, caring, and compassionate parent), the identification of His Father with the father of the prodigal son, the elevation of love to the highest commandment, and the definition of love (*agapē*) through the Beatitudes. We have also seen it in the Person and actions of Jesus—His care and compassion for sinners, the sick, and the poor; His genuine affection for His friends and disciples; and most importantly, His self-sacrificial love manifest in His body and blood poured out on the Cross.

We have seen the source of Jesus' unconditional love, in His perfect communion with the Father and sharing in the Father's life and power ("All things have been delivered to me by my Father; and no one knows the Son except the Father, and no one knows the Father except the Son" [Mt 11:27]).

As John and Paul reflected upon the mystery of Jesus' and the Father's perfect love, they could not help but conclude that "God is love" (1 Jn 4:8) and that the fullness of God is the fullness of love with all of its positive, life-giving, powerful, beautiful, and joy-filled qualities. John says in his first letter:

> Beloved, let us love one another; for love is of God, and he who loves is born of God and knows God. He who does not love does not know God; for God is love. In this the love of God was made manifest

among us, that God sent his only-begotten Son into the world, so that
we might live through him. In this is love, not that we loved God
but that he loved us and sent his Son to be the expiation for our sins.
(1 Jn 4:7–10)

Paul speaks of the immensity and incomprehensibility of God's love
in his Letter to the Ephesians:

[And I pray] that you, being rooted and grounded in love, may have
power to comprehend with all the saints what is the breadth and
length and height and depth, and to know the love of Christ which
surpasses knowledge, that you may be filled with all the fulness of
God. (Eph 3:17–19)

Paul's prayer for the Ephesians is not only a prayer for the present,
but also a prayer for the future. It is a prayer for their salvation in
the Kingdom of Heaven, the only place where they will be able to
behold "the breadth and length and height and depth, and to know
the love of Christ", which is "the fulness of God."

If the Kingdom of Heaven is a reflection of the fullness of God,
then it must be, according to Jesus, John, and Paul, the *kingdom of perfect love*. If we are not to leave this idea of "perfect love" at the level of
abstraction, we will have to apply Paul's and Jesus' definitions of love
to it. So what would the Kingdom of Heaven be according to Paul's
definition of love in 1 Corinthians 13? It would be a state of perfect
patience and kindness and rejoicing in the truth. It would be the
complete absence of envy, boasting, pride, contempt, egocentricity,
anger, resentments, and evil. It would be a perfect state of protection,
trust, hope, and constant affirmation.

Jesus' definition of love is contained within the Beatitudes (see
Chapters 1 and 2). Accordingly, the Kingdom of Heaven would
be a state of perfect humble-heartedness ("poor in spirit"), gentle-
heartedness ("the meek"), forgiveness, caring, compassion ("the merciful"), purity of heart, and peace. Yet, even with these specifications,
the kingdom of love still seems abstract. Is there any way we can
combine the concreteness of Jesus' image of the messianic banquet
with the definitions of love given by Paul and Jesus? The following
reflection may help to do this.

C. A Reflection on the Kingdom of Heaven

We might begin our reflection with Jesus' definition of love (*agapē*) in the Beatitudes and the two great parables of love, the Prodigal Son and the Good Samaritan. For Jesus, love at its core is genuine care and compassion for others (which requires humility and gentleness). If in Heaven God brings our love to perfection, then He will help us to become our truly good and authentic selves so that we can see the unique goodness and lovability of others as they see our unique goodness and lovability. This lays the groundwork for an act of empathy that so closely bonds us with others that we naturally give our whole selves to them. Let us examine this idea more deeply.

When our goodness or virtue is brought to perfection, our alienation from self and others is removed. We see people in their true and most beautiful state with their unique inner light and integrity. This vision of ourselves and others brings an overwhelming sense of joy. We know this to be true by assessing our own experience of joy when we encounter truly *good* people.

Jesus' followers (and even total strangers) saw His goodness and found Him quite irresistible. They not only enjoyed being around Him; they wanted to remain with Him. We may have noticed this in some particularly good friends or acquaintances who have deep faith, humility, gentleness, and compassion. Their transparent goodness evokes trust, and that trust becomes the foundation for a relationship that opens upon ever-deepening friendship, love, and joy.

We not only experience this in our encounters with truly good people; we may also have noticed it in ourselves. When we become more humble, gentle, virtuous, forgiving, compassionate, and empathetic, people enjoy us more. They feel enhanced and ennobled by being in our company. They trust us more, and they enter into a deeper relationship with us. When our unique goodness is purified, we become more lovable and we are able to more deeply see the unique goodness and lovability of others. If we assume that all of us have a virtually inexhaustible depth of unique goodness and lovability, then each person in the Kingdom of Heaven presents every other person in the Kingdom of Heaven with a reality of unique goodness, lovability, beauty, trustworthiness, and joy—a virtually inexhaustible supply.

Now imagine for a moment that you are that person, that you could bring people out of their darkness with your unique ennobling and virtuous spirit. Now imagine further that every single person in Heaven was brought to this state of perfection through God's grace (perfect humility, virtue, authenticity, courage, and generosity), but each one has it in his own unique way, so that no manifestation of these qualities is the same. Now imagine further that you could get a sense of the *collective* goodness of all these unique manifestations of perfect goodness. They would be like notes constituting a perfect melody and harmony, like a symphony. What could we do except behold and enjoy all of these perfect notes within the symphony of unique goodness orchestrated by God? It would be unbelievably joyful.

When the darkness of egocentricity and narcissism is removed, one sees the radiant splendor of other people that is far more beautiful than lights or sounds, spectra or symphonies, because each person has a virtually inexhaustible depth. Now imagine being in Heaven and seeing yourself and others in one huge collective vision just like this, all orchestrated by God, who is truly infinite goodness. You would never be bored because you would be probing a depth of spiritual beauty giving rise to ever-increasing joy.

By now it will be evident that goodness and love are interrelated. When our goodness is brought to perfection, so also is our love. Recall that love begins with recognizing the "good news" in the other, not only the goodness of the other but the lovability of the other. When we see the good news of the other in all of its splendor and perfection, perfect empathy (connectedness of feeling and thinking) ensues. Recall that empathy not only *connects* us with others; it also breaks down the enmity between us, making it just as easy, if not easier, to *do* the good for others as doing the good for ourselves.

When goodness is brought to perfection in every unique person, it makes all of them perfectly lovable; there is not a single defect in their lovability. We want to behold them in their perfection, but we want to go beyond this; we want to enter into a relationship with them, to do the good for them, and to give ourselves to them. This is what it means to have our love brought to perfection. We are not completed by simply enjoying others; we are completed when we give ourselves over to the beloved. This idea of giving ourselves, being accepted by the other, and having the other give back to us is the perfection of interpersonal personhood, a reflection of what is taking place in the Holy Trinity itself.

This perfection of *interpersonal* personhood is also the perfection of joy. In the Gospel of John, Jesus brings together the themes of the love of God, the love of one another, and perfection of joy:

> As the Father has loved me, so have I loved you; abide in my love. If you keep my commandments, you will abide in my love, just as I have kept my Father's commandments and abide in his love. These things I have spoken to you, that my joy may be in you, and that your joy may be full. (Jn 15:9–11)

All of these images of love, joy, and fulfillment are synthesized in Jesus' image of the banquet. Think about a time when you were gathered around a dining room table in a restaurant with a group of intimate friends. As the evening went on, the topics of conversation seemed to fade into the background while the people who were speaking came more to the foreground. Everybody seemed to have a sense of others' goodness, lovability, loyalty, friendship, and willingness to serve. These characteristics emerged out of stories, humor, affection, and depth of personality. At certain points the sense of community becomes almost palpable. Finally, someone looks at his watch and says, "Wow, its two o'clock in the morning! Where did the time go?" Time seems to disappear when we lose ourselves in the goodness, lovability, and beauty of others, as we give ourselves to them in a perfect act of empathy.

Now imagine what it would be like to be in Heaven, where everybody's goodness and lovability are brought to perfection. As we gaze upon each of these transcendent mysteries, we find ourselves perfectly connected to them and giving ourselves over to them. They experience the very same thing when they gaze upon *us* in our unique, transcendent goodness, lovability, and beauty. You would not have to stop at some surface dimension of their lovability, because there would be no egocentricity or narcissism in you or in them to block the full scope of their unique lovability. This love is so profound that you find a home in the other, complete the other, and are completed by the other through mutual gift of self. You are as lost in the depth of the mystery of their unique lovability as they are in your unique lovability.

Now imagine further that you have the capacity to enter into this kind of relationship with billions upon billions of people, and that you can have complete empathy with them as they can for you. We are now beginning to touch on the love intrinsic to the Kingdom of Heaven. Yet, we have barely scratched the surface, because at the center of it all—orchestrating it all—is the *infinite* love of Father, Son, and Holy Spirit.

Inasmuch as the three divine Persons are unrestricted and unconditional love for each other, they are unrestrictedly and unconditionally empathetic, self-giving, and joyful. Inasmuch as they desire to share themselves totally with us, they call us into a relationship with them, a relationship of *unrestricted and unconditional* goodness, lovability, self-gift, and joy. They offer an infinite outpouring of themselves as well as an infinite acceptance of everyone in the Kingdom of Heaven. They unify all of the unique lovable inner worlds of everyone in that kingdom. Now imagine that you get to participate in this, without egocentricity or narcissism, by giving yourself to that incredible array of beloveds through the unrestricted and unconditional love of the Trinity. You would be completely fulfilled, completely accepted, completely needed, completely contributive, completely at home, completely immersed in billions of people brought to loving perfection by the ineffable mystery of infinite love.

The sixteenth-century Carmelite mystic Saint Teresa of Avila gives a faint glimmer of the ecstasy of this infinite love in describing some of her experiences of the love of God in prayer:

> The *loving* exchange that takes place between the soul and God is so sweet that I beg Him in His goodness to give a taste of this love to anyone who thinks I am lying. On the days this lasted I went about as though stupefied. I desired neither to see nor to speak.... It seems the Lord carries the soul away and places it in *ecstasy*; thus there is no room for pain or suffering, because *joy* soon enters in.[22]

---

[22] Teresa of Avila, "The Book of Her Life", in *The Collected Works of St. Teresa of Avila*, trans. Kieran Kavanaugh and Otilio Rodriguez, vol. 1 (Washington, D.C.: ICS Publications, 1976), p. 194; emphasis mine.

If this is only a finite taste of the infinite love that is to come, the reality of our spiritual destiny will be nothing less than perfect ecstasy through the billions upon billions of loving relationships drawn together in perfect communion with the infinitely loving God.

Is Heaven even more? Does it go beyond the ecstasy of perfect goodness and love? It does inasmuch as it includes the fulfillment of the other two transcendental desires (truth and beauty). Recall the four transcendental desires addressed in Volume II, Chapter 4: truth, love, goodness, and beauty. The fulfillment of two of these desires (for perfect love and goodness) is directly addressed by Jesus, but the other two (for truth and beauty) are seen only in the light of love and goodness.

Jesus does not restrict truth to the "mind's reasons"—seeking the complete intelligibility of reality through physics, mathematics, logic, metaphysics, and the other major disciplines. Rather, He begins with the truth of the heart, and the highest truth of the heart is His relationship with the Father. Thus when He says that "no one knows the Son except the Father, and no one knows the Father except the Son" (Mt 11:27), He is pointing to the highest truth: the lived awareness of the Father's love and goodness, which reveals His life, power, and creative activity. Thus, Jesus sees the created world through the eyes of His Father, who *lovingly* made it and shared His creative activity with His Son.

In what does the fulfillment of our desire for perfect truth consist? It would partially consist in a beholding of the intelligibility of the created world (from the fundamental equations of physics to the mathematics that underlies them, from the transcendental powers and nature of individuals to the moral religious laws that govern them, and so forth). As fascinating and beautiful as all this is, it is not the fulfilment of our desire for perfect truth (the beatific vision[23]). The vision of truth itself must include an insight into the unrestricted act of thinking that created the world of complete intelligibility, and not only an insight into its thinking, but most importantly, for Jesus, into

---

[23] Saint Thomas Aquinas defines the beatific vision as the consummate happiness that comes from the perfect satisfaction of all our desires (the desire for perfect truth, perfect love, perfect goodness, and perfect beauty). Nothing can satisfy these desires for perfection except an absolutely perfect being that is itself perfect truth, love, goodness, and beauty—namely, God. See *Summa Theologica* I–II, q. 3, a. 8 and I–II, q. 2, a. 8.

its love and goodness. Thus, the fulfillment of our desire for perfect truth must be a beholding of the unconditionally loving, unrestricted mind and heart of God lovingly creating the world of complete intelligibility for transcendent creatures like ourselves. As the name "beatific" suggests, this vision brings with it not only the satisfaction of intellectual curiosity, but the satisfaction of being immersed in tremendous beauty, the beauty of complete intelligibility, perfect symmetry, perfect creativity, perfect mind, and the perfect love behind it all. In the beatific vision, truth is beauty and beauty is truth; love and goodness are truth and beauty; and truth and beauty are love and goodness. To behold it all in the midst of real interpersonal love is yet another dimension of joy that surpasses all understanding.

This brings us to the idea of perfect home. Jesus uses many expressions such as "family, rooms, and houses" that convey a sense of ultimate home. When we are immersed in the perfect love of the Trinity and all others in the Kingdom of Heaven, there can be no alienation from self or others—no emptiness, no darkness, no negation, no loneliness, no pain that arises out of egocentricity, narcissism, or evil. We are in complete harmony with self and others and at peace with self and others; this perfect harmony and peace may be described as perfect home. This is our true calling, what the unconditionally loving God has prepared for us—what we were created for.

As can be seen, Jesus' view of Heaven is anything but boring; it does not lack emotion and excitement, for it exudes these at the highest levels of joy and ecstasy; it is not lackluster, but the complete satisfaction of our curiosity, the overwhelming satisfaction of our desire for beauty, and the continuous satisfaction of our desire for love and goodness.

D. Correlation with Near-Death Experiences

As noted in Volume II (Chapter 5, Section V), contemporary studies of near-death experiences reveal some interesting parallels with the Christian view of resurrection—specifically, that God is immensely loving, and that Heaven is centered on this immensity of love. Near-death experiences cannot validate the unconditional nature or eternal status of this "immensity of love", because they cannot penetrate the knowledge and will of God. However, they can show that the experience of a large number of clinically dead individuals has intense love at its center. This finding is most powerfully described in a patient's experience of a loving white light. Raymond Moody expresses it as follows:

> What is perhaps the most incredible common element in the accounts I have studied, and is certainly the element which has the most profound effect upon the individual, is the encounter with a very bright light. Typically, at its first appearance this light is dim, but it rapidly gets brighter until it reaches an unearthly brilliance. Yet, even though this light (usually said to be white or "clear") is of an indescribable brilliance, many make the specific point that it does not in any way hurt their eyes, or dazzle them, or keep them from seeing other things around them.... Despite the light's unusual manifestation, however, not one person has expressed any doubt whatsoever that it was a being, a being of light. Not only that, it is a *personal* being. It has a very definite personality. The *love* and the warmth which emanate from this being to the dying person are utterly beyond words, and he feels completely surrounded by it and taken up in it, completely at ease and *accepted* in the presence of this being. He senses an irresistible magnetic attraction to this light. He is ineluctably drawn to it.[24]

This being of light is invariably described as loving and accepting. Some people associate it with God, Jesus, or an angel. Given the large numbers of patients in different studies who have witnessed this loving white light,[25] we might infer that it is a beginning point of what Jesus described as the messianic banquet and what Paul described as the wide and long and high and deep love of Christ, which is the fullness of God (Eph 3:17–19).

We now encounter a seeming contradiction of Jesus' presentation of His unconditionally loving Father and the eternal banquet of unconditional love—the possibility and/or reality of Hell. How could such a God, who loves us so much, allow anyone to go to a domain of darkness, away from the light?

---

[24] Raymond Moody, *Life After Life* (New York: HarperCollins, 1975), p. 49; emphasis mine.

[25] See the sixteen different studies in Volume II, Chapter 5, Section III.

III. Why Would an Unconditionally
Loving God Allow Hell?

Jesus preached the reality of a domain "prepared for the devil and his angels" (Mt 25:41). He describes it as a place of pain, darkness, exclusion, and emptiness. He gives several warnings about the dangers of pursuing a life of self-absorption and self-idolatry giving rise to a lack of forgiveness and compassion.

Two words are used for this domain. The more frequent word is "Gehenna", but occasionally "Hades" (which is a Greek translation of the Hebrew *Sheol*, the abode of the dead) is used. Gehenna is a fiery pit outside of Jerusalem that was associated with barrenness and ongoing torment. Luke uses the term "Hades" to have a similar meaning in the parable of Lazarus and the Rich Man (Lk 16:19–31). These uses are not the invention of Jesus, but rather that of the Old Testament and extratestamental literature.[26]

How can Jesus' view of Hell be squared with His view of the unconditional love of God and the intrinsic goodness of every person? When we define love as Jesus did (humble-heartedness, gentle-heartedness, compassion, patience, kindness, not growing angry, etc.), Jesus' view of Hell seems to contradict love, and therefore the nature of God.

One of the most concise definitions of Hell that gives an important insight into how Hell can be reconciled with the unconditional love of God comes from the *Catechism of the Catholic Church*, which states that Hell is a "state of definitive self-exclusion from communion with God and the blessed".[27] This definition comes from centuries of reflection on three New Testament teachings that influence the doctrine of Hell.

1. Jesus' teaching on the pains of Hell implied by His use of "Gehenna" and His expression "into the outer darkness, where there will be weeping and gnashing of teeth" (Mt 22:13).
2. The association of Hell with a lack of compassion and love for others (e.g., the Parable of Lazarus and the Rich Man [Lk

[26] See McKenzie, *Dictionary of the Bible*, pp. 299–300.
[27] *Catechism of the Catholic Church*, no. 1033.

16:19–31], and the Parable of the Sheep and the Goats [Mt 25:31–46]).

3. Jesus' revelation of the unconditional love of God (seen in the Parable of the Prodigal Son [Lk 15:11–32], and the Parable of the Lost Sheep [Lk 15:1–7]).

When these three New Testament teachings are put together systematically, they point to the above definition of Hell given in the *Catechism of the Catholic Church*. This definition is quite dense and requires considerable explanation.

Let us begin with the most basic part of the definition: "self-exclusion from communion". "Communion" is derived from the early Christian use of *Koinōnia*, which refers to "the idealized state of love, unity, and community that exists within the Kingdom of God, and toward which the Body of Christ—the Christian church—aspires." So at a very basic level, Hell is the absence of love, unity, and community with God and the blessed. Though Hell is sometimes portrayed as flames, darkness, and "weeping and gnashing of teeth", these images are *metaphors* for the *pain* of a domain without love.[28] The absence of love is emptiness, darkness, coldness, and loneliness; it is also envy, contempt, anger, resentment, egocentricity, narcissism, self-idolatry, and hatred. All of these dimensions of "unlove" or "anti-love" are painful, and so Hell is associated with this pain.

The next part of the definition concerns the reason why the unconditionally loving God would allow a state of Hell—namely, the free choice of individuals to reject love, God, and others. The definition says that Hell is "*self*-exclusion from communion with God and the blessed." This means that the all-loving God does not *send* people to Hell, but rather *allows* people to *choose* Hell through an act of definitive, self-determining freedom.

[28] The Synoptic Gospels, (particularly Matthew [Mt 5:22 and 18:9, Mk 9:43]), the Letter of James (Jas 3:6), and the Book of Revelation (Rev 14:10, 17:16, and 18:8) are the only New Testament writings that make reference to the imagery of "flames, a fiery pit, and prison". These authors refer to popular Jewish Apocalyptic that was prevalent in the intertestamental period. Paul, John, Peter, Hebrews, and other New Testament writers prefer other descriptions of this negative condition. Paul views it as "death" and "separation from the Kingdom of God" (Rom 6:23, 1 Cor 6:10, and Gal 5:9–12). John also speaks of this negative condition as "death", as well as "judgment", "darkness", and "exclusion from the eternal life communicated by the Son" (Jn 5:29, 8:24, 10:28, 11:25, and 12:25). Evidently, Paul's and John's definitions of this negative condition are much closer to the definition given in the *Catechism of the Catholic Church*. See McKenzie, *Dictionary of the Bible*, p. 300.

Why would anyone choose Hell and the pain associated with it? In brief, some people may prefer to endure the above-mentioned pain to live in unbounded self-absorption, egocentricity, dominion over others, and to become a "god" for self and others. For these people, love, God, and others are all negatives, while self, power, autonomy, and dominion are supreme. They definitively choose as their meaning in life "godlike" status, the rejection of truly divine sovereignty, and the subjugation of others to themselves. This *requires* that they reject the love of God and others because they cannot simultaneously make both self and love their highest priority. For them, love gets in the way of self-absorption and self-idolatry, and so God and love must be rejected.

As explained in Chapter 3 (Section I.A), we explained that for Jesus and the Christian Church, the purpose of our life in this world is to define ourselves. We must choose between two fundamental options: (1) God, others, and love, or (2) self-absorption and self-idolatry. We accomplish this process of self-definition through our decisions and actions during the course of our lives. Eventually those decisions and actions form habits (a second nature), and they become stronger and stronger, gradually forming our essence (our self-definition).

We don't have to define ourselves perfectly before leaving this world. It is doubtful that any person could do this. Nevertheless, we do need to make a committed decision toward one set of goals or the other (because we cannot hold both sets of goals at the same time, for they are contradictory). Thus, our lives are characterized by choosing to move in the direction of either self or others, autonomy or love, and worship of self or worship of God. Even if our intention is to choose love, others, and God, we could choose courses of action that run contrary to this intention. Nevertheless, we are not locked into these bad choices, for the Lord of unconditional love allows us to repent and return to Him, even an endless number of times.[29] When we do repent, the Lord not only forgives us, but gives us grace

---

[29]Jesus' response to Peter that he should forgive his neighbor "seventy times seven" times (Mt 18:22) reflects Gods own heart and attitude, for He would not ask us to do what He Himself would not do. "Seventy times seven" refers to the perfect prime number (seven) times ten times the perfect prime number (seven), which for a Semite means "an endless number of times". This is commensurate with Jesus' proclamation that the Father will take us back fully into His family—even if we have sinned as gravely as the prodigal son.

to reorient our lives toward love. Eventually a "mindset" begins to form, a leaning toward love rather than autonomy, toward others rather than self, and toward divine worship rather than self-worship. In this way, our complex network of decisions, actions, acts of repentance, struggles to stay on the right road, and the little improvements we make define us as beings of love, worship, and community.

Alternatively, we might make decisions that lead us into darkness, in favor of self, autonomy, and self-idolatry—decisions that show no regard for others, and that choose dominion and narcissistic satisfaction above empathy and compassion for others. We don't care if we plunge others into suffering, darkness, emptiness, or hopelessness, so long as we get what we want. We can even experience the *opposite* of an act of repentance and become hardened in our resolve to intensify others' misery. For example, we might have a "weak" moment in our journey toward complete self-obsession and self-idolatry, and show some empathy or compassion for another person, and then have second thoughts, and even regrets. We might think to ourselves, "I could have taken far more advantage of him; I won't be compassionate again." As we make these decisions, another kind of "mindset" develops, and we gradually define ourselves in terms of "unlove" and "anti-love". Eventually we get to the point of preferring "unlove" and "anti-love", which could lead to a choice of an eternity of self-absorption, autonomy, dominion, self-obsession, and self-idolatry above an eternity of love, others, and God.[30]

Hell is oftentimes viewed as a punishment for past sin, and there are implications of this in both the New Testament Scriptures and in

---

[30] Readers interested in how people might be able to make a definitive free choice to remain in an atmosphere of egocentricity, dominion of others, and self-idolatry, instead of choosing the kingdom of love, beauty, and truth, will want to read the modern parable by C. S. Lewis, *The Great Divorce*. He tells a story about a bus ride from Hell to Heaven. The bus parks on the outskirts of Heaven, at which point, "the wispy ghosts" from the grey city of Hell are greeted by bright spirits—deceased relatives, friends, and emissaries of the loving God—who come to persuade and help them make the *choice* of Heaven. Most of the ghosts *choose* to return to Hell because the love (*agapē*) of the Kingdom of Heaven is either unintelligible or "simply too much to endure". One ghost cannot believe that there are so many golden apples, freely available to *anyone*, in the Kingdom of Heaven. He reasons that they could not have any "value" in this overly generous environment, and so spends the rest of his time at the outskirts of Heaven trying to stuff his pockets with golden apples (which are heavy for him) so that he can take them to Hell where they will be highly unusual and have a "much greater value". Another self-conscious ghost keeps hiding in the bushes while her friend pleads with her to stop worrying about her appearance so that she can take in the splendor of Heaven, but

theological reflection throughout the centuries.[31] The idea of punishment is not accentuated in the definition from the *Catechism of the Catholic Church*, which emphasizes the *self*-exclusion of people from communion with God and the blessed. How can the views of "punishment" from the Synoptic Gospels and the Church tradition be reconciled with the notion of "*self*-exclusion from communion" given in the *Catechism of the Catholic Church*?

As noted above, the Catholic Church had to reconcile several different New Testament passages to synthesize her doctrine on Hell. In addition to the passages on punishment from the Synoptic Gospels, there are also passages on the unconditional love of God (Lk 15:1–7;11–32) and passages on people without compassion or empathy straying on the path to Hell (Lk 16:19–31; Mt 25:31–46). The Church reconciles the tension in these passages by taking the emphasis off of punishment as "*God's* action" and placing it on "the actions of a person who freely rejects love and communion with God and others" (a form of *self-punishment*).

Self-punishment can come from a "trade-off" in which one accepts a negative consequence in order to procure something intensely desired, such as Faust selling his soul to the devil for worldly fame and power.[32] Sometimes self-punishment can come from self-hatred, which can come from hatred and contempt for others. It seems that

---

she can't seem to break away from her self-absorption. Lewis ingeniously gives many other portrayals of ghosts with other preferences—a ghost who prefers to hang on to her resentment of God in Hell (for taking her child on earth) rather than see her child in Heaven with the loving God; a bishop who prefers "to continue his search for God in hell" rather than actually finding God in Heaven; and many others. See C. S. Lewis, *The Great Divorce* (New York: HarperOne, 2009).

[31] Gehenna is generally associated with the punishment of evildoers, particularly in the Gospel of Matthew. Gehenna can also refer to a place of eternal punishment (Mt 18:8) or to a place of definitive destruction (Mt 10:28), implying that it is a place of annihilation rather than eternal punishment. This resembles the rabbinical use of the term in extratestamental Judaism. Jesus apparently uses the term with both of these rabbinical meanings, which would have been familiar to His audiences. See McKenzie, *Dictionary of the Bible*, pp. 299–300. Additionally, many Church theologians have considered Hell to be a place of punishment. See Ludwig Ott, *The Fundamentals of Catholic Dogma* (Rockford, Ill.: Tan Books, 1955), p. 479.

[32] The legend of Dr. Faustus (or the "Faust Legend") is a late medieval (ca. 1500) German story about a dissatisfied scholar who made a pact with the devil to exchange his immortal soul for immense worldly power and knowledge. There are many versions of this story including that of the English author Christopher Marlowe and of Johann von Goethe. The latter revised the original story (in which Faust is condemned) so that Faust's pleading and God's mercy rescue him from the clutches of Mephistopheles (the devil) with whom he made the pact.

we eventually apply the criterion we use for others to ourselves. Thus, self-punishment is not as unusual as it might first seem. There may actually be people like Faust who would choose Hell for a diabolical reward, or people who choose Hell out of a sense of self-hatred emanating from their hatred of others.

The definition of "Hell" in the *Catechism* emphasizes *self*-punishment (self-exclusion) instead of "punishment by God". This position is consistent with other teachings of Jesus, such as God's unconditional love and the definitive power of personal freedom to reject God, love, and others. This emphasis assures that God is not viewed as either a "justice machine" (meting out justice in a heartless, mechanical fashion) or "an angry God who needs to get even with sinners with whom He has run out of patience". Both of these notions of "God" are irreconcilable with Jesus' teaching about the Father of the Prodigal Son, Abba, the Beatitudes, and love as the highest commandment.

The unconditionally loving God (the Father of Jesus) has no interest in punishing anyone, either out of vengeance or a sense of strict justice. He gives people what they really want for their eternal "happiness". If their decisions and actions consistently manifest (without repentance) a desire for autonomy, self-absorption, narcissism, and contempt for and abuse of others as well as a continual rejection (without repentance) of God, the blessed, and love, they come very close to a *definitive*[33] preference or choice to be "excused" from Heaven and to go to a place where unlove and anti-love reign supreme, where they can have what they truly want.

They will join other people who have the very same preference, which has the consequence of creating an atmosphere of abuse, contempt, hatred, emptiness, and darkness, with its attendant deep psychological pain. It seems that some people might think that this pain is "worth it" in order to procure the "benefits" of Hell—more enmity, narcissism, contempt, abuse, and hatred. It is as if convinced sadists will embrace masochism in order to obtain greater levels of sadistic pleasure.

Is personal freedom capable of this? Jesus suggests that it is. However, this attitude of "anti-love" cannot exist in the Kingdom of Heaven. It completely contradicts the love of the Kingdom, and

---

[33] The *Catechism*'s use of "definitive" in its definition of Hell will be taken up in detail below in this section.

therefore it requires a completely separate place in which people with that attitude can continue to stoke and endure the flames of psychological pain in order to obtain sadistic pleasure and self-idolatry.

Thus, God does not create the pain of Hell. Rather, He allows people to enter a state in which they can create pain for others and self, and so obtain their true preference and lifelong desire. When people choose this domain, God is incredibly saddened, not only because they have rejected Him and the love He has provided, but also because they choose agony above the joy of communion with others. An all-loving God could not hate these people; He would continue to love them just as the father in the parable continues to love his prodigal son. Nevertheless, because of their definitive choice to reject love, He allows them, with great sadness, to have their hearts' desire.

Is Hell eternal? The Synoptic Gospels indicate that Jesus said that it is. The *Catechism*'s definition indicates *why* Hell is eternal, because those who choose Hell *definitively* choose to reject love, God, and others. Thus, the eternity of Hell *follows* from the *definitive* decision of those who choose Hell, not vice versa. If a person definitively chooses Hell, and God recognizes the definitiveness of that decision, He grants him his eternal desire. However, the opposite is not the case; God does not create an eternally painful domain in which to cast evil people. Hence, the eternity of Hell comes from *people's* definitive choice to reject love, but not from God's decision.

The above interpretation is borne out by the *Catechism*'s choice to define Hell as "a *state* of definitive self-exclusion" instead of "a *place* of definitive self-exclusion". There has been considerable theological debate about this topic, and it is noteworthy that the *Catechism* has decided in favor of the theological view expressed by many modern theologians such as Karl Rahner and Hans Urs von Balthasar.[34]

---

[34]Saints Augustine and Gregory held that Hell was a *place* under the earth. Other theologians held that Hell is a place whose location is unspecified. Still other theologians, such as Karl Rahner, Bernard A. Marthaler, and Hans Urs von Balthasar, favor the position that Hell is a *state*. Von Balthasar has taken the strongest position, declaring that "hell is not an object that is 'full' or 'empty' of human individuals, but a possibility that is not 'created' by God but in any case by the free individuals who choose it." See Jack Mulder, *Kierkegaard and the Catholic Tradition* (Bloomington: Indiana University Press, 2010), p. 145. The official Catholic Church teaching has moved in the direction of "a state" and has indicated this in both the *Catechism of the Catholic Church* as well as in the work by Brian Singer-Towns entitled *The Catholic Faith Handbook for Youth* (Winona, Minn.: St. Mary's Press, 2008).

If it had decided instead to define Hell as a *place*, it would imply that God created an eternal domain for the condemned, which is difficult to reconcile with the unconditional love of God.

Could a person change his mind after experiencing the pain of Hell and plead to God to rescue him? The question is really a moot point because when the all-loving God allows a person to choose *definitively* a state of self-exclusion from Him and the blessed, He does so with complete certitude that the person's decision *is* definitive (eternal). This belief is grounded in God's omniscience, which enables Him to know every nuance and potential of every person. Therefore God would be certain that a person *would not* change his mind, but rather would *perpetually* prefer the "rejection of love" to communion with Him and the blessed. He would be certain that a person's choice was to endure the pain of separation eternally from Him and love to procure the "privileges" of Hell—the supremacy of self and unmitigated contempt for others.

What if a person does not *definitively* choose self-exclusion from communion with God and the blessed? Or, asked the other way around, what if a person only *imperfectly* chooses communion with God and the blessed? This condition indicates that the person in question is in some respect open to communion with God and the blessed, but in other respects is impeded from desiring it completely (and entering into this communion perfectly in the Kingdom of Heaven). The Catholic Church provides for this condition of imperfect freedom to love (obscured by egotistical desires) in its doctrine on Purgatory, which holds that there is a state of purification of desire, choice, and action after death. In this state, God allows individuals through His grace to purge remnant desires for egocentricity, dominion, and self-idolatry. These individuals will not remain in Purgatory forever (nor will they regress to Hell), but eventually will be ushered into Heaven when their purification is complete.

In conclusion, the unconditionally loving God does not make a mechanical judgment about our salvation. God's will is to save *every* person who chooses to be saved (through repentance and faith) and who wants to be brought into a Kingdom where "love, others, and God" take precedence over "autonomy and egocentricity".[35]

---

[35] God's desire to save everyone is thoroughly discussed in Section I above.

Though an all-loving God desires to save *everyone*, He allows individuals to refuse His salvific intention, and to choose definitively a kingdom without love.

This interpretation of Hell (the state of definitive self-exclusion from God and the blessed) requires that we make distinctions concerning God's intention; He *desires* to save everyone, but He *allows* people to reject His salvation, and He *judges* everyone omnisciently—seeing into the depths of our hearts, and perfectly discerning our *definitive* intention to choose self-exclusion or self-inclusion in His Kingdom.

We can now summarize this interpretation of the *Catechism*'s definition of Hell. God wills to save everyone who chooses loving communion with Him and the blessed (and who is willing to be purified in love to enter into that communion). He is able to discern and judge perfectly the intentions of every person, and so He knows whether a person definitively rejects communion with Him and others, and who would therefore be unwilling to be purified in love through the purging of egotistical desires. The all-loving God does not *send people* to Hell; He accommodates their definitive choice to reject Him, others, and love. He is incredibly saddened by those who make this decision because they choose a negative and destructive form of happiness in favor of true happiness in the beatific vision. He does everything possible (through the Holy Spirit and His "conspiracy of Providence") to bring people back to their senses, to the goodness and beauty of love and communion with others, but He will not take away their freedom to definitively choose what they think will make them "happy". He subordinates His will to their will, for this is what is required to create creatures capable of love.

God is caught in the tension between freedom and love. He cannot make truly loving creatures unless He gives them the choice *not* to love (and even the choice to undermine love), because without that choice, we would be restricted to *only* loving behaviors, in which case our love would not be chosen by us, but would be programmed into us by the Creator (who would act as a kind of "divine programmer"). However, the unconditionally loving God did not want to create "robots programmed for loving behaviors". He wanted to make creatures in His own image (capable of love) and, in the future, capable of unconditional love with Him and others in His heavenly Kingdom. Inasmuch as God wanted to make loving creatures, He had to give them freedom *not* to love, and even the freedom to definitively reject love (which entails rejecting Him and others who are committed to love). The irony of freedom and love is that the Creator must allow His creatures the freedom to choose "definitive self-exclusion from him and the blessed" in order to give them the capacity to love in His own image. He has to subordinate His will (for universal salvation of all His "beloveds") to our freedom to choose, allowing us the possibility of definitively rejecting the love we have been given. God does not send anyone to Hell; Hell is the result of the freedom to love brought to the opposite extreme for which it was intended.

IV. The Path to Salvation

We now arrive at the critical question: How can we assure that we are moving on the path to the Kingdom of Heaven (and away from the path of definitive self-exclusion from God and the blessed)? Jesus gives us the answer in the central message of His preaching during His ministry: "The time is fulfilled, and the kingdom of God has come near; repent, and believe in the good news" (Mk 1:15, my translation). Jesus indicates that there are two dimensions for entering into the Kingdom of God: repentance and belief in the good news. What does He mean by these expressions?

A. "Repent and Believe in the Good News"

"Repentance" (*metanoia*) has two aspects: (1) turning *away* from what is sinful, and (2) turning *toward* the goodness of God. Jesus defines the first dimension for a young man who approaches Him and asks, "[W]hat good deed must I do, to have eternal life?" Jesus responds by telling him to heed the five central commandments: do not kill; do not commit adultery; do not steal; do not bear false witness; and honor your father and your mother. Then He adds His own commandment taken from Leviticus 19:18: "[L]ove your neighbor as yourself" (Mt 19:16–19).

The following question now arises: What happens if people do not obey these commandments? This brings us to the second dimension of Jesus' proclamation: "Believe in the good news." Recall that Jesus reveals the Father to be unconditional love and that He intensely desires to lose no one, not even the most errant sinner (portrayed, for example, in the Parables of the Lost Sheep and the Prodigal Son), and so He will bring us back into His fold if we sincerely ask Him for forgiveness, even if we have sinned gravely. We see this in several passages, among which the following three are prominent:

1. the repentance of the prodigal son: "Father, I have sinned against heaven and before you; I am no longer worthy to be called your son" (Lk 15:21), after which the father restores the son to full membership within the family;
2. the story of the Pharisee and the tax collector in the Temple, in which the tax collector pleads, "God, be merciful to me a sinner!" to which Jesus responds, "I tell you, this man went down to his house justified" (Lk 18:13–14); and
3. the good thief on the cross who asks, "Jesus, remember me when you come into your kingly power," to which Jesus responds, "Truly, I say to you, today you will be with me in Paradise" (Lk 23:42–43).

So how do we assure that we are on the path to the Kingdom of Heaven (rather than the path of definitive self-exclusion from God and the blessed)? Jesus indicates that we should try to adhere to six basic commandments, and if we fail in them, to sincerely seek His compassion and forgiveness like the prodigal son, the tax collector, and the good thief. He says that God will give His mercy to those who do make sincere acts of repentance and He will invite them into His Kingdom.

Recall from the previous chapter that for Jesus, an act of repentance (*metanoia*) is an entrance into the Kingdom He brought to the world. When we enter this Kingdom, we embark on a journey toward the future Kingdom of Heaven. This journey will have many challenges as well as opportunities to build the Kingdom. In His parables, Jesus indicates that *perseverance* will be essential. We will have to allow His word to take deep root in our hearts so that when challenge and persecution comes, we will not wither and fade (the seed that fell on shallow ground in the Parable of the Sower). We will also have to contend with evil and suffering in the world by trusting in God, obtaining support from the Church community, and following the Holy Spirit (the seed that fell in with the thorns); and if we persevere, we will not only reach our goal of the heavenly Kingdom; we will produce a yield, thirty, sixty, and even a hundred times (the seed that fell on good soil).

This yield will include being compassionate toward those in need, forgiving those who ask for mercy, trying to make the world a better place, helping people to see the light and love of Jesus Christ, bringing hope and consolation to the suffering, and helping people to enter and persevere in their journey to the Kingdom of Heaven. When we contend well with suffering and evil, the Holy Spirit opens doors of opportunity for us to be companions with Jesus in building the Kingdom, and this becomes our joy, because there cannot be any more significant and fulfilling life than this. Thus repentance goes far beyond sincere contrition for sins and trust in the unconditionally loving God. It is the acceptance of Jesus' invitation to enter into the Kingdom He brought to the world, with all its challenges and opportunities, that leads ultimately to an eternity of unconditional love with the Trinity and the blessed. We may find ourselves falling off the path (through neglect or sin), but we know that God will pull us back on the path if we ask Him with a sincere heart. When we get back on the path to the heavenly Kingdom, we find ourselves further along, despite our failures, thanks to the Holy Spirit and the mystery of divine Providence.

B. Jesus' Four Gifts to Inspire and Build His Kingdom

Jesus does not leave us alone on the journey. He provided us with four gifts to help us persevere on the journey in the midst of temptation, suffering, and evil, and to seize opportunities to help the needy, promote the common good, and build the Kingdom:

1. The Church community
2. The Holy Spirit
3. The Holy Eucharist
4. His word

1. *The Church community:* The Church community provides not only the support of Church leaders, ministers, and members, but also a means of public worship, a teaching authority to interpret Scripture, a source of spiritual wisdom, and opportunities for service. Jesus set up this Church by choosing disciples (Mt 4:18–22); giving them authority and power to heal the sick and expel unclean spirits (Mt 10 1–4); giving them the power to forgive and retain sins (Mt 16:19; 18:18; Jn 20:23), the authority to celebrate the Holy Eucharist ("do this in memory of me" [Lk 22:19; 1 Cor 11:24]), and the power to impart the Holy Spirit to new members ("Go therefore and make disciples of all nations, baptizing them" [Mt 28:19]); and appointing Peter as the highest authority ("you are Peter, and on this rock, I will build my Church. . . . I will give you the keys of the kingdom of heaven" [Mt 16:18–19]). He promised to inspire and guide the Church by the Holy Spirit, and to protect it so that the powers of Satan will not prevail against it.

The Church is a tremendous gift because she not only helps us to continue our act of repentance (*metanoia*) on the path to salvation, but also to deepen our spiritual conviction and to join with others in serving the needy and building the Kingdom. Some people might think that participating in the Church (through worship, learning, and service) is a duty or a hassle, but Jesus did not intend it that way. He intended to build a community in which we would *want* to participate, because it provides support for our faith, support in times of suffering, a source of inspired learning and worship, and a means of deepening prayer and wisdom. No doubt the Church has her high and low moments of inspiration and service, but at base she provides help and inspiration to stay on the path to salvation. This is explained in detail in Volume I (Chapter 6).

2. *The Holy Spirit:* Though the Holy Spirit inspires all people, cultures, and religions,[36] Jesus gave Christians an additional gift or charism of His Spirit through Baptism (His indwelling in our hearts) to further

[36] See the explanation in the Pastoral Constitution on the Church in the Modern World (*Gaudium et Spes*) above in Sections I.C and I.D. The passage reads: "For since Christ died for all, and since all men are in fact called to one and the same destiny, which is divine, we must hold that the Holy Spirit offers to *all* the possibility of being made partners, in a way known to God, in the paschal mystery" (no. 22).

inspire us, guide us, protect us, deepen us in our relationship with the Father, deepen our trust, hope, and love, and fill us with the joy of the Kingdom. The Spirit deepens our spiritual life and our connection with one another in "Christ's body". Additionally, the Spirit inspires us to serve the community and the Kingdom of God by opening doors of opportunity, galvanizing friendships and *esprit de corps* for common mission, and organizing the people and events around us. This was discussed in detail in Volume I (Chapter 8) and in this volume (Chapter 5, Section II).

3. *The Holy Eucharist:* At the Last Supper Jesus gave all future generations the gift of His body and blood poured out in unconditional love. He indicated that this gift would be a means of forgiveness for sin, freedom from the slavery of evil, transformation in His own heart, and a grace toward eternal life. Additionally, Saint Paul sees the Eucharist as a grace to integrate us more fully into Christ's own body—the Church and the communion of saints. This deeper integration into Christ's mystical body enables us to build up the Church and the Kingdom of God. It also enables us to receive more deeply from the Church—its joys become our joys; its challenges, our challenges. This was discussed in Volume I (Chapter 6) and in this volume (Chapter 3, Section IV.A).

4. *Jesus' word:* Jesus is the Word of God (Jn 1:1), and so His preaching is the word of the Father. His preaching consists in His definition of love in the Beatitudes, His advancement of the law in the Sermon on the Mount, His many parables on entering fully into the Kingdom, His proverbs and prayers, and even His polemic with Jewish authorities. His actions spoke even louder than His words—His love and defense of sinners, His miracles, His relationship with His disciples, and His care for the poor. These words provide instruction, example, inspiration, and a vehicle for prayer and grace that can help us deal with suffering and challenges and pursue opportunities to serve others and build the Kingdom. *Lectio Divina* and Ignatian meditation help us to use Jesus' words to deepen our relationship with Him in contemplation and continued conversion. This was explained in Volume I, Chapters 7 and 9, as well as in this volume, Chapters 5 and 6.

C. Jesus Himself as the Way to the Kingdom of God

The above four gifts given by Jesus do not exhaust the grace Jesus gave us to persevere on the path to the Kingdom of Heaven; He gave us *his whole self* as the source of the other four gifts. Saint Paul calls the *Church* (the baptized) "the body of Christ" (1 Cor 12:27). Thus, Jesus is not only the source of the Church; He *is* the unity and the integrating fabric of the Church. Jesus is not only the source of the *Holy Eucharist*; His crucified and risen body *is* the Holy Eucharist. Finally, Jesus is the source of *His word*, not just the words on the pages of the New Testament, but His living word that inspires us to know and love His wisdom, truth, and love for us and the world.

Therefore, if we are to engage and use the four gifts Jesus has given to us, we will want first to bond ourselves to *Him*; we will want to form a personal relationship, a friendship with Him so that our involvement in the Church, our inspiration by the Spirit, our reception of the Holy Eucharist, and our reflection on His word are embedded with His loving personal presence. Thus, we will want to come to a loving awareness of Jesus (and His presence to us) to make His gifts come fully alive within us. This is the reason for contemplative prayer, *Lectio Divina*, and Ignatian meditation, as explained in Volume I, Chapter 7.

Recall from Volume I (Chapter 7) that contemplative prayer is the act of placing ourselves in the presence of Jesus or His Father (or His Mother)[37] simply to be with them or connect with them. The form of this prayer is not as important as *being aware of the presence of Jesus, His Father, or His Mother*. As you begin your prayer, you might want to say to Jesus, the Father, or His Mother, "I know you are here with me and I know you love me." Frankly, I do this all the time, and I know they are present, and it brings their loving presence into my prayer, which makes all the difference.

The effectiveness of contemplative prayer cannot be underestimated. It completely transforms the quality and depth of our relationship to the Church, the inspiration of the Holy Spirit, our reception of Jesus' body and blood, and our reflection on His word. The more

[37] See Volume I, Chapter 7, Section III, "The Rosary as Contemplative Prayer".

we know Jesus and His Father (and Mother), the better we can persevere in the path of salvation toward the Kingdom of Heaven. Our awareness of their loving presence gives us the wisdom, trust, and patience to contend with life's hardships and sufferings as well as with the temptations and wiles of the evil one (see Volume IV of this Quartet). Their loving presence also animates us to serve the needy, bring hope to the world, and build the Church.

In sum, the assured path to salvation, according to Jesus, is repentance (the sincere contrition for sins, a renewed desire to live according to the commandments, and a trust in God's unconditional, forgiving love). Jesus assures us that God's love is so great that this action alone is sufficient to set us on the path to salvation, and if we should die the next minute, it would bring us into His Kingdom, even if we have sinned as egregiously as the good thief on the cross, the prodigal son, and the repentant tax collector.

Repentance also includes entering into the kingdom brought by Jesus (which ultimately leads to the Kingdom of Heaven). Jesus tells us that this will require perseverance, because there will be many temptations, challenges, hardships, and sufferings along the path. We can turn these temptations and challenges into opportunities to serve the needy and build the kingdom (yielding a harvest thirty, sixty, or even a hundredfold), or we can be overcome by them, allowing ourselves to wilt in the burning heat or be choked by thorns. Yet, if we are overcome, we are never lost, for the Father will always restore us to full membership in the family if we turn back to Him with a repentant spirit. If we persevere on the path to salvation (or return to the path after leaving it, through the grace of God), we can be sure that God will bring us to the goal for which we were destined, for no suffering, hardship, trial, demon, principality, or power will be able to separate us from the love of God given to us through Christ Jesus our Lord (see Rom 8:34–39).

D. Six Steps on the Path to Salvation

How can we best stay on the path to salvation? The following six steps summarize the teaching of Jesus:

1. Try to follow the commands of God, maintaining a repentant spirit, and if you should fall away, turn back to the Lord in humility like the prodigal son or the repentant tax collector.
2. Join a church community through Baptism, if you have not already done so (see Volume I, Chapter 6).
3. Try to deepen your relationship with the Lord in prayer; begin with acknowledging the presence of Jesus, His Father, or His Mother, and find some appropriate ways to ask for what you need and to give thanks and praise for His creation, redemption, and love (see Volume I, Chapter 7).
4. Ask for the inspiration and guidance of the Holy Spirit, and follow it through the rules of discernment (see Volume I, Chapter 8).
5. Receive the Eucharist as often as possible (see this volume, Chapter 3, Section IV.A).
6. Reflect on the Word of God, particularly the New Testament (see Volume I, Chapter 7).

Joining a church community (step 2 above) requires special attention. One need not join a church community to make a sincere act of repentance and to believe in Jesus Christ (step 1 above), so I would recommend that readers who are considering belief in God and Jesus for the first time make peace with the Lord *now* (through an act of repentance in faith) and then consider joining a church community through Baptism. It is not necessary to join a church to express repentance and faith, but a church community can be essential for *remaining in the faith*, and it can provide important guidance and support in pursuing the other four steps on the path to salvation (steps 3 through 6). Furthermore, it is not necessary to join a church in order to have a *personal relationship* with God and Jesus (step 3 above). Nevertheless the spiritual guidance, traditions, practices, teachings, direction, and devotions of a church community can significantly strengthen and enhance this personal relationship.

A church community *is* necessary for steps 4 and 5, for Baptism (the indwelling of the Holy Spirit) normally occurs through a Christian church community, and the Holy Eucharist must be received through a Catholic Church community. Step 6 (reflection on the

Word of God) can occur outside a church community, but it can be significantly enhanced by the learning and spiritual guidance of teachers within a church.

E. My Personal Journey into the Catholic Church

Given the importance of church community, it is essential to make a thoughtful and careful decision about which community to join. I thought it might be helpful to share the criteria of church membership I used as a college student that led me to *freely choose* the Catholic Church, the church in which I had been raised. Three principal criteria seemed important to me at that time, and I still believe they are valid today:

1. a church that was given perpetual teaching authority by Jesus;
2. a church that celebrates the Holy Eucharist conceived as the real presence of the crucified and risen Jesus; and
3. a church with a diverse and deep spiritual tradition.

The first criterion came from a need I experienced in college (see Volume I, Chapter 6). I was taken aback by the myriad of different interpretations for so many passages of Scripture, and knew that I would not be able to make the decision as to which interpretation best reflected what Jesus intended. It seemed to me that Jesus would have to have anticipated this problem and would have provided for an ongoing teaching authority capable of making a definitive interpretation of Scripture, so that people like me would be able to live the faith as He intended. Furthermore, I was aware that disagreements about Scripture and doctrine had led to considerable dissension and disunification within the Christian Church over the centuries, and so I reasoned that Jesus would have to have invested primary juridical authority not only in an individual like Peter, but in the *office* to which He appointed Peter. Without this teaching authority and teaching office, it seemed to me that the church founded by Jesus would never be able to maintain a core identity. Since I wanted to belong to a church that could give me personal clarity about the will of Jesus and could maintain unity amid diversity, I chose a

church with a primary teaching office and a defined juridical structure. Furthermore, from my reading of Scripture, I believed that Jesus
intended to establish such a primary juridical and teaching authority
in His selection of Peter as the first holder of this primary juridical
office (Mt 16:18–20).[38]

The second criterion goes back to my early childhood—to my
first Holy Communion. As I reflected on the significance of the Holy
Eucharist in my personal spiritual life, I came to realize how central it was. Even as a child, I had an intuitive sense of the extreme
significance of receiving the Person, body, and blood of Jesus; a
sense of the sacrifice He made to give me this gift of Himself; and
a sense of its importance in bringing me to salvation. Even when
I was plagued with doubts about various parts of my faith (in high
school), I continued to go to Mass, because I had a strong intuition
that the Holy Eucharist (the Lord's presence, body and blood) was
saving me, pulling me toward salvation. In college, I resolved that I
wanted to belong to a church who believed and practiced the centrality of this great gift (conceived as Jesus' real presence and not just
a symbolic presence), and I eventually became a daily communicant.
When I later studied Scripture in my graduate theological programs,
I came to understand how true my childhood intuitions really were.
Jeremias' *The Eucharistic Words of Jesus* revealed the heart of Jesus'
intention in the Eucharist (see Chapter 3, Section IV.A), and I was
perplexed as to how I could have had such a deep awareness of the
Eucharist before formally studying its historical background. Clearly,
some of my knowledge came from the Church herself, but much of
it came from the Spirit within me.

[38] As explained in Volume I (Chapter 6), there is ample reason to believe that Jesus did
impart primary juridical authority to Peter. If He did not, this passage (as well as Peter's primary role in the early Church) would have been disputed, but it was not. The power Peter
is given is immense; according to Viviano: "God shall bind and loose what Peter binds and
looses. This verse gives enormous authority to Peter. What is the nature of this authority?
Binding and loosing are rabbinic technical terms that can refer to binding the devil in exorcism, to the juridical acts of excommunication and of definitive decision making (a form of
teaching through legislation, policy setting). See J. Jeremias, *TDNT* 3 744–53. The authority
to bind and loose is given to the disciples in 18:18, but to Peter alone are accorded the revelation, the role of the rock of foundation (Eph 2:20), and especially the keys". Benedict T.
Viviano, O.P., "The Gospel according to Matthew", in *The New Jerome Biblical Commentary*,
eds. Raymond E. Brown, Joseph A. Fitzmyer, and Roland E. Murphy (Englewood Cliffs,
N.J.: Prentice-Hall, 1990), p. 630.

The third criterion also goes back to my childhood years, when I became familiar with the lives of the saints, especially the apostles and Saints Paul, Peter Damian, Francis, and Clare. I was not only impressed by these heroic figures' stories and actions, but by the devotions and spiritual traditions they initiated. In college, I was fascinated by Saints Augustine, Thomas Aquinas, Bonaventure, Teresa of Avila, John of the Cross, and Ignatius of Loyola. As I reflected on their theological and spiritual depth, I felt as if I was experiencing different melodies, harmonies, and movements within a single symphony—composed by Jesus. I could sense their love for the Lord, and it strengthened my love for Him as well; I could feel their heart for the poor, deprived, and depressed, and I desired to imitate them where I could; and above all, I felt their zeal for spreading the faith, and I shared that zeal, and so I selected a church that not only had a strong, deep, and diverse spiritual tradition, but also one that kept that tradition alive in its current practice.

There were many other reasons for why I chose to remain within the Catholic Church and even to pursue a priestly vocation within it—not the least of which was my mother's faith and love of the Church. However, as I made this important decision, the above three stood out not simply as *rational* criteria, but as *spiritual* imperatives; so I followed what I believed was the lead of the Holy Spirit into the heart of a church that I came to know as the gift of Jesus Christ. I was not disappointed.

V. Conclusion

We may now return to the six steps mentioned above. If we maintain a spirit of repentance (*metanoia*—turning away from sin and turning toward the unconditionally loving God), take part in a church community, connect daily with the Lord in prayer, and use the four gifts He has given us, we will be true companions of Jesus in serving others and building His kingdom of light against darkness, hope against despair, love against hatred, and good against evil. This will become our life's purpose, our living legacy, and our joy. Our journey to salvation will not only reach its goal; we will have the honor of working with the one we love to be instruments of eternal salvation in imitation of Him. The promise of Jesus is not only the heavenly Kingdom but a grace-filled adventure to advancing the cause of the world's Savior.

The moment we profess that Jesus is Emmanuel, the whole of our life changes. We see our true happiness, purpose, dignity, and destiny in light of the kingdom He brought and the kingdom of unconditional love we will inherit. We know that there is no ultimate tragedy, that God will bring good out of all suffering, that we can be effective instruments in the cosmic struggle between good and evil, that we will be able to build an eternal legacy, and that faith, hope, and love (*agapē*) is the way to live our lives.

If we affirm these central truths, we will not underlive our lives, underestimate our dignity, undermine our true destiny, or undervalue our neighbor. We will live up to our true transcendent potential and, in so doing, find transcendent happiness, not only in the Kingdom of Heaven, but also on the journey to it—even in the midst of suffering and challenge. The affirmation of Jesus as Emmanuel makes every other judgment and decision in our lives pale by comparison, for faith in Jesus is nothing less than the path and reality of salvation.

CONCLUSION

Our Journey to Transcendence—Thus Far

In Volume I of this Quartet (*Finding True Happiness: Satisfying Our Restless Hearts*), we began our journey to transcendence by examining four levels of happiness and showed that our highest form of happiness—the one that is most pervasive, enduring, and deep—is embedded in an interior awareness of, desire for, and "call" to the transcendent. We proposed that transcendent happiness (Level Four) is also our highest dignity and destiny, and that ignoring it would be tantamount not only to underestimating that dignity and destiny, but also to underliving our lives and wasting our transcendent potential. Yet, we did not fully engage the question of the evidence for our transcendent nature and destiny, deferring it instead to the second and third volumes of the Quartet.

I. The Clues to Our Transcendent Nature from Experience and Reason

We took up the second part of our journey to transcendence in Volume II of the Quartet (*The Soul's Upward Yearning: Clues to Our Transcendent Nature from Experience and Reason*). In Chapter 1, we first probed into Rudolf Otto's numinous experience—our awareness of the presence of the numen to us. We saw in Otto's "first pole of religious experience" the elements of dread, awe, dauntingness, and creatureliness, and in the second pole the elements of fascination, desire, love, and joy. We noted that even if these elements are not experienced in a vivid way, they create an awareness of and yearning for the spiritual and the sacred.[1]

---

[1] See Rudolf Otto, *The Idea of the Holy: An Inquiry into the Non-Rational Factor in the Idea of the Divine and Its Relation to the Rational* (New York: Oxford University Press, 1958).

We then explored how this numinous experience expressed itself in world religions, using the extensive research of Mircea Eliade (Chapter 2, Section I). In his work *The Sacred and the Profane*,[2] we saw the universal belief that the sacred had broken into the profane world, and that we could draw closer to it in sacred places as well as sacred times that could be relived through myth and ritual. We considered the deep satisfaction that comes from drawing close to the sacred through religious places, Scripture, and ritual, and also noted the sense of alienation that comes from rejecting the sacred—marked increases in suicide, substance abuse, alienation within families, and lost sense of purpose (as reported by the American Psychiatric Association[3]). This suggests that we are by nature religious (*homo religiosus*, according to Eliade[4]), and that alienation from our transcendent nature is really alienation from ourselves.

This led to an inquiry about conscience through the work of Immanuel Kant and John Henry Newman (Chapter 2, Section II). We saw that conscience is a felt awareness of and attraction to good and a fear of and revulsion toward evil. We noted that this "felt awareness toward the good" accompanies certain moral contents—for example, justice, love, integrity, and honesty—while a "felt awareness of alienation and evil" accompanies such actions as injustice, dishonesty, unnecessary harm, lying, cheating, and stealing. Using the reflections of Newman, we discovered a dialogical character of conscience in which our sense of moral obligation appears to be given by a benevolent (almost fatherly) moral authority, which manifests the presence of God within us.

We then saw that our natural awareness of the sacred is intertwined with our conscience through an archetypal myth (and symbols), revealing a cosmic struggle between good and evil (Chapter 2, Section III). Tolkien's *Lord of the Rings*, Lucas' *Star Wars*, and Rowling's *Harry Potter* typify the archetypal myth within us, calling us to a heroic mission to join the side of cosmic good against that of cosmic evil.

---

[2] Mircea Eliade, *The Sacred and the Profane: The Nature of Religion* (New York: Harcourt Brace Jovanovich, 1987).

[3] The statistical analysis for this conclusion may be found in Kanita Dervic et al., "Religious Affiliation and Suicide Attempt", *American Journal of Psychiatry* 161, no. 12 (December 2004): 2303–8, http://ajp.psychiatryonline.org/article.aspx?articleid=177228.

[4] Eliade, *Sacred and the Profane*, p. 202.

We concluded that the numinous experience, the awareness of the sacred, conscience, and the archetypal myth reveal something curious about us: we have a deep interior sense of a good transcendent entity calling us toward itself, beckoning us toward the good, and inviting us to join it in a struggle against cosmic evil. If there really isn't a transcendent reality present to us, we might justifiably wonder where this universal sense of the transcendent comes from, why we believe we are in relation to it, why we feel alienated when we reject it, and why we feel invited to enter into its sacred goodness and mission.

In Chapter 3 of Volume II, we looked at another set of interior experiences that led us deeply into the domain of reason: our five transcendental desires. We began by looking at our desire for perfect truth—the desire to know everything about everything, the complete set of correct answers to the complete set of questions. We turned to Bernard Lonergan's analysis in *Insight: A Study of Human Understanding*,[5] and saw that we not only had an unrestricted desire to know, but the capacity to know when we had not reached perfect knowledge—about everything. This revealed an awareness of what Lonergan calls "the notion of being" (the tacit awareness of the complete intelligibility of all reality).[6]

This compelled us to ask whether reality was in fact completely intelligible, which led in turn to Lonergan's proof for the existence of a unique unrestricted act of thinking that creates all else in reality (God). This unique unrestricted Creator cannot be denied without implying that there is nothing in reality (obviously counterfactual) or asserting an intrinsic contradiction (which is impossible).[7] We then saw that this God is the only possible source of our tacit awareness of the complete intelligibility of reality, meaning that God is present to us as the source of our questioning and creativity, allowing us to

[5] Bernard Lonergan, *Insight: A Study of Human Understanding in Collected Works of Bernard Lonergan* 3, ed. Frederick E. Crowe and Robert M. Doran (Toronto: University of Toronto Press, 1992).

[6] See ibid., pp. 380–81.

[7] In Appendix I of Volume II, we provided additional evidence for God, showing that contemporary science (particularly the combination of the Borde-Vilenkin-Guth proof, entropy, and the anthropic values of universal constants) points to an intelligent transcendent Creator beyond our universe (or even a multiverse). In Appendix II we provided another proof of God from a contemporary interpretation of Thomistic philosophy that correlates well with Lonergan's proof given in Chapter 3.

transcend the parameters of merely artificial intelligence, and to pursue the answers to all questions.

We then explored the other three transcendental desires, the desire for perfect love, justice or goodness, and beauty (Chapter 4). Once again, we noticed that we are aware of every imperfection in these three areas. This seemingly unrestricted awareness of imperfection in these three areas reveals our tacit awareness of *perfect* love, *perfect* justice or goodness, and *perfect* beauty. The awareness of these three "transcendentals" continuously manifests imperfections in the love we experience, the justice of people and institutions, and the beauty surrounding us, causing us to desire and strive for more, until we reach the perfection that incites our desire.

These three "transcendentals" can accommodate higher and higher orders of unity—the unity of empathy (love), the unity of harmonious society (justice or goodness), and the unity of physical form (beauty). This bears a striking resemblance to the unity of perfect thinking (which grasps the whole of intelligible reality). We showed that there can be only one perfect unity because it must be unrestricted (and there can only be one unrestricted reality). This means that perfect love, perfect justice or goodness, and perfect beauty would have to be the *same* reality as the unique unrestricted act of thinking, implying not only that God is perfectly loving, good, and beautiful, but also that He is present to us, causing us to strive creatively for greater heights of thought, love, goodness, and beauty.

In Chapter 5, we turned to the recent studies of near-death experiences reported in medical journals during the last thirty-five years. We gleaned from those studies that between 9 percent and 20 percent of patients leave their physical bodies after clinical death and maintain their capacity to see, hear, think, remember, and recall. Their new nonphysical form is not subject to physical laws and can pass through walls, and defy gravity. There are literally thousands of veridical cases of this phenomenon in which unusual (nonrecurring) data reported by patients during clinical death were verified (as perfectly accurate) by independent researchers after the patient had been revived. Furthermore, 80 percent of blind people are able to see (most of them for the first time) during a near-death experience. Many patients also moved from the physical universe to "the other side" in which many met deceased family members and friends who spoke to them about hitherto unknown information. This was also verified by independent researchers after the patient's revival. Many also reported encountering a loving white light, Jesus, and a beautiful "heavenly" surrounding. The prolific and veridical nature of the data enabled us to conclude reasonably that we have some transphysical dimension of consciousness capable of surviving bodily death, and that it can move to "the other side" in which we would most likely encounter love—the overwhelming love of the white light, the love of Jesus, and the love of deceased relatives and friends.

In Chapter 6, we faced the challenge of proposing the existence of a *transphysical* soul and proposed a theory for how a transphysical soul could interact with and orient the physical brain. We reviewed the five major indications of transphysical self-consciousness (soul) presented in the previous five chapters:

1. the necessity of heuristic notions to form conceptual ideas,
2. the need for a transalgorithmic awareness of mathematical intelligibility to explain Gödel's proof,
3. the requirement for "a tacit awareness of the complete intelligibility of reality" to explain our unrestricted desire to know,
4. the need for a transphysical ground of consciousness to explain the data of near-death experiences, and
5. the need for transphysical *self*-consciousness (which can be in two relative positions with respect to itself simultaneously) to explain the hard problem of consciousness (experiencing ourselves experiencing).

These five indications of *transphysical self-consciousness* required an explanation for how it could interact with a physical brain. Borrowing from the theory of trialistic interactionism (formulated by Sir John Eccles, Carl Popper, and Friedrich Beck) and the theory of contemporary hylomorphism (proposed by Michael Polanyi and Bernard Lonergan), we showed how the soul's activities could interact with and orient the brain through quantum fields. This enabled us to conclude the likelihood of our transphysical nature—capable of transcendental awareness and survival of bodily death.

This brought us to the end of our inquiry into transphysical self-consciousness from experience and reason in Volume II (Appendixes

1 and 2). We combined the data of experience and reason in what Newman called "an informal inference"[8]—beginning with the numinous experience, then proceeding to a proof of a unique, unrestricted act of thinking that is loving, good, and beautiful, and concluding with the existence of a transphysical soul interacting with our physical brain. This led us to infer the existence of a mysterious, sacred, personal, good, loving, and fascinating Being that is present to our consciousness, inviting us into itself, to seek it in community through sacred places and rituals, to grow in justice and goodness, and to join it in the struggle against cosmic evil. We as individuals are truly mysterious and transphysical. We not only manifest the capacity to survive bodily death and to pursue transcendental objectives in truth, love, goodness and beauty; we are aware of being called by a sacred presence to a transcendent destiny to which we cannot bring ourselves—an adventure leading into the very heart of empathy and the sublime.

II. The Need for Revelation and the Plausibility of "Emmanuel"

At this juncture, we reached the boundaries of experience and reason, and found ourselves presented with more questions about the transcendent than experience and reason could answer. We began the third stage of our journey to transcendence (in this volume) by asking how we should relate to a unique, unrestrictedly intelligent, loving, and good transcendent Being; what It intended for us; and what our transcendent reality means for our life and destiny. Reason and experience could only provide clues to the existence, intelligence, love, goodness, and beauty of the transcendent Being, but they could not answer questions that would require "reading the mind of God". We would need God's self-revelation to answer them—questions about God's love, will, guidance, inspiration, and salvific intention; questions about suffering (and how to deal with it), the presence of evil (and how to combat it), and our ultimate destiny

---

[8] See John Henry Newman, *An Essay in Aid of a Grammar of Assent* (Notre Dame, Ind.: University of Notre Dame Press, 1992), pp. 259–342 (Chapter 8).

(and how to attain it). This provoked us to investigate the domain of God's self-revelation.

After reflecting on the likelihood that a good and loving God would not leave us without answers to life's most important questions (concerning our true nature, dignity, and ultimate destiny), we concluded that God would want to reveal Himself to every individual and culture. This conclusion was confirmed by the findings of Eliade regarding the universal awareness of and desire for the sacred, and also the findings of Friedrich Heiler regarding the seven common themes of world religions. We were then moved to ask the question of whether this good, loving, and self-revealing God would want to make a *personal* and *ultimate* appearance to us—and enter into our reality in a perfect act of empathy, peer-to-peer and face-to-face. This led to six questions that opened upon the likelihood of God wanting and coming to be with us (Emmanuel).

We began by asking what our most positive and meaningful capacity is, and concluded that love (*agapē*) was the most promising candidate. We then asked whether the transcendent Creator-God could be devoid of love (if He were ultimately responsible for creating us with that capacity), and concluded that He must be loving (in some sense). This led to a third question of whether we were content with imperfect love or really wanted *perfect* love. Turning to the analysis of Volume II (Chapter 4), we concluded that we wanted perfect love (because we could detect every imperfect manifestation of love and were dissatisfied with it).

In view of our desire for perfect love, we asked whether God might Himself be *perfectly* loving. We concluded that He is, because perfect love must be the source of our awareness of it. Furthermore, we showed that perfect love must be a perfect unity, and that there can be *only one* perfect unity. This meant that perfect love must be the *same reality* as all other manifestations of perfect unity—that is, the unique unrestricted act of thinking, perfect justice or goodness, and perfect beauty. We concluded from this that God is the only reality that can be perfect and unrestricted love, and therefore, the only possible source of our desire for it.

We then asked whether an unconditionally loving God would want to make a personal appearance to us in a perfect act of empathy—face-to-face and peer-to-peer. Drawing from the definition of love (*agapē*—given in Chapter 1 of this volume), we concluded that this is precisely what an unconditionally loving God would want to do.

III. The Evidence for Jesus-Emmanuel

The above conclusion led to our final question: Is Jesus the One, the "unconditionally loving God with us"? This led to a historical investigation of Jesus from both New Testament and nonbiblical sources. In Chapter 2, we began with an investigation of Jesus' preaching about God, whom He called "His Father". We discerned from His presentation of the father in the Parable of the Prodigal Son; from the name with which He addressed God—"Abba" (affectionate, patient, loving parent, i.e., "daddy"); and from His raising of love to the highest commandment, that He knew His Father to be unconditional love—unconditionally forgiving of repentant sinners and unconditionally desirous of our salvation.

In Chapter 3, we turned to Jesus himself and discovered that He too exemplified unconditional love in His love of sinners, the poor, and the sick, and we saw this unconditional love brought to its fulfillment in an act of total self-sacrifice for the redemption of the world—poured out for everyone for all time and made directly accessible to us through the gift of the Eucharist at the Last Supper.

In light of this, Jesus seemed to be a very plausible candidate for "the unconditionally loving God with us". However, a question still remained: How can we know that He is not merely a man, but really *God* with us? We explored four major clues that lay at the center of the apostolic Church's conviction about His divine Sonship:

- His Resurrection in glory
- His miracles (particularly raising the dead)
- His gift of the Holy Spirit
- His self-revelation

We noted that these four clues were so powerful to the first members of the Church that they were willing to (and did in fact) sacrifice everything to proclaim Jesus as "the Lord" and "the Son of God". They sacrificed their religious status, social status, financial status, and even their lives to proclaim a truth that was apologetically unappealing—and even repulsive to their Jewish brethren.

In Chapter 4, we investigated recent evidence for the historicity of Jesus' Resurrection in glory. We saw that the vast majority of contemporary exegetes believe that Jesus did rise and appear in a spiritual, glorified body (the Habermas study); and then we examined Saint Paul's argument for the reliability of the first witnesses—Peter, the Twelve, five hundred of the brothers, James, the apostles who were destined for missionary activity, and Paul himself. They had everything to lose—from their salvation to their livelihood—and nothing to gain, if they had lied about the Resurrection of Jesus.

We then looked at N. T. Wright's historical examination of messianic movements around the time of Jesus, and noticed that all of them came to a speedy end with the execution of their so-called Messiah, with a notable exception of Christianity, which experienced huge growth, remarkable missionary activity, and a fervor and hope that cannot be explained without an appropriate cause. Such an appropriate cause would have to be something powerful, like Jesus' Resurrection in glory and His gift of the Holy Spirit to the apostles (enabling them to perform miracles in His name).

We then examined Wright's Christian mutations of Second Temple Judaism. Recognizing that the apostolic Church did not want to be separated from the synagogue and relied very heavily on Second Temple Judaism for her doctrine, it seemed quite strange that she should have so drastically altered the Jewish view of the doctrine of the resurrection—from resurrection as resuscitated *physical* embodiment (Judaism) to resurrection as glorified *spiritual* embodiment (Christianity); from resurrection of a *group* at the *end* of time (Judaism) to resurrection of an *individual* at the *present* moment (Christianity); from resurrection as a minor doctrine (Judaism) to resurrection as the central doctrine upon which all other doctrines depend (Christianity). After seeking a suitable cause for these highly unusual mutations and after looking at Wright's analysis of various explanations, we concluded that Jesus' Resurrection in glory (as reported by the Gospels and Paul) is the only current plausible explanation for them.

In view of the above evidence for Jesus' Resurrection in glory, the early Church's willingness to sacrifice everything becomes more understandable—the early witnesses truly believed that they would be risen in glory too, and that Jesus' Father had vindicated everything that Jesus had said about being the exclusive Son of the Father.

In Chapter 5, we deepened our investigation into Jesus' divine status by examining His miracles. We first noticed that they were unique in the history of Judaism and Hellenism—not a display of magic or power, but a means of bringing God's Kingdom into the world, manifesting God's love, requiring the faith of believers, and done by His own command.

We examined nonbiblical historical sources for His miracles (specifically Josephus and the Babylonian Talmud) as well as the Jewish polemic that revealed the Jewish authorities' awareness of His prolific ministry of miracles. We then examined the many instances of multiple attestation, the criterion of embarrassment, and the criterion of coherence in the different miracle accounts, paying special attention to His raising the dead by His own command. We concluded again that there was an abundance of evidence to support reasonable belief that Jesus performed many miracles by His own command (including raising the dead), that He saw these miracles as a means of bringing God's Kingdom into the world (and defeating Satan), and that He believed He had the power and authority of God within Himself in order to do this.

We then proceeded to a brief investigation of Jesus' gift of the Holy Spirit, which the apostolic Church called "the power of God", because it gave the apostles and early witnesses the power to perform the same miracles as Jesus, except they did it through Jesus' *name* (and not by their own authority). We also examined the interior gifts of the Holy Spirit—from prophesy, inspiration, and guidance, to prayer, faith, hope, and love. We then showed that the Spirit is just as active today as during the time of Jesus—in exorcisms, healings, and the interior gifts. We concluded that there is abundant evidence to show that the Holy Spirit, "the personal power of God", resided in Jesus, and that He had the authority to give God's power to whomever He wished.

At this juncture, Jesus' status as Emmanuel became increasingly clear—He appeared in the glory of *God* after His Resurrection; He possessed the power and authority of God to exorcise, heal, and raise the dead by His own command; and He gave the Holy Spirit (the power of God) to His followers in perpetuity. Everything about Him exuded the power and presence of God.

In Chapter 6, we arrived at the final stage of our investigation, inquiring into what Jesus said about Himself, recognizing that He did not call Himself "the Son of God" or "the Lord" (because it would have brought about a premature end to His ministry). We saw instead that He called Himself the Son of Man, referring to the preexistent eschatological judge sent by God into the world to initiate the final time. He told His disciples that He knew the Father as the Father knows Him, implying that He shared not only the Father's divine life, but also the fullness of His power. In the cleansing of the Temple, Jesus showed the religious authorities that He believed Himself to be the final messianic judge of Israel, and used the allegory of the Wicked Tenants to justify His actions; He is the only beloved Son of the Vineyard Owner (God) who has the right to initiate the new age and the New Jerusalem. If Jesus did not think He was the exclusive Son of the Father—sharing in His life and power—the above claims would not be intelligible. Equally unintelligible would be His claim to bring the Kingdom of God in His own Person, defeat Satan, fulfill the Torah, and engage in His ministries of healing, exorcism, and raising the dead by His own authority and word. Nested within these different dimensions of Jesus' mission is the mission reserved by Scripture to Yahweh alone, implying that Jesus believed He was not just Yahweh's emissary, but Yahweh's *reality* in the world. We concluded with Wright: "He believed he had to do and be, for Israel and the world, that which according to scripture only YHWH himself could do and be."[9]

From this we concluded that there is ample evidence for believing that Jesus is "the unconditional love of God with us". The historicity of His Resurrection is compellingly grounded, and the presence of the Holy Spirit is clearly manifest today. The prolific and distinct nature of His ministry of miracles was not even denied by His enemies, and His claim to be the exclusive Son of the Father is set out in a clear way—precisely as Jesus the Semite would have done it, carefully designed to keep His ministry alive until His appointed time.

[9] N. T. Wright, *Jesus and the Victory of God* (Minneapolis: Fortress Press, 1996), 2:653.

When we combine these data with His definition of love (*agapē*), His preaching of the unconditional love of His Father, His own unconditional love manifest in His ministry and self-sacrificial death, the conclusion of His divine status is almost irresistible. Yet, as we noted earlier, all the evidence in the world will not convince a person who does not want to believe it, either because he does not want to be responsible to a divine authority, sees no darkness in himself that requires redemption, or rejects a life of love (and therefore the loving God). If, however, we are open to belief and see a need for divine redemption and salvation, then the evidence for Jesus' divine status is likely to be both probative and persuasive. The affirmation of this in a profession of faith will change the direction, meaning, and significance of our lives. It will also tell us about our transcendent destiny and how best to reach it.

IV. Our Transcendent Destiny through Jesus

The above conclusion brought us to the final part of our investigation (Chapter 7), in which we studied Jesus' view of the four principle doctrines of salvation:

1. God's universal offer of salvation
2. The heavenly Kingdom
3. The reason why an unconditionally loving God would allow Hell
4. The path to salvation through Jesus

With respect to the first doctrine, there is considerable evidence from New Testament Scripture and Jesus' Eucharistic words that Jesus' offer of salvation is extended to the whole of mankind for all time. We concluded with the Catholic Church in her Dogmatic Constitution on the Church, *Lumen Gentium*, that

> those who, through no fault of their own, do not know the Gospel of Christ or his Church, but who nevertheless seek God with a sincere heart, and, moved by grace, try in their actions to do his will as

they know it through the dictates of their conscience—those too may achieve eternal salvation.[10]

With respect to Heaven, we explored Jesus' use of the image of the messianic banquet as well as Saint Paul's and Saint John's implicit doctrine of "the kingdom of love", and concluded that our true transcendent destiny is to be in a loving relationship with the triune God and all the blessed in the Kingdom of Heaven. There would be no pain in these relationships, because there would be no remnant of egocentricity, self-obsession, dominion over others, darkness, suffering, or evil. We would be free to see one another in our unique goodness, lovability, and transcendence. This "seeing and being seen" through the eyes of perfect love is what Jesus called our fulfillment in joy (Jn 15:11). It never ceases to be intensely interesting, passionate, accepting, and giving; it is so intense that we no longer sense the passage of time. It is also a beholding of the complete intelligibility of reality, as it is unified by and arises out of the loving power of the Creator. Thus we see the beauty of truth, the truth of beauty, the goodness and beauty of love, and the lovability and goodness of truth's beauty. In a single unified "beatific vision" all our desires are fulfilled, as we participate in our own uniquely lovable way in the satisfaction of others' desire for love, goodness, truth, and beauty. It is the true destiny for which the unconditionally loving God created us—and it is our eternal and unconditional joy.

Jesus' view of the universality of salvation and the Kingdom of Heaven provoked us to ask why His loving Father would allow for Hell (the absence of God, love, and the blessed). Respecting Jesus' view that there is such a state, we turn to the definition of Hell in the *Catechism of the Catholic Church* to explain how this doctrine could be reconciled with that of the unconditionally loving God. The *Catechism* explains that Hell is a "state of definitive self-exclusion from communion with God and the blessed."[11] After examining each word in the definition, we concluded that God sends no one to Hell, but rather that individuals exclude themselves from communion

---

[10] *Lumen Gentium*, no. 16, in Austin Flannery, *Vatican Council II, Vol. 1: The Conciliar and Postconciliar Documents* (Northport, N.Y.: Costello, 1975), p. 376.

[11] *Catechism of the Catholic Church*, 2nd ed. (Washington, D.C.: Libreria Editrice Vaticana—United States Conference of Catholic Bishops, 2000), no. 1033.

with God and the blessed by rejecting love in favor of egocentricity, rejecting self-gift in favor of dominion over others, and rejecting God in favor of self-idolatry.

Though God continues to love every individual who has made such a definitive choice, He allows them to pursue their preferences in a state that will not affect the love or joy of the blessed. Though it may be difficult to imagine a person giving up the Kingdom of Heaven for an eternity of egocentricity, dominion, and self-idolatry, Jesus was concerned that some people might make this choice, and so He warned them about the pain and darkness that would accompany such a life, hoping to incite repentance (*metanoia*) through which the Father would lovingly accept them back into full membership with His family.

In sum, Hell is not the "vindictiveness of an angry God"; it is the unfortunate consequence of creating creatures with the freedom to love. In order to do this, the unconditionally loving God had to allow those creatures the choice *not* to love, which allows for the possibility of a definitive and eternal rejection of love, God, and others.

This reflection brought us to the fourth and final point about our transcendent destiny—namely, the path to salvation. We returned to Jesus' preaching about the Kingdom of God and noted the initial step that must be taken: "repent and believe in the good news" (Mk 1:15). We saw that for Jesus, repentance is primarily a contrite heart for violating the law of God written in our hearts (which He describes through the six universal commandments: do not kill, commit adultery, steal, and bear false witness; honor our parents; and love our neighbor as ourselves). The "good news" of which Jesus speaks is the unconditional love of His Father, who wants to save all of us who seek Him with a sincere heart. In view of this, we can be sure that our Father will restore us to full membership in His family with the same unconditional joy as the father of the prodigal son—even if we have sinned gravely.

We also noted that for Jesus, repentance is entrance into the kingdom He brought to the world that leads ultimately to the Kingdom of Heaven (described above). As Jesus indicates in the Parable of the Sower, entrance into the kingdom carries with it both challenges and opportunities. We will have to persevere through suffering and deprivation, and contend with temptation and evil, but there will be great opportunity to become like Jesus, serve others, and build the kingdom—all of which will last into eternity.

We can stay on the path to salvation through six steps:

1. Try to follow the commands of God, maintaining a repentant spirit, and if you should fall away, turn back to the Lord in humility like the prodigal son or the repentant tax collector.
2. Join a church community through Baptism, if you have not already done so (see Volume I, Chapter 6).
3. Try to deepen your relationship with the Lord in prayer—begin with acknowledging the presence of Jesus, His Father, or His Mother, and find some appropriate ways to ask for what you need and to give thanks and praise for His creation, redemption, and love (see Volume I, Chapter 7).
4. Ask for the inspiration and guidance of the Holy Spirit, and follow it through the rules of discernment (see Volume I, Chapter 8).
5. Receive the Eucharist as often as possible (see this Volume, Chapter 3, Section IV.A).
6. Reflect on the Word of God, particularly the New Testament (see Volume I, Chapter 7).

If we try to persevere on the path of salvation through these six steps, we will be able to transform life's challenges (trials, hardships, sufferings, temptations, and confrontations with evil) into opportunities to serve the needy, bring hope to the world, and build the kingdom. In so doing, we will not only allow God to bring us into the Kingdom of Heaven; we will also leave an eternal legacy, through the grace of Jesus Christ, which is our true transcendent dignity and destiny.

V. Where Do We Go from Here?

There are two major challenges intertwined with the path to salvation: suffering and evil. Up to now we have only touched upon them in Jesus' life and teaching. We saw how Jesus gives eternal significance to suffering (Chapter 3, Section I) and His mission to

defeat Satan (Chapter 6, Section II), but we have left many questions either unanswered or partially answered. We will devote
the first part of Volume IV of this Quartet to the exploration of
suffering, love, and redemption by addressing such questions as the
following: Why would an all-loving God allow suffering, caused
by ourselves, others, or nature? How does God bring good out of
suffering? How can we suffer well through our faith? How can we
help others contend with suffering? We will then devote the second
part of Volume IV to contending with evil through faith. This will
lead to such questions as the following: Why is there evil in the
world, and how does it present itself or hide itself? How does evil
influence us, and how do we resist it? How do we help others contend with evil? How do we engage in the cosmic struggle between
good and evil?

The dark side of life can sometimes be quite daunting, but the love
of Christ, prayer, the Church community, the Holy Spirit, the Holy
Eucharist, and the Word of God can bring light into the darkness.
This gives rise to a great mystery that most people of faith will well
recognize (if we persevere on the path to salvation)—that challenge
oftentimes turns into opportunity, suffering into new viewpoints
and ways of life, dejection into strengthened hope, fear into trust in
God, weakness into spiritual strength, temptation into strengthened
virtue, and confrontation with evil into the triumph of love.

You might ask, "Why do we have to see God's light through
darkness? Why can't we just see His light without the darkness?" You
might already know at least some of the answers from the themes
discussed in the previous three volumes. It has something to do with
personal freedom, fundamental choices, a life of love, self-definition,
and the struggle between the forces of good and evil.

By reflecting on these themes we will discover the complexity and
beauty of God's providential hand—how He tries to orchestrate optimal good, love, and salvation from the myriad of interrelated freely
acting individuals; how He sends His Spirit into our midst to inspire
us interiorly and guide us exteriorly, not merely to any superficial
form of happiness, but to true happiness that brings to fulfillment all
our transcendental desires for perfect truth, love, goodness, beauty,
and home; how He helps this huge array of uniquely good and lovable people to reach true happiness without violating their freedom;

how He orchestrates us to help one another toward our salvation; and how He uses the diversity of talents, personalities, histories, and cultural backgrounds to fill out the body of His Son so that we might together inherit the perfect love relationship of the Kingdom of Heaven symbolized by the messianic banquet.

Some people ask why God remains so hidden in this process. The above considerations give an inkling of an answer. The Lord of love will not take away our freedom to define ourselves through love, virtue, courage, and faith. Moreover, we cannot possibly understand how we are connected with the billions of other people in this world (not to mention the whole communion of saints) and how our destiny is tied up with theirs. We cannot possibly grasp where an "enemy came and sowed weeds among the wheat", and how the Lord must work to protect the wheat as well as the freedom of those who attempt to choke it (Mt 13:24–30). We cannot fully understand the past that led up to our present, the future that will proceed from it, and even the present itself—and so we cannot understand how God's providential hand is working in our personal history and on a grand scale, in the history of the world. In short, the Lord's providential hand remains hidden because He is trying to preserve our freedom, lead us through that freedom to our salvation, and allow us to be His instruments in leading others to the same; His hand remains hidden because we cannot see it—it is like looking to the end of the horizon; we know that there is an entire world out there, but it is beyond our ability to see.

As we move into the mystery of suffering and evil, we cannot leave behind the lessons of the previous three volumes, for they provide the foundation for the tools we will use to contend bravely with suffering and evil through our faith—the indispensable tools to remain on the path to salvation. Above all we will need to retain the hope and confidence of Saint Paul, who realized that all suffering will be redeemed and all evil defeated in the love of Jesus Christ:

> [W]ho is to condemn? Is it Christ Jesus, who died, yes, who was raised from the dead, who is at the right hand of God, who indeed intercedes for us? Who shall separate us from the love of Christ? Shall tribulation, or distress, or persecution, or famine, or nakedness, or peril, or sword? ... No, in all these things we are more than conquerors

through him who loved us. For I am sure that neither death, nor life, nor angels, nor principalities, nor things present, nor things to come, nor powers, nor height, nor depth, nor anything else in all creation, will be able to separate us from the love of God in Christ Jesus our Lord. (Rom 8:34–35, 37–39)

Appendix One

The Shroud of Turin

Introduction

The evidence for the historical Jesus given in this book stands on its own. It does not need to be substantiated by a relic like the Shroud of Turin. However, since there is such an abundance of evidence for the authenticity of the Shroud it is worth investigating as additional corroborating evidence for His Crucifixion, Resurrection, and the New Testament accounts of these events. So what is this seeming relic of Jesus' Passion, death, and Resurrection?

The Shroud of Turin is a burial shroud (a linen cloth woven in a 3-over-1 herringbone pattern) measuring 14 feet 3 inches in length by 3 feet 7 inches in width. It apparently covered a man who suffered the wounds of crucifixion in a way very similar to Jesus of Nazareth.

The Shroud has deposits of real human blood. Dr. Alan Adler (expert on porphyrins, the colored compounds seen in blood) and John Heller (physician) studied the blood flecks gathered on the STURP (Shroud of Turin Research Project) tapes in 1978. They compared the porphyrin with the spectra of blood spots and determined that the blood on the Shroud is real.[1] Furthermore, as Dr. Raymond Rogers (leading expert in thermal analytical chemistry) notes:

> The x-ray fluorescence spectra taken by STURP showed excess iron in blood areas, as expected for blood. Microchemical tests for proteins were positive in blood areas but not in any other parts of the Shroud.[2]

[1] See John Heller and Alan Adler, "Blood on the Shroud of Turin", *Applied Optics* 19, no. 16 (1980): 2742–44.

[2] Raymond Rogers, "Shroud of Turin Guide to the Facts", 2004, Question no. 2, https://shroudstory.wordpress.com/2012/02/26/introduction-to-ray-rogers-shroud-of-turin-faq/.

Some researchers have found that male DNA and an AB blood type are also present on the cloth. Though genetic testing confirms these findings, there is no guarantee that they belong to the man on the Shroud. The samples are so old and the possibility of contamination is so great, that they could have originated with someone else.[3] However, the blood stains on the Shroud match those of the Sudarium (face cloth) of Oviedo, which touched the same face. The match of the blood stains themselves, the blood type, and the male genetic character suggest that these characteristics came from the same face that touched both cloths (see below, II.C.3).

The image on the Shroud is anatomically perfect and a perfect photographic negative. The image was formed after the blood stains congealed on the cloth, and the image and blood stains, relative to one another, are anatomically correct. The image was not produced by any paint, dye, powder, or other artistic chemical or biological agent and has no brush strokes. This was confirmed by multiple tests that were overseen by Dr. Raymond Rogers, who noted:

> The Shroud was observed by visible and ultraviolet spectrometry, infrared spectrometry, x-ray fluorescence spectrometry, and thermography. Later observations were made by pyrolysis–mass–spectrometry, lasermicroprobe Raman analyses, and microchemical testing. No evidence for pigments or media was found.[4]

There are some microscopic particles of paint on the cloth unrelated to the image, but these are explained by a medieval custom called "sanctification of paintings", in which an artist would paint a copy of the Shroud and then touch the painting to the Shroud to sanctify it. This contact led to the transfer of some microscopic particles of paint onto the Shroud, which moved around it when the Shroud was folded and rolled.[5]

Inasmuch as the blood is real, and the image was not produced by a medieval forger (see below, Section III), the Shroud seems to have

[3] See ibid.

[4] See ibid., Question no. 1.

[5] See John Iannone, "The Shroud of Turin—Evidence It Is Authentic", *New Geology*, 2015, http://www.newgeology.us/presentation24.html.

enveloped a *real* man who was crucified in a similar way to Jesus of Nazareth, who underwent a very unique kind of crucifixion, including being crowned with thorns (pertinent to the charge leveled against Jesus to be "King of the Jews" [Jn 19:3]), being flogged (which Pilate ordered for Jesus before presenting Him to the crowds [Jn 19:1–5]), and being pierced in the side by a spear similar to a Roman pilium (which was thrust into Jesus' side to assure that He had already died [Jn 19:34]). The precise nature of the torments undergone by the man on the Shroud is detailed by the French physician Pierre Barbet in his famous work *A Doctor at Calvary*.[6]

The confluence between the Shroud and the Gospels is so close that it is difficult to imagine how it could be anyone other than Jesus. But we are getting ahead of ourselves here, for we still have to present the evidence for this claim coming from the multifold scientific investigation of it.

Prior to the 1988 carbon 14 dating, the Shroud was considered by many experts to be the authentic burial cloth of Jesus, for the reasons mentioned above. Some physicists also thought that it might indicate His Resurrection, because of the way in which the image was likely formed (see below, Section III). Furthermore, the presence of pollen grains dating back to first-century Palestine (see below, Section II.C.1) and the presence of Tiberian coins minted in Judea in A.D. 29—coins that were on the eyes of the man in the Shroud (see below, Section II.C.2)—indicated an origin of the Shroud around the time of Jesus' death. Then came the 1988 carbon testing that showed a date of origin between A.D. 1260 and 1390 (around 1350).

Since the laboratories involved in the 1988 carbon 14 test were beyond reproach and the fibers taken for the test *seemed to be* from the Shroud itself (and not from thread or cloth used to mend the Shroud or provide a backing for it), the result appeared unquestionable, which cast doubt on all the evidence mentioned above. Though carbon 14 testing is by no means incontrovertible,[7] and there were significant problems following the protocols for the 1988 test, the

[6]Pierre Barbet, *A Doctor at Calvary: The Passion of Our Lord Jesus Christ as Described by a Surgeon* (New York: P.J. Kennedy, 1953).

[7]See William Meacham and Roger Sparks, "C-14 Debate from the Shroud Newsgroup: alt.turin-shroud", Shroud.com, February 4, 1998, http://www.shroud.com/c14debat.htm.

result shocked most of the 1978 STURP committee of scientists as well as the religious community.

The negative result of the 1988 carbon 14 test did not discourage researchers who felt that the evidence for the Shroud's authenticity was too great to simply be abandoned in the face of one negative test that could be fallible for many reasons. Ironically, this led to a resurgence of new creative Shroud research that gave rise to four new testing methods (see below, Section II.B.1–4); comparisons with the Sudarium of Oviedo, the facecloth of Jesus (see below, Section II.C.3); and new studies of the image formation on the Shroud (see below, Section III). This new research seriously calls into question the result obtained from the 1988 carbon 14 test because it overwhelmingly shows that the Shroud not only dates back to the time of Jesus, but also could not have been a forgery and possibly shows a "relic" of His Resurrection. At the very least, this calls for a new carbon dating test to be performed with all of the standards recommended by the scientists who found flaws in the 1988 procedure—Raymond Rogers, Giulio Fanti, Leoncia Garza-Valdes, Stephen J. Mattingly, John Jackson, and Mario Moroni (see below, Section II.A.1–3).

At present the preponderance of scientific and historical evidence favors the authenticity of the Shroud (see below, Sections II and III). In fact, the preponderance is so great that a change in carbon 14 dating should be expected from new tests—with the swing back in time of approximately one thousand to sixteen hundred years from the date given by the 1988 carbon testing (1260–1390). This would put the date of the cloth between 250 B.C. and A.D. 350 (see below, Section II.A–II.B). Thus, the mean predictable date of the Shroud's origin would be approximately A.D. 50—quite near the time of Jesus' Crucifixion.

The following exposition gives a brief summary of the scientific and historical data connected to the Shroud, both before and after the 1988 carbon 14 test. It will be divided into three sections:

1. A brief documentable history of the Shroud of Turin from 1349 to the present
2. The Shroud's date and place of origin
3. The formation of the Shroud's image

I. A Brief Documented History of the Shroud from 1349 to the Present[8]

The Shroud surfaced in Europe in 1349 in Lirey, France, in the possession of French nobleman Geoffrey de Charny, who married Jeanne de Vergy, a fifth-generation descendent of a Burgundian leader of the Fourth Crusade, Othon de la Roche. Othon occupied the area of Constantinople from which the Shroud had been taken in 1204 and was documented to have transferred it to his lands in Greece and then to Besançon, France, in 1206 (see below, Section II.E). He reported to Pope Clement VI that he was in possession of the burial Shroud of Christ. The Shroud was subsequently given to the canons of Lirey and then went into the possession of Margaret de Charny, who after displaying it traded it to Duke Louis I of Savoy for a castle and estate in 1453. In 1464 an accord was drawn up between Duke Louis I and the canons of Lirey indicating the above history of the Shroud. The Shroud was taken with the Savoy family on its travels, and in 1502, it found a resting place in the Sainte Chapelle in Chambery, France.

In 1532 a fire broke out in the Sainte Chapelle, and the Shroud was damaged. The Poor Clare nuns repaired the Shroud, sewing it onto a backing cloth (the Holland cloth), and put repair patches on the most damaged parts (this will become important in the dating evidence mentioned below in Section II). After France invaded Savoy, the Shroud was moved by the Savoy family to Piedmont (a northern region of Italy), where it was displayed in Turin and Milan. The Shroud was moved to various towns but was ultimately brought to Turin in 1578 (where it was seen by Saint Charles Borromeo). It has remained there since that time and was displayed on multiple occasions.

In 1898 during a public exposition, an Italian photographer, Secondo Pia, photographed the Shroud and noticed the perfect positive image on his negative. This indicated that the Shroud was a perfect photographic *negative image* (though the blood was not an image— and therefore appeared on photographic negatives as a negative). This

---

[8] The historical dates and facts reported throughout this section are all taken from Ian Wilson, "Highlight of the Undisputed History", 1996, Shroud of Turin Website, https://www.shroud.com/history.htm.

led to the first scientific investigation of the Shroud in which its anatomical perfection (in the photographic negatives) was discovered.

In 1931–1932 Pierre Barbet performed anatomical studies on cadavers to determine the accuracy of the bloodstains on the shroud, and to check the historicity of the Gospel accounts of the Crucifixion. He reported his findings in his book *A Doctor at Calvary*, which remains a classic today in which he proved both of his hypotheses—the accuracy of the blood marks and the accuracy of the Gospel accounts.

In 1939, the first scientific Congress on Shroud Studies was held that examined not only physiology, blood, and image formation, but also the Shroud's image in iconography, and likely historical scenarios of its travels.

In 1973 several scientific experts were allowed to examine the Shroud and remove fabric samples and surface dust. In 1976 Dr. John Jackson and Bill Mottern (from Sandia Labs in Albuquerque, New Mexico) showed that the Shroud is encoded with information sufficient for 3-D imaging. This gave rise to considerable interest in the Shroud from scientists in diverse disciplines, which eventually led to STURP in 1978.

The STURP Investigation of the Shroud occurred over 120 hours, after which a comprehensive report was published indicating the likelihood of the Shroud's blood evidence as well its dating in first-century Jerusalem (from the indigenous pollen evidence collected by Dr. Max Frei). The investigation was so positive that it called for a carbon 14 testing. In 1988, the famous three-lab test (University of Oxford, University of Arizona, and University of Zurich) was performed with the unanimous result that the Shroud originated about 1350 (between 1260 and 1390), implying that it is a medieval fake. Though these three tests were carefully carried out with the technology of the time, they did not observe many of the protocols for the collection of the fibers to be used in the tests (see below, II.A.1).

Furthermore, the samples used in the test were not cleaned appropriately. In 1993, Professor Leonicio Garza-Valdes showed the presence of a bioplastic coating on fibers of the Shroud that he obtained from Professor Giovanni Riggi (obtained in 1988). The coating was observed by several other scientists who admitted that it could have skewed the dating of the Shroud (see below, Section II.A.2).

In January 2005, Dr. Raymond Rogers, former Fellow of the Los Alamos National Laboratory, performed mass spectrometry and microchemical tests from fibers that were part of the sample used in the 1988 carbon testing (which he obtained from Giovanni Riggi). He wrote an important article controverting the carbon dating result obtained in 1988, claiming that all three tests were based on a sample of cloth that was not part of the original Shroud (see below, Section II.A.1).

Since Rogers' negation of the sample used in the 1988 carbon testing, four additional tests were devised and performed on Shroud fibers—the vanillin test of Rogers and three new dating techniques introduced by Giulio Fanti (see below, Section II.B). Additionally, it was determined that the Shroud touched the same face as that touched by the Sudarium of Oviedo (the facecloth of Jesus), which can be dated to A.D. 616—much earlier than 1350, the date proposed by the 1988 carbon testing (see below, Section II.C.3).

Furthermore, considerable scientific testing was done on the Shroud's image by John Jackson, Giulio Fanti, and Paolo Di Lazzaro. This revealed five enigmas that were likely caused by an intense burst of vacuum ultraviolet radiation emitted from every three-dimensional point within a mechanically transparent body (see Section III below). Since this extraordinary phenomenon seems to have a *transphysical* cause, and reflects some of the unusual features of Jesus' Resurrection (by comparison with Jewish and pagan views), some theorists consider the Shroud to be a relic of Jesus' Resurrection in glory.

We may now proceed to an examination of the 1988 carbon test and the likely date of the Shroud's origin.

II. Dating the Shroud

Prior to the 1988 carbon testing, there were three major indicators of the Shroud's date of origin:

1. Max Frei's analysis of pollen fossils embedded in the Shroud
2. The striking resemblance of the Shroud to the Crucifixion of Jesus—which is not a scientific test, but interesting in light of its anatomical perfection and the absence of forgery

3. Coins identified on the eyes of the man on the Shroud with raised lettering indicating a Roman lepton minted in Palestine in A.D. 29

Since these three indications of the Shroud's age did not come from a direct test of the age of the Shroud's fiber (but only from features of the Shroud and its image), the STURP Investigation team strongly recommended a carbon 14 test of fibers from the Shroud. This dating method was the only one available to scientists in 1988.

As noted in the history above, the carbon testing showed that the *fibers* removed from the Shroud were 638 years old (with a probable origin at around 1350). Note that this test did not show that the Shroud originated in A.D. 1350, but only that the fibers extracted from the Shroud did (which could have come from a later source). As we shall see, the fibers removed from the Shroud were probably not from the original Shroud, but from dyed cloth added to the Shroud at a later time (probably 1532—the time of the fire of Chambery). Furthermore, the testing did not account for microbiological contaminants or the additional carbon that would have been added by the fire. These problems indicate that the 1988 carbon 14 testing was very likely invalid and skewed toward a much younger age (see below, II.A).

The 1988 carbon 14 testing was further challenged by four additional dating techniques discovered after 2005 (see below, Section II.B). These four tests indicate a much earlier date of the Shroud's origin—around A.D. 50 (with 95 percent confidence). These controverting results strongly suggest that the 1988 carbon test was not performed on original Shroud fibers but rather on fibers introduced at a later time (presumably to mend the cloth).

A. Problems with the 1988 Carbon Test

At the very outset, there were problems associated with the sampling of fibers used for the 1988 carbon 14 test. The STURP team recommended that seven different samples from different parts of the Shroud be sent to seven labs across Europe and the United States. This was inexplicably changed. Instead of taking fibers from many parts of the Shroud, the samples were taken from a single strip from a questionable part of it. This one sample was divided into three parts and sent to only three labs. To make matters worse, chemical and microscopic testing on the single strip was not performed (even though there were experts present who could have done so). Though arguments broke out about these problems, the samples were sent to the three labs, which no doubt performed the tests professionally. The problem was not with the carbon testing, but rather with the gathering of the samples.

Since the 1988 carbon 14 testing of the Shroud, three important discoveries were made indicating that it did not reflect the Shroud's proper age, but rather underestimated it by thirteen hundred years.

1. Problems with the samples used to make the tests (discovered by Dr. Raymond Rogers)
2. Microbiological contaminants producing additional carbon content that were not removed prior to the 1988 testing (discovered by Drs. Garza-Valdes and Mattingly)
3. Additional carbon content embedded in the Shroud from the fire of Chambery and other carbon contaminants (discovered by Kouznetsov and Jackson—and modified by Moroni and associates)

We will discuss each of these findings in turn.

1. Raymond Rogers on Aberrant Samples Used in the 1988 Carbon 14 Testing

Though the carbon 14 testing at the three laboratories at the University of Arizona, University of Oxford, and University of Zurich was done very professionally, the collection of the sample to be tested was seriously flawed in two respects. First, the sample came from a *single* strip from a *single* site on the Shroud. According to Rogers:

> The use of a single sample, assuming it was representative of the whole cloth, defied normal procedures and protocols established before the radiocarbon study. It was a serious mistake.[9]

[9] Rogers, "Shroud of Turin Guide to the Facts", Question no. 5.

Though this single sample seemed to avoid the many patches and charred areas (from the fire of Chambery), there was no guarantee that it represented the *original* part of the cloth. Such a guarantee could have only come from following ordinary protocols—namely, obtaining fibers from *multiple* sites of the cloth.

Second, the two scientists charged with certifying the originality of the single strip (Franco Testore, professor of textile technology at the Turin Polytechnic, and Gabriel Vial, curator of the Ancient Textile Museum, Lyon, France) approved the single sample for carbon 14 testing without making any serious chemical or microscopic characterization of it.[10]

These two flaws in the collection procedure made it impossible to guarantee the validity of the sample by normal carbon 14 sampling protocol. Indeed, the procedure was wide open to an invalid sample, which Rogers later discovered to be the case:

> The area where the radiocarbon sample was obtained had been photographed in 1978 with an ultraviolet source.... While making the UV photographs, the source was heavily filtered to exclude visible light and the camera was heavily filtered to exclude any effect of the UV on the film.... The area where the radiocarbon sample was taken is relatively dark, a fact that is not the result of dirt, image color, or scorching. The cloth is much less fluorescent in that area, brightening into more typical fluorescence to the right. The photograph proves that the radiocarbon area has a different chemical composition than the main part of the cloth. This was obviously not considered before the sample was cut.[11]

The ultraviolet photography should indicate fluorescence where the carbon 14 sample was taken, if it were free of dyes (like the other parts of the cloth). However, the 1978 UV photography shows that the sample was taken from a darkened (nonfluorescing) area, which suggests the presence of a darkening agent, such as dye.

Rogers and Adler discovered the chemical source of this darkening through further analysis. According to Rogers:

[10] Ibid.
[11] Ibid.

I found that the radiocarbon sample was uniquely coated with a plant gum (probably gum Arabic), a hydrous aluminum oxide mordant (the aluminum found by Adler), and Madder root dye (alizarin and purpurin). *Nothing similar* exists on *any other* part of the Shroud. The photomicrograph shows several fibers from the center of the radiocarbon sample in water. The gum is swelling and slowly detaching from the fibers.[12]

Rogers explained the significance of this discovery in an important article published in the peer-reviewed journal *Thermochimica Acta* in 2005:

A gum/dye/mordant [(for affixing dye)] coating is easy to observe on radiocarbon [sample] yarns. No other part of the shroud shows such a coating. [This indicates that] the radiocarbon sample had been *dyed.* Dyeing was probably done intentionally on pristine replacement material to match the color of the older, sepia-colored cloth. The dye found on the radiocarbon sample was not used in Europe before about 1291 AD and was not common until more than 100 years later. Specifically, the color and distribution of the coating implies that repairs were made at an unknown time with foreign linen dyed to match the older original material. The consequence of this conclusion is that the radiocarbon sample was not representative of the original cloth. The combined evidence from chemical kinetics, analytical chemistry, cotton content, and pyrolysis-mass-spectrometry *proves* that the material from the radiocarbon area of the shroud is significantly different from that of the main cloth. The radiocarbon sample was thus not part of the original cloth and is invalid for determining the age of the shroud.[13]

Rogers' results speak for themselves. If the sample was drawn from a piece of linen that was dyed in the fourteenth century (by a dye available in Europe only after 1291), one should expect a carbon dating result from the fourteenth century—in *all three labs* that took fibers from the same dyed strip used for the sample. As yet, there has been no scientific response to rebut Rogers' chemical and microscopic

---

[12] Ibid.; emphasis mine.
[13] Raymond N. Rogers, "Studies on the Radiocarbon Sample from the Shroud of Turin", *Thermochimica Acta* 425, nos. 1–2 (January 20, 2005): 189–94; emphasis mine.

analysis and his contention that the sample came from fabric of much later origin.

2. Garza-Valdes and Mattingly on Microbiological Contaminants

Dr. Leonicio Garza-Valdes (professor of archaeology and pediatrics) in conjunction with Dr. Stephen J. Mattingly (renowned microbiologist) discovered a bioplastic coating of bacteria and fungus on the linen fibers (60 percent by weight) caused by living microbes that absorb and add carbon 14 to the cloth and thereby skew the date by several centuries. These microbes were not known at the time of the 1988 test and were not removed by the carbon 14 cleaning protocol.

In the journal of the University of Texas Health Science Center at San Antonio, Jim Barrett reported on the research of Garza-Valdes and Mattingly:

> Dr. Garza said the shroud's fibers are coated with bacteria and fungi that have grown for centuries. Carbon dating, he said, had sampled the contaminants as well as the fibers' cellulose.[14]

Barrett also interviewed Dr. Harry Gove (co-inventor of the use of accelerator mass spectrometry for carbon dating and professor emeritus of physics at the University of Rochester in New York) who noted: "This is not a crazy idea. A swing of 1,000 years would be a big change, but it's not wildly out of the question, and the issue needs to be resolved."[15]

3. Kouznetsov, Jackson, and Moroni on Carbon Contaminants from Fire and Other Sources

The Fire-Model Tests of Dr. Dmitri Kouznetsov in 1994 (and Dr. John Jackson and others in 1998) replicated the Chambery fire of 1532. They showed that the fire added carbon isotopes to the linen.

Later tests, principally by Mario Moroni and associates, showed that Kouznetsov's and Jackson's estimates of elevated carbon seemed to be exaggerated. In Moroni's model, the carbon content from the fire

---

[14] Jim Barrett, "Science and the Shroud Microbiology Meets Archaeology in a Renewed Quest for Answers", *Mission*, Spring 1996, http://www.sindone.info/BARRETT.PDF.
[15] Ibid.

would have only made the age of the Shroud younger by three hundred years. This means that the Shroud's date of origin—calculated from the result of the 1988 carbon 14 testing—should be 1050 instead of 1350. Antonacci reported the team's findings as follows: "Moroni's fire model results yielded a 300 year younger result with a pretreatment method that removed 37 percent of the original sample."[16]

4. Summary and Conclusions

If the Kouznetsov-Jackson-Moroni skewing of the 1988 carbon 14 tests were the only problem, it would be quite puzzling because it would imply a medieval forgery in 1050 instead of 1350. However, when this finding is combined with the skewing discovered by Garza-Valdes and Mattingly (perhaps three hundred years or more) and the radical skewing produced by "non-original fibers" used in the 1988 carbon 14 test (discovered by Raymond Rogers—see above, II. A.1), it seems increasingly apparent that the 1988 carbon 14 test was invalid—and the result may be skewed by a factor of thirteen hundred years. If this problem is to be resolved, other carbon 14 tests will have to be performed according to the specifications and protocols listed below in Section II.B.5. Since carbon 14 tests are by no means infallible, these new tests will have to be compared to the four new tests developed by Rogers and Fanti (see below, Section II.B) to obtain an optimal result.

B. Four New Scientific Dating Methods

Dr. Raymond Rogers and Dr. Giulio Fanti (professor of mechanical and thermal measurement at the University of Padua's engineering faculty) developed four new tests for dating ancient materials, unrelated to carbon 14 dating. Rogers' test results were reported in the *Thermochimica Acta* in 2005[17] and Fanti's results in a book published in 2013.[18] These tests show a strong likelihood that the Shroud

---

[16] Mark Antonacci, "Appendix F: Fire Simulation Model", *The Resurrection of the Shroud: New Scientific, Medical, and Archeological Evidence* (New York: M. Evans, 1998), pp. 270–71.

[17] Rogers, "Studies on the Radiocarbon Sample", pp. 189–94.

[18] See Giulio Fanti and Saverio Gaeta, *Il Mistero della Sindone: Le Sorprendenti Scoperte Scientifiche sull'enigma del Telo di Gesu* (Milan: Editore Rizzoli, 2013).

originated around the time of Jesus and that the 1988 carbon 14 testing was seriously in error (probably for the reasons mentioned above
in II.A). We will examine each of the test results in turn.

1. Raymond Rogers' Vanillin Test

Rogers developed a vanillin test to measure the age of cellulose in
ancient fabrics. Lignin (lignocellulose) can be converted to vanillin, an
organic compound that decays with age. By measuring the percentage of vanillin in cellulose fibers in various materials of ancient origin,
the age of fabrics (within a defined range of error) can be reasonably
estimated. Rogers performed these vanillin tests on several ancient
fabrics, and then compared them to the Shroud. He concluded that
the 1988 carbon 14 test was not consistent with the vanillin test:

> If the shroud had been produced between 1260 and 1390 AD, as indi-
> cated by the radiocarbon analyses, lignin should be easy to detect.
> A linen produced in 1260 AD would have retained about 37% of its
> vanillin in 1978.... The Holland cloth and all other medieval linens
> gave the test [i.e., tested positive] for vanillin wherever lignin could
> be observed on growth nodes. The disappearance of all traces of van-
> illin from the lignin in the [S]hroud indicates a *much older age* than the
> radiocarbon laboratories reported.[19]

Rogers anticipated the objection that the fire of Chambery would
have heated the Shroud, accelerating the disappearance of vanillin
in the cellulose fibers, but he responds that the fire alone could not
have been responsible for the disappearance of all the vanillin in the
Shroud, because the Shroud was folded, and therefore was not exposed
evenly to the heat. Moreover, the Shroud was not situated near the
fire long enough to produce a complete disappearance of vanillin in it
(if it originated in the thirteenth or fourteenth centuries, as supposedly
indicated by the carbon 14 testing). He notes in this regard:

> The fire of 1532 could not have greatly affected the vanillin con-
> tent of lignin in all parts of the shroud equally. The thermal conduc-
> tivity of linen is very low ... therefore, the unscorched parts of the

[19] Rogers, "Studies on the Radiocarbon Sample", p. 192; emphasis mine.

folded cloth could not have become very hot.... The cloth's center would not have heated at all in the time available. The rapid change in color from black to white at the margins of the scorches illustrates this fact.... Different amounts of vanillin would have been lost in different areas. No samples from *any location* on the shroud gave the vanillin test [i.e., tested positive].[20]

If the fire of Chambery cannot explain the absence of vanillin in the Shroud, then what can? Rogers says we will have to make recourse to the same process that explains vanillin's complete absence in the Dead Sea Scrolls and other ancient materials (which are over fifteen hundred years old)—namely, the *aging* process:

> Because the shroud and other very old linens do not give the vanillin test [i.e., test negative], the cloth must be quite old.... A determination of the kinetics of vanillin loss suggests that the shroud is between 1300 and 3000 years old. Even allowing for errors in the measurements and assumptions about storage conditions, the cloth is unlikely to be as young as 840 years.[21]

The median age of the Shroud (within Rogers' broad margins of error) is 2,150 years old, which allows the origin of the Shroud to be situated near the Crucifixion of Jesus (A.D. 30). This result agrees with the three new dating tests performed by Giulio Fanti (and colleagues) at six laboratories in Italy and the U.K.

2. Giulio Fanti's Fourier Transformed Infrared Spectroscopy Test of Cellulose Degradation

Dr. Giulio Fanti carried out three new dating tests on fibers from the Shroud he procured from Giovanni Riggi:

1. Fourier Transformed Infrared Spectroscopy Testing of Cellulose Degradation
2. Raman Spectroscopy (Laser) Testing of Cellulose Degradation
3. Mechanical Tests of Compressibility and Breaking Strength of Fibers

[20] Ibid., pp. 192–93.
[21] Ibid., p. 194.

Fanti carried out his test with six teams in six different laboratories throughout Italy and the U.K.—Padua, Bologna, Modena, Udine, Parma, and London. In 2013, he published his results in a new book entitled *Il Mistero della Sindone*, which in combination with the vanillin test of Raymond Rogers shows the strong likelihood that the 1988 carbon 14 dating was in error by a large factor. We will give a basic description of each testing procedure and the results obtained by Fanti in his six labs in this and the following two subsections.

In his Fourier Transformed Infrared Spectroscopy Test of Cellulose Degradation, Fanti used a specially transformed infrared light beam to excite the molecules of the material. The resulting reflections made it possible to evaluate the concentration of particular substances contained in the cellulose of the linen fibers. According to Fanti, since cellulose degrades over time, it is possible to determine a correlation with the age of the fabric.

Fanti examined nine different ancient textiles of varying ages (five from Egypt, three from Israel, and one from Peru), along with two modern fabrics, and developed a calibration curve that represented how the trend of degradation varies with age. Then he measured the same parameters on the Shroud and derived an estimate of its age by making a comparison with the calibration curve. He determined that the origin of the Shroud (at a 95 percent confidence level) occurred around 300 B.C. (within a margin of error of four hundred years), therefore between 700 B.C. and A.D. 100.[22]

3. Giulio Fanti's Raman Spectroscopy Test for Cellulose Degradation

The Raman Laser Spectroscopy Test for cellulose degradation is similar to the Fourier Transformed Infrared Spectroscopy Test, but uses a different method to excite the molecules. Once again, the resulting reflections made it possible to evaluate the concentration of particular substances contained in the cellulose of the linen fibers. He then generated a new calibration curve from the same nine ancient materials

---

[22] Fanti's book (*Il Mistero della Sindone*) is not yet translated into English. Stephen E. Jones translated the results of Fanti's three new dating tests in Stephen E. Jones, "New Tests by Prof. Giulio Fanti Show the Shroud of Turin Could Date from the Time of Christ", *Shroud of Turin* (blog), April 2, 2013, http://theshroudofturin.blogspot.com/2013/04/new-tests-by-prof-giulio-fanti-show.html.

(and two modern materials), and compared this to the measurements obtained from the Shroud. He then determined that the origin of the cloth (with a 95 percent confidence level) occurred at 200 B.C. (within a margin of error of five hundred years), therefore between 700 B.C. and A.D. 300.[23]

4. Giulio Fanti's Mechanical Test of Compressibility and Breaking Strength of Fibers

This mechanical test is substantially different from the first two spectrographic tests. Instead of measuring the level of particular substances in the cellulose (as above), this test used a multiparametric mechanical method made possible by constructing a new mechanism capable of loading and unloading cycles of single linen fibers. Using a petrographic microscope, Fanti was able to separate Shroud linen fibers from dust particles vacuumed from the Shroud. He then mounted them on supports for testing. In collaboration with Dr. Pierandred Malfi, he performed tests of tension and compression on the nine ancient fabrics from Egypt, Israel, and Peru. He developed five mechanical parameters (tensile strength, Young's modulus in direct cycle, Young's modulus in reverse cycle, loss factor in direct cycle, and loss factor in reverse cycle) to give five different age-dependent curves of the samples. He then measured the corresponding mechanical properties of the Shroud, and compared them to the five age-dependent curves generated from the nine ancient materials. He determined from this that the origin of the Shroud occurred (with a 95 percent confidence level) around A.D. 400 (within a margin of error of four hundred years), therefore between A.D. 1 and A.D. 800.[24]

5. Summary of the Fanti and Rogers Dating Tests

Fanti averaged the results of his three tests and obtained a mean origin date of 33 B.C. (within a margin of error of 250 years) with a confidence level of 95 percent. The three techniques used by Fanti were used and verified in other labs in Italy and the U.K. (see above). This means that there is a strong likelihood that the Shroud originated between 283

---

[23] See the comment and references in the previous note.
[24] See the comment and references in footnote 22.

B.C. and A.D. 217—which allows the origin of the Shroud to be situated near the time of Jesus' Crucifixion (A.D. 30). Recall from II.B.1 above that Raymond Rogers obtained a similar result, within broader parameters, from his vanillin tests of the Shroud.

If Fanti's and Rogers' dating techniques continue to bear scientific scrutiny, then a rescheduling of carbon 14 testing will be unavoidable. When this occurs, the deficiencies of the past will have to be remedied. This will entail scheduling the tests at seven laboratories (instead of three) and assuring that the selection of the samples comes from different parts of the Shroud that are not near darkened (nonfluorescing) regions. Furthermore, the selection will have to be done with expert thermal chemists and archaeologists present who can perform the chemical, microscopic, and textile tests necessary to avoid gross errors such as a selection of dyed fibers. Additionally, the threads will have to be cleaned to remove the bioplastic covering from microorganisms, and the age estimates will have to be adjusted to account for the carbon buildup from the Chambery fire.

If all these procedures are followed, the result will be significantly different from the 1988 carbon 14 test, indicating an older age of the Shroud, probably corresponding to the age shown by the other four chemical, spectroscopic, and mechanical tests performed by Rogers and Fanti. If the carbon testing does not show this result, and the other four tests continue to bear scientific scrutiny, the carbon 14 test may have to be "bracketed" because it will likely have too high a degree of carbon contamination to give accurate aging data.

C. Other Indications of the Shroud's Age

The above analysis was restricted to five directly measurable tests of age (within defined parameters and margins of error). But these do not exhaust the age indicators of the Shroud of Turin. As we saw above, there are three additional circumstantial indications of the Shroud's origin at the time of Jesus:

1. The presence of pollen grains discovered by Max Frei
2. The presence of two Roman coins (leptons) on the eyes of the man in the Shroud

3. Similarities to the face cloth of Oviedo (known as the "Sudarium Christi") indicating that the same face touched both cloths

We will examine each of these age indicators in turn.

1. Max Frei's Evidence of Pollen Grains

Max Frei was a Swiss botanist and a criminologist who was a professor at the University of Zúrich and one of the best-known criminol-
ogists in Europe. He was the science editor of the German periodical
Kriminalistik and carried out several pollen classifications on both the
Shroud and the face cloth of Oviedo (see below, Section II.C.3).

Frei used adhesive tapes to collect dust samples from the Shroud
during the 1978 STURP investigation. He later classified fifty-eight
pollen grains by comparing them to pollen grains in the largest botanical museums around the world. He concluded that of the fifty-eight
pollen grains discovered on the Shroud, the largest number (forty-
five) were from the region of Israel (specifically from sedimentary
layers from two thousand years ago near the area of the Sea of Galilee), and six grains from the eastern Middle East (two grains from
Edessa, Turkey, and one growing exclusively in Istanbul [Constan-
tinople]). The remaining grains came from France and Italy. Importantly, thirteen of the pollen grains are *unique* to Israel and are found
at the bottom of both the Sea of Galilee and the Dead Sea.[25]

The botanist Avinoam Danin of the Hebrew University of Jerusalem noted:

> As far as establishing the Shroud's provenance, Zygophyllum dumo-
> sum is the most significant plant on the list. Max Frei identified pollen
> grains of this species on the adhesive tapes he examined. The north-
> ernmost extent of the distribution of this plant in the world coincides
> with the line between Jericho and the sea level marker on the road
> leading from Jerusalem to Jericho. As Zygophyllum dumosum grows

[25] See Max Frei, "Identificazione e classificazione dei nuovi pollini della Sindone", *La
Sindone, Scienza e Fede, Atti del II Convegno Nazionale di Sindonologia*, Bologna, November 27–29, 1981; CLUEB, Bologna 1983, p. 281. See also P.C. Maloney, "A Contribution toward a History of Botanical Research on the Shroud of Turin", in *Proceedings of the
1999 Shroud of Turin International Research Conference* (Richmond: Magisterium Press, 1999),
pp. 244–46.

only in Israel, Jordan and Sinai, its appearance helps to definitively limit the Shroud's place of origin.[26]

The three major regional similarities of pollen grain groupings indicate a high probability of the Shroud's origin and travels. The abundance of grains, and unique grains, indigenous to Palestine indicate a high probability that the Shroud originated there. It was probably manufactured there and exposed to the open air for a considerable period of time. Frei also believed that some of the grains came from the aloes used to anoint the body and from grains that adhered to the wetness of the body after the Crucifixion.

Since we know where the Shroud surfaced in Europe (Lirey, France, in the possession of Geoffrey de Charny in 1349), we can deduce from the pollen grains that the Shroud must have traveled to Turkey (Edessa and Constantinople) before its arrival in France. The previously mentioned fact that Geoffrey de Charny was married to Jeanne de Vergy, a fifth-generation descendant of Othon de la Roche (a leader of the Fourth Crusade who occupied the area of Constantinople in which the Shroud was kept) corroborates this (see below, II.E). Frei also helped to make a connection between the Shroud of Turin and the Sudarium (facecloth) of Oviedo by showing a similar origin in Palestine from the presence of indigenous pollen grains from that region on the Sudarium.

As we shall see, the Sudarium also bears the same blood and aloe stains as the Shroud (see below, Section II.C.3). Frei first used dust samples not taken by him from an investigation of the face cloth in 1978 and then used his own samples obtained in 1979. According to Emanuela Marinelli:

As on the Shroud, also on the Sudarium he found cells of the epidermis of Aloe socotrina. He also identified the pollen of 13 plants, four of which do not grow in Europe but are frequently encountered in Palestine, in the deserts, in salt places or on rocks, and five others are Mediterranean plants that grow also in Palestine. Frei stressed: "The Acacia albida is typical for the Dead Sea area and the Hyoscyamus

[26]Avinoam Danin, "Pressed Flowers", *Eretz Magazine* 55 (1997): 35–37 and 69.

aureus still grows on the walls of the Old Citadel of Jerusalem. These two plants are represented also on the Shroud".[27]

Frei's studies were complemented and completed by the studies of the biologist Carmen Gómez Ferreras, of the *Universidad Complutense* of Madrid.

The work of Frei and Gómez Ferreras is important for showing that the two cloths had a similar geographical origin—namely, Palestine. The blood and aloe evidence is even more important because it reveals that both cloths touched the same face (see below, Section II.C.3). Since the Sudarium can be dated to A.D. 616, we must assume that both the Shroud and the Sudarium originated prior to that time. Thus, when we combine the pollen, blood, and aloe evidence on both the Shroud and the Sudarium, we may conclude that both cloths originated in Palestine before A.D. 616, which casts doubt on the 1988 carbon 14 test and the medieval forgery hypothesis.

2. Roman Coins on the Eyes of the Man in the Image

The presence of coins on the eyelids of the man on the Shroud was first identified by the Greek classical numismatist Michael Marx, who saw their images in the photographs of Enrie (1931) and those of Secondo Pia (1898). Marx identified four raised letters (UCAI) on coins that looked like Jewish lepta ("widow's mite" coins, copper coins minted by Pontius Pilate in A.D. 29 in Judea). This discovery was initially challenged by some numismatists who claimed that such a coin would not have had a Roman "C" but rather a Greek "K", because this was the way Tiberius' coins were typically minted. However, Fr. Francis Filas (professor at Loyola University Chicago) responded when he was given a lepton with the "C" inscription on it. Later, Filas and Duke University Professor Alan Whanger discovered five additional leptons with the same inscription, indicating that it was unusual, but by no means rare.

[27]Emanuela Marinelli, "The Question of Pollen Grains on the Shroud of Turin and the Sudarium of Oviedo", Shroud.com, accessed November 4, 2015, https://www.shroud.com/pdfs/marinelli2veng.pdf.

These coins enabled Whanger (and others) to use a polarized over-lay photographic analysis to show that the images of the coins (on the eyes of the man of the Shroud) corresponded almost perfectly to the actual coins with the unusual "C" mint. Whanger described the discovery as follows:

> We have done this by means of the polarized image overlay technique that we developed which enables the highly accurate comparison of two different images and the documentation of the various points of congruence.... Using the forensic criteria for matching finger prints, we feel that there is *overwhelming evidence* for the identification of the images and the matches with the coins.[28]

Whanger has made these results well-known internationally through a variety of media:

> We have published these findings in the referenced professional lit-erature and in many lay publications, have issued an international press and video release in 1982, have shown the findings personally to many thousands of people, and have produced detailed documentary videotapes showing the identification of these images and their con-gruence to two Pontius Pilate lepta.[29]

Whanger's polarized imaging overlay analysis is complemented and corroborated by the *digital* imaging analysis of Professor Rob-ert Haralick (an internationally known computer imaging expert). Haralick's results show evidence of "OUCAIC" on the coins on the eyelids of the man in the Shroud. This is a more extensive result than the previous one (UCAI) by Marx, Filas, and Whanger. He notes in this regard:

> The evidence is definitely supporting evidence because there is some degree of match between what one would expect to find if the Shroud

---

[28] Alan D. Whanger, "A Reply to Doubts concerning the Coins over the Eyes", Shroud of Turin Website, 1997, https://www.shroud.com/lombatti.htm; emphasis mine. See also Alan D. Whanger and Mary Whanger, "Polarized Image Overlay Technique: A New Image Comparison Method and Its Applications", *Applied Optics* 24, no. 6 (March 15, 1985): 766–72.

[29] Whanger, "Reply to Doubts".

did indeed contain a faint image of the Pilate coin and what we can in fact observe in the original and in the digitally processed images.[30]

If Whanger is correct in assessing the evidence as "overwhelming" and Haralick is correct in assessing it as "definitive", then it is highly probable that the image of the man on the Shroud of Turin has two Jewish lepta, minted in A.D. 29 by Pontius Pilate in Judea at the time of Jesus, on his eyelids. If this is the case, then it agrees strongly with the pollen grain evidence of Frei and Danin, which further challenges the medieval forger hypothesis and the 1988 carbon dating test.

3. The Sudarium of Oviedo

The Sudarium Christi (the face cloth of Christ) is kept in the Cathedral of Oviedo (in northern Spain). It is a poor quality linen cloth measuring 84 by 53 centimeters. Though it does not have an image of a face (as does the Shroud of Turin), it has features indicating that it was applied to the face of a man who was newly deceased. It has bloodstains and serum stains from pulmonary edema fluid that match the blood and serum patterns and blood type AB of the Shroud of Turin. The length of the nose on both cloths is eight centimeters (three inches). The similarities between the two cloths indicate the high probability that they touched the face of the same crucified man who was crowned with thorns. The evidence of pollen grains on both cloths (see above, II.C.1) corroborates their origin in Judea.

Why is this cloth significant for dating the Shroud of Turin? Its history going back to A.D. 616 can be better documented than the Shroud of Turin. If both cloths touched the same face, then the Shroud of Turin must also go back to A.D. 616, approximately eight hundred years earlier than the age determined by the 1988 carbon 14 tests. In order to establish this, we will first examine the blood, pulmonary fluid, and other stains on both cloths, and then investigate the documented history of the Sudarium Christi.

The Sudarium was applied to the face of a crucified man at a time proximate to his death in an upright position (if we suppose the face

---

[30] Robert M. Haralick, *Analysis of Digital Images of the Shroud of Turin* (Blacksburg, Va.: Publication of Spatial Data Analysis Laboratory, Virginia Polytechnic Institute and State University, 1983).

is that of Jesus, it would have been applied to His face while He was still upright on the Cross). This was a typical part of Jewish burial custom (out of respect for the deceased) and frequently done for people whose faces had been disfigured (out of respect for the deceased and the mourners).[31] According to the Investigation Team of the Spanish Centre for Sindonology (who performed the analysis on the stains) and Dr. José Villalain (who performed the medical examination),[32] the main stains are composed of one part blood and six parts fluid from the pleural oedema. According to Guscin:

> This liquid collects in the lungs when a crucified person dies of asphyxiation, and if the body subsequently suffers jolting movements, can come out through the nostrils. These are in fact the main stains visible on the Sudarium.[33]

The investigation team determined that the cloth was folded over, which left four stains for every imprint of fluid on the face of the crucified man—the front and back surfaces of the part touching the face as well as the back and front surfaces furthest from the face (the folded over part). This fold enabled the Investigation Team to create a timeline for the events that occurred immediately after the cloth had been applied to the dead man:

> [The first stain was made while the body was still on the Cross.] The second stain [on the back side of the part touching the face] was made about an hour later, when the body was taken down. The third stain [the back side of the part folded over] was made when the body was lifted from the ground about forty five minutes later. The body was lying at the foot of the cross for about forty-five minutes before being buried. The marks (not fingerprints) of the fingers that held the cloth to the nose are also visible.[34]

---

[31] See Mark Guscin, "The Sudarium of Oviedo: Its History and Relationship to the Shroud of Turin", *Proceedings of the Nice Symposium on the Shroud of Turin*, May 1997, https://www.shroud.com/guscin.htm#top.

[32] Guillermo Heras, J.D. Villalain, and J.M. Rodriguez, *Comparative Studies of the Sudarium of Oviedo and the Shroud of Turin* (Turin: III Congreso Internazionale de Studi sulla Sindone, 1998), pp. 1–17, http://www.teachingfaith.com/files/books/Sudarium.PDF.

[33] Guscin, "Sudarium of Oviedo".

[34] Ibid.

The presence of a fluid that would have formed in the lungs during asphyxiation and the drying patterns of the blood and fluids on all four sides of the cloth indicate a series of events strikingly similar to those recounted about the burial of Jesus. Furthermore, it is evident that the face cloth was taken off the dead man's face before the main Shroud was applied (prior to the burial). This corresponds to the account of the empty tomb in the Gospel of John:

> Simon Peter came, following him, and went into the tomb; he saw the linen cloths lying, and the napkin, which had been on his head, not lying with the linen cloths but rolled up in a place by itself. (Jn 20:6–7)

How can the investigators be so certain that the Sudarium touched the same face as the Shroud of Turin? There are six major kinds of coincidences between the two cloths:

1. The blood stains contain human male DNA and are the rare type AB.[35]
2. The length of the nose through which the pleural oedema fluid was discharged was just over three inches (eight centimeters), the same size as the man on the Shroud of Turin.[36]
3. Since the Sudarium was not used to wipe the face, but only placed on the face in a stable position, the stains on the Sudarium can be laid over the image of the face on the Shroud of Turin. The positioning of the wounds relative to the beard is an exact fit. This would be extremely difficult to duplicate unless the face that touched the Sudarium and the Shroud were very similar.[37]
4. The stain on the side of the mouth (visible on the Sudarium) was confirmed to be present on the Shroud through the VP-8 photo enhancements of Dr. John Jackson (of the STURP Investigation Team).[38]

[35] See Heras, Villalain, and Rodriguez, *Comparative Studies of the Sudarium*, p. 15, and ibid., p. 12.

[36] See Heras, Villalain, and Rodriguez, *Comparative Studies of the Sudarium*, p. 15, and Guscin, "Sudarium of Oviedo", p. 11.

[37] See ibid.

[38] See ibid.

5. The blood stains resulting from the thorns on the nape of the neck on the Sudarium correspond perfectly to the blood stains on the Shroud of Turin.[39]

6. Dr. Alan Whanger used Polarized Image Overlay Technique on photographs of both cloths and discovered seventy coincidences on the frontal stains of the Sudarium and the Shroud, and fifty points of coincidence on the rear side of the Sudarium and Shroud. There are so many coincidences between the wounds and fluid markings of both cloths that Guscin notes, "The only possible conclusion is that the Oviedo Sudarium covered the same face as the Turin Shroud."[40]

In view of the similarities in blood type and facial features, as well as the 120 points of coincidence in the positioning of blood and fluids on the two cloths, it is difficult to avoid Guscin's conclusion—that the two cloths touched the same face of a man crowned with thorns and severely beaten.

So why is this coincidence so important for purposes of dating the Shroud of Turin? As noted above, the documented history of the Shroud of Turin begins in 1349 in the possession of Geoffrey de Charny, which is compatible with the 1988 carbon dating of the Shroud. However, the documented history of the Sudarium of Oviedo goes back much earlier, to 616 in the Middle East.

The twelfth-century bishop and historian Pelagius wrote a history of the Sudarium in the *Book of the Testaments of Oviedo* and the *Chronicon Regum Legionensium* (1121). He was presiding bishop in Oviedo and expanded the cathedral in which the Sudarium was kept. As a historian, he traced the history of the Sudarium (along with other relics) from its arrival in Spain at Cartagena in 616 to its arrival at Oviedo, where it was placed in a chapel built by King Alfonso II (around 792). Pelagius was able to trace the history of the Sudarium prior to the time of King Alfonso II by recording the history of the Spanish bishops who had received it for safekeeping from the Muslim invaders. The first bishop to receive it was Fulgentius (bishop of Cartagena) in 616. It was given to him in a chest with other relics

[39] See Heras, Villalain, and Rodriguez, *Comparative Studies of the Sudarium*, p. 15, and Guscin, "Sudarium of Oviedo", p. 3.
[40] Guscin, "Sudarium of Oviedo", p. 4.

transported from Alexandria at the time when Chosroes II (King of Persia) conquered it. Bishop Fulgentius surrendered the relics to Bishop Leandro of Seville. The Sudarium remained in Seville and was in the custody of Saint Isidore (bishop of Seville). Saint Isidore was the teacher of Saint Ildefonso, who in turn became bishop of Toledo. When he assumed his see in Toledo, he took the Sudarium with him. In 718, as the Muslims continued to invade the Iberian Peninsula, the Sudarium was moved to a cave outside of Oviedo named Monsacro, where it remained until King Alfonso II built a chapel for it around 792. It was then transported to the Cathedral of Oviedo, where it remains to this day.

Let us now return to the high probability that the Sudarium touched the same face as the Shroud of Turin. If the two cloths originated at the same time by touching the same face, and the Sudarium can be documented to the time of Bishop Fulgentius in Cartagena in 616, then we must conclude that the Shroud also goes back to 616, and very probably prior to it in Jerusalem. Why? Because the Sudarium left Jerusalem in 614 and came to Cartagena in 616 after a brief stop in Alexandria. How can we be so sure that the Sudarium originated in Palestine? Once again the pollen evidence is telling. Thirteen of the pollen grains on the Sudarium are from Israel, and four of them are unique to that region.[41]

The logical conclusion is that the Sudarium was in Israel for a long period of time prior to the Muslim conquest in 614. Since the Sudarium's pollen evidence corresponds to that on the Shroud of Turin (which touched the same face as the Sudarium), we conclude that the Shroud was also in Jerusalem prior to 614.

This throws the 1988 carbon testing into question (which dates the Shroud to 1350). If the Sudarium and the Shroud touched the same face, then the carbon dating is in error by at least 734 years.

D. Summary of the Dating Evidence

The 1988 carbon dating of the Shroud of Turin has cast doubts on its origin in the first century, and therefore on its authenticity as the burial cloth of Jesus. As we have said, carbon 14 dating is by no

[41] Marinelli, "Question of Pollen Grains".

means infallible. William Meacham, an archaeologist and carbon dating expert, has noted in this regard:

> Over the years a whole host of difficulties have come to light with C14, e.g. modern living samples which give ages of hundreds or thousands of years, or centuries-old samples which give dates in the future. The causes of these phenomena are known, but in many other cases anomalous dates have not been satisfactorily explained.[42]

As we have seen above, the carbon 14 dating of the Shroud conflicts with four other dating methods (Roger's vanillin test, Fanti's infrared spectroscopy, Fanti's Raman laser spectroscopy, and Fanti's mechanical compressibility and breaking strength test) and three other reliable circumstantial methods of dating the Shroud (Frei's pollen evidence, Whanger's polarized photographic overlay analysis of the coins, and the evidence for the Sudarium having touched the same face as the Shroud from the analysis of Heras, Villalain, and Rodriguez). Each of these seven kinds of evidence can stand on its own, but in combination they corroborate one another in pointing to a first-century origin of the Shroud. It is truly difficult to imagine that all four of the above tests and the three circumstantial methods of dating the Shroud are fallacious, and it is even more difficult to imagine that they are off by a factor of 1,350 years! When a single carbon 14 test departs so radically from so many other kinds of equally substantial evidence, Meacham recommends:

> As an archaeologist with 25 years of experience using C14 for the dating of excavated samples, I know what most archaeologists do when C14 produces a date which conflicts strongly with other evidence from a site: 1) run more dates on different samples from the same context, and then 2) put the aberrant dates down to some unidentified problem (usually in a footnote to the site report if mentioned at all).... This happens often in archaeology, even on sites and samples which were thought to be ideal for C14 dating. Very rarely is the problem of these individual aberrant dates ever resolved or even addressed.[43]

[42] Meacham, "C-14 Debate".
[43] Ibid.

In the case of the Shroud of Turin, considerable work has been done to explain the aberrant finding of the 1988 carbon 14 test:

1. Roger's discovery of dye on the fibers used for the carbon 14 test (indicating the likelihood that the fibers were of later origin, and not from the original Shroud),
2. Garza-Valdes' and Mattingly's discovery of a bioplastic coating on the fibers (produced by microorganisms over the centuries) that could have affected the carbon dating by a factor of several centuries, and
3. Marone's analysis of the carbon buildup in the cloth from the fire of Chambery and other sources that could have affected the carbon dating by a factor of three hundred years.

In the face of these problems, the 1988 carbon dating cannot be given much credibility, and a new carbon 14 dating will have to be performed according to the specifications given above in Section II.B.5. It is difficult to imagine that a new carbon 14 testing—with the above protocols in place—would not result in a much earlier date of the Shroud's origin. If it did result in a finding substantially different from the seven other dating techniques mentioned above (around the time of Jesus, within a suitable margin of error), then the new carbon dating test would have to fall into the category of what Meacham calls "an anomalous date which has not been satisfactorily explained".[44]

E. A Probable Journey of the Shroud from First-Century Jerusalem to Fourteenth-Century France

As explained above, there is considerable evidence that the Shroud originated in first-century Palestine. The above seven dating techniques indicate an origin in the first century. Furthermore, the burial Shroud itself, its pollens grains, and the coins on the man's eyes indicate a Palestinian origin. We also know that the Shroud surfaced in Lirey, France, in 1349 in the possession of Geoffrey de

[44] Ibid.

Charny, who was connected by marriage to a leader of the Fourth Crusade who was involved in the sacking of Constantinople (Othon de la Roche). Finally we know that it traveled to Edessa, Turkey, and then to Constantinople, Turkey, because of the presence of indigenous pollen grains from those regions (identified by Max Frei and others). Can we put together the probable history of the Shroud's travel from first-century Palestine into Edessa, Constantinople, and finally to Lirey, France?

Professor Ian Wilson made a study of the iconography of Edessa and Constantinople and reconstructed a credible informal history of the Shroud's movements from Palestine to Lirey, France.[45] He based his work on the research of Paul Vignon, who identified twenty unusual facial markings on the Shroud of Turin, which first appear in the art of Edessa and Constantinople after the sixth century A.D. These markings did not appear on the standard iconography of the period in regions outside of Edessa. Standard iconography portrayed Jesus as a beardless, Roman- (non-Semitic-) looking young man, but the new icons of Edessa and Constantinople portray Him as having a beard, long hair parted in the middle, and a Semitic nose. Additionally, there are fifteen other facial peculiarities having no artistic function that seem to be unique to the Shroud and the new icons of Edessa and Constantinople in that period (sixth century A.D.), such as an open top square on the forehead, V-shaped markings near the bridge of the nose, a raised eyebrow, accentuated cheeks, enlarged nostril, hairless area between the lips and beard, and large owlish eyes.[46] This agrees with Max Frei's discovery of pollen grains on the Shroud that are indigenous to Edessa and Constantinople, corroborating its appearance in those two cities.

The change in iconography in post-sixth-century Edessa and Constantinople corresponds with historical accounts of the appearance of the "Holy Image of Edessa" (the Mandylion), which is first reported by Evagrius Scholasticus in 593 in his *Ecclesiastical History*. He notes there that the Holy Image of Edessa was of divine origin—not made

---

[45] Ian Wilson, *The Shroud of Turin* (New York: Doubleday, 1978).

[46] See John Long, "The Shroud of Turin's Earlier History: Part One: To Edessa", *Bible and Spade*, Spring 2007, http://www.biblearchaeology.org/post/2013/03/14/The-Shroud-of-Turins-Earlier-History-Part-One-To-Edessa.aspx. See also Paul De Gail, S.J., "Paul Vignon", *Shroud Spectrum International*, no. 6 (1983), https://www.shroud.com/pdfs/ssi06part7.pdf.

by human hands. Other histories and legends suggest that it came from touching the face of Christ. Was the Holy Image of Edessa the folded and framed Shroud of Turin?

It probably was—for wherever it went, the iconography of the region changed to conform to the peculiar features of the face of the man on the Shroud.[47] Furthermore, there are several accounts indicating that some observers of the Holy Image of Edessa were aware that it was more than the *face* of Jesus. As John Long notes: "The superficial view during this period that the Edessa Icon was a small cloth containing just Jesus' face is challenged by other descriptions obviously dependent on special knowledge (someone's personal observation) and suggesting a semblance to the Turin Shroud."[48] Long notes further:

> A 12th century Latin text from the monk Odericus Vitalis reporting a full-body image was one of the earliest evidences of the truth's disclosure. However, 19th century historian Ernest von Dobschutz had already observed that this and similar Latin documents reporting a full-body image from about this time could trace their source to a Syriac text from about 800. In 1993 Italian classical scholar Gino Zaninotto announced the discovery of such an earlier Latin text from the 10th century, Vossianus Latinus Q69. These related manuscripts contain the "Oldest Latin Abgar Legend" asserting that the Edessa Image was of Jesus' full-body and probably derived from a Syriac text even before 769. (Scavone 1999: 18).[49]

In view of the above, it is reasonable to believe that the Holy Image of Edessa was in fact the folded and framed Shroud. Its popularity was so great that it brought Christian pilgrims (and great prestige) to Edessa even during the Islamic conquest of the city. Its Muslim rulers (who were ordinarily iconoclasts) allowed the Shroud to be preserved and protected, because it brought so much commerce and prestige.

[47] See John Long, "The Shroud of Turin's Earlier History: Part Two: To the Great City", *Bible and Spade*, Fall 2007, http://www.biblearchaeology.org/post/2013/03/20/The-Shroud-of-Turins-Earlier-History-Part-Two-To-the-Great-City.aspx.

[48] Ibid.

[49] See ibid. See also Daniel Scavone, "Joseph of Arimathea, the Holy Grail, and the Edessa Icon", *Arthuriana* 9, no. 4 (Winter 1999): 3–31.

In 943 the Byzantine emperor Roman Lacapenus laid siege to Edessa in order to obtain the Holy Image. By discontinuing the siege and granting payment to Edessa's rulers, he procured it in 944 and displayed it in various churches in Constantinople—Saint Mary Blachernae and then in Hagia Sophia.[50] Ultimately "it found a resting place in the secret Pharos Chapel—a depository for precious treasures inside the emperor's Great Palace."[51] In the eleventh century the treasury in Constantinople reports not only having the Mandylion (the Holy Image of Edessa), but also the burial Shroud of Christ with the markings of His Crucifixion.[52] According to Wilson and Long, it is likely that the Holy Image was removed from its frame, unfolded, and shown to be a burial cloth with wounds resembling those of Jesus' Crucifixion.[53] From that point until its disappearance in 1204, the burial Shroud of Christ was kept in the emperor's treasury.

Is there any evidence indicating that the Shroud spent centuries being folded in a frame to look like the Holy Image of Edessa? Long appeals to the research of John Jackson to answer this question:

> If it did spend centuries folded or "doubled in four" there might still be some traces, even though faint, among the cloth's creases. Dr. John Jackson, one of the scientific leaders in the 1978 Shroud of Turin Research team, has noticed "a series of fold marks which argue strongly for the identification of the Shroud as the Mandylion ..." (Jackson 1995: 303). These occur at one-eighth length intervals on the Turin Shroud and, as Dr. Jackson discovered, no such folding arrangement is known during its "good" history since the 14th century.[54]

Was the shroud in the treasury of Constantinople the Shroud of Turin? It probably was. In addition to the folding evidence discovered by Jackson, and the change in iconography corresponding to the unusual facial markings discovered by Paul Vignon, there were reliable reports from Constantinople that the shroud had a very unusual,

---

[50] See Long, " Part Two: To the Great City".
[51] Ibid.
[52] See ibid.
[53] See ibid.
[54] Ibid.

if not unique, feature—an image—and specifically, an image of a crucified man. According to Long:

> Robert de Clari, an ordinary knight in the western army, wrote about the many wonders to be seen in Constantinople as the visiting soldiers toured the city in 1203, including, "another church called My Lady St. Mary of Blachernae, where there was the shroud [*sydoines*] in which our Lord had been wrapped, which every Friday raised itself upright, so that one could see the figure of Our Lord on it" (Wilson 1991: 156).[55]

Assuming that this imaged Shroud of Constantinople was the unfolded Mandylion (Holy Image of Edessa), we now have a history of the Shroud prior to its arrival in Lirey, France, that corresponds to the three geographical areas of indigenous pollen grains found on the Shroud by Max Frei and others—Palestine, Edessa, and Constantinople. So how did the Shroud move from Constantinople to Lirey, France?

Assuming Scavone's theory to be the most credible (because of documentation), it seems likely that the Shroud was taken by (or fell into the custody of) a French knight of the Fourth Crusade who occupied the Church of Saint Mary Blachernae—Othon de la Roche. He was a high-ranking lord among the French forces who was granted Greek lands by the Crusade leaders.[56] According to Long, two documents support Scavone's theory:

> In August 1205, Byzantine nobleman Theodore Angelos wrote a letter to Pope Innocent III complaining of the theft of precious objects from Constantinople including the "linen cloth of our Lord Jesus Christ in which he was wrapped after his death and before his resurrection" (Barta 2008: 1); Theodore named Athens as the place where the Latin invaders took it. A second document discovered by Scavone

---

[55] John Long, "The Shroud of Turin's Earlier History: Part Three: The Shroud of Constantinople", Associates for Biblical Research, March 28, 2013, http://www.biblearchaeology.org/post/2013/03/28/The-Shroud-of-Turins-Earlier-History-Part-Three-The-Shroud-of-Constantinople.aspx. See also Wilson, *Shroud of Turin*, p. 156.

[56] See John Long, "The Shroud of Turin's Earlier History: Part 4: To Little Lirey", Associates for Biblical Research, September 5, 2013, http://www.biblearchaeology.org/post/2013/09/05/The-Shroud-of-Turins-Earlier-History-Part-4-To-Little-Lirey.aspx.

in 1989 stated that Nicolas of Otranto, an Italian abbot who accompanied the new Latin Patriarch on a trip to the East in 1206, says that he "saw with our own eyes" Christ's burial linens. Both Constantinople and Athens were on his travel itinerary with his language more likely referring to the latter (Scavone 2008: 5–6).[57]

According to an anonymous document (MS 826 of the Besançon archives), Othon shipped the relic from Athens to his lands in Besançon (France) perhaps as early as 1206.[58] He may have deposited it in Saint Stephen's Cathedral in Besançon. According to Long:

> It was customary for relics to be donated to local churches and MS 826 claims that Othon's family passed the Shroud to a Bishop Amadeus de Tramelay for depositing it in St. Stephen's Cathedral in Besancon (Scavone 1989: 98).[59]

The cathedral was destroyed in a fire in 1349, but the Shroud, if it was in the cathedral at the time of the fire, was safely removed. Shortly thereafter, it makes its uncontested appearance in Lirey, France, in the possession of Geoffrey de Charny, who, as previously mentioned, married Jeanne de Vergy—a fifth-generation descendent of Othon de la Roche. At this point, the Shroud's history is well documented (see Section I above).

III. The Image on the Shroud

Explanations of the formation of the Shroud's image remain in the category of "scientifically plausible hypotheses". We currently do not have a *definitive* explanation for how this unique and mysterious image was created from the body of a deceased man. The most plausible current hypothesis comes from a combination of two teams of researchers:

[57] Ibid. See also Daniel C. Scavone, "Besançon and Other Hypotheses for the Missing Years: The Shroud from 1200 to 1400", Shroud Science Group International Conference, Ohio State University, Columbus, August 14–17, 2008.

[58] See Long, "Part 4: To Little Lirey".

[59] See ibid. See also Scavone, "Besançon and Other Hypotheses".

1. John Jackson's team, who proposed the vacuum ultraviolet radiation hypothesis in 2008 to explain three (out of five) enigmas of the Shroud's image, and
2. Paolo Di Lazzaro's team, who experimentally substantiated Jackson's hypothesis in 2010.

According to Jackson, an intense burst of vacuum ultraviolet radiation produced a discoloration on the uppermost surface of the Shroud's fibrils (without scorching it), which gave rise to a perfect three-dimensional negative image of both the frontal and dorsal parts of the body wrapped in it.

As will be shown below, this hypothesis (and its corroboration by Di Lazzaro) explains only three out of five enigmas on the Shroud. In order to explain the final two enigmas, Jackson had to propose a more "unconventional" (and possibly scientifically uncorroborated) hypothesis that the burst of intense vacuum ultraviolet radiation be emitted from every three-dimensional point within a mechanically transparent body. This hypothesis still stands today as the only explanation of the Shroud's double image as well as the interior (skeletal) and exterior images of the hands.

Currently, we know of no *natural* explanation for the seemingly unique occurrence of such a burst of vacuum ultraviolet radiation from either a decomposing body or the geological and atmospheric conditions within a tomb. Though this is suggestive of a possible *supernatural* origin of the radiation, perhaps as a part of Jesus' Resurrection, we cannot prove this scientifically, because we cannot construct a scientific test for a supernatural cause; all we can do is eliminate every *known* natural cause of this seemingly unique radiation. The uniqueness and current inexplicability of this phenomenon gives us room to *believe* that God has given us evidence of Jesus' Resurrection. This belief can be strengthened by further understanding of the light phenomenon that seems to be the source of the image as well as the continued elimination of natural causes for it.

We will explain this conclusion in three steps:

1. The 1978 STURP investigation of the image
2. The hypothesis of John Jackson
3. The experimental substantiation by Paolo Di Lazzaro

A. The 1978 STURP Investigation of the Shroud's Image

Prior to the STURP investigation, Secondo Pia and subsequent photographers discovered that the Shroud image was a perfect photographic negative (as distinct from the blood that is a positive image). Furthermore, the work of Dr. Pierre Barbet (and others) showed that the image of the Shroud, relative to the blood stains, was anatomically perfect. These two early findings suggested that medieval forgery was unlikely. The results of the STURP investigation in 1978 and the 3-D imaging of the Shroud by Jackson, Jumper, and Ercoline in 1982[60] showed how exceedingly unlikely a medieval forgery would be.

So what did the STURP investigation find in 1978? The image was caused by rapid dehydration, oxidation, and degradation of the linen by an unidentified process, coloring it a sepia or straw yellow. The range of possible causes is restricted by the unusual characteristics of the image—namely, its *superficial* character limited to the uppermost surface of the cloth and the fact that the image does not fluoresce. This meant that the surface was likely produced by light radiation, but *not* by *heat radiation*.[61] Dr. John Jackson (and other physicists) theorized that a plausible cause of such "light radiation" might be a short intense burst of vacuum ultraviolet radiation.

B. The Hypothesis of John Jackson

Why did Jackson select a radiation hypothesis instead of a chemical one? Because a dye, powder, ointment, or other chemical source

---

[60] See J. P. Jackson, E. J. Jumper, and W. R. Ercoline, "Three Dimensional Characteristic of the Shroud Image", *IEEE 1982 Proceedings of the International Conference on Cybernetics and Society*, October 1982, pp. 559–75; J. P. Jackson, E. J. Jumper, and W. R. Ercoline, "Correlation of Image Intensity on the Turin Shroud with the 3-D Structure of a Human Body Shape", *Applied Optics* 23, no. 14 (July 15, 1984): 2244–70.

[61] See E. J. Jumper and R. W. Mottern, "Scientific Investigation of the Shroud of Turin", *Applied Optics* 19, no. 12 (1980): 1909–12; E. J. Jumper, "An Overview of the Testing Performed by the Shroud of Turin Research Project with a Summary of Results", *IEEE 1982 Proceedings of the International Conference on Cybernetics and Society*, October 1982, pp. 535–37; E. J. Jumper et al., "A Comprehensive Examination of the Various Stains and Images on the Shroud of Turin", *Archaeological Chemistry III, ACS Advances in Chemistry*, no. 205 (1984): 447–76.

of the image could not explain three enigmatic dimensions of the image adequately:

1. Chemicals cannot explain the superficiality of the Shroud image (limited to the uppermost surface of the fibrils without penetration to the medulla of the fiber). Chemicals that touched the Shroud would have in many places penetrated beyond that surface.
2. Chemicals do not explain how the image is evenly present on the many areas of the cloth that did *not* touch the body.
3. Vapors from chemicals on the body (or from the body itself) could not have produced a perfect photographic image on the areas of the cloth that did not touch the body.

In view of this, Jackson moved into the realm of radiation—which held out the potential of resolving all three of these enigmatic features.[62]

There is only one problem with a radiation hypothesis—radiation not only gives off light (which could produce discoloration of the fabric), but also heat, which could scorch or burn the cloth. The STURP investigation showed that the image on the cloth was not the result of a scorch, because it did not fluoresce.[63] So Jackson needed to find a kind of radiation that would not produce an accompanying heat radiation sufficient to scorch the cloth.

[62] Jackson's supposition was later confirmed when it was found that the cloth has a *double image*—one on the front surface of the cloth and a fainter, but nonetheless distinct image on the back surface of the cloth; however, there is *nothing* in between the front and back surface images! Chemicals and vapors could not have done this, and it requires that the body in the Shroud be mechanically transparent. See below, Section III.B.

[63] According to Barry Schwortz, a well-known Shroud expert, "Since the color of the image is very similar to the color of the scorches, STURP understood the need to test this theory and performed specific experiments for that purpose. A primary test was to photograph the Shroud using ultraviolet fluorescence photography, since true scorches on linen will always fluoresce in the red. As there are many documented scorches on the Shroud from the 1532 fire, testing this was not difficult and the results of the tests were published in this peer reviewed reference: Miller, V.D. and S. F. Pellicori, 'Ultraviolet Fluorescence Photography of the Shroud of Turin,' *Journal of Biological Photography*, Vol. 49, No. 3, 1981, pp. 71–85. Every documented scorch on the Shroud fluoresced in the red, as expected. However, the *image* did NOT fluoresce and in fact, even quenched the background fluorescence in the image areas. The only conclusion possible from these observations is that the Shroud image is NOT the product of scorched or heated linen." Barry Schwortz, comment in "The Image on the Shroud of Turin Is Not a Scorch", *The Shroud of Turin* (blog), Shroudstory.com, February 10, 2012, http://shroudstory.com/2012/02/10/the-image-on-the-shroud-of-turin-is-not-a-scorch/.

Vacuum ultraviolet radiation is an excellent candidate for explaining the Shroud image because VUV radiation would not have scorched the cloth. It dissipates so quickly that its initial energy could discolor the cloth in a brief burst without destroying it in the process.[64] Furthermore, vacuum ultraviolet radiation could be limited to the surface of the fibrils without penetrating the medulla of the fibers:

> Of particular note, are the observations that the image discolorations reside on the surfaces of the image fibrils and that the inside medullas are not colored. We point out, again, that vacuum ultraviolet radiation would be absorbed at the surface of the fibrils, which would leave the medullas unaffected, thereby satisfying those requirements.[65]

Finally, a short burst of ultraviolet radiation would also explain how the image was perfectly present (sufficient to produce a perfect photographic negative) on the many parts of the cloth that did *not* touch the body. Thus the Jackson hypothesis is able to explain all three enigmas of the image on the cloth.

Yet, there is another enigma. A cursory glance at the image reveals the bones of the hand encased within flesh, as if the image recorded both the inside of the hand (the skeleton) and the outside of the hand (the flesh surrounding the skeleton) at the same time. As Jackson notes:

> There is, however, one particular observation that definitively places the Shroud image in a unique category.... If we examine this image region carefully, we can see ... that the finger bones are visible well into the palm of the hands, extending right up to the base of the wrist. These cannot be interpreted as tendons, because tendons and ligaments are much too narrow. Rather, we see that the thickness of the fingers are individually preserved well into the palm of the hand. It thus seems as though we are looking at the internal skeletal structure of the hand imaged through the intervening flesh tissues onto the Shroud cloth.[66]

---

[64] See John P. Jackson, "Is the Image on the Shroud Due to a Process Heretofore Unknown to Modern Science?" *Shroud Spectrum International*, no. 34 (March 1990): 3–29.

[65] John P. Jackson and Keith E. Propp, "Comments on Rogers' 'Testing the Jackson Theory' of Image Formation", Shroud of Turin Website, 2004, http://www.shroud.com/pdfs/jacksonpropp.pdf.

[66] John P. Jackson, "An Unconventional Hypothesis to Explain All Image Characteristics Found on the Shroud Image", in *History, Science, Theology and the Shroud*, ed. A. Berard (St. Louis: Symposium Proceedings, 1991), http://theshroudofturin.blogspot.com/2012/01/john-p-jackson-unconventional.html.

How could this unique image-forming process occur? It would require that the frontal part of the cloth *collapse* into the dorsal part of the cloth during the process of image formation, as if the body were completely transparent, not impeding the collapse of the cloth. If the cloth had not collapsed, only the outside of the body would have been in the image, which is clearly not the case (because the skeleton of the hand is visible along with the flesh surrounding it). It seems that the vacuum ultraviolet radiation is emanating evenly throughout the body, and that the body presents no obstacle to the collapse of the cloth. In Jackson's words:

> I propose that, as the Shroud collapsed through the underlying body, radiation emitted from all points within that body and discolored the cloth so as to produce the observed image. As will be seen below, this assumption [also] explains the superficiality of the Shroud image and, perhaps, the differentiation in fibril coloring.[67]

If Jackson is correct, then when the blood attached to the Shroud, the body impeded the collapse of the cloth; however, during the time of image formation, the body became mechanically transparent; it still remained a three-dimensional source of light, but lost the mechanical quality of solidity that would have impeded a collapse of the cloth. The loss of "mechanical solidity" enabled the newly configured body to emit a burst of evenly distributed intense radiation while the cloth collapsed through it, giving rise to the flattened 3-D image. Jackson explains:

> We must assume that the Shroud initially covered a body shape [at the time that blood was being transferred to the cloth], but, for some reason, that body did not impede the collapse of the Shroud during the time of image formation.[68]

Despite the unconventional nature of this hypothesis, Jackson believes that it is warranted, because it is currently the only explanation for all of the observed data on the cloth:

> In the case of the Shroud image, the cloth did collapse *into* and *through* the underlying body structure. As a physicist, I admit to having my

[67] Ibid.
[68] Ibid. See also Jackson, "Image on the Shroud", pp. 3–29.

own difficulties with this concept, but I also know that scientists must be ready to overturn even their most hallowed principles if observation warrants.[69]

Jackson's hypothesis seems to break completely with everything we know about bodily decomposition—and verges on the miraculous. How could a decomposing body give rise to such an intense burst of radiation? How could it become transparent so that this ultraviolet radiation could emanate evenly through it during the process of image formation?

We may here be on the verge of having to use a *transphysical* explanation to explain the observational data. Nevertheless, Jackson and others persist in this line of thinking, because no other *natural* explanation seems to meet the requirements of the enigmatic image on the Shroud. If Jackson's hypothesis could be experimentally confirmed in the laboratory—with short bursts of vacuum ultraviolet radiation producing an image similar to that on the Shroud—it would confirm his hypothesis as realistic and tenable. It would not answer the question of how a decomposing body could produce this very special kind of radiation, or how the cloth could collapse through the body while vacuum ultraviolet radiation emanated evenly from every point within it; but it would show that the Jackson hypothesis could explain at least three enigmas on the Shroud: the restriction of the discoloration to the uppermost surface of the fibrils, the absence of scorching in the image areas, and the perfect three-dimensional negative image in places where the body did not touch the cloth.

The first step in this experimental verification occurred in 2010 (see below, III.C), but before discussing it, we will want to examine yet another enigma of the Shroud image that can also be answered by Jackson's hypothesis—the *double* image on the frontal part of the Shroud discovered by Fanti and Maggiolo in 2004.[70]

The Shroud of Turin has a *double* image—that is, a superficial discoloration on the front surface of the cloth, closest to the body—and a fainter image on the back surface of the cloth, furthest from the

[69]Jackson, "Unconventional Hypothesis"; emphasis in original.

[70]Giulio Fanti and Roberto Maggiolo, "The Double Superficiality of the Frontal Image of the Turin Shroud", *Journal of Optics A: Pure and Applied Optics* 6, no. 6 (2004): 491.

body. However, there is no discoloration on the fibers *between* the front surface and back surface of the cloth. Both images correspond to each other anatomically—though the one on the back surface of the cloth is fainter than the one on the front surface. The double image is evident only on the frontal part of the Shroud (but not on the dorsal part), particularly in the area of the face and the hands.[71]

Chemical and vapor explanations of this double image are inadequate, because none of them can explain an image occurring on the front surface and the back surface of a cloth without leaving any residue in-between. In order for chemicals or vapors to reach the back surface of the cloth, they would have to go *through* the cloth, leaving an obvious residue in the process. Given that the image could not have been produced by slowly dissipating radiation (which would leave a scorch), we are left with Jackson's explanation of a short intense burst of vacuum ultraviolet radiation (which dissipates before scorching the cloth) emitted evenly throughout a mechanically transparent body.

Could this kind of radiation produce the *double* image on the frontal part of the Shroud? It would if we accept the validity of Jackson's mechanically transparent man (collapsing cloth) hypothesis. If the cloth collapsed, the light energy would have made superficial images on both the front surface and the back surface of the cloth without penetrating more deeply. Think of it this way: the vacuum ultraviolet radiation is completely *surrounding* the cloth collapsing through the body. Thus, it is making contact with both the front surface and the back surface of the frontal part of the collapsing cloth. However, it does not penetrate either surface of the cloth deeply, because the vacuum ultraviolet energy dissipates so quickly. Thus, the radiation hits both the front and back surface of the collapsing cloth simultaneously, but dissipates so quickly that it does not penetrate into the center of the cloth from either side.

---

[71] See ibid. No researcher has yet been able to make a digital scan of the back surface of the frontal part of the cloth, because there is a backing that was made to protect it, and the custodians of the Shroud are reluctant to have it removed. However, Fanti and Maggiolo enhanced photographs of the back surface of the cloth by a special method: "This was based on convolution with Gaussian filters, summation of images, and filtering in spatial frequency by direct and inverse bidimensional Fourier transformations." Ibid. This brings the image of the face into perspective sufficiently for matching with the front surface of the cloth.

Jackson predicted that such a double image would be the consequence of his hypothesis before its discovery by Fanti and Maggiolo. Jackson and Keith E. Propp reasserted this prediction in 2004:

> In 1990, one of us (Jackson) offered a [mechanically transparent man] hypothesis as an attempt to explain simultaneously all observations regarding the Shroud image. This hypothesis was ventured only after a systematic study of alternatives had failed to account for various image characteristics and, though unconventional, this hypothesis makes a variety of testable predictions that are a-priori falsifiable by means of the Scientific Method. Recently, one important prediction of the hypothesis, that a double superficial frontal image without an associated dorsal image should exist on the Shroud, was reported by Fanti and Maggiolo.[72]

In sum, there are five major enigmas of the Shroud image:

1. The fact exists that the image is limited to the uppermost surface of the fibrils and does not penetrate to the medulla of the fibers. This implies that the image was not produced by chemicals or vapors of any kind.
2. The fact exists that the image is not a scorch (but rather discoloration coming from dehydration). This implies that the image could not have been produced by slowly dissipating radiation (which would have scorched it).
3. The image is a perfect photographic negative in which the image intensity is related to the distance of the cloth from the body. Thus, the image was present regardless of whether the cloth touched the body. This implies that radiation, and not chemicals, was the source of image formation.
4. There is a double image on the frontal part of the cloth (a more intense image on the front surface, nearest the body, and a less intense image on the back surface, furthest from the body, without any effects between the two surfaces). This implies that the radiation was surrounding both surfaces of the cloth, further

---

[72] Jackson and Propp, "Comments on Rogers' 'Testing the Jackson Theory'". Jackson and Propp refer to three previous investigations for this conclusion. See Jackson, "Image on the Shroud". See also Jackson et al., "Correlation of Image Intensity", pp. 2244–70.

implying that the cloth collapsed into a mechanically transparent body.

5. Parts of the frontal image, particularly the hands, show an image that is resolvable into three dimensions, in which the inside skeletal parts of the hand are proportionately related to the surrounding exterior flesh on the hand. This implies that the cloth collapsed into *and through* a mechanically transparent body.

The more conventional part of Jackson's hypothesis—that a short intense burst of vacuum ultraviolet radiation emitted from the decomposing body—can explain the first three enigmas. However, the fourth and fifth enigmas—the double image on the frontal part of the Shroud as well as the inside (skeletal) and outside (flesh) characteristics—require the unconventional part of Jackson's hypothesis, in which the body became mechanically transparent, allowing the cloth to collapse as light emanated evenly from every part of the transparent body.

C. Partial Confirmation of the Jackson Hypothesis in 2010

In 2010, six physicists from three research centers (Frascati Research Center, the University of Padua, and the Casaccia Research Center) were able to confirm the Jackson hypothesis under experimental conditions by creating a burst of ultraviolet radiation through an excimer laser. According to Paolo Di Lazzaro, director of the six-member team,

> We have irradiated a linen fabric having the same absolute spectral reflectance of the Turin Shroud ... with pulsed deep-UV radiation emitted by an ArF excimer laser. We have shown that 12 ns, 193 nm laser pulses are able to color a very thin layer on the linen yarn.... The colorless inner part of a few fibers ... suggests that we have locally achieved a coloration of the outermost part of the fibers. To the best of our knowledge, this is the first coloration of a linen material resembling the very shallow depth of coloration ... observed in the Turin Shroud fibers.[73]

[73] Paolo Di Lazzaro et al., "Deep Ultraviolet Radiation Simulates the Turin Shroud Image", *Journal of Imaging Science and Technology*, July-August 2010, p. 6.

The team specified that three of the above five enigmas were explained and experimentally confirmed by this method, precisely as Jackson predicted. In an interview with Sci-News, Di Lazzaro said:

> In particular, vacuum ultraviolet photons account for [1] the very thin coloration depth, [2] the hue of color and [3] the presence of image in linen parts not in contact with the body. Obviously, it does not mean the image was produced by a laser. Rather, the laser is a powerful tool to test and obtain the light parameters suitable for a shroud-like coloration.[74]

He adds that a single laser alone could not explain the image over the full length of the body. In fact, it would have taken fourteen thousand lasers like the one used by Di Lazzaro to produce a full-body image like the one on the Shroud. The characteristics of the kind of light impulse that would be needed to produce an image like that on the Shroud are quite remarkable. According to Di Lazzaro:

> [The ultraviolet light necessary to form the image] exceeds the maximum power released by all ultraviolet light sources available today says Di Lazzaro. It would require "pulses having durations shorter than one forty-billionth of a second, and intensities on the order of several billion watts."[75]

How *in the world* could a normal decomposing body do something like this? The image on the Shroud is completely unique. There is no other known image resembling it having the first three enigmas— let alone all five enigmas. If the only way of reproducing the image requires an intense burst of vacuum ultraviolet radiation tantamount to several billion watts (dissipating in less than one–forty billionth of a second), then it would imply a supernatural cause. In sum, Di Lazzaro's research confirms Jackson's theory that a short intense burst of vacuum ultraviolet radiation can produce an image on the uppermost

---

[74] Sergio Prostak, "Scientists Suggest Turin Shroud Authentic", Sci-News.com, December 21, 2011, http://www.sci-news.com/physics/scientists-suggest-turin-shroud-authentic.html.

[75] Frank Viviano, "Why Shroud of Turin's Secrets Continue to Elude Science", *National Geographic*, April 17, 2015, http://news.nationalgeographic.com/2015/04/150417-shroud-turin-relics-jesus-catholic-church-religion-science/.

surface of the fibrils that is discolored through dehydration (rather than a scorch), yielding a perfect photographic negative image, on parts of the cloth not in contact with the body. However, his experiment did not confirm how the other two enigmas of the image originated, the double image as well as the image of the inside and outside of the hands.

Recall that Jackson had to supplement his vacuum ultraviolet radiation hypothesis with the more unconventional hypothesis of a mechanically transparent man to account for these other two enigmas. We should not be surprised that Di Lazzaro and his team were not able to confirm the fourth and fifth enigmas of the image because they were not able to reproduce a mechanically transparent body in which light emanated evenly from every part. These two enigmas may never be reproducible under experimental conditions, because the only known explanation of them (from Jackson) supersedes the known laws of physics. Thus, we may be left with a plausible explanation for the image that cannot be, strictly speaking, physically reproducible, and experimentally verifiable.

D. Does the Shroud Give Evidence of Jesus' Resurrection?

The research of the 1978 STURP Investigation, as well as subsequent research of John Jackson, Giulio Fanti, Paolo Di Lazzaro, and their teams, shows the likelihood that sometime after the blood deposits had dried on the Shroud, the decomposing body in the Shroud emitted a short intense burst of vacuum ultraviolet radiation that led to a dehydration and discoloration of the frontal and dorsal parts of the Shroud, giving rise to a perfect photographic negative image. Jackson's research also suggests that the body inside the Shroud became mechanically transparent and emitted light evenly from every three-dimensional point within it. This allowed the frontal part of the Shroud to collapse, creating an image (of both the inside and outside of the hands) as well as a double image on the frontal part of the Shroud.

So where do we stand? The first three of the above five enigmas (see above, III.B) of image formation can be explained by a short intense burst of vacuum ultraviolet radiation emitted from the body. This explanation has been shown to be realistic through experimental replication (by Paolo Di Lazzaro). The fourth and fifth enigmas imply that the body in the Shroud became mechanically transparent and emitted light evenly from every three-dimensional point within it.

Jackson, Fanti, and Di Lazzaro show that alternative physical explanations either contradict the above enigmas or fail to explain them:

- *Chemical and vapor explanations* fail to explain four of the above five enigmas (one, three, four, and five). With respect to the first enigma, chemicals and vapors would not be limited only to the uppermost surface of the fibrils, but would have penetrated to the medulla of the fibers on many parts of the cloth. Furthermore, with respect to the third enigma, chemicals and vapors would not give rise to a perfect photographic image; even the most recent ingenious attempts to do this have resulted in multiple imperfections and "clumping".[76] With respect to the fourth and fifth enigmas, chemicals and vapors cannot reproduce the double image (with nothing in between) and the interior image of the skeleton of the hand.
- *Heating or scorching explanations* violate the second enigma because the image is not a scorch as shown by its failure to fluoresce.
- *Other radiation hypotheses* besides vacuum ultraviolet radiation will likely violate the second enigma because they would not dissipate quickly enough to prevent scorching on the cloth.

---

[76] An organic chemistry professor at the University of Pavia (Luigi Garlaschelli) and his team, who were funded by an Italian association of atheists and agnostics, tried to reproduce the Shroud image by using ochre, acid, and a special heating technique. According to the Catholic News Agency, "They created their image by placing the linen over a volunteer before rubbing it with a pigment called ochre with traces of acid. The linen was then 'aged' by heating it in an oven and washing it with water." They then added blood stains. Though the image bore some resemblance to that on the Shroud superficially, it was by no means a replica of it. First, adding the blood stains afterward is not consistent with what happened on the Shroud, but if the attempted forgers had placed the blood stains on the cloth first, they would have ruined them when adding the ochre and acid to produce the image. Furthermore, the image they produced was quite distorted. As Jackson noted, "While the images of Garlaschelli's shroud on the internet look authentic, when taken from a 3-D perspective, "it's really rather grotesque. The hands are embedded into the body and the legs have unnatural looking lumps and bumps." Catholic News Agency, "Experts Question Scientist's Claim of Reproducing Shroud of Turin", October 6, 2009, http://www.catholicnewsagency.com /news/experts_question_scientists_claim_of_reproducing_shroud_of_turin/.

Furthermore, heat radiation of this kind would penetrate to the medulla of the fiber, violating the first enigma.

At present, there is no alternative physical explanation for all five enigmas on the Shroud besides the two-part explanation of John Jackson:

1. a short intense burst of vacuum ultraviolet radiation that was
2. emitted evenly by a mechanically transparent body from every three-dimensional point within it.

Currently, the known laws of physics cannot explain how a decomposing body can emit an intense burst of vacuum ultraviolet radiation. Furthermore, they cannot explain how such a body could become mechanically transparent and emit light from every three-dimensional point within it.

So, where does that leave us? If Jackson's explanation continues to be the only one that explains all five enigmas, and if future articulations of the laws of physics cannot explain how a decomposing body could become mechanically transparent and evenly emit vacuum ultraviolet radiation from every three-dimensional point within it, then we are left at the brink of a *transphysical* or *metaphysical* explanation. Under these conditions, it would be both reasonable and responsible to *believe* that a *transphysical cause* interacted with the decomposing body to transform it into an intense burst of light.

Evidently, we cannot *scientifically prove* a transphysical cause, because science is restricted to the domain of physical causation. However, if the above conditions hold, we can reasonably *infer* the possibility and perhaps the likelihood of such a transphysical cause. This is sufficient for reasonable and responsible belief.

Does this transphysical explanation of the Shroud's image point to the Resurrection of Jesus? Recall from Chapter 4 that Jesus' Resurrection was not a resuscitation of a material corpse, but rather a transforming event that gave rise to what Saint Paul called a "spiritual body" (1 Cor 15:44)—a body transformed in glory, spirit, and power. Could this transformation of a material body into a burst of intense light signify a beginning point of the transformation of Jesus' body from a physical one to a spiritual-glorified one? Though there can be no scientific proof of this, it is a reasonable inference from the parallels between the explanation of the Shroud's enigmatic image and the testimony of Saint Paul and the Gospel writers. In this sense, we might say that the image on the Shroud presents a clue, even a relic, of Jesus' Resurrection.

IV. Conclusion

Why would we think the body in the Shroud was that of *Jesus*? As explained above, it is exceedingly improbable that the Shroud is a medieval forgery. First, there are no paints, dyes, or other pigments on the Shroud (except for the small flecks coming from the sanctification of icons and paintings that touched it). Second, the anatomical precision of the blood stains—which are real human blood that congealed on the Shroud *before* the formation of the image—are in precise anatomical correlation to the image itself. How could a medieval forger have accomplished this? Third, it is exceedingly difficult to explain how pollen grains indigenous to Palestine appeared in abundance on a shroud of probable Semitic origin (if it originated in medieval Europe) and how coins minted in A.D. 29 in Palestine appeared on the eyes of the man on the Shroud. How could a medieval forger have duplicated these first-century Palestinian characteristics of the Shroud? Fourth, the five enigmas of the image on the Shroud almost certainly preclude a forgery. How could a medieval forger have used vacuum ultraviolet radiation to discolor the cloth on the uppermost surface of the fibrils? How could he have created a perfect photographic negative image? How could he have created a double image on the frontal part of the Shroud? And how could he have known how to duplicate the interior and exterior of the hands in perfect proportion to each other? Thus, it does not seem reasonable or responsible to believe that the Shroud is a medieval forgery.

Beyond this, there are three probative kinds of evidence pointing specifically to *Jesus'* place and time of origin and to His *unique* Crucifixion and Resurrection:

1. The material of the Shroud, the pollen grains on it, and the coins on the man's eyes all have their origin in first-century Palestine, the place where Jesus was purported to have died.

2. The blood stains come from a crucifixion event identical to the one described in the four Gospels, which was very unusual, if not unique, in many respects, such as the man being crowned with thorns, being flogged, and being pierced with a Roman pilium (see above, the Introduction to this Appendix).

3. The five enigmas of the Shroud's image point to a *transphysically* caused burst of vacuum ultraviolet radiation from a mechanically transparent body. This is suggestive of the transformation of Jesus' body from a physical one to a spiritual-glorified one (as reported by Saint Paul and the four Gospels). Recall that the spiritual-glorified transformation of Jesus' body was *unique* to the Christian view of resurrection (see Chapter 4). It was not known in Judaism (which held to a resuscitation of the flesh) or pagan cults (which held to ethereal or ghostlike views of immortality). Thus, the enigmas on the Shroud's image point to the *uniquely* Christian view of resurrection implied by Jesus' risen appearance.

The odds of this first-century Palestinian burial shroud, with the unique features of Jesus' Crucifixion and Resurrection, being that of anyone else is exceedingly remote. Inasmuch as the image is not a forgery, it would have to have come from a real person living at that specific time, killed in that unique way, and producing a burst of intense vacuum ultraviolet radiation from his decomposing body. Given all this, we might reasonably infer that the Shroud is the burial cloth of Jesus, which contains not only a relic of His Crucifixion, but also of His Resurrection in glory. If so, it shows both the truth of the most significant event in history as well as the accuracy of the Gospel accounts of it.

Appendix Two

Making Sense of the Trinity and Incarnation

Introduction

At the end of Chapter 6, we concluded that there was abundant evidence to show that Jesus is the unconditional love of God with us—from His glorious Resurrection, His gift of the Holy Spirit, the miracles by His command alone, His claims to be the exclusive Son of the Father, His view of love (*agapē*), His preaching of His Father's unconditional love, and His life and self-sacrifice exemplifying *His* unconditional love. This evidence is significant only if we have an affinity for His teaching on love and sense a need for His redemption and salvation. Even if we favorably assess the evidence for Jesus' claim to be the exclusive Son of the Father, we still face the problem of how to conceive of the Trinity and the Incarnation. How can God be three in one, and how can the Son of *God* become human? This Appendix attempts to make sense out of what might at first appear to be confusing or even contradictory, but is in fact consistent and coherent. As will be seen, these doctrines reflect the unconditional love of God, which is commensurate not only with Jesus' preaching, but with the name He gives to Himself: the only *beloved* Son of the Father (see Lk 20:13 and also footnote 5, below).

I. Divine Nature versus Divine Person

How can Jesus be divine in human form? Isn't that a contradiction? It would be if the early Church had claimed that Jesus' Incarnation was "*divinity* becoming human", or "the divine taking human form", or "the Infinite taking finite form". But it did not, because it was very much aware of the contradiction implied by these statements.

Hence, the early Church, reflecting Jesus' preaching, found other forms of expression that avoided these problems. It declared early on that it was not "the infinite God" who became "man", but the "Son of God" who became man.

As the Church developed her doctrine into the third, fourth, and fifth centuries, she worked out a distinction between "Person" and "nature". She subsequently declared that the *second Person* of the Trinity (the Son) became human (took finite form). However, she was careful to note that the one, divine (infinite) *nature* did *not* become human (finite), because that would have been an obvious contradiction.[1] So what is the distinction between "Person" and "nature"? And why is it that "the Person of the Son taking on a finite nature" is not a contradiction?

A. One Divine Nature

"Nature" within a Platonic context refers to the form or essence of a thing. In an Aristotelian context, it refers to the substance (what is not accidental or incidental) or the "to ti ēn einai" (the "what it was to be"). Perhaps the easiest way of finding the common ground between these two great ancient Greek traditions is to use the word "power" or "act". A thing's nature is the *acting power* that is most central to its being, and allows it to be compared to other beings (making it intelligible and susceptible to definition).

Thus, the "nature of God" would be equivalent to the "acting power of God". We can know the most fundamental characteristic of the acting power of God through natural reason—namely, that it must be an acting power *existing through itself.* We can prove this because

---

[1] It should not be thought that the apostolic Church was altogether ignorant of a distinction between what was later termed "Person" and "nature". Though it did not make a clear, defined distinction between these realities (as did later Church councils), it *implicitly* distinguished between the Father and Son (later termed "Persons") and the divine nature. For example, the Philippians Hymn (Phil 2:6–11) makes the implicit distinction between "the form of God" (*morphē Theou*—a neo-Platonic precursor to "divine nature") and Jesus Christ (who had the "form of God" and also took on the form of a servant—*morphē doulou*). Similarly, John 1:1–2 makes an implicit distinction between "the Word" (the Son) and "ho Theos" (with the definite article—*the* Father), who are divine *Persons*, and *Theos* (without the definite article—"divine *nature*"). See Chapter 6, Section III, for a detailed explanation.

there must be at least one uncaused cause, existing through itself, in order for everything else to exist (see Volume II, Appendix II, Section I, step 1 of the Thomistic metaphysical proof). We then showed in steps 2 and 3 of the Thomistic metaphysical proof that there can be *no restriction* in "an acting power existing through itself", because that restriction could not exist through itself and would therefore have to be caused. Thus a pure "acting power existing through itself" must be unrestricted.[2]

In step 4 of the Thomistic metaphysical proof, we showed that an *unrestricted* acting power would have to be *unique* (one and only one), because two unrestricted acting powers is a contradiction.[3] We might summarize that proof as follows: Suppose there are two unrestricted powers. Then one of them would have to have something, or be something, or be somewhere, or be in some other dimension that the other one was *not*. If there were no difference of any kind between the two unrestricted powers—no difference as to power, act, qualities, space-time point, dimension, and so on—then they would be the *self-same* power; in other words, they would be only *one*.

Now consider the following. If there has to be some difference between the two unrestricted powers (in order for them to be "two"), and that difference requires that one of the "unrestricted" powers *not* have "something", *not* be "something", *not* be at a particular space-time point, or *not* be in a particular dimension—then the one that does *not* have or *is* not those "things" would have to be *finite* (*restricted*), because it *lacks* something that the other one has. Therefore, every hypothetical *second* unrestricted power is a contradiction, a "restricted-unrestricted power", which is impossible. Hence, there can only be one *unrestricted power*, meaning that there can only be one nature in God. The power and nature of God must be unique.

The Church councils of Nicaea (A.D. 325) and Chalcedon (A.D. 451) were well aware that there could be only one unrestricted power, and therefore, one nature in God, and so they knew that they would have to clarify how there could be three "Persons" in that one unrestricted power and nature. They were also aware

---

[2] See Volume II, Appendix II, Section I, steps 3 and 4 of the Thomistic metaphysical proof.
[3] See Volume II, Appendix II, Section I, step 4 of the Thomistic metaphysical proof.

that the one unrestricted power and nature of God could not have become incarnate (i.e., could not have taken on a human or finite form), because that would imply a contradiction, a "restricted unrestricted reality" or a "finite infinite reality". The Church never advocated such a contradictory position, but instead advocated that the second *Person* of the Trinity (the Son) became incarnate.

So how might we distinguish the one unrestricted power and nature of God from the three Persons within that one nature? Recall that the three Persons cannot be "unrestricted powers or natures" (implying three Gods), because there can only be one unrestricted power and nature (for the reasons mentioned above). Furthermore, the "three Persons" cannot be *parts* within the one unrestricted power and nature of God, because that would imply *restrictions* (to make the parts) within that one *unrestricted* power and nature. So how can we understand "person" so that we do not confuse it with "the one unrestricted power and nature of God" or "a part within the one unrestricted power and nature of God"? The idea of "*self-consciousness*" has considerable explanatory potential.

B. "Person" and Self-Consciousness

The Church declared the Father, Son, and Holy Spirit to be "divine persons". Jean Galot presents a penetrating explanation of "person" as "the subject of *consciousness* and freedom",[4] from which we can provide a basic resolution to the tension in the Christian claim that there are "*three* Persons in the *one* God". Following Galot's insight that "person signifies self-consciousness", we can make a fundamental distinction between the "*one* unrestricted power (nature) of God" and the "*three Persons* (who may be seen as 'distinct acts of self-consciousness making use of that one unrestricted power')". Let us begin with the idea of "person as self-consciousness".

How might "self-consciousness" be understood? Let us begin with "consciousness". Recall from Volume II (Chapter 6) that consciousness is an act of awareness of, or attention to, a specific content. For

[4] See Jean Galot, *Who Is Christ? A Theology of the Incarnation* (Chicago: Franciscan Herald, 1980), p. 284.

example, I am aware of the computer in front of me. Now, when I attend to the computer, everything else within my visual field moves into the background, and my act of consciousness, as it were, moves only the computer (as the only item of interest) into the foreground.

Self-consciousness is awareness of one's awareness, a consciousness of one's consciousness, or a grasping of one's act of grasping. For example, I am not only aware of my computer; I am also aware of being *aware* of my computer. It is as if I doubled back on myself and caught myself catching the computer or grasped myself grasping the computer.

I can even be aware of being aware of my awareness (that is, aware of my *self*-awareness). Seemingly, I have the power not only to grasp my grasping of the computer, but also to grasp myself grasping myself.

This remarkable power seems to defy *physical* explanation, because it can be in two relative positions with respect to itself simultaneously (see Volume II, Chapter 6, Section III.C). If we use a spatial analogy to describe it (which cannot describe it perfectly), it would be like my consciousness doubling back on itself at an *infinite* velocity, so that it can be "inside" itself, and even inside itself inside itself. But my objective here is not to address the specialness of this power of self-awareness or self-consciousness within the world of physical limits, but only to point to the *effects* of this power—namely, its capacity to create an inner world or "inner universe".

This power enables me to divide consciously the world into two parts: "my inner world", and "the world out there", which gives rise to two fundamental drives: to bring the outer world under the control or dominion of my inner world (ego-control), or to invest my inner world in the outer world—that is, to give my inner world over to the good and enhancement of the outer world (love).

Love requires self-consciousness. Recall for a moment that love, according to Jesus, is "gift of self", and it is evident that I cannot give myself away unless I have appropriated myself, and I cannot appropriate myself unless I am aware of myself. The same holds true for ego-control. If I wish to dominate another, I must first appropriate the "I" that will do the dominating, and this requires self-awareness. Thus, self-awareness might be viewed as a mixed blessing, for it empowers both love and ego-control, the freedom to give oneself away or to impose one's will on others.

Now, let us return to the matter of the Trinity. As noted earlier, there can be *only one* unrestricted power, but Christian revelation holds that there are three Persons in this one power. If we follow the clue given by Jean Galot and associate "person" with "self-consciousness", then we might say that there are three distinct acts of self-consciousness sharing in the one unrestricted power and nature. This is not contradictory because an unrestricted power can accommodate multiple acts of self-consciousness. We might characterize this as three distinct acts of self-consciousness (Father, Son, and Spirit) making an unconditional use of the one unrestricted power. The one unrestricted power acts as a single "power source" for the three distinct acts of self-consciousness. Notice that the Church is not postulating three unrestricted powers (which would be intrinsically contradictory), but only one unrestricted power of which the three distinct acts of self-consciousness are making an unconditional use.

II. Making Sense of the Trinity

What are these three distinct acts of self-consciousness doing (according to Christian revelation)? In addition to making an unconditional use of the one unrestricted power (nature), they are in *love*. The clue to this is found in the Father's twofold name for the Son: "This is my Son, the beloved one (*ho agapētos*)".[5] The reader will notice

---

[5] See the use of *ho agapētos* (the beloved one) as the Father's name for Jesus in the Baptism and Transfiguration stories of Matthew, Mark, and Luke (Mt 3:17; 17:5; Mk 1:11; 9:7; Lk 3:22; 20:13). John's Gospel elaborates this: "The Father loves the Son, and has given all things into his hand" (Jn 3:35); "For the Father loves the Son, and shows him all that he himself is doing" (Jn 5:20); "As the Father has loved me ..." (Jn 15:9); "[Y]ou [Father] have sent me and loved them even as you have loved me" (Jn 17:23); "Father, I desire that they also, whom you have given me, may be with me where I am, to behold my glory which you have given me in *your love for me* before the foundation of the world" (Jn 17:24; emphasis mine); "I have made known to them your name, and I will make it known, that the love with which you have loved me may be in them, and I in them" (Jn 17:26). This is confirmed by Jesus' self-reference as "the beloved son" in the Parable of the Wicked Tenants (Lk 20:13). Note also Saint Paul's many references to the love between the Father and the Son. In Romans 5:8, he shows the love between the Father and the Son in the love given to us in Christ's sacrificial death: "God shows his love for us in that while we were yet sinners Christ died for us." Again, in Romans 8:38–39, the love between the Father and the Son is manifest in the love of God, which cannot be separated from us in Christ: "[N]either death ... nor anything else in all creation, will be able to separate us from the love of God [the Father] in Christ Jesus our Lord."

the familiar root *agapē* in *ho agapētos* (the beloved one). Inasmuch as the three distinct acts of self-consciousness are capable of making an unconditional use of the one infinite power source, they are also capable of three distinct *unconditional* acts of love.

If the Son's core identity is the Beloved One, then it stands to reason that the Father's core identity is the Lover of the Beloved One. The Father (the first act of self-consciousness) loves the Son (the Beloved One, the second act of self-consciousness) in an *unconditional* way, because this is commensurate with His unconditional use of the one unrestricted power.

When the Son (the Beloved, the second act of self-consciousness) receives the love of the Father, He is completely aware of the goodness and beauty of the Father's love, and responds to the Father with all His love (which includes the love arising out of His being beloved by the Father). Like the Father, the Son is making an unconditional use of the one infinite power; so His act of love is also unconditional. Thus, the two Persons form a unity of interpersonal love through the one unrestricted power (nature). The Father is a "giver-receiver", while the Son is a "receiver-giver".

But what about the Holy Spirit? The Holy Spirit (the third distinct act of self-consciousness) is also a beloved, but not simply the beloved of *either* the Father *or* the Son. The Spirit is beloved of the *union* between the Father and the Son.[6]

---

[6]John strongly implies this in Jesus' final discourse with His disciples: "I will ask the Father, and he will give you another Counselor, to be with you for ever, even the Spirit of truth ... for he dwells with you, and will *be in you*. ... In that day you will know that I am in my Father, and you in me, and I in you. ... *[W]e* will come to him and make *our* home with him" (Jn 14:16–17, 20, 23; emphasis mine). Notice the parallel between the Spirit being *in* the disciples and the Father and the Son being *in* the disciples, implying that the Spirit proceeds from the love between the Father and the Son.

Paul also implies that the Spirit proceeds from the love of the Father and the Son. In Romans 5:5, Paul shows the unity of the Father and the Spirit through the love poured into our hearts: "God's [the *Father's*] love has been poured into our hearts through the *Holy Spirit* who has been given to us"; in Galatians 5:22, 24, he shows the unity between Christ and the Holy Spirit in the overcoming of the desire of the flesh: "[T]he fruit of the *Spirit* is love. ... And those who belong to *Christ Jesus* have crucified the flesh with its passions and desires" (emphasis mine). But Paul goes beyond the unity of Father and Spirit, and the unity of Christ and Spirit. He shows that the unity between the Father and the Son is also in loving union with the Spirit (Rom 15:30): "I appeal to you, brethren, by our *Lord Jesus Christ* and by the love of the *Spirit*, to strive together with me in your prayers to God [the *Father*]" (emphasis mine).

How does the union of the Father and the Son love? Love always acts beyond itself. When love is from an individual, it is termed "gift of self"; but love need not be only an outpouring of *self*—it can also be an outpouring of an *"us"* (that is, a union among selves). This occurs in marriage where a couple can give its "us" (its collective self) to another person by welcoming that person into the relationship. One can generally tell when a couple has this loving quality as a relational whole because their invitation is harmonious and welcoming. If this loving quality of the "us" is not there, or if there is a problem causing a disruption of the relationship, it is immediately discernable. But when this quality is present, it constitutes a new relationship between the "us" and another beloved. When this other beloved receives the love of the "us", he returns it (much like a child or a friend) to the union (the *collective* self), not merely to the *individual* selves (separately). When a child, for example, reflects love back to his parents, it is qualitatively different than reflecting it back to one parent or another (independently of their relationship). The Holy Spirit, then, is the "beloved of the union between the Father and the Son". The Spirit is welcomed into the love of their relationship and reflects this love back to them (in their relationship to one another). The Holy Spirit completes the loving relationship within the Trinity just as a child completes the loving relationship within a family. Just as a child brings fulfillment and joy to the parents (through their love for the child), so also the love of the Holy Spirit brings completion and joy to the love of the Father and the Son (through their love of the Spirit).

Therefore, when Christians say that God is love, they do not mean only that the attribute of love belongs to the one infinite nature of God; they mean that there is real *interpersonal* love (gift of self and gift of the "us") taking place through three perfect acts of self-consciousness, making unconditional use of the one unrestricted power.

III. Making Sense of the Incarnation

As implied above, the Incarnation does not mean that the one unrestricted power and nature of God became human (finite/restricted), because that would be intrinsically contradictory. Rather, Christian tradition declares that the second *Person* (*self-consciousness*, making an unconditional use of the one unrestricted power and nature) entered into a finite human nature.

Self-consciousness can act through either an infinite nature or a finite nature, but it will take on the conditions of the power or nature in which it inheres. If self-consciousness inheres (makes use of) a finite nature, it will be subject to the limitations of that nature. However, if self-consciousness inheres in (makes use of) an *unrestricted* power and nature, then there is no limit to the power of its understanding, creativity, freedom, and will.

Thus, when the *Son* (second self-consciousness) makes use of His unrestricted nature, His acts of understanding, creativity, and will are similarly unrestricted. However, when the Son inheres in a finite nature (appropriated after the Incarnation), His understanding, creativity, and will are limited by the restrictions of that finite nature.

For this reason, Christianity holds that Jesus Christ, after the Incarnation, is *one Person* (one self-consciousness having one inner domain from which free acts can arise) who makes use of *two natures*, one unrestricted and the other restricted. Hence, the one Person of the Son is both true God and true man.

Christianity holds that the second Person (self-consciousness) did not stop using the divine nature when He took on the limitations of human nature, but rather continued operating through His divine nature so that the one self-consciousness had the perspective, understanding, and will of *both* an unrestricted nature and a restricted and finite nature.

One might ask the question of how a single self-consciousness could have two such different perspectives. One analogy that comes to mind is our dream state, but I hesitate to use it, because it presents so many disanalogous elements. If one bears in mind that the Incarnation is not anything like a human dream state, but a human dream state illustrates how one self-consciousness can have two different perspectives, then perhaps the analogy may render some benefit.

When I am dreaming, my self-consciousness (self-awareness) does not exit out of my material body. Rather, while present to my "real world body", my self-consciousness enters into a dream world with states and laws quite different from the physical world. I might be able to fly, run the one-hundred-yard dash in less than nine seconds (not likely in my condition within the physical world), and even quarterback better than Joe Montana. I can feel fear and elation within that world, which is not commensurate with anything going on in the physical world. Nevertheless, the fear seems quite real, even when my self-consciousness experiences it in the dream world.

One might use this analogy (recognizing its limitations) to think of the second Person (self-consciousness) in the Trinity. While still using His unrestricted power, He enters into His thought of creation, and takes on the particularity of Jesus of Nazareth. The self-consciousness of the Son does not have to stop using His infinite nature in order to enter into the perspective of a finite nature any more than my self-consciousness has to leave my physical body in order to enter into a dream world with altogether different laws and perspectives.

IV. Conclusion

If the above analysis has not thoroughly confused the reader, consider three essential themes that show how Jesus' revelation of the Trinity and Incarnation connect with His (and the Father's) unconditional love:

1. The Trinity is the interpersonal love taking place among three Persons (self-consciousnesses) making an unconditional use of the one unrestricted, divine power (nature). These three Persons relate to each other as follows: the Father loves the Son, while the Son receives the love of the Father and returns it to Him. The loving relationship between the Father and the Son constitutes a unity, which unity gives itself to another beloved (the Spirit) who receives the love of the Father and the Son (in their unity), and returns it to them (collectively).

2. Jesus-Emmanuel is not the one unrestricted *nature* of God becoming human (finite). Rather, He is the second Person (*self-consciousness*—the Son, the Beloved) of the Trinity entering into a finite human nature.

3. The reason why the second Person of the Trinity entered human nature was to achieve a face-to-face, peer-to-peer relationship

with humanity, a perfect act of empathy arising out of His *unconditional love*. Why else would the second self-consciousness subject Himself to finitude, transitoriness, and pain[7] when He could have avoided these restrictions and sufferings by remaining within the infinite divine nature alone? Only the "logic of *unconditional love*" can explain this self-sacrifice, which He turns into *complete* self-sacrifice through His Passion and death.

Thus it seems that the interpersonal love of the Trinity desires to move out of itself into the domain of creatures through the Person of the Beloved, who can make us co-beloveds in His union with the Father and the Spirit, and can give us His Spirit to course through our community and bring that community back to the Father as perfect gift. This is the logic of love, or better, the logic of *unconditional love*.

[7] Self-emptying, *kenosis*; see Philippians 2:7.

BIBLIOGRAPHY

Ambrose. *De obitu Valent*. In *The Fundamentals of Catholic Dogma*, by Ludwig Ott, translated by Patrick Lynch. Rockford, Ill.: Tan Books, 1955.

Antonacci, Mark. "Appendix F: Fire Simulation Model". *The Resurrection of the Shroud: New Scientific, Medical, and Archeological Evidence*. New York: M. Evans, 1998.

Augustine. *Confessions*. Translated by Henry Chadwick. New York: Oxford University Press, 1991.

———. *De Baptismo Contra Donatistas Libri Septem*. In *The Fundamentals of Catholic Dogma*, by Ludwig Ott, translated by Patrick Lynch. Rockford, Ill.: Tan Books and Publishers, 1955.

Aquinas, Thomas. *The Summa Theologica of St. Thomas Aquinas*. Translated by the Fathers of the English Dominican Province. New York: Benziger Brothers, 1947.

Aune, David E. "Magic in Early Christianity". In *Aufstieg und Niedergang der römischen Welt*, edited by Wolfgang Haase, II, 23.2, pp. 1507–57. Berlin: Walter de Gruyter, 1980.

Barbet, Pierre. *A Doctor at Calvary: The Passion of Our Lord Jesus Christ as Described by a Surgeon*. New York: P.J. Kennedy, 1953.

Barrett, Jim. "Science and the Shroud Microbiology Meets Archaeology in a Renewed Quest for Answers". *Mission*, Spring 1996. http://www.sindone.info/BARRETT.PDF.

Bennett, Jonathan Francis. *Rationality: An Essay towards an Analysis*. 1964. Reprint, Indianapolis: Hackett, 1989.

Bernhard, Andrew, trans. "The Infancy Gospel of Thomas". In *Other Early Christian Gospels: A Critical Edition of the Surviving Greek Manuscripts*. T&T Clark Library of Biblical Studies. London; New York: T&T Clark, 2006. http://gnosis.org/library/inftoma.htm.

Betz, Johannes. "Eucharist". In *Sacramentum Mundi*, edited by Karl Rahner, 2:257–67. London: Burns and Oates, 1968.

Bromiley, Geoffrey. *The International Standard Bible Encyclopedia.* Grand Rapids, Mich.: William B. Eerdmans, 1988.

Brown, Raymond. *The Death of the Messiah: From Gethsemane to the Grave; A Commentary on the Passion Narratives in the Four Gospels.* New York: Doubleday, 1994.

———. *The Gospel according to John XIII-XXI.* Vol. 2. In *The Anchor Bible,* vol. 29A. New York: Doubleday, 1970.

———. *An Introduction to New Testament Christology.* New York: Paulist Press, 1994.

———. *The Virginal Conception and Bodily Resurrection of Jesus.* New York: Paulist Press, 1973.

Burpo, Todd, and Lynn Vincent. "Jesus *Really* Loves the Children". Chapter 19 in *Heaven Is for Real: A Little Boy's Astounding Story of His Trip to Heaven and Back.* Nashville: Thomas Nelson, 2010.

Callaway, Ewen. "Sex and Violence Linked in the Brain". *Nature News,* February 9, 2011. http://www.nature.com/news/2011/110209/full/news.2011.82.html.

Catechism of Catholic Church. 2nd ed. Washington, D.C.: Libreria Editrice Vaticana—United States Conference of Catholic Bishops, 2000.

Catholic News Agency. "Experts Question Scientist's Claim of Reproducing Shroud of Turin", October 6, 2009. http://www.catholicnewsagency.com/news/experts_question_scientists_claim_of_reproducing_shroud_of_turin?.

Cerfaux, Lucien. "L hymne au Christ-Serviteur de Dieu (Phil., II, 6–11 - Is., LII, 13,–LIII, 12)". In *Miscellanea historica in honorem Alberti de Meyer Universitatis Catholicae in oppido Lovaniensi iam annos XXV professoris,* 1:117–30. Louvain: Bibliothèque de l'Université, 1946.

Charles, R. H. *Apocrypha and Pseudepigrapha of the Old Testament.* Oxford: Oxford University Press, 1913.

Charlesworth, James H., ed. *Jesus and Archaeology.* Grand Rapids, Mich.: William B. Eerdmans, 2006.

———. "Jesus Research and Archaeology: A New Perspective". In *Jesus and Archaeology,* edited by James H. Charlesworth, pp. 30–50. Grand Rapids, Mich.: William B. Eerdmans, 2006.

Coles, Robert. *The Spiritual Life of Children.* New York: Mariner Books, 1991.

Cornwall, M., S.L. Albrecht, P.H. Cunningham, and B.L. Pitcher. "The Dimensions of Religiosity: A Conceptual Model with an

Empirical Test". *Review of Religious Research* 27, no. 3 (1986): 266–44.

Danin, Avinoam. "Pressed Flowers". *Eretz Magazine* 55 (1997): https://www.shroud.com/danin.htm.

D'Arcy, Martin. *The Mind and Heart of Love: Lion and Unicorn; A Study in Eros and Agape*. New York: Meridian Books, 1956.

Davis, Stephen T. "Is Belief in the Resurrection Rational?" *Philo* 2 (1999): 51–61.

De Gail, Paul. "Paul Vignon". *Shroud Spectrum International*, no. 6 (1983). https://www.shroud.com/pdfs/ssio6part7.pdf.

Denzinger, H., and A. Schönmetzer. *Enchiridion Symbolorum*. New York: Herder, 1965.

Dervic, Kanita, Maria A. Oquendo, Michael F. Grunebaum, Steve Ellis, Ainsley Burke, and J. John Mann. "Religious Affiliation and Suicide Attempt". *American Journal of Psychiatry* 161, no. 12 (December 2004): 2303–8. http://ajp.psychiatryonline.org/article.aspx?articleid=177228.

Di Lazzaro, Paolo, D. Murra, A. Santoni, G. Fanti, E. Nichelatti, and G. Baldacchini. "Deep Ultraviolet Radiation Simulates the Turin Shroud Image". *Journal of Imaging Science and Technology*, July-August 2010, pp. 40302-1–40302-6. www.ingentaconnect.com/content/ist/jist/2010/00000054/00000004/art00003.

Dodd, C. H. *The Apostolic Preaching and Its Developments*. New York: Harper and Brothers, 1962.

Dunn, James D. G. *Jesus and the Spirit: A Study of the Religious and Charismatic Experience of Jesus and the First Christians as Reflected in the New Testament*. Philadelphia: Westminster Press, 1975.

———. *The Partings of Ways between Christianity and Judaism and Their Significance for the Character of Christianity*. London: SCM, 1991.

Eliade, Mircea. *The Myth of the Eternal Return: Or, Cosmos and History*. Princeton, N.J.: Princeton University Press, 1971.

———. *Myths, Dreams, and Mysteries*. New York: Harper and Row, 1975.

———. *The Sacred and the Profane: The Nature of Religion*. New York: Harcourt Brace Jovanovich, 1987.

Fanti, Giulio, and Saverio Gaeta. *Il Mistero della Sindone: Le Sorprendenti Scoperte Scientifiche sull'enigma del Telo di Gesu*. Milan: Editore Rizzoli, 2013.

Fanti, Giulio, and R. Maggiolo. "The Double Superficiality of the Frontal Image on the Turin Shroud". *Journal of Optics A: Pure and Applied Optics* 6, no. 6 (2004): 491–503.

Ferch, Shan Ray. *Forgiveness and Power in the Age of Atrocity: Servant Leadership as a Way of Life*. Lanham, Md.: Lexington Books, 2011.

Fitzmyer, Joseph A. "The Aramaic Background of Philippians 2:6–11". *The Catholic Biblical Quarterly* 50 (1988): 470–83.

———. "Pauline Theology". In *The New Jerome Biblical Commentary*, edited by Raymond E. Brown, Joseph A. Fitzmyer, and Roland E. Murphy, pp. 1382–416. Englewood Cliffs, N.J.: Prentice Hall, 1990.

Flannery, Austin. *Vatican Council II, Vol. 1: The Conciliar and Postconciliar Documents*. Northport, N.Y.: Costello Publishing, 1975.

Frei, Max. "Identificazione e classificazione dei nuovi pollini della Sindone". *La Sindone, Scienza e Fede, Atti del II Convegno Nazionale di Sindonologia*, Bologna, November 27–29, 1981; CLUEB, Bologna 1983, pp. 277–28.

Fry, Roger. "Retrospect". In *Vision and Design*, edited by J.B. Bullen, pp. 199–212. Mineola, N.Y.: Dover, 1998.

Fuller, Reginald H. *The Formation of the Resurrection Narratives*. New York: Macmillan, 1971.

Galot, Jean. *Who Is Christ? A Theology of the Incarnation*. Chicago: Franciscan Herald Press, 1980.

Greenleaf, Robert K., Larry C. Spears, and Stephen R. Covey. *Servant Leadership: A Journey into the Nature of Legitimate Power and Greatness*. Mahwah, N.J.: Paulist Press, 2002.

Groeschel, Benedict. *Spiritual Passages: The Psychology of Spiritual Development*. New York: Crossroads, 1984.

Gunkel, H. *Die Wirkungen des heiligen Geistes nach der populären Anschauung der apostolischen Zeit und nach der Lehre des Apostels Paulus*. Göttingen, 1888.

Guscin, Mark. "The Sudarium of Oviedo: Its History and Relationship to the Shroud of Turin". *Proceedings of the Nice Symposium on the Shroud of Turin*, May 1997. https://www.shroud.com/guscin.htm#top.

Habermas, Gary R. "Mapping the Recent Trend toward the Bodily Resurrection Appearances of Jesus in Light of Other Prominent Critical Positions". In *The Resurrection of Jesus: John Dominic*

Crossan and N. T. Wright in Dialogue, edited by Robert B. Stewart, pp. 78–92. Minneapolis: Fortress Press, 2006.

Haralick, Robert M. *Analysis of Digital Images of the Shroud of Turin*. Blacksburg, Va.: Publication of Spatial Data Analysis Laboratory Virginia Polytechnic Institute and State University, 1983.

Harvey, Anthony Ernest. *Jesus and the Constraints of History: The Bampton Lectures, 1980*. London: Duckworth, 1982.

Heiler, Friedrich. "The History of Religions as a Preparation for the Cooperation of Religions". In *The History of Religions*, edited by Mircea Eliade and J. Kitagawa, pp. 142–53. Chicago: Chicago University Press, 1959.

Heller, John, and A. Adler. "Blood on the Shroud of Turin". *Applied Optics* 19, no. 16 (1980): 2742–44.

Hengel, Martin. *Acts and the History of Earliest Christianity*. Translated by John Bowden. Philadelphia: Fortress Press, 1980.

Heras, Guillermo, J. Villalain, and J. Rodriguez. *Comparative Studies of the Sudarium of Oviedo and the Shroud of Turin*. Turin: III Congreso Internazionale de Studi sulla Sindone, 1998. http://www.teachingfaith.com/files/books/Sudarium.PDF.

Hillenbrand, Laura. *Unbroken: A World War II Story of Survival, Resilience and Redemption*. New York: Random House, 2010.

Hilton, Donald L., Jr. "Pornography Addiction—A Supranormal Stimulus Considered in the Context of Neuroplasticity". *Socioaffective Neuroscience and Psychology* 3 (July 19, 2013). http://www.socioaffectiveneuroscipsychol.net/index.php/snp/article/view/20767/29179.

Hurd, R. Scott. *Forgiveness: A Catholic Approach*. Los Angeles: Pauline Books, 2011.

Iannone, John. "The Shroud of Turin—Evidence it is Authentic". *New Geology*, 2015. http://www.newgeology.us/presentation24.html.

Ignatius of Loyola. *The Spiritual Exercises of St. Ignatius*. Translated by Louis J. Puhl, S.J. Chicago: Loyola University Press, 1951.

International Association for Near-Death Studies. "Distressing Near-Death Experiences". Last updated July 17, 2012. http://iands.org/about-ndes/distressing-ndes.html#a.

Isenberg, Wesley W., trans. "The Gospel of Philip". In *The Nag Hammadi Library in English*, rev. ed., edited by James M. Robinson. San

Francisco: HarperCollins, 1990. http://www.gnosis.org/naghamm
/gop.html.

Jackson, John P. "Is the Image on the Shroud Due to a Process Heretofore Unknown to Modern Science?" *Shroud Spectrum International*, no. 34 (March 1990): 3–29.

———. "An Unconventional Hypothesis to Explain All Image
Characteristics Found on the Shroud Image". In *History, Science,
Theology and the Shroud*, edited by A. Berard. St. Louis: Symposium Proceedings, 1991. http://theshroudofturin.blogspot.com
/2012/01/john-p-jackson-unconventional.html.

Jackson, John, E.J. Jumper, and W.R. Ercoline. "Correlation of
Image Intensity on the Turin Shroud with the 3-D Structure
of a Human Body Shape". *Applied Optics* 23, no. 14 (July 15,
1984): 2244–70.

———. "Three Dimensional Characteristic of the Shroud Image".
*IEEE 1982 Proceedings of the International Conference on Cybernetics
and Society*, October 1982, pp. 559–75.

Jackson, John P., and Keith E. Propp. "Comments on Rogers' 'Testing the Jackson Theory' of Image Formation". Shroud of Turin
Website, 2004. http://www.shroud.com/pdfs/jacksonpropp.pdf.

James, M.R., trans. "The Gospel of Peter". In *The Apocryphal New
Testament*. Oxford: Clarendon Press, 1924. http://www.gnosis.org
/library/gospete.htm.

Jeremias, Joachim. *The Eucharistic Words of Jesus*. London: SCM Press,
1966.

———. *Heiligengräber in Jesu Umwelt (Mt. 23, 29; Lk. 11, 47): eine
Untersuchung zur Volksreligion der Zeit Jesu*. Göttingen: Vandenhoeck and Ruprecht, 1958.

———. *New Testament Theology*. Vol. 1. New York: Charles Scribner's Sons, 1971.

———. *The Parables of Jesus*. London: SCM Press, 1972.

———. "The Problem of the Historical Jesus". In *In Search of the
Historical Jesus*, edited by Harvey K. McArthur, pp. 125–30. London: Charles Scribner's Sons, 1969.

Johann, Robert, S.J. *The Meaning of Love*. Glen Rock, N.J.: Paulist
Press, 1966.

John of the Cross. "The Living Flame of Love". In *The Collected
Works of St. John of the Cross*, translated by Kieran Kavanaugh and

Otilio Rodriguez, pp. 613–718. Washington, D.C.: ICS Publications, 1979.

Johnson, Luke Timothy. *The Gospel according to Luke*. Sacra Pagina Series, edited by Daniel J. Harrington, vol. 3. Collegeville, Minn.: Liturgical Press, 1991.

Jones, Stephen E. "New Tests by Prof. Giulio Fanti Show the Shroud of Turin Could Date from the Time of Christ". *Shroud of Turin* (blog), April 2, 2013. http://theshroudofturin.blogspot.com/2013/04/new-tests-by-prof-giulio-fanti-show.html.

Josephus, Flavius. *Jewish Antiquities*. Edited and translated by Louis H. Feldman. Loeb Classical Library. Cambridge, Mass.: Harvard University Press, 1965.

Jumper, Eric J. "An Overview of the Testing Performed by the Shroud of Turin Research Project with a Summary of Results". *IEEE 1982 Proceedings of the International Conference on Cybernetics and Society*, October 1982, pp. 535–37.

Jumper, Eric J., A. Adler, J. Jackson, S. Pellicori, J. Heller, and J. R. Drusik. "A Comprehensive Examination of the Various Stains and Images on the Shroud of Turin". *Archaeological Chemistry III, ACS Advances in Chemistry*, no. 205 (1984): 447–76.

Jumper, Eric J., and R. W. Mottern. "Scientific Investigation of the Shroud of Turin". *Applied Optics* 19, no. 12 (1980): 1909–12.

Karris, Robert J. "The Gospel according to Luke". In *The New Jerome Biblical Commentary*, edited by Raymond E. Brown, Joseph A. Fitzmyer, and Roland E. Murphy, pp. 675–721. Englewood Cliffs, N.J.: Prentice Hall, 1990.

Keener, Craig. *Miracles: The Credibility of the New Testament*. 2 vols. Grand Rapids, Mich.: Baker Academic Publishing, 2011.

Kirby, Peter. "Cornelius Tacitus". *Early Christian Writings*. Accessed October 16, 2015. http://www.earlychristianwritings.com/tacitus.html.

Krohn, Paysach. *Bris Milah: Circumcision*. Artscroll Mesorah Series. Brooklyn: Mesorah Publications, 1986. http://www.torah.org/features/par-kids/names.html.

Küng, Hans. *On Being a Christian*. Translated by Edward Quinn. Glascow: Fount Paperbacks, 1978.

Latourelle, René. *Finding Jesus through the Gospels: History and Hermeneutics*. New York: Alba House, 1979.

Lepp, Ignace. *The Psychology of Loving*. New York: Mentor-Omega Books, 1963.

Lewis, C. S. *The Four Loves*. New York: Harcourt, 1960.

———. *The Great Divorce*. New York: HarperOne, 2009.

———. *Surprised by Joy: The Shape of My Early Life*. New York: Harcourt, Brace, Jovanovich, 1966.

Lin, Dayu, Maureen P. Boyle, Piotr Dollar, Hyosang Lee, E. S. Lein, Pietro Perona, and David J. Anderson. "Functional Identification of an Aggression Locus in the Mouse Hypothalamus". *Nature* 470 (February 10, 2011): 221–26.

Lohmeyer, Ernst. "Kyrios Jesus: Eine Untersuchung zu Phil 2:5–11". *Sitzungsberichte der Heidelberger Akademie der Wissenschaften, Philosophisch-historische Klasse* 1927–28/4. Heidelberg: Winter, 1928.

Lonergan, Bernard. *Insight: A Study of Human Understanding*. In *Collected Works of Bernard Lonergan* 3, edited by Frederick E. Crowe and Robert M. Doran. Toronto: University of Toronto Press, 1992.

———. *Method in Theology*. New York: Herder and Herder, 1972.

———. *Verbum: Word and Idea in Aquinas*. In *Collected Works of Bernard J. F. Lonergan*, vol. 2, edited by Frederick E. Crowe. Toronto: University of Toronto Press, 1994.

Long, John. "The Shroud of Turin's Earlier History: Part One: To Edessa". *Bible and Spade*, Spring 2007. http://www.biblearchaeology.org/post/2013/03/14/The-Shroud-of-Turins-Earlier-History-Part-One-To-Edessa.aspx.

———. "The Shroud of Turin's Earlier History: Part Three: The Shroud of Constantinople". Associates for Biblical Research, March 28, 2013. http://www.biblearchaeology.org/post/2013/03/28/The-Shroud-of-Turins-Earlier-History-Part-Three-The-Shroud-of-Constantinople.aspx.

———. "The Shroud of Turin's Earlier History: Part Two: To the Great City". *Bible and Spade*, Fall 2007. http://www.biblearchaeology.org/post/2013/03/20/The-Shroud-of-Turins-Earlier-History-Part-Two-To-the-Great-City.aspx.

———. "The Shroud of Turin's Earlier History: Part 4: To Little Lirey". Associates for Biblical Research, September 5, 2013. http://www.biblearchaeology.org/post/2013/09/05/The-Shroud-of-Turins-Earlier-History-Part-4-To-Little-Lirey.aspx.

Lüdemann, Gerd. *The Resurrection of Jesus: History, Experience, Theology*. Translated by John Bowden. Minneapolis: Fortress Press, 1994.

Mally, Edward J. "The Gospel according to Mark". In *The Jerome Biblical Commentary*, edited by Raymond Brown, Joseph A. Fitmyer, and Roland E. Murphy, 2:21–61. Englewood Cliffs, N.J.: Prentice-Hall, 1968.

Maloney, P.C. "A Contribution toward a History of Botanical Research on the Shroud of Turin". In *Proceedings of the 1999 Shroud of Turin International Research Conference*, pp. 241–66. Richmond: Magisterium Press, 2000.

Marinelli, Emanuela. "The Question of Pollen Grains on the Shroud of Turin and the Sudarium of Oviedo". Shroud.com. Accessed November 4, 2015. https://www.shroud.com/pdfs/marinelli2veng.pdf.

Marxsen, Willi. *The Resurrection of Jesus of Nazareth*. Translated by Margaret Kohl. Philadelphia: Fortress Press, 1970.

McArthur, Harvey K., ed. "Basic Issues: A Survey of Recent Gospel Research". In *In Search of the Historical Jesus*, edited by H.K. McArthur, pp. 138–42. London: Charles Scribner's Sons, 1969.

———. *In Search of the Historical Jesus*. London: Charles Scribner's Sons, 1969.

McKenzie, John L. *Dictionary of the Bible*. New York: Macmillan, 1965.

———. "The Gospel according to Matthew". In *The Jerome Biblical Commentary*, edited by Raymond Brown, Joseph A. Fitzmyer, and Roland E. Murphy, 2:62–114. Englewood Cliffs, N.J.: Prentice-Hall, 1968.

Meacham, William, and Roger Sparks. "C-14 Debate from the Shroud Newsgroup: alt.turin-shroud". Shroud.com, February 4, 1998. http://www.shroud.com/c14debat.htm.

Meier, John P. *A Marginal Jew: Rethinking the Historical Jesus*. Vol. 1, *The Roots of the Problem and the Person*. New York: Doubleday, 1991.

———. *A Marginal Jew: Rethinking the Historical Jesus*. Vol. 2, *Mentor, Message, and Miracles*. New York: Doubleday, 1994.

———. "The Present State of the 'Third Quest' for the Historical Jesus: Loss and Gain". *Biblica* 80 (1999): 459–87.

Miller, Vernon, and S. Pellicori. "Ultraviolet Fluorescence Photography of the Shroud of Turin". *Journal of Biological Photography* 49, no. 3 (1981): 71–85.

Moody, Raymond A. *Life After Life*. New York: HarperCollins, 1975.

Mulder, Jack. *Kierkegaard and the Catholic Tradition*. Bloomington: Indiana University Press, 2010.

Mullins, Terence Y. "Jewish Wisdom Literature in the New Testament". *Journal of Biblical Literature* 68, no. 4 (1949): 335–39.

Murphy, Roland E. "Psalms". In *The Jerome Biblical Commentary*, edited by Raymond Brown, Joseph A. Fitmyer, and Roland E. Murphy, 569–602. Englewood Cliffs, N.J.: Prentice-Hall, 1968.

Newman, John Henry. *An Essay in Aid of a Grammar of Assent*. Notre Dame: University of Notre Dame Press, 1992.

———. *An Essay in Aid of a Grammar of Assent*. Worcester, Mass: Assumption Press, 2013.

———. *Sermons on Various Occasions*. London: Longmans, Green, 1908.

Ott, Ludwig. *The Fundamentals of Catholic Dogma*. Rockford, Ill.: Tan Books, 1955.

Otto, Rudolf. *The Idea of the Holy: An Inquiry into the Non-Rational Factor in the Idea of the Divine and Its Relation to the Rational*. New York: Oxford University Press, 1958.

Parnia, Sam, et al. "AWARE—AWAreness during REsuscitation—A Prospective Study". *Journal of Resuscitation*, October 6, 2014, pp. 1799–805. http://www.resuscitationjournal.com/article/S0300-9572%2814%2900739-4/fulltext.

Peck, M. Scott. *Glimpses of the Devil: A Psychiatrist's Personal Accounts of Possession, Exorcism, and Redemption*. New York: Simon and Schuster, 2005.

Pew Research Center. "The Global Religious Landscape". December 18, 2012. http://www.pewforum.org/2012/12/18/global-religious-landscape-exec.

Pieper, Josef. *About Love*. Translated by Richard Winston and Clara Winston. Chicago: Franciscan Herald Press, 1974.

Pitre, Brant. "Jesus, the Messianic Banquet, and the Kingdom of God". *Letter and Spirit* 5 (2009): 145–66.

Plato. *The Collected Dialogues of Plato*. Edited by Edith Hamilton and Huntington Cairns. Princeton, N.J.: Princeton University Press, 1961.

———. *Symposium and Phaedrus*. Translated by Benjamin Jowett. New York: Dover, 1993.

Powell, John. *Unconditional Love*. New York: Argus, 1978.

Prayer, Frances. "What Drives a Sex Addict? Is Sex Addiction about Love or an Insatiable Craving?" *Psychology Today*, October 7, 2009. http://www.psychologytoday.com/blog/love-doc/200910/what-drives-sex-addict.

Prostak, Sergio. "Scientists Suggest Turin Shroud Authentic". Sci-News.com, December 21, 2011. http://www.sci-news.com/physics/scientists-suggest-turin-shroud-authentic.html.

Quarles, Charles. "The Gospel of Peter: Does It Contain a Precanonical Resurrection Narrative?" In *The Resurrection of Jesus: John Dominic Crossan and N. T. Wright in Dialogue*, edited by Robert B. Stewart, pp. 106–20. Minneapolis: Fortress Press, 2006.

Rahner, Karl. *Foundations of Christian Faith*. New York: Crossroad, 1982.

———. *Spirit in the World*. New York: Herder and Herder, 1968.

———. *Spirit in the World*. Bloomsbury Academic, 1994.

Rigaux, Béda. "L'historicité de Jésus devant l'exégese récente". *Revue Biblique* 68 (1958): 481–522.

Rochais, Gérard. *Les Recits De Resurrection Des Morts Dans Le Nouveau Testament*. Cambridge: Cambridge University Press, 1981.

Rogers, Raymond N. "Shroud of Turin Guide to the Facts". 2004. https://shroudstory.wordpress.com/2012/02/26/introduction-to-ray-rogers-shroud-of-turin-faq/.

———. "Studies on the Radiocarbon Sample from the Shroud of Turin". *Thermochimica Acta* 425, nos. 1–2 (January 20, 2005): 189–94.

Sanders, E. P. *Jesus and Judaism*. Philadelphia: Fortress, 1985.

Scavone, Daniel C. 2008. "Besançon and Other Hypotheses for the Missing Years: The Shroud from 1200 to 1400". Shroud Science Group International Conference, Ohio State University, Columbus, August 14–17, 2008.

———. "Joseph of Arimathea, the Holy Grail, and the Edessa Icon". *Arthuriana* 9, no. 4 (Winter 1999): 3–31.

Seneca, Lucius. *De Clementia*. In *World Essays*, translated by John W. Basore, vol. 1. The Loeb Classical Library. London: W. Heinemann, 1928.

Shwortz, Barry. "The Image on the Shroud of Turin Is Not a Scorch". *Shroud of Turin* (blog), Shroudstory.com, February 10, 2012. http://shroudstor.com/2012/02/10/the-image-on-the-shroud-of-turin-is-not-a-scorch/.

Singer-Towns, Brian. *The Catholic Faith Handbook for Youth*. Winona, Minn.: St. Mary's Press, 2008.

Spitzer, Robert J. *Five Pillars of the Spiritual Life: A Practical Guide to Prayer for Active People*. San Francisco: Ignatius Press, 2008.

——. *Healing the Culture: A Common-Sense Philosophy of Happiness, Freedom, and the Life Issues*. San Francisco: Ignatius Press, 2000.

——. *Indications of Creation in Contemporary Big Bang Cosmology*. Vol. 10 of *Philosophy in Science*. Tucson: Pachart, 2003.

——. *New Proofs for the Existence of God: Contributions of Contemporary Physics and Philosophy*. Grand Rapids, Mich.: William B. Eerdmans, 2010.

Stein, Edith. *On the Problem of Empathy*. Translated by Waltraut Stein. Washington, D.C.: Institute of Carmelite Studies, 1989.

Stewart, Robert B., ed. *The Resurrection of Jesus: John Dominic Crossan and N. T. Wright in Dialogue*. Minneapolis: Fortress Press, 2006.

Stone, Michael E. *Fourth Ezra*. Minneapolis, Minn.: Fortress, 1990.

Suenens, Léon Joseph Cardinal. *Love and Control*. Westminster, Md.: Newman Press, 1962.

Tacitus, Cornelius. *Annals*. In *Complete Works of Tacitus,* edited by Alfred John Church and William Jackson Brodribb. New York: Random House, 1942. Perseus Digital Library. http://www.perseus.tufts.edu/hopper/text?doc=Perseus%3Atext%3A1999.02.0078%3Abook%3D15%3Achapter%3D44.

Tanqueray, Adolphe. *The Spiritual Life: A Treatise on Ascetical and Mystical Theology*. Rockford, Ill: Tan Books, 2013.

Teresa of Avila. "The Book of Her Life". In *The Collected Works of St. Teresa of Avila,* translated by Kieran Kavanaugh and Otilio Rodriguez, 1:31–308. Washington, D.C.: ICS Publications, 1976.

Torrey, Charles Cutler. *The Composition and Date of Acts*. Cambridge: Harvard University Press, 1916.

Turner, J. H. *The Institutional Order*. New York: Addison-Wesley Educational Publishers, 1997.

Underhill, Evelyn. *Mysticism: A Study in the Nature and Development of Spiritual Consciousness*. New York: Renaissance Classics, 2012.

Viviano, Benedict T., O.P. "The Gospel according to Matthew". In *The New Jerome Biblical Commentary*, edited by Raymond E. Brown, Joseph A. Fitzmyer, and Roland E. Murphy, pp. 630–74. Englewood Cliffs, N.J.: Prentice-Hall, 1990.

———. "Why Shroud of Turin's Secrets Continue to Elude Science". *National Geographic*, April 17, 2015. http://news.nationalgeo graphic.com/2015/04/150417-shroud-turin-relics-jesus-catholic -church-religion-science/.

Von Balthasar, Hans Urs. *The Glory of the Lord: A Theological Aesthetics*. Vol. I. Translated by Erasmo Leiva-Merikakis. Edinburgh: T&T Clark, 1982.

Von Wahlde, Urban C. "Archeology and John's Gospel". In *Jesus and Archaeology*, edited by James H. Charlesworth. Grand Rapids, Mich.: William B. Eerdmans, 2006.

Weaver, G.R., and B.R. Agle. "Religiosity and Ethical Behavior in Organizations: A Symbolic Interactionist Perspective". *Academy of Management Review* 27, no. 1 (2002): 77–97.

Whanger, Alan D. "A Reply to Doubts concerning the Coins Over the Eyes". Shroud of Turin Website, 1997. https://www.shroud .com/lombatti.htm.

Whanger, Alan, and Mary Whanger. "Polarized Image Overlay Technique: A New Image Comparison Method and Its Applications". *Applied Optics* 24, no. 6 (March 15, 1985): 766–72.

Wilson, Ian. *The Shroud of Turin*. New York: Doubleday, 1978.

Wright, N.T. *The Contemporary Quest for Jesus*. Minneapolis: Fortress Press, 2002.

———. *Jesus and the Victory of God*. Vol. 2. Minneapolis: Fortress Press, 1996.

———. *The New Testament and the People of God*. Vol. 1. Minneapolis: Fortress Press, 1992.

———. *The Resurrection of the Son of God*. Minneapolis: Fortress Press, 2003.

NAME INDEX

SUBJECT INDEX

Abba
  defined, 79
  as father figure in Parable of the
    Prodigal Son, 81–88, 332
  identity of Jesus and, 250–52, 269–70
  Resurrection and, 181n56
  transcendence and, 276, 294, 308, 332
  unconditional love of God and, 19,
    79–81
acting power, 394–95
acts of self-consciousness, 396, 398–99,
  400
addiction (sexual), 38–39, 38n9
affection (*storgē*), 32–33, 40–41, 47
agapē
  defined, 32–33, 32nn7–8, 92
  as highest commandment, 74–79,
    75n24, 77n29
  identity of Jesus and, 272–73
  philia and, 34
  power of, 42–47, 46n15
  Resurrection and, 181n56
  storgē and, 39–42
  supremacy of love and, 39–42, 48–52
  transcendence and, 278, 306–7n30,
    322, 331–32, 336
  as unconditional love of God, 53,
    56–57, 61–64, 88
  as unconditional love of Jesus, 93,
    95–96, 106, 110, 122–23, 141
aggression (sexual), 38–39, 38n9,
  38–39n10, 48
agony, 309
alienation, 17, 185–86, 272–73, 296,
  301, 326–27
Allegory of the Wicked Tenants, 243,
  250, 255–58, 266, 335, 398n5
American Psychiatric Association, 326

anamnesis, 128
angels, 100–101
Annals (Tacitus), 65–66
anti-love, 304, 306, 308–9
antipathy, 26–27, 29–30
Antiquities (Josephus), 66–67
apartheid, 43, 46
apostolic proclamations, 68–71, 168,
  191
appearance (outward) of others, 28–29,
  40–41, 49, 57
archaeological coherence, 211, 219
archetypal myth, 326–27
attitudes. *See* interior attitudes and
  dispositions
authenticity. *See* purity of heart
autonomy, 305–6, 308, 310

Babylonian Talmud, 65, 68, 190n3, 228,
  334
Baptism, 287–89, 290n17, 315–16, 319,
  339
beatific vision, 49, 51, 53–54, 300–301,
  300n23, 311, 327, 337
Beatitudes
  first, 91, 108
  third, 91, 92n1
  fifth, 109
  transcendence and, 294–96, 308,
    316
  unconditional love of God and, 16,
    25–26, 78
  unconditional love of Jesus and, 91,
    142, 144
beauty. *See also* perfect beauty
  eros and, 34–38, 40
  Heaven and, 337
  identity of Jesus and, 271–72

423

Happiness, Suffering, and Transcendence Quartet

Finding True Happiness: Satisfying Our Restless Hearts

The Soul's Upward Yearning: Clues to Our Transcendent Nature from Experience and Reason

God So Loved the World: Clues to Our Transcendent Destiny from the Revelation of Jesus

The Light Shines On in the Darkness: Contending with Suffering through Faith